East Asian Integration

The growth of world trade has been stagnant in recent years and trade liberalisation has now been challenged. The recent rise of antiglobalisation calls for a better integration in East Asia. How should East Asia manage its openness? This book provides profound analyses on how FTAs affect trade in the region, rules of origins, non-tariff measures and restrictiveness in services and investment. It gives insight into how East Asian countries should shape their trade, investment and industrial policies. This book helps to answer the question of what kind of a better integration this should be and how East Asia can realise it.

Lili Yan Ing is Lead Advisor, the Ministry of Trade of Republic of Indonesia. She was a Senior Economist at the Economic Research Institute for ASEAN and East Asia (ERIA) and Senior Lecturer at University of Indonesia.

Martin Richardson is Professor of Economics at the Australian National University.

Shujiro Urata is Professor of Economics at Waseda University and Senior Advisor to the President of ERIA.

Routledge-ERIA Studies in Development Economics

ASEAN and Regional Free Trade Agreements
Edited by Christopher Findlay

Age Related Pension Expenditure and Fiscal Space
Modelling Techniques and Case Studies from East Asia
Edited by Mukul G. Asher and Fauziah Zen

Production Networks in Southeast Asia
Edited by Lili Yan Ing and Fukunari Kimura

The Indonesian Economy
Trade and Industrial Policies
Edited by Lili Yan Ing, Gordon H. Hanson and Sri Mulyani Indrawati

Social Protection Goals in East Asia
Strategies and Methods to Generate Fiscal Space
Edited by Mukul G. Asher, Fauziah Zen and Astrid Dita

World Trade Evolution
Growth, Productivity and Employment
Edited by Lili Yan Ing and Miaojie Yu

Emerging Global Trade Governance
Mega Free Trade Agreements and Implications for ASEAN
Edited by Lurong Chen, Shujiro Urata, Junji Nakagawa and Masahito Ambashi

East Asian Integration
Goods, Services and Investment
Edited by Lili Yan Ing, Martin Richardson and Shujiro Urata

For more information about this series, please visit www.routledge.com/Routledge-ERIA-Studies-in-Development-Economics/book-series/ERIA

East Asian Integration

Goods, Services and Investment

Edited by Lili Yan Ing, Martin Richardson and Shujiro Urata

First published 2019
by Routledge
2 Park Square, Milton Park, Abingdon, Oxon OX14 4RN

and by Routledge
52 Vanderbilt Avenue, New York, NY 10017

Routledge is an imprint of the Taylor & Francis Group, an informa business

British Library Cataloguing-in-Publication Data
A catalogue record for this book is available from the British Library

Library of Congress Cataloging-in-Publication Data
Names: Ing, Lili Yan, editor. | Richardson, Martin, 1960– editor. | Urata, Shujiro, 1950– editor.
Title: East Asian integration : goods, services and investment / edited by Lili Yan Ing, Martin Richardson and Shujiro Urata.
Description: Abingdon, Oxon ; New York, NY : Routledge, 2019. | Series: Routledge-ERIA studies in development economics | Includes bibliographical references and index.
Identifiers: LCCN 2018060179
Subjects: LCSH: East Asia—Economic integration. | East Asia—Foreign economic relations. | East Asia—Commerce. | Regionalism—East Asia.
Classification: LCC HC460.5 .E2744 2019 | DDC 337.1/5—dc23
LC record available at https://lccn.loc.gov/2018060179

ISBN: 978-1-138-35962-8 (hbk)
ISBN: 978-1-03-209228-7 (pbk)
ISBN: 978-0-429-43360-3 (ebk)

Typeset in Galliard
by codeMantra

Dedicated to Our Children with Much Love

Michelle and Han Na
L.Y.I.

James and Emmett
M.R.

Shuzo, Shinji and Shiro
S.U.

Professor Olivier Cadot, a significant contributor to this volume, passed away on March 20th, 2019. Olivier was not only an outstanding economist, he was a fine human being and a friend to many, all over the world. He is a wonderful friend with a beautiful mind. He will be missed professionally and personally. The editors also wish to dedicate this volume to his family and to his memory. Vale, Olivier.

Contents

List of figures

List of tables

Acknowledgements

We are indebted to constructive comments from Masahiro Kawaii, Mari Pangestu, Erlinda Medalla, Wing Thye Woo, Jaime de Melo, Peter Drysdale, Yoshifumi Fukunaga, Simon Tay, Shiro Amstrong and Chia Seo Yuew, as well as beneficial discussions with the ASEAN Secretariat and our East Asian government official counterparts. During our writing, we have also been invited to provide insights at RCEP negotiations. We thank Jaysa Prana and Abigail Ho for their excellent research assistance. We specially thank Assunta Petrone and Fadriani Trianingsih, our book production managers. Elisa Ayu provided very helpful administrative support.

Last, we are very grateful for all the love and support that has been poured to us unconditionally by our parents, spouses, colleagues and friends.

Material from the following articles reproduced with permission:

Olivier Cadot, Lili Yan Ing, 'How Restrictive Are ASEAN's Rules of Origin?', Asian Economic Papers, 15:3 (Fall, 2016), pp. 115–134. © 2016 by The Earth Institute at Columbia University and the Massachusetts Institute of Technology.

Shujiro Urata, Free Trade Agreements and Patterns of Trade in East Asia from the 1990s to 2010s', East Asian Community Review (Palgrave Macmillan), 1 (2018), pp. 61–73. © 2016 by Asiatic Research Institute

Notes on contributors

Cosimo Beverelli is Research Economist at the Economic Research and Statistics Division, World Trade Organization.

Olivier Cadot was Professor at the University of Lausanne, Research Fellow at the Centre for Economic Policy Research (CEPR) and Senior Fellow at the Foundation for Studies and Research on International Development.

Matteo Fiorini is Fellow at the Global Governance Programme, Robert Schuman Centre for Advanced Studies, European University Institute.

Bernard Hoekman is Professor and Director at the Global Governance Programme, Robert Schuman Centre for Advanced Studies, European University Institute, and Research Fellow at the CEPR.

Lili Yan Ing is Lead Advisor, the Ministry of Trade of Republic of Indonesia. She was a Senior Economist at the ERIA and Senior Lecturer at University of Indonesia.

Ken Itakura is Professor at the Graduate School of Economics, Nagoya City University.

Juthathip Jongwanich is Associate Professor at the Faculty of Economics, Thammasat University.

Archanun Kohpaiboon is Associate Professor at the Faculty of Economics, Thammasat University.

Junianto James Losari is Lawyer at the International Arbitration Department, Allen & Overy LLP, Singapore.

Misa Okabe is Associate Professor at the Faculty of Economics, Wakayama University.

Martin Richardson is Professor of Economics at the Australian National University.

Shujiro Urata is Professor at Waseda University and Advisor to the President of ERIA.

Zhihong Yu is Associate Professor at the School of Economics, University of Nottingham.

1 Introduction

Lili Yan Ing, Martin Richardson and Shujiro Urata

Right after the World Trade Organization (WTO) was established in January 1995, the number of bilateral and regional agreements began to mushroom. The number of free trade areas (FTAs) grew from 44 in 1995 to 290 in November 2018. The Association of Southeast Asian Nations (ASEAN) also experienced an increase in the number of FTAs from 5 to 47 over the same period. As of November 2018, ASEAN as a group had six FTAs, of which one is among ASEAN countries, and the others are with its six main trading partners: the ASEAN Free Trade Area (AFTA), ASEAN-Australia-New Zealand FTA, ASEAN-China FTA, ASEAN-India FTA, ASEAN-Japan CEPA and ASEAN-Korea FTA. To improve the level of liberalisation in goods, services and investment, ASEAN and its six main trading partners have agreed to consider a new FTA: the Regional Comprehensive Economic Partnership (RCEP).

The RCEP has been under negotiation since November 2012. Six years later, by the time of the final stage of editing this book, November 2018, the RCEP has been through more than 20 rounds of negotiations. We hope this volume will serve as meaningful analyses to academics, practitioners and policymakers in providing not just an understanding of regional integration and cooperation in East Asia to date but also a profound base that provides insights in designing better preferential trade agreements or economic cooperation in the region. The book comprises ten chapters which analyse trade in goods, trade in services and investment.

In Chapter 2, Urata starts the book with an overview of regionalism in East Asia. East Asia has witnessed the proliferation of FTAs during the last three decades, beginning with the AFTA in 1993. A series of bilateral and regional FTAs have been discussed and enacted since around the turn of the century in a competitive pattern, involving many East Asian countries, including ASEAN member states China, Japan and Korea. Despite the active formation of FTAs, a region-wide mega-FTA involving all East Asian countries has not yet been established. The closest one is the Comprehensive and Progressive Trans-Pacific Partnership (CPTPP) agreement, which is scheduled to be enacted towards the end of 2018, but it only includes a few East Asian countries.

The RCEP agreement, which includes all 16 East Asian countries, has been in negotiation since May 2013 without concluding. The importance of establishing

DOI: 10.4324/9780429433603-1

a rules-based trading system such as RCEP has increased because of intensifying protectionism by the US under the Trump administration and the stalemate in multilateral trade negotiations in the WTO. This chapter reviews the trend in FTAs in East Asia by referring to their competitive nature and identifying their special characteristics, and provides suggestions to overcome the challenges to reach an agreement for the RCEP negotiation.

Chapter 3 by Itakura estimates the economic effects of the integration of 16 East Asian countries in the RCEP. Itakura estimates how the formation of the RCEP will affect individual ASEAN member economies' gross domestic product (GDP) growth, exports, imports and total welfare. By applying a recursively dynamic computable general equilibrium model of global trade, the chapter considers three policy scenarios: Scenario 1 is tariff rate reductions, Scenario 2 is this plus services trade cost reductions and Scenario 3 is Scenario 2 plus investment liberalisation.

Applying Global Trade Analysis Project (GTAP)-11, the simulation experiments of RCEP explore the potential economic gains from liberalising goods and services trade, improving logistics of merchandise goods and fostering investment in the region. The simulation results suggest that all the participating countries in RCEP will gain in terms of real GDP, ASEAN's real GDP rising by 4.7 percent from the baseline, in 2035. For each ASEAN Member States, RCEP has varying degrees of impact, reflecting the economic size and depth of liberalisation. As RCEP commits to promoting investment, the increase in real GDP is boosted even more. Investment in all member countries rises as RCEP is implemented, and trade volumes expand for the participating countries.

In Chapter 4, Zhinhong Yu provides an anatomy of the evolution of the structure of China's trade with Southeast Asian countries (namely ASEAN), using detailed Chinese Customs data. The analysis discovers dramatic compositional changes in ASEAN-China trade across ownership, product and the processing trade regime over the last two decades. In particular, since the late 1990s China's active engagement in the global production network has led to the reorientation of China-ASEAN trade towards intermediate goods and machinery sectors, which are characterised by high processing trade intensities and are dominated by foreign-owned firms located in China. As a result, ASEAN's exports to China have surged, leading to sizeable trade surpluses.

However, this trend has not continued in recent years and, if anything, has reversed. Indeed, the growth of China's imports from ASEAN firms has slowed down since 2011, accompanied by decreasing shares of the machinery and intermediate good sectors, and declining processing trade intensity. On the other hand, non-processing exports from indigenous Chinese firms to ASEAN have risen sharply, especially in these same sectors. Taken together, these forces turned ASEAN's trade surplus against China into a trade deficit, which might even widen in the years to come. The results imply that policymakers in ASEAN countries must make appropriate policy adjustments to cope with China's structural transformation towards a "new normal" model of trade growth in order to achieve a healthier trade balance with China in future.

In Chapter 5, Okabe analyses the impacts of ASEAN's FTAs on trade in goods in Southeast Asia using disaggregated trade data. Using overall FTA dummies and the preferential tariff margins under all FTAs that are formed by each ASEAN member, she estimates the impact of each ASEAN FTA on exports and imports in 26 sectors in a gravity model. The major findings are as follows: first, AFTA increases trade in natural resources, industrial materials and consumption goods between members, while ASEAN's regional trade in the manufacturing sectors, which have well-developed regional production networks, decreases under AFTA. Instead, trade in these sectors increases under the ASEAN-China FTA and the ASEAN-Korea FTA.

The result suggests that the ASEAN-China FTA and the ASEAN-Korea FTA have trade diverting effects on trade among ASEAN members. Second, ASEAN FTAs have the potential to facilitate the newer members' catching-up process by enhancing their participation in regional production networks. Third, the impact of tariff reductions under the FTA is a small portion of the overall impact of the FTA. Liberalisation measures other than tariff reductions have a much larger impact on facilitating trade among members. Fourth, new FTAs have little impact if the members already have FTAs among the same members. New FTAs should have a greater degree of liberalisation or lower utilisation costs than existing FTAs. Last, the results of the newer ASEAN FTAs suggest that FTAs need several years to have an effect on trade flows.

Chapter 6 by Kohpaiboon and Jongwanich examines in depth the uptake of FTA provisions by firms in Thailand to shed light on ongoing negotiations for the RCEP. The key finding is that while certificates of origin records significantly increased over the period under consideration, their value remained less than one-third of total trade. Utilisation on the import side was even lower (one-fifth of total imports). Products that are often traded under an FTA preferential trade scheme are highly concentrated and dominated by automotive products (both vehicles and auto parts), electrical appliances, petrochemical products and processed foods, all of which have special characteristics that place them in a better position for applying the preferential schemes.

The key policy inference is that while the use of FTAs by Thai firms suggests that the RCEP has the potential to promote trade among members, the negotiations must focus on the problems of existing agreements. The negotiations should prioritise further liberalisation of the exclusion lists of previously signed FTAs as well as the designing of the rules of origin. In addition, the scope of the negotiations for the RCEP should go beyond opening up trade in goods to eventually facilitate trade and investment among RCEP members.

Chapter 7 by Cadot and Ing estimates the cost of ASEAN's rules of origin. Cadot and Ing use a disaggregated (product-level) gravity approach to estimate the effect of ASEAN's product-specific rules of origin on regional trade, using original data on rules applicable at the 6-digit level of the Harmonized System. Overall, they find that the average *ad valorem* equivalent of the ASEAN's rules of origin is 3.40 percent across all instruments and sectors. The trade-weighted average is 2.09 percent. This moderate estimate is in line with the existing literature.

However, they also find fairly high average *ad valorem* equivalents for some sectors, including leather, textiles and apparel, footwear and automobiles. They also find that some rules appear more restrictive than others; in this regard, the Textile Rule seems to stand out as a relatively more trade-inhibiting rule than others.

In Chapter 8, Cadot and Ing raise a growing issue in trade in the region: non-tariff measures (NTMs). The ongoing RCEP is a critical element of regional integration in East Asia and the Pacific. While tariffs are already low in the region, NTMs remain a key issue in trade in goods.

NTMs may bring consequences for sourcing and enforcement costs, and may affect the structure of an industry. ASEAN countries have similar patterns of NTM imposition at the product level. International experience shows that regional trade agreements could reduce regulatory distance – that is, the difference among regulations across countries – by 41 percent. The RCEP could bring East Asian countries to improve the transparency of their NTMs and encourage mutual recognition.

Chapter 9 by Beverelli, Fiorini and Hoekman conducts a quantification exercise on the effects of services trade liberalisation for the ten Asian economies, including several members of the RCEP. The analysis highlights substantial heterogeneity among the covered RCEP economies. Differences exist not only in terms of the effort required to reach further openness in services markets but also with respect to the quality of governance institutions, which is likely to shape the effects of services trade policy across the partnership's members.

The empirical exercise in this chapter consists of the quantitative assessment of the effects of services trade policy reforms on the productivity of downstream manufacturing industries. The exercise is based on a hypothesised policy reform of the complete removal of all barriers to Mode 3 services trade in four producer services sectors – finance, transport, communications and professional services. The analysis shows that good governance institutions, as captured by broad indicators of the control of corruption, regulatory quality and the rule of law, are important factors for the positive impact of services trade liberalisation on downstream economic performance.

The key implication in the context of the RCEP is that the objective of removing barriers to services trade should not be pursued in isolation or unconditionally. The existing quality of domestic economic governance and the operation of the relevant institutions across RCEP members should be accounted for. The RCEP should explicitly consider the relationships between services trade and investment restrictions, and the quality of economic governance and regulation. It should also include provisions that target the performance of economic governance institutions. The quantitative estimates of the potential gains from services liberalisation suggest that these can be substantial but are conditional on the quality of domestic economic governance: if weaknesses in the latter are not addressed, gains from services liberalisation may not materialise. Addressing economic governance weaknesses in trade agreements will enhance the gains from services trade liberalisation while at the same time improving the prospect of attaining good institutions.

In Chapter 10, Losari explains how International Investment Agreements (IIAs) have evolved significantly from the era of Treaties of Friendship, Commerce and Navigation. This is inevitable as the era changes – investors need more protection, and, at the same time, states need to ensure they can take measures for their own citizens. While earlier generation IIAs tended to evolve more rapidly in the West, particularly with the conclusion of the North American Free Trade Agreement, the East did catch up with a similar evolution, particularly with the conclusion of ASEAN's Comprehensive Investment Agreement. Admittedly, a multilateral investment regime would be ideal without distinction between the West and the East. However, the current development is still a better compromise compared to the era of bilateral investment treaties. The new IIAs have taken in inputs provided by stakeholders and have attempted to incorporate more balanced provisions, namely protecting foreign investors without sacrificing public interests.

The exercise aims to provide further input for future East Asian Integration, particularly the RCEP, based on existing IIAs, which can be the building blocks for more refined provisions for addressing the concerns of the negotiating states – including lessons learned from past disputes arising from similar provisions – and ways for states to address them. In addition, inputs are proposed based on various IIAs that have been concluded recently, particularly the Comprehensive Economic and Trade Agreement, the EU-Viet Nam Investment Protection Agreement and the CPTPP.

Based on these exercises, East Asia should consider designing a much better Investment Chapter in its future integration agenda, including having deeper and broader investment liberalisation commitments, more concrete investment facilitation provisions, limitations on the applicability of the most-favoured-nation clause and improvements to the investor-state dispute settlement mechanism. With these improvements, a Preferential Trade Agreement (PTA) – in whatever form – can provide a better and more balanced legal framework for investment and eventually contribute to a better investment climate in the region.

2 Trends of FTAs in East Asia from the 1990s to the 2010s

Defensive and competitive regionalism

Shujiro Urata

2.1 Introduction

East Asia witnessed a rapid expansion of intra-regional trade in the late 1980s and 1990s, resulting in de facto regional economic integration. Behind this development was the formation of regional production networks by multinational corporations (MNCs). MNCs adopted the fragmentation strategy, under which they break up a production process into a number of sub-production processes (blocks) and locate them in a country or a region where the sub-production processes can be performed most efficiently. MNCs actively trade in parts and components by connecting subprocesses, and they produce final products by assembling parts and components procured from various locations. MNCs were able to adopt the fragmentation strategy because of the free and open business environment, which was established by liberalisation in trade and foreign direct investment (FDI) policies by East Asian countries, and because of the reduction in transportation costs due to technological progress and deregulation.

The construction and use of regional production networks contributed to economic growth, which in turn led to further liberalisation of trade and FDI policies, resulting in greater and deeper regional economic integration. Because of the increased importance of market forces, resulting from trade and FDI policy liberalisation, in the formation of regional economic integration, such integration is characterised as market-driven regional economic integration.[1]

In the late 1990s, East Asia began to observe the emergence of institution-driven regionalisation, which was promoted mainly by the establishment of free trade agreements (FTAs). An FTA is a trade policy through which tariffs on trade between and among FTA members are eliminated, while tariffs on imports from non-FTA members remain at the same level. East Asia was a latecomer in the FTA frenzy as other regions, including Europe, North America, and South America, began to establish FTAs in the late 1980s. Although East Asia was a late starter in the FTA race, it caught up with the rest of the world very quickly, first establishing mostly bilateral FTAs involving two countries before later moving to plurilateral and multilateral FTAs.

The objective of this chapter is to provide an overview of the FTA developments in East Asia in order to set the stage for the detailed analyses conducted

DOI: 10.4324/9780429433603-2

in the other chapters of this book.[2] Specifically, this chapter attempts to examine the patterns of FTA developments in East Asia and then identify the factors that led to the active formation of FTAs. The analysis of the developments of FTAs is performed more or less in chronological order, beginning with the 1990s, then the 2000s, and finally in the 2010s before presenting some concluding remarks. Although there are both economic and non-economic, particularly political, factors at work, this chapter focusses on the economic factors. It further attempts to analyse the implications for region-wide FTAs. The main geographical focus is East Asia, but discussions are extended to include those countries in the Asia-Pacific when such extensions are appropriate. A special focus is placed on the two region-wide FTAs. One is the Regional Comprehensive Economic Partnership (RCEP), which involves 16 East Asian countries, and the other is the Trans-Pacific Partnership (TPP), which involved 12 Asia-Pacific countries originally but later became the Comprehensive and Progressive TPP (CPTPP) with 11 countries, after the US withdrew from the TPP. In the discussion of FTAs, the competitive nature of the relationship between and among FTAs, particularly the alleged rivalry between the RCEP and TPP (CPTPP), is highlighted.

2.2 1990s: the ASEAN Free Trade Area and the emergence of discussions on bilateral FTAs

Starting in the latter half of the 1980s, the movement towards forming regional economic integration, that is, regionalisation in terms of institutions, became active among the regions of the world. In Europe, the movement towards regional economic integration in institutions that started in the 1950s accelerated. The European single market, in which goods, services, labour, and capital could move freely, was formed in 1992. The European Union (EU), an economic and political union, was established in 1993, and the currency union was established in 1999 by introducing a common currency, the euro. In North America, through the formation of FTAs starting in the mid-1980s, the US promoted institutional regional economic integration. Among the FTAs to which the US is a party, the North American Free Trade Area (NAFTA), founded with Canada and Mexico in 1994, is the largest in economic scale.

In contrast with other regions in the world, East Asia was not active in pursuing institutional regional economic integration in the form of FTAs until the end of the 1990s. In fact, the Association of Southeast Asian Nations (ASEAN) Free Trade Area (AFTA), comprised of ASEAN countries, was the only major FTA established in East Asia before the turn of the century. ASEAN was founded in 1967 with political objectives but became increasingly active as an economic framework after the end of the East-West Cold War in 1989. AFTA was created by the ASEAN members (Brunei Darussalam, Indonesia, Malaysia, the Philippines, Singapore and Thailand) at the time and came into effect in 1993. Viet Nam, Myanmar, Lao PDR, and Cambodia later acceded to AFTA after joining ASEAN. Through AFTA, tariffs were reduced in stages, and for the six original member countries, tariffs on trade among the member nations (intra-regional tariffs) were abolished by 2010 for all products except those which were considered exceptions to liberalisation. For the four newer member countries, intra-regional tariffs on 93 percent of the products, excluding sensitive products, were eliminated by 2015, and the remaining tariffs are planned to be removed by 2018. Within ASEAN, there is not only the FTA regarding goods in the framework of AFTA[3] but also an FTA on trade in services (AFAS) and an agreement regarding investment (AIA).[4] These policy and institutional initiatives for economic integration in ASEAN culminated with the establishment of the ASEAN Economic Community (AEC) at the end of 2015. The main objective of the AEC is to set up a single market and production base for establishing the free movement of goods, services, investment and skilled personnel.[5] While remarkable progress has been made to achieve the AEC, there remain unfinished goals. The ASEAN economic ministers have agreed to a new target year of 2025 for dealing with the remaining issues and completing the AEC.[6]

Several factors may be behind the formation of AFTA and the AEC.[7] Two important external motives are the formation of regional economic integration frameworks in the rest of the world and the competitive threat from China. As discussed earlier, moves towards strengthening regional economic groups became active in the latter half of the 1980s. Intensified moves towards regional economic groupings in major areas in the world made ASEAN realise that an FTA could be an important policy option to promote trade and not to be left out from the major markets.

Another factor was the increasing importance of China as a recipient of FDI. China began to attract FDI notably in the late 1980s as MNCs from developed countries found it an attractive FDI destination. This was largely because of the abundant availability of low-wage labour and the potentially huge market in the future. Furthermore, the Chinese government improved the inward FDI environment by implementing reforms and market opening policies, improving infrastructure, and providing various incentives to foreign investors. Faced with increasing FDI to China, ASEAN leaders and government officials became concerned with the further expansion of FDI inflows to China at the expense of inflows to the ASEAN region. One response for dealing with this concern was to set up a region-wide market by establishing a free trade area. Indeed, for ASEAN, China had always been regarded as a competitor in various aspects, including as an FDI host country and region, and as an exporter in overseas markets, such as the US. Indeed, ASEAN's schedule for the completion of AFTA and the AEC was moved forward as ASEAN thought the competitive threat from China had increased remarkably. The fact that these two external factors pushed the ASEAN member countries to form AFTA indicates that defensive motive played an important role for the formation to AFTA.

The internal dynamic of ASEAN has also contributed to deeper integration in the form of the AEC. Specifically, the Asian financial crisis of 1997–1998 made the ASEAN leaders realise the need for promoting cooperation in order to avoid another crisis. They expected that the various types of economic cooperation under the AEC would contribute to making ASEAN a resilient and competitive region and a region with equitable economic development.

The impacts of AFTA on intra-ASEAN trade have been shown to be positive in several empirical studies, although the patterns of trade differ among different products. Okabe and Urata (2014) investigate the impacts of tariff reductions on intra-ASEAN trade. They find that the share of intra-ASEAN trade in overall ASEAN trade increased after the enactment of AFTA. Specifically, the share of intra-ASEAN exports and imports in total ASEAN exports and imports increased from around 20 percent and 16 percent in 1993 to 25 percent and 24 percent in 2010, respectively, with some fluctuations during the 1993–2010 period. Their econometric analysis using trade data at the product level reveals positive and statistically significant trade creation effects for a wide range of products. They also find that the trade creation effects were smaller for the newer AFTA members compared to the original members. They argue that the information about the merits of using AFTA may not have been spread to exporters in new AFTA member countries.

Towards the end of the 1990s, several countries in East Asia began to consider the establishment of bilateral FTAs. Among the ASEAN countries, Singapore actively pursued FTAs. Singapore approached Japan and the Republic of Korea (henceforth, Korea) for possible FTAs in 1998. Among the Northeast Asian countries, Korea was the first country to begin discussing FTAs. Korea and Chile began bilateral FTA negotiations in 1999. Compared to Korea, Japan was passive in pursuing FTAs. Mexico approached Japan to discuss a possible bilateral FTA in 1998, while Korea and Singapore each approached Japan in 1998 and 1999, respectively. Japan and Korea were the two major World Trade Organization (WTO) members that did not have any FTAs at that time. Japan and Korea shared the view that they should not be involved in preferential and discriminatory trade agreements such as FTAs because they would violate the basic principle of non-discrimination of the WTO, thereby complicating the trading environment and discouraging trade.

However, both Japan and Korea changed their attitudes towards FTAs and began to examine their feasibility. Several reasons can be identified as the reasons behind their change in attitude. One was the rapid increase in FTAs in the world. As discussed earlier, FTAs began to increase rapidly in the 1990s (Figure 2.1). One reason behind this rapid expansion of FTAs was the slow progress in multinational trade liberalisation under the General Agreement on Tariffs and Trade (GATT) until 1994 and the WTO after 1995. Faced with the situation, those countries interested in trade liberalisation opted for FTAs with like-minded countries. FTAs tend to trigger a domino effect because they are discriminatory trade policies. Countries that are excluded from FTAs suffer from discrimination. In order to deal with this disadvantage, excluded countries can try to join existing FTAs or set up their own new FTAs. This way, the number of FTAs expands.

Faced with a discriminatory situation resulting from the rapid expansion of FTAs, Japan and Korea changed their attitude towards FTAs from negative to

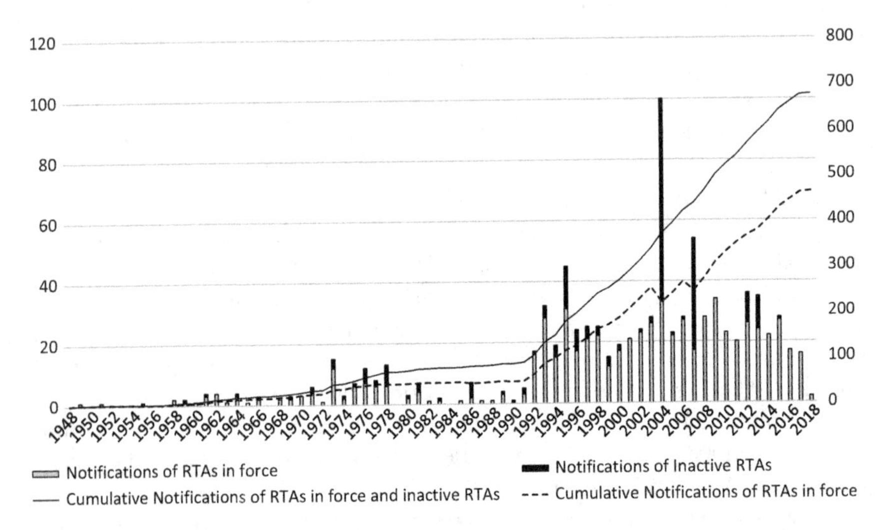

Figure 2.1 Regional Trade Agreements (FTAs and Customs Unions) in the World.

positive, in order to defend their overseas markets. Another reason was the outbreak of the Asian financial crisis. Korea suffered severely from the crisis, which began in June 1997 in Thailand and spread through other Asian countries, including Indonesia, Korea, the Philippines and Malaysia. Faced with the crisis situation, Korea approached Japan and other countries to cooperate in various ways, including the provision of emergency loans, and the leaders also sought the formation of FTAs. Many bilateral FTAs that were proposed and studied were later negotiated and then enacted in the 21st century; we turn to these in the next section.

2.3 2000s: ASEAN+1 FTAs and the beginning of discussions on region-wide FTAs – ASEAN+3 FTA, ASEAN+6 FTA, CJK FTA, and TPP

The early 2000s saw the enactment of a series of bilateral FTAs involving East Asian countries, beginning with the Japan-Singapore FTA in 2002. While Japan and Korea became active in establishing FTAs, China did not show an interest in forming agreements. However, after China joined the WTO in 2001 and established its access to the world market, it started to pursue regional strategies through FTAs. China's approach towards FTAs was quite different from those of other countries in several respects, and thus, many East Asian countries, especially Japan and Korea, were caught by surprise. First, unlike Japan and Korea, which pursued bilateral FTAs, China approached ASEAN as a group to form an FTA. Second, the China-ASEAN FTA contained components that had not been incorporated in other FTAs. Specifically, China offered various schemes that were attractive to ASEAN and, particularly, to its newer members, such as economic cooperation for the newer ASEAN members and advanced trade liberalisation (early harvest) in tropical foods and other products.

Several factors were behind China's active FTA policy. One was the desire to maintain and expand export markets, and another was the reduced adjustment costs for trade liberalisation as a result of the substantial trade liberalisation committed to before its entry into the WTO. China started to have concerns about its export market because of the increase in FTAs and the increase in protectionist measures against Chinese exports, particularly in the form of antidumping charges. Faced with these obstacles to the expansion of its exports, China considered FTAs as a possible solution. China's positive attitude resulted from the realisation that it may not have to incur many additional adjustment costs from FTAs because it had already committed to substantial trade liberalisation under the WTO. Besides these economic motives, it is commonly perceived that China used FTAs as regional policies to increase its economic and non-economic positions in East Asia.

The China-ASEAN FTA unleashed competitive pressure on Japan, Korea, Australia-New Zealand and India, and thus triggered a domino effect through which these East Asian countries individually approached ASEAN to establish FTAs. Although there was a strong tendency for the respective countries to propose the FTAs to ASEAN rather than ASEAN approaching them, the fact that the partner countries were aware of the political and economic importance of ASEAN indicates the high diplomatic abilities of ASEAN. The China-ASEAN FTA was enacted in 2005. Other FTAs involving ASEAN as a group were enacted during the subsequent period, and by 2010, five ASEAN+1 FTAs (each with China, Japan, Korea, India, and Australia-New Zealand) were enacted, making ASEAN the regional hub of FTAs in East Asia. Table 2.1 shows the levels of trade liberalisation for the five ASEAN+1 FTAs. The figures show the percentages of the total tariff lines (HS 6-digit) that are committed for tariff elimination. The ASEAN+ANZ (Australia-New Zealand) FTA has the highest level of tariff elimination, while the ASEAN+India FTA has the lowest. These differences led to difficulty in forming a region-wide FTA, which will be discussed in Section 2.4.

The concept of an FTA encompassing all countries in East Asia emerged in the late 1990s. At the ASEAN+3 (China, Japan and Korea) summit meeting in 1998, the establishment of the East Asia Vision group was suggested by President Kim Dae Jung of Korea to examine the goals for long-term economic cooperation. This group submitted a policy proposal including the formation of an East Asian FTA (EAFTA) to its leaders in 2002. In 2005, a research group of private-sector experts was formed to examine the feasibility of achieving an EAFTA, and, after completing a first and second phase, compiled a 2009 proposal for intergovernmental discussions to begin. Thereafter, a working group led by the Chinese government was formed to discuss important themes, such as the definition of rules of origin for the creation of an FTA at the regional level.

Table 2.1 Tariff Elimination Rates for ASEAN+1 FTAs

	ASEAN-ANZ (%)	*ASEAN-China (%)*	*ASEAN-India (%)*	*ASEAN-Japan (%)*	*ASEAN-Korea (%)*	*Average (%)*
Brunei	99.2	98.3	85.3	97.5	99.1	95.9
Cambodia	89.1	89.9	88.4	85.1	90.8	88.7
Indonesia	93.1	92.3	48.6	91.2	91.1	83.3
Lao PDR	91.8	97.4	80.1	86.3	90.0	89.1
Malaysia	97.3	92.6	79.7	93.9	92.4	91.2
Myanmar	88.1	93.6	76.6	84.9	91.6	86.9
Philippines	95.1	92.5	80.9	97.1	89.6	91.1
Singapore	100.0	100.0	100.0	100.0	100.0	100.0
Thailand	98.9	93.5	78.1	96.4	95.1	92.4
Viet Nam	94.8	92.2	79.5	94.2	89.3	90.0
Australia	100.0					
China		94.7				
India			78.8			
Japan				91.9		
Korea					90.4	
New Zealand	100.0					
Average	95.6	94.3	79.6	92.6	92.7	90.9

Note: The share of tariff elimination in total tariff lines, computed at HS 6-digit level.
Source: Kuno et al. (2015).

Soon after the research group for EAFTA was formed, Japan proposed the idea of a Comprehensive Economic Partnership for East Asia (CEPEA) in 2006 as an economic partnership agreement to include an FTA with the member countries of ASEAN+3+3 (ASEAN, China, Japan, Korea, India, and Australia-New Zealand). ASEAN+3+3 (ASEAN+6) also comprises the members of the East Asian Summit meeting that was launched in 2005.[8] Considering the rivalry between Japan and China, and keeping in mind that China was the country that took the initiative in discussing the EAFTA, it can be understood that the backdrop to the CEPEA concept was Japan's strategy to play a leadership role in creating regional institutions in East Asia. A research group of private-sector researchers began to study the feasibility of the CEPEA in 2007, passing through the first and second phases and proposing in 2009 that discussions between governments should begin. From this recommendation, as in the case of the EAFTA, the governments extracted important themes for achieving the CEPEA, including the rules of origin, and further discussions were pursued under a working group.

The activities and research surrounding the EAFTA and CEPEA moved in parallel, often through back-to-back discussions. China and Japan respectively took the leadership role in each group, but ASEAN countries, which did not want to deepen opposition by aligning with one or the other, participated in both activities with equal weight. Amidst these circumstances, ASEAN countries strengthened their voices in both frameworks and began to engage actively in leading the discussions on regional integration in East Asia. Japan and China both participated in EAFTA and CEPEA activities for the reason that there was a common understanding that maintaining favourable relations between the two countries was important for the promotion of regional integration in East Asia. In fact, through the EAFTA and CEPEA activities, the rivalry between Japan and China seemed to decrease.

One goal of founding the EAFTA and CEPEA was to increase the level of economic activity by forming an integrated market in East Asia. In the 2000s, five ASEAN+1 FTAs were completed, but these FTAs did not result in a unified single market. FTAs connecting the +6 countries (China, Japan, Korea, India, Australia and New Zealand) were missing. If a single market like that of Europe were to be created in East Asia as well, the elements that carry out an important role in economic activity, such as goods and capital, would come to move freely and actively by avoiding the 'spaghetti/noodle bowl effect', which arose due to different rules being adopted by the five ASEAN+1 FTAs, and economic growth and prosperity could be expected. More specifically, the expansion and smoother utilisation of the regional production network that extends through East Asia would become possible as a result of forming a free and open single market, leading to higher economic growth.

There is a view that an EAFTA or CEPEA that encompasses the East Asian countries could be founded by combining the existing ASEAN+1 FTAs.[9] Theoretically, this is not incorrect, but the contents of each ASEAN+1 FTAs are quite different, meaning it would not be easy in reality. Furthermore, it is the delay in moving towards creating FTAs among the three countries of China, Japan, and Korea that is hindering the founding of the EAFTA and CEPEA. Negotiations for a Japan-Korea FTA began in 2003 but were broken off in 2004 without coming to an agreement regarding the framework for negotiations. Japan wants to avoid market opening for its agricultural and fishery industries, and Korea fears a negative effect on small- and medium-sized enterprises resulting from market opening in the area of manufactured products. As such, opposing opinions over the market opening between these countries have acted as a barrier. Japan's industrial sector is extremely forward-looking regarding a Japan-China FTA, but Japanese agriculture fears damage from market opening and is firm in its stance of opposition. Factors that make a Japan-Korea FTA and a Japan-China FTA difficult not only include the economic factors mentioned but also include problems of history and politics.

The idea of a China-Japan-Korea (CJK) FTA was proposed informally by Chinese Premier Zhu Rongi at the Leaders' Meeting in 2002. This proposal led to the initiation of a private-sector study involving the three countries. The study began in 2003 and continued until 2009 with a recommendation to begin a feasibility study involving government, business, and academics. A joint research group of government, business, and academia was founded in 2010 by the Chinese, Japanese, and Korean leaders to consider the feasibility of a trilateral FTA. The research group produced a report in December 2011 indicating that a trilateral FTA would bring benefits to all three countries and recommending governments to decide on how to proceed.

While East Asian countries became active in discussing the possible formation of region-wide FTAs, some economies and countries belonging to the Asia-Pacific Economic Cooperation (APEC) began to discuss the formation of a region-wide FTA with a high level of trade liberalisation. At several APEC meetings in the 1990s, Australia, Chile, New Zealand, Singapore and the US (P5) held informal discussions intended to discuss mechanisms for creating a new type of trade agreement among 'like-minded' states.[10] Of the P5 countries, Chile, Singapore and New Zealand, which shared very high enthusiasm for establishing a high-level FTA, launched the negotiations at the APEC Leaders' Summit in 2002. Brunei joined the negotiations in 2005.[11] P4, consisting of Chile, Singapore, New Zealand and Brunei, was enacted in 2006.

It may be important to note that several attempts at trade liberalisation under the APEC framework had been unsuccessful, leading to the formulation of P4. The reasons for the previous failed attempts include the slow progress towards achieving the Bogor Goals of free trade and investment and the failure of the Early Voluntary Sectoral Liberalisation (EVSL). In Bogor in 1994, the APEC Leaders committed to achieving free trade and investment by 2010 for industrialised economies and by 2020 for developing economies. The APEC Leaders introduced the Osaka Action Agenda (OAA) in 1995 and the Manila Action Plan in 1996 to further progress towards the Bogor Goals, but the progress was disappointingly little and slow. The EVSL was an initiative developed by the APEC trade ministers in 1997 to liberalise selected sectors, which were agreed upon by the APEC members, as a way of pursuing the OAA.[12] The EVSL was not implemented as Japan refused to liberalise forestry and fish products, and the food and oilseed sectors. It should be added that slow progress on multilateral trade liberalisation negotiations under the WTO and the increasing number of FTAs in many parts of the world were also factors leading to the formation of P4.

P4 is a comprehensive FTA covering a broad range of issues, including trade in goods and services, rules of origin, trade remedies, sanitary and phytosanitary measures, technical barriers to trade, competition policy, intellectual property, government procurement, economic cooperation, and dispute settlement.[13] P4 is a high-level FTA requiring members to eliminate tariffs on basically all products by 2015. The primary objective of P4 is the establishment of a business-friendly environment under which free trade and investment are achieved with fair competition and the effective protection and enforcement of intellectual property rights.[14] Another important objective of the agreement is to support the APEC process towards the goals of free and open trade and investment. In other words, the founding members hoped for P4 to become a foundation for a larger trade agreement by accepting new members.

In March 2008, the P4 members began negotiations on trade in financial services and investment in order to broaden the agreement's issues coverage. Broadening the issues coverage to meet the demands and needs of businesses was one of the notable characteristics of P4, which is known as a living agreement. In September 2008, the US, which was interested in the liberalisation of financial services and investment, made an announcement seeking to join the expanded

P4 negotiations. The Obama administration, which took over in January 2009, joined the expanded P4 negotiations in November 2009. Australia, Peru and Viet Nam quickly joined the US in expressing their intention to join the negotiations. During this period, P4 became the TPP. It should be noted that the emergence of the discussions on the formulation of region-wide FTAs in East Asia in the form of the ASEAN+3 and ASEAN+6 FTAs sparked the US's interest in TPP (which encompasses countries on both sides of the Pacific) as it did not want to be kept out of East Asia.

Before closing this section on the discussion of region-wide FTA developments in the 2000s, it should be noted that in 2006, the US proposed a Free Trade Area of the Asia-Pacific (FTAAP), which includes all APEC member economies. The idea for the FTAAP was first presented in 2005 by the APEC Business Advisory Council, which represents the business community. The idea was taken up by the US government, which thought the FTAAP would play an important role for US businesses in maintaining access to the fast-growing East Asian market. At the APEC summit meeting held in Yokohama in 2010, the FTAAP was considered a primary means for regional economic integration in the Asia-Pacific, and the EAFTA, CEPEA and TPP were considered the pathways to realising the FTAAP. China proposed a feasibility study for the realisation of the FTAAP at an APEC meeting in Beijing in 2014. A feasibility study entitled *Collective Strategic Study on Issues Related to the Realization of the FTAAP* and headed jointly by China and the US was launched, and the report was delivered at the APEC Leaders' Meeting in Peru in 2016. Although a roadmap to the realisation of the FTAAP was expected from the study, the report did not provide concrete plans for meeting the expectation (APEC, 2016).

2.4 2010s: the negotiation of the mega-regional FTAs – RCEP and TPP

Enlarged TPP negotiations with eight countries, Brunei, Chile, New Zealand, Singapore, Australia, Peru, the US and Viet Nam, began in March 2010. After the negotiations began, four countries joined: Malaysia in October 2010, Canada and Mexico in 2012, and Japan in 2013. The fact that the number of negotiating countries increased during the negotiation process is quite unusual and reflects the importance of the TPP for many countries. The TPP negotiations lasted for five years and seven months before the countries reached an agreement in October 2015. The TPP agreement was signed by the TPP negotiating members in February 2016. The ratification process began after the signing. The ratification process stopped after Japan and New Zealand ratified the TPP treaty because the newly elected US president, Donald Trump, withdrew the US from the TPP Treaty on his third day in office in January 2017. US ratification was a necessary condition for the enactment of the treaty.[15]

Now that the TPP was not going to enter into force, the remaining TPP members decided to pursue TPP11 without the US. The TPP11 trade ministers held a sideline meeting at the APEC trade ministers' meeting in May and agreed to revive the stalled agreement. They tasked senior trade officials with assessing the options to bring the TPP11 into force expeditiously before the APEC Leaders' Meeting in November 2017.[16] Several reasons were identified for pursuing TPP11. First, the TPP, with its high-level trade and FDI liberalisation and its comprehensive issue coverage, could be a model FTA for future FTAs.[17] Second, the enactment of the TPP11 could put pressure on other mega-regional FTAs, such as the RCEP, so that the momentum for forming FTAs could be maintained and resistance against protectionism strengthened. Third, although very unlikely under the Trump Administration, the US may come back to the TPP. For such an eventuality, the TPP11 needs to be in force to receive the US. The negotiation of the TPP11 reached an agreement rather quickly in January 2018 and the TPP11 treaty, or formally the CPTPP, was signed in March 2018. The ratification process began and at the time of writing (31 October), six members have ratified the treaty, so that the CPTPP is scheduled to enter into force on 30 December 2018.[18] Several countries including South Korea, Indonesia, Thailand, Colombia and the United Kingdom expressed an interest in joining the CPTPP.

Turning to the EAFTA and the CEPEA, government-level discussions began in 2010 following recommendations by feasibility studies. Discussions proceeded in parallel until 2011, when Japan and China jointly proposed the founding of a working group in order to accelerate the formation of an EAFTA and CEPEA. This joint move by China and Japan, which were competing for a leadership role in the establishment of a region-wide FTA, resulted from a desire on the part of China to move forward either the EAFTA or CEPEA in light of the fact that TPP negotiations had begun to make progress. In other words, the start of the TPP negotiations apparently put the pressure on China to make a move towards a region-wide FTA in East Asia.

While China and Japan were taking the lead in the formation of a region-wide FTA in East Asia, the ASEAN countries, which did not wish to deepen opposition by deciding an order of precedence, participated in both activities (EAFTA and CEPEA) with equal weight. However, the joint proposal by China and Japan for accelerating the EAFTA and CEPEA pushed the ASEAN countries, which feared losing a central role in the movement towards an East Asian regional framework, to respond by proposing the RCEP in 2011. The RCEP is a framework that does not specify membership, such as ASEAN+3 or ASEAN+6, and that can be joined by East Asian countries that are prepared to sign an FTA with ASEAN. A statement was released to launch RCEP negotiations at the ASEAN+6 summit meeting held in November 2012, and, as a result, the movement towards founding an EAFTA and CEPEA was unified in RCEP. Negotiations did not begin until May 2013. It is argued that Japan's announcement of its participation in TPP negotiations in March 2013 pushed RCEP members, especially non-TPP members, such as China, to begin negotiations. Indeed, it is interesting to note that the negotiations for the CJK FTA and the Trans-Atlantic Trade and Investment Partnership (involving the US and the EU) began in March and July 2013, respectively, possibly triggered by the intensification of

TPP negotiations. This kind of chain reaction or domino effect has been discerned concerning FTAs, and such a phenomenon is described as 'competitive regionalism' (Solis et al., 2009). RCEP negotiations missed several targets for conclusion. The 24th round of negotiations finished in October 2018. The momentum for reaching an agreement has been strengthened since the signing of the CPTPP agreement, a rival mega-FTA. We will return to the reasons behind the slow progress of RCEP negotiations in the concluding section.

The remainder of this section provides a comparison of CPTPP and RCEP to discern the special characteristics of RCEP.[19] The CPTPP text has been released, and thus its content is known. However, RCEP is still under negotiation, and thus discussions on its content are bound to suffer from uncertainty. In the discussion on RCEP, we rely on the limited information obtained from various sources, including official documents and press reports.

Let us compare the CPTPP and the RCEP in terms of the objectives, content, and quality of the agreements. The objectives of the CPTPP and the RCEP seem quite similar.[20] Both the CPTPP and the RCEP aim to be high-quality and comprehensive trade agreements for promoting economic growth and development. Indeed, the issues coverage of both frameworks is broader than that of the WTO (Table 2.2). Despite the common objective of promoting economic growth and development, there are differences in CPTPP and RCEP's emphasis on economic growth and economic development. One of the most important elements of the RCEP is achieving equitable economic development through economic cooperation. By contrast, the CPTPP does not put much emphasis on economic cooperation. It is only natural that RCEP emphasises economic cooperation as the RCEP members include least-developed countries, such as Cambodia, Lao PDR and Myanmar, whose successful economic development is important for the sustainable economic growth and social stability in the region.

The coverage of the issues for the CPTPP and the RCEP is different. As shown in Table 2.2, both CPTPP and RCEP cover the following issues: market access for goods, rules of origin, customs cooperation and trade facilitation, sanitary and phytosanitary measures, technical barriers to trade, investment, trade in services, e-commerce, government procurement, competition policy, intellectual property, economic cooperation and capacity building, economic development, small- and medium-sized enterprises, and dispute settlement. However, there are issues that are only covered by TPP and not by RCEP. These are state-owned enterprises and designated monopolies, labour, environment, competitiveness and business facilitation, regulatory coherence, and transparency and anti-corruption. These issues are regarded as important for developed countries, such as Japan and Australia, for achieving a level playing field in competition and for achieving sustainable economic growth with protection of labour and environment, but pose challenges for developing countries, especially those with strong government control of their economies. One should note that the CPTPP adopted 'cumulation' in the definition of rules of origin, which treats products produced in CPTPP countries as CPTPP products. Thus, they are traded tariff free, facilitating the construction and management of regional production

Table 2.2 Comparison of Issues Coverage for CPTPP and RCEP

	CPTPP	*RCEP*	*WTO*
Market access for goods	●	●	●
Rules of origin and origin procedures	●	●	●
Textiles and apparel	●	●	●
Customs administration and trade facilitation	●	●	●
Trade remedies	●	●	●
Sanitary and phytosanitary measures	●	●	●
Technical barriers to trade	●	●	●
Investment	●	●	▲
Cross-border trade in services	●	●	●
Financial services	●	●	●
Temporary entry for business persons	●	●	●
Telecommunications	●	●	●
Electronic commerce	●	●	
Government procurement	●	●	▲
Competition policy	●	●	
State-owned enterprises and designated monopolies	●		
Intellectual property	●	●	●
Labour	●		
Environment	●		
Cooperation and capacity building	●	●	
Competitiveness and business facilitation	●		
Development	●	●	
Small- and medium-sized enterprises	●	●	
Regulatory coherence	●		
Transparency and anti-corruption	●		
Administrative and institutional provisions	●	●	
Dispute settlement	●	●	●

Note: ● indicates the issue is covered; ▲ indicates the issue is partially covered.
Sources: CPTPP are taken from the CPTPP text and RCEP are based on the information given by RCEP 'Guiding Principle and Objectives for Negotiating RCEP' and other sources.

networks, or supply chains. RCEP is likely to adopt a similar arrangement, contributing to the development and promotion of regional production networks.

A closer look at the CPTPP and the RCEP reveals that content that may appear similar turns out to be quite different in terms of quality or the level of commitment. One of the areas where the differences in the level of commitment can be clearly seen is the level of trade liberalisation, or market access in goods trade. The CPTPP is seeking for complete elimination of tariffs, or 100 percent trade liberalisation, although in reality, trade liberalisation rates (the proportion of the number of tariff lines subject to tariff elimination in the total number of tariff lines) for some members are lower than 100 percent because of political sensitivities concerning some products, such as rice for Japan (Table 2.3).

In contrast, the trade liberalisation rate for the RCEP is likely to be substantially lower compared to that of the TPP. Some observers predict a maximum of 90 percent, or more than 80 percent, trade liberalisation, considering the trade

Table 2.3 Tariff Elimination Rate for CPTPP (% Share in Total Number of Tariff Lines)

	Actual Figures (2015)					*TPP Commitments*			
	Agricultural Products		*Manufactured Products*		*Total*	*Agricultural Products*		*Manufactured Products*	
	Final Bound	*MFN Applied*	*Final Bound*	*MFN Applied*	*Eventual Elimination*	*Immediate Elimination*	*Eventual Elimination*	*Immediate Elimination*	*Eventual Elimination*
Australia	31.3	77.0	18.8	45.9	100	99.5	100	91.8	99.8
Brunei	0.0	98.5	0.0	78.5	100	98.6	100	70.2	96.4
Canada	46.0	59.6	25.8	78.5	99	86.2	94.1	96.9	100
Chile	0.0	0.0	0.0	0.3	100	96.3	99.5	94.7	100
Japan	34.1	36.5	55.9	55.7	95	51.3	81	95.3	100
Malaysia	12.9	75.0	5.0	64.1	100	96.7	99.6	78.8	100
Mexico	0.4	19.6	0.3	55.2	99	74.1	96.4	77	99.6
New Zealand	54.8	72.4	46.4	62.5	100	97.7	100	93.9	100
Peru	0.0	52.6	2.2	70.0	99	82.1	96	80.2	100
Singapore	4.1	99.8	17.0	100.0	100	100	100	100	100
Viet Nam	8.7	15.5	15.0	38.8	100	42.6	99.4	70.2	100

Source: WTO Tariff Profiles, and Japanese Government, Cabinet Secretariat.

liberalisation achieved by the five ASEAN+1 FTAs. ASEAN countries achieved nearly 90 percent trade liberalisation in each of the ASEAN+1 FTAs (Table 2.1), while only 73.1 percent of tariff lines were commonly eliminated vis-à-vis their ASEAN+1 FTA partners (Fukunaga and Kuno, 2012). Considering that common tariff concessions are adopted in RCEP negotiations, even achieving 80 percent trade liberalisation requires significant efforts on the part of ASEAN members. Furthermore, it should be pointed out that India has the lowest trade liberalisation rate, at 78.8 percent, in its FTA with ASEAN, indicating substantial difficulty in achieving 80 percent or 90 percent trade liberalisation. If one considers that India is very much concerned with the possible increase of imports from China, India is not likely to achieve the rate achieved in its FTA with ASEAN (78.8 percent). Non-ASEAN RCEP members also have to make enormous efforts to achieve 90 percent trade liberalisation, except for Australia and New Zealand, which have achieved 100 percent trade liberalisation in their FTA with ASEAN.

Another major difference between the CPTPP and the RCEP is their treatment of the least-developed countries. The ASEAN+6 Trade Ministers agreed to provide special and differential treatment to the least-developed ASEAN Member States in the RCEP. Considering the substantial differences in the levels of economic development of the RCEP negotiating members, this special and differential treatment is understandable and consistent with the arrangements adopted in the ASEAN+1 FTAs. Specific examples of this treatment include the postponement of trade liberalisation by new ASEAN members in the ASEAN-China FTA. The CPTPP does not provide special or differential treatment to its least-developed members in terms of the content of the agreement.

It should also be noted that the modes of agreement are likely to be different between the CPTPP and the RCEP. Despite CPTPP's comprehensive content, its members need to accept all the contents and components from the outset in the form of a single undertaking. Unlike the CPTPP, the RCEP may adopt a gradual and sequential approach, where different components are negotiated and implemented under different time schedules, depending on the difficulty in reaching an agreement.

Last, having discussed several differences between the CPTPP and the RCEP, one may wonder if the relationship between these two mega-regional FTAs would be competing/substitutable or complementary as a region-wide mega-FTA. They tended to be considered competing when the US was a member of the TPP because of rivalry relationship between the US in the TPP and China in the RCEP. However, a view emphasising complementary relationship seems to be growing. For example, Urata (2014b) presents the stages approach to East Asian regionalism in that East Asian countries that cannot accept high-standard, comprehensive rules required to join the CPTPP should first join the RCEP (first stage) and achieve economic development. These countries should join the CPTPP (second stage) once they have grown successfully and become able to accept these rules.

In this way the CPTPP and the RCEP are in complementary relationship.

2.5 Concluding remarks

East Asia has witnessed rapid expansion of FTAs during the last three decades. It began with the establishment of the AFTA comprising of ASEAN Member States in 1993. The momentum of FTA creation accelerated around the turn of the century as a large number of bilateral and regional FTAs became in existence. Mega-regional FTAs began to be discussed in the 2000s and the negotiation of some of these mega FTAs began in the 2010s. The TPP, which later became the CPTPP, and the RCEP are two major mega-regional FTAs in East Asia. A defensive motive has been behind the proliferation of FTAs in East Asia as countries faced with the external competitive pressure either in the form of rapidly growing countries or the establishment of FTAs turned to establish FTAs in order to attract FDI and/or protect their market shares in their export markets. Recognising that trade negotiation under the auspices of the WTO has faced difficulty in making progress, realising FTAs, particularly mega-regional FTAs, is important for promoting trade and investment, which in turn would contribute to economic growth.

The CPTPP, which includes 11 Asia-Pacific countries, is scheduled to be enacted on 30 December 2018, but it does not include all East Asian countries. After its enactment, new members from East Asia are likely to join as several East Asian countries including Thailand, South Korea and Indonesia have expressed an interest. Now that the CPTPP is likely to be realised soon, the importance of the RCEP, which includes practically all East Asian countries, for establishing a rule-based, open, competitive, fair, stable and transparent business environment in East Asia has increased. The RCEP negotiation began in 2013, but after five years, the negotiations have not yet reached an agreement. Difficult issues have been identified, and discussions on these issues have not progressed smoothly. One of the most contentious issues is the level of tariff elimination in the market access negotiations. Developed countries, such as Australia and Japan, demand high levels of tariff elimination exceeding 90–95 percent of overall tariff lines, while some developing countries, including India and China, particularly India, insist on much lower levels of tariff elimination.

It should be noted that the countries included in the missing FTA links in East Asia are involved in heated controversy about market access because of the differences in the competitiveness of different sectors between these countries. Specifically, India is not ready to open its market for manufactured products vis-à-vis China for the fear that market opening would have disastrous impacts on India's manufacturing sector. China is hesitant to open its market for high-technology products vis-à-vis Japan, while Japan is keen on maintaining the protection of its agricultural sector vis-à-vis China. India is keen on relaxing restrictions on the mobility of software engineers, while ASEAN is reluctant to accept it.

Besides the sectoral and country-specific issues, the absence of a leader or leaders has been an obstacle for accelerating the negotiations. In the case of the TPP, the US and Japan played important roles in leading the negotiations and reaching an agreement, while in the case of the CPTPP Japan played a leading role. In the case of the RCEP, ASEAN is expected to play that role because it was

ASEAN that proposed RCEP. However, ASEAN does not seem to be proactive about leading the negotiations, probably because it is preoccupied with its own economic integration under the AEC and because ASEAN faces difficulty in having common views on various issues among its members.

Some argue that RCEP cannot be established without a CJK FTA. Certainly, the conclusion of the RCEP negotiations could be more easily reached if CJK FTA negotiations were to be concluded, but the conclusion of a CJK FTA does not seem necessary for the establishment of RCEP. RCEP negotiations can reach an agreement if its contents are agreeable for China, Japan, and Korea, while a CJK FTA can be at a higher level in terms of trade liberalisation and other areas and of more comprehensive coverage compared to RCEP.

Having discussed the obstacles preventing the progress of RCEP negotiations, one must emphasise that the most serious obstacle is the lack of strong political will by the RCEP Country Leaders for the establishment of the RCEP. Without strong political will, negotiators cannot make any commitments for the conclusion of the negotiations.

To successfully conclude the negotiations, the RCEP Leaders need to be convinced about the importance of the RCEP in promoting economic growth and give appropriate guidance to the negotiators. In order for the leaders to commit to the RCEP, they need strong support from the business community and the general public. Researchers and journalists, who have a strong influence on the opinion of the general public, need to provide evidence of the possible benefits of the RCEP to the public. Once the commitment of the RCEP Leaders is established, there are possible ways to deal with the controversial issues successfully.

Possible conclusion may require either one of the following three options regarding tariff elimination. One is to accept a low level of tariff elimination. Another is to drop the countries that cannot accept high-level tariff elimination. The final option, which may be the best, is flexible in that a high-level target can be set, and countries can be allowed to achieve the target within a transition period. A similar approach could be adopted for other controversial issues.

It should be added that the provision of safety nets, such as temporary income compensation and education and training for those negatively affected by the trade liberalisation, is necessary for the RCEP countries for dealing with opposition groups. Furthermore, economic cooperation, which is included in the RCEP, should be undertaken effectively to narrow the development gap among the RCEP members.

Notes

1 See Urata (2004) for discussions on market-driven and institution-driven regional economic integration in East Asia.

2 A number of studies on FTA developments in East Asia have been undertaken. Some useful studies include Solis et al. (2009), Kawai and Wignaraja (2011), Das and Kawai (2016) and Urata (2014a).

3 The ASEAN Trade in Goods Agreement was enacted in 2010.
4 The ASEAN Framework Agreement in Services (AFAS) was founded in 1995 and the ASEAN Investment Area (AIA) in 1998. In 2009, the AIA developed into the ASEAN Comprehensive Investment Area (ACIA), which contains more comprehensive contents.
5 On ASEAN Economic Community, see, for example, ASEAN (2008).
6 See ASEAN (2017) on this point.
7 See ERIA (2014) on AFTA and the AEC.
8 Since then, the US and Russia joined the East Asian Summit group.
9 Among ASEAN+6 countries, the pairs of countries that are not linked by FTAs are China-Japan, China-India, Japan-Korea, Japan-New Zealand, India-Australia, and India-New Zealand.
10 Elms and Lim (2012) provide detailed discussions on the origin and evolution of FTA discussions in the Asia-Pacific region.
11 New Zealand Ministry of Foreign Affairs (www.mfat.govt.nz/Trade-and-Economic-Relations/2-Trade-Relationships-and-Agreements/Trans-Pacific/2-P4.php).
12 See Okamoto (2000), for a detailed account of the discussions regarding the EVSL.
13 Trans-Pacific Strategic Economic Partnership Agreement (www.mfat.govt.nz/downloads/trade-agreement/transpacific/main-agreement.pdf).
14 Trans-Pacific Strategic Economic Partnership Agreement (www.mfat.govt.nz/downloads/trade-agreement/transpacific/main-agreement.pdf).
15 According to the agreement, the TPP enters into force if at least six TPP governments, accounting for 85 percent of the combined GDP of the 12 countries, have ratified. US ratification is necessary because the share of the US in the combined GDP is 60.3 percent.
16 Nikkei Asian Review, 21 May 2017, (https://asia.nikkei.com/Politics-Economy/International-Relations/TPP-11-ministers-pledge-to-revive-stalled-agreement?page=2).
17 The notable characteristics of the TPP will be discussed later.
18 According to the agreement, the CPTPP enters into force if at least six CPTPP members have ratified. As of 31 October 2018, Mexico, Japan, Singapore, New Zealand, Canada, and Australia have ratified the CPTPP treaty.
19 The contents of TPP basically remain the same in the CPTPP. In the CPTPP treaty 22 provisions in the TPP are suspended. The suspended provisions are mostly advocated by the US and faced opposition from other TPP members. Most important suspensions are investment and intellectual property right provisions. See New Zealand Foreign Affairs and Trade Ministry website for the details.
www.mfat.govt.nz/en/trade/free-trade-agreements/free-trade-agreements-concluded-but-not-in-force/cptpp/tpp-and-cptpp-the-differences-explained/#what.
20 The text of the CPTPP is available in the following website.
www.mfat.govt.nz/assets/CPTPP/Comprehensive-and-Progressive-Agreement-for-Trans-Pacific-Partnership-CPTPP-English.pdf. The information on RCEP is obtained from RCEP (2012) 'Guiding Principles and Objectives for Negotiating the Regional Comprehensive Economic Partnership' (https://dfat.gov.au/trade/agreements/rcep/Documents/guiding-principles-rcep.pdf).

References

APEC (2016) *Collective Strategic Study on Issues Related to the Realization of the FTAAP.* Appendix 6. 2016 CTI Report to Ministers. www.apec.org/-/media/Files/Groups?CTI?2016/Appendix-8---Recommendations-of-FTAAP-Study.pdf.
ASEAN (2008) *ASEAN Economic Community Blue Print.* Jakarta: ASEAN.
ASEAN (2017) *ASEAN Economic Community 2025 Consolidated Strategic Action Plan.* http://asean.org/storage/2017/02/Consolidated-Strategic-Action-Plan.pdf.

Das, S.B. and M. Kawai, eds. (2016) *Trade Regionalism in the Asia-Pacific: Developments and Future Challenges*. Singapore: ISEAS-Yusof Ishak Institute.

Economic Research Institute for ASEAN and East Asia [ERIA] (2014) *ASEAN Rising: ASEAN and AEC Beyond 2015*. www.eria.org/publications/key_reports/ASEAN-Rising.html.

Elms, D.K. and C.L. Lim (2012) "An Overview and Snapshot of the TPP Negotiations." In C.L. Lim, D.K. Elms, and P. Low eds. *The Trans-Pacific Partnership: A Quest for a Twenty-first-Century Trade Agreement*. Cambridge: Cambridge University Press.

Fukunaga, Y. and A. Kuno (2012) "Toward a Consolidated Preferential Tariff Structure in East Asia: Going beyond ASEAN+1 FTAs." *ERIA Policy Brief*. No. 2012-03, May.

Kawai, M. and G. Wignaraja (2011) "Asian FTAs: Trends, Prospects and Challenges." *Journal of Asian Economics*, 22:1 (February), pp. 1–22.

Kuno, A., Y. Fukunaga, and F. Kimura (2015) "Pursuing a Consolidated Tariff Structure in the RCEP: Sensitivity and Inconsistency in ASEAN's Trade Protection." In Christopher Findlay ed. *ASEAN and Regional Free Trade Agreements*. London: Routledge, pp. 167–188.

Okabe, M. and S. Urata (2014) "The Impact of AFTA on Intra-AFTA Trade." *Journal of Asian Economics*, 35, pp. 12–31.

Okamoto, J. (2000) "The Political Process of APEC Early Voluntary Sectoral Liberalization: Setting the Research Agenda." Working Paper Series 99/00-No.1, APEC Study Center, Institute of Developing Economies.

Solis, M., B. Stallings, and S. Katada, eds. (2009) *Competitive Regionalism: FTA Diffusion in the Pacific Rim*. Basingstoke: Palgrave Macmillan.

Urata, S. (2004) "The Shift from 'Market-led' to 'Institution-led' Regional Economic Integration in East Asia in the late 1990s." RIETI Discussion Paper, 04-E-012. www.rieti.go.jp/jp/publications/dp/04e012.pdf.

Urata, S. (2014a) "Managing East Asia's Free Trade Agreements." In G. Capannelli and M. Kawai, eds. *The Political Economy of Asian Regionalism*. Tokyo: Springer, pp. 59–83.

Urata, S. (2014b) "A Stages Approach to Regional Economic Integration in Asia Pacific: The RCEP, TPP, and FTAAP." In T. Guoqiang and Peter A. Petri, eds. *New Directions in Asia-Pacific Economic Integration*. Hawaii: East-West Center, pp. 119–130.

3 Economic effects of East Asian integration on Southeast Asia

Ken Itakura

3.1 Introduction

The ten Association of Southeast Asian Nations (ASEAN) Member States have steadily engaged in establishing freer trading markets, not only among the Member States but also with their six neighbouring countries. The ASEAN Economic Community (AEC) was established in December 2015 as the single market and production base among the ASEAN Member States. Prior to the AEC's inauguration, ASEAN formed bilateral free trade agreements (FTAs) with Australia and New Zealand, China, India, Japan and the Republic of Korea (henceforth, Korea). Aiming for the integration of these FTAs with a higher level of liberalisation, negotiations for the Regional Comprehensive Economic Partnership (RCEP) were launched in Brunei Darussalam in May 2013 by the ASEAN Member States and their six partners.

The RCEP aims to go beyond the conventional trade liberalisation of tariff reduction or elimination; it aims to liberalise trade in services, facilitate trade and promote investment in the region. In our simulation experiments of the RCEP, using a set of economic data and empirical estimates for the global economy, we explore the potential economic gains from the liberalising of goods and services trade, improving the logistics for merchandise goods trade and fostering investment in the region.

A number of studies quantify the economic effects of the RCEP using computable general equilibrium (CGE) models: for example, Kawai and Wignaraja (2008), Lee et al. (2009), Cheong and Tongzon (2013), Itakura (2014), Urata (2014) and Lee and Itakura (2017). We contribute to the existing studies in two ways. First, we update the underlying economic structure by utilising a recently released public database to simulate the impacts of the RCEP on the RCEP economies, using a CGE model. Second, we incorporate into our RCEP simulation not only the liberalisation of tariffs and tariff equivalents of trade barriers, which have been the key ingredients in the previous studies, but also the investment commitment of the RCEP members. Itakura (2015) experiments with the investment commitment by assuming an exogenously higher rate of return on investment. However, in this study, we link the empirical estimates of a gravity model of foreign direct investment (FDI) to the CGE model.

DOI: 10.4324/9780429433603-3

The RCEP countries account for about half of the world's population and one-third of world trade and gross domestic product (GDP) in 2017 based on estimates by the United Nations and the International Monetary Fund. Given this economic size, implementation of the RCEP may have profound economic effects on the ASEAN Member States, which, combined, represent about 9 percent of world population, 7 percent of world trade and 4 percent of world GDP. Our simulation results show that RCEP raises ASEAN's real GDP by 4.7 percent, amounting to a GDP of 344 billion US dollar higher than the baseline in 2035 (in constant US dollars). RCEP's impact on the real GDP of members varies, reflecting the economic size and the depth of the liberalisation commitments by the ASEAN Member States, ranging from 538 million US dollar for Brunei to 120 billion US dollar for the Philippines.

We outline the methodology used in this study in the next section and describe the databases, model and simulation scenarios. Section 3.3 reports the simulation results followed by a concluding summary.

3.2 Methodology

We attempt to obtain quantitative measures that can capture the potential economic effects of RCEP. For this purpose, we conduct a set of numerical simulations using a recursively dynamic CGE model of global trade. Since RCEP will have economy-wide effects on the economies of the ASEAN Member States, Australia, China, India, Japan, Korea and New Zealand, it is reasonable to use a global CGE model for evaluating the repercussions arising from the multi-sector and multi-region interactions induced by the agreement's implementation. In this section, we describe the database, the CGE model and the scenarios for the simulation.

3.2.1 Database

To reflect the current and prospective states of the global economy in our simulation analysis, we rely on the Global Trade Analysis Project (GTAP) Data Base version 9 (Aguiar et al., 2016) and economic forecasts from international organisations. The GTAP Data Base records the entire global economy with detailed information on 57 industrial sectors in 140 regions. With this database, we are able to observe the economic structure of production, international trade and protection, and consumption, benchmarked at the year 2011. The GTAP Data Base is supplemented with international factor income flows due to domestic and foreign asset holdings. To reduce the computational burden, we aggregated the GTAP Data Base to 24 countries and regions and 25 sectors, and the mappings from the original disaggregated data are reported in Tables 3.A1 and 3.A2. The GTAP Data Base covers nine ASEAN Member States – Brunei, Cambodia, Indonesia, Lao PDR, Malaysia, the Philippines, Singapore, Thailand and Viet Nam. Because of data limitations, Myanmar is included in 'rest of Southeast Asia' (RoSEAsia) along with Timor-Leste.

Our first task is to construct a baseline scenario, which is a hypothetical future state of the global economy that forms the basis of the comparisons against the RCEP policy simulations. We rely on projections for the total population, working-age population and GDP as well as gross investment. Projections for the total and working-age population growth rates are computed from the United Nations' *World Population Prospects* (United Nations, 2015) based on the medium projection variant. Projections for the growth rates of real GDP and gross investment are from the International Monetary Fund's *World Economic Outlook* (International Monetary Fund, 2017). We extrapolate the real GDP growth rates in 2022 to the end of the simulation period of 2035. Given the projections of the total population, working-age population, and real GDP for 2011–2035, the model can compute technological change as a measure of productivity. The baseline includes the trade accords that have already been agreed: the AEC, ASEAN-China FTA, ASEAN-Korea FTA, ASEAN-Japan FTA, ASEAN-Australia New Zealand FTA, ASEAN-India FTA, China-Korea FTA, Australia-Japan FTA, Australia-Korea FTA and Australia-China FTA. We assume a gradual reduction of import tariffs, and the tariffs are reduced by 80 percent.

Figure 3.1 illustrates an example of a tariff reduction schedule for the baseline and a policy scenario. The GTAP Data Base version 9 provides us with estimates of bilateral import tariffs for 2011, t_{11}. The tariff data in the GTAP Data Base originate from the Market Access Map (MAcMap) data set developed by Centre d'Études Prospectives et d'Informations Internationales and International Trade Center, which constructs the aggregated tariff information from the tariff-line level to the harmonised commodity coding systems (HS-6), including ad valorem equivalents of tariff rate quotas and specific tariffs as well as the ad valorem tariffs of most-favoured nation (MFN) and preferential tariffs (Pichot et al., 2014). The first target is specified by the year 2019, t_{19} in Figure 3.1. For all 25 sectoral trade flows of the 24 regions, we make sure that the baseline simulation passes through the bilateral tariffs of the 2019 target. The second target is specified by

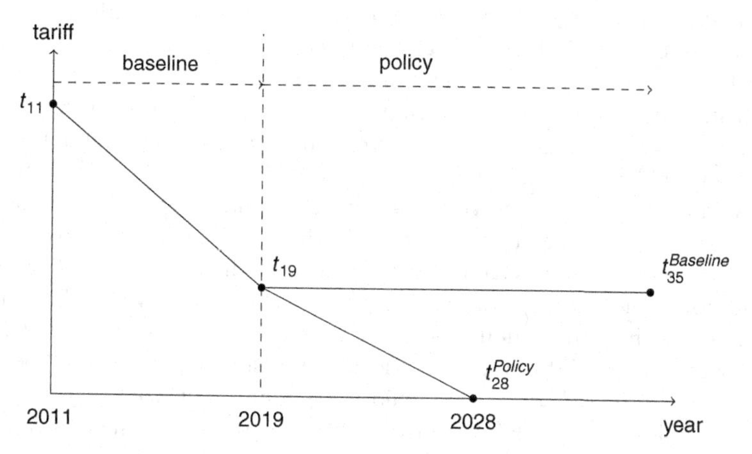

Figure 3.1 Tariff Reduction Schedule, 2011–2035.

Note: t_{11} is given by Dynamic GTAP Database v.9 (Aguiar et al., 2016). $t_{19} = (1.0 - 0.8)\ t_{11}$ if FTA is assumed in the baseline.

Source: Author's simulation scenarios.

the year 2028, t_{28}^{Policy}, which corresponds to the end of the RCEP implementation period of 2019–2028. The tariff rates in 2019 are gradually eliminated over the 2019–2028 period. All the simulations run from 2011 to 2035, and the difference between the baseline and the policy simulations emerges after 2019.

Table 3.1 reports the average applied tariff rates by sector for the ASEAN Member States for 2019, with the estimates obtained from the baseline simulation results. Average applied tariff rates on merchandise imports are computed for the sectors from primary to other manufacturing (OthMnfct). Ad valorem tariff equivalents of barriers in services trade, from utilities to other services, are computed as the unweighted averages of the gravity-model estimates of Wang et al. (2009) and the values used in the Michigan Model of World Production and Trade (Brown et al., 2010).

3.2.2 Overview of the dynamic GTAP model

For all simulations in this study, we use the dynamic GTAP model developed by Ianchovichina and McDougall (2001) and updated by Walmsley and Ianchovichina (2012). Ianchovichina and McDougall (2001) extended the comparative static standard GTAP model (Hertel, 1997; McDougall, 2003) by introducing international capital mobility and capital accumulation. In the standard GTAP model, capital is assumed to be mobile across sectors in a country but not across borders. The dynamic GTAP model preserves all the main features of the standard GTAP model: constant return to scale of production technology; perfectly competitive markets; and product differentiation by origin, known as the Armington assumption (Armington, 1969). The dynamic GTAP model uses as its core inputs the GTAP Data Base (Aguiar et al., 2016) augmented with foreign income data from the Balance of Payments Statistics of the International Monetary Fund to infer international capital ownership and foreign wealth.

In the dynamic GTAP model, each region is endowed with a fixed physical capital stock, and physical capital is accumulated over time with new investments. This dynamic is driven by net investment, which is sourced from regional households' savings. Net investment in a region is a composite of domestic investment and foreign investment from 'global trust', which is assumed to be the sole financial intermediary for all foreign investments. Regional households own indirect claims to the physical capital in the form of equity of two types – equity in domestic firms and equity in foreign firms. A regional household directly owns domestic equity but only indirectly owns foreign equity by holding shares in a portfolio of foreign equities provided by the global trust. The values of the household's equity holdings in domestic firms and in the global trust change over time, and the household allocates savings for investment. Collecting such investment funds from regions, the global trust reinvests the funds in firms around the world and offers a portfolio of equities to households. The sum of the household's equity holdings in the global trust is equal to the global trust's equity holdings in firms around the world.

Incentives for investments or equity holdings are governed by rates of return, which would be equal across regions if capital were to be perfectly mobile. However,

Table 3.1 Average Applied Tariff Rates for the ASEAN Member States (%), 2019

	Brunei	*Cambodia*	*Indonesia*	*Lao PDR*	*Malaysia*	*Philippines*	*Singapore*	*Thailand*	*Viet Nam*	*RoSEAsia*
Primary	0.6	2.8	2.3	2.4	3.0	3.3	0.0	5.3	2.7	1.3
Energy	0.0	0.0	0.0	0.4	1.3	0.0	0.0	0.0	0.6	1.9
BvrgTbcc	20.0	4.5	9.0	3.8	53.9	4.0	1.3	13.4	26.9	2.7
Textile	0.4	2.0	1.1	1.0	2.3	1.1	0.0	1.9	2.7	2.3
Apparel	0.1	7.8	3.0	1.2	2.8	1.2	0.0	6.6	4.3	3.2
Leather	0.9	2.7	1.0	1.6	1.4	1.2	0.0	5.3	3.9	1.3
Wood	1.1	5.8	0.6	5.2	1.0	1.5	0.0	2.9	1.9	2.7
Paper	0.0	2.2	1.3	1.4	3.3	2.6	0.0	1.7	3.1	0.7
PetCoProduct	0.2	3.3	0.8	1.0	0.2	0.0	0.0	1.4	2.9	0.4
Chemical	0.5	2.1	1.9	0.9	2.0	1.1	0.0	2.8	1.2	0.7
Minerals	0.0	2.4	1.6	0.5	6.0	0.9	0.0	2.3	3.8	0.4
FerrousMetal	0.0	1.6	1.3	0.4	7.0	0.5	0.0	1.1	0.7	0.3
OtherMetal	0.0	0.9	0.7	3.1	1.3	0.3	0.0	0.1	0.5	0.7
MetalProduct	0.0	3.4	1.7	0.9	3.6	1.3	0.0	3.3	2.3	0.8
Motorvehicle	5.2	8.0	2.9	5.7	5.0	3.0	0.0	7.3	6.1	2.5
TrnsprtEquip	0.1	3.1	0.6	4.9	0.5	2.4	0.0	3.0	5.0	0.6
ElecEquip	1.6	3.7	0.1	0.9	0.1	0.4	0.0	0.7	0.4	1.6
Machinery	4.6	3.3	1.7	1.1	1.3	0.6	0.0	2.1	1.1	0.5
OthMnfct	1.8	2.7	1.5	2.9	2.1	0.7	0.0	2.9	5.6	1.3
Utilities	20.6	20.6	64.4	20.6	17.4	52.6	0.0	44.9	53.7	20.6
Construction	20.6	20.6	64.4	20.6	17.4	52.6	0.0	44.9	53.7	20.6
Trade	32.5	32.5	98.5	32.5	36.0	80.2	1.3	63.5	82.7	32.5
TransComm	24.7	24.7	86.3	24.7	28.8	69.7	1.3	54.5	71.6	24.7
FinsBusi	20.0	20.0	92.5	20.0	30.2	72.6	1.5	58.1	74.7	20.0
OthSrvc	15.7	15.7	94.5	15.7	33.2	73.9	2.2	58.2	79.0	15.7

BvrgTbcc = beverages and tobacco, FinsBusi = financial business services, OthMnfct = other manufacturies, OthSrvc = other services, TrnsprtEquip = transport equipment. Table A.3.2 lists the sector description.

Note: Average applied tariff rates for merchandise trades from Primary to OthMnfct. Ad valorem equivalents of services trade barriers from Utilities to OthSrvc.

Source: Author's calculation based on Aguiar et al. (2016), Wang et al. (2009) and Brown et al. (2010).

this equalisation of the rates of return seems impractical, at least in the short run. Further, there are empirical observations of the so-called 'home bias' in savings and investment, equity holdings by households, and capital flows. Home bias refers to the empirical observations that domestic markets are preferred to foreign markets. These empirical observations suggest that capital is not perfectly mobile, leading to varying rates of return across regions. The dynamic GTAP model allows interregional differences in rates of return in the short run, which are eventually equalised in the long run.[1] Differences in the rates of return are attributed to the errors in investors' expectations about the future rates of return. However, the errors in expectation are gradually adjusted to the actual rate of return. Eventually, the errors are eliminated and the unique rate of return across regions can be attained. Therefore, we assume perfect capital mobility applies only in the long run.

Participating in the RCEP could lead to more investment from abroad. Trade liberalisation often makes prices of goods from a participating country cheaper due to the removal of tariffs, creating increased demand for the goods. Responding to the increased demand, production of the goods may expand in the exporting country. To increase production, more intermediate goods, labour, capital and other primary factors are demanded. This derived demand for production inputs raises the corresponding prices, wage rates and rental rates in the competitive markets. Higher rental rates can be translated into higher rates of return, attracting more investment from both home and foreign countries. These are part of the expected repercussions induced by RCEP liberalisation.

3.2.3 Scenarios for simulation

Three policy scenarios were designed for our simulation experiments of RCEP implementation. The baseline is constructed to reflect the hypothetical future state of the world economy without RCEP implementation for the period 2011–2035. During this period, average applied tariff rates are gradually reduced for the first target given by 2019, as discussed previously (see Figure 3.1).

Three policy scenarios for the RCEP are implemented over the period 2019–2035, comprising the RCEP implementation period of 2019–2028 and the post RCEP period of 2029–2035. Each policy scenario is designed to evaluate different liberalisation components of the RCEP.

Scenario 1: Tariff rate reductions over the years. Import tariffs are gradually removed for the RCEP members.

Scenario 2: Ad valorem equivalents of services trade barriers are gradually reduced by 20 percent for the RCEP members. On merchandise goods, logistic improvements reduce time and cost of crossing border (namely, 'services trade costs'), thereby their trade costs among the RCEP members are gradually lowered by 20 percent. These liberalisation components are added to Scenario 1.

Scenario 3: The investment liberalisation commitments by the RCEP members are added to Scenario 2.

In Scenario 1, bilateral tariff rates on goods among RCEP countries begin linearly decreasing from the level in 2019, t_{19} in Figure 3.1, towards the complete removal, t_{28}^{Policy}. For example, Brunei's average applied tariff rate on beverage and tobacco (20 percent in Table 3.1) is lowering towards zero for the partner countries at constant degree. Given the fact that the RCEP covers economic linkages not only trade in goods but also trade in services as well as investment, Scenario 1 can be regarded as a fraction of the entire coverage.

In Scenario 2, in addition to the import tariff removal, we consider the reduction in services trade costs to trade due to RCEP's measures to improve logistics for merchandise goods. Services trade costs that measure time-cost to trade can be considered as the product of the average cost of a one-day delay in trade multiplied by the number of days of shipping delays. For example, shipping delays arising from regulatory procedures and inadequate infrastructure incur services trade costs. Hummels and Schaur (2013) provide empirical estimates of the average costs of time delays in trade. Minor (2013) compiles information about time in transit and the empirical estimates in a database. We use the database to compute the reduction in services trade costs by 20 percent over the 2019–2028 period of RCEP's implementation. We also include the reduction in ad valorem equivalents of services trade barriers (Table 3.1).

In Scenario 3, for the investment commitment, we incorporate the empirically estimated relation between inward FDI flows and investment treaties, on top of Scenario 2. There are several empirical studies we consider for this analysis, for example, Busse et al. (2010), Urata (2015) and Honda et al. (2015). The latter explores the relation between inward or outward FDI and investment treaties, collecting data on 201 countries for 1995–2012 for their estimation. Their estimating model of the inward FDI is

$$lnFDI_{it+1} = \alpha + \beta_1 lnBIT_{it} + \beta_2 lnGDP_{it} + \beta_3 lnCO_{it} + \beta_4 lnTO_{it} + \varepsilon_{it}$$

where *BIT* is for bilateral investment treaties, *GDP* for gross domestic product, *CO* for capital openness, and *TO* for trade openness. They find a statistically significant coefficient for $\beta_1 = 0.196$, which can be interpreted that, on average, the inward FDI flow following the year of establishing a bilateral investment treaty tends to be 19.6 percent higher. For the RCEP simulation in this study, the increased FDI inflow is captured by country-specific factors in the rate of return on investment in the CGE model, matching the targeted increase in investment.

3.3 Simulation results

Figure 3.2 shows the annual growth rate of ASEAN's real GDP from 2011 to 2035 for the baseline and the RCEP simulation (Scenario 3). We can clearly see that the real GDP growth rates for ASEAN are higher than those in the baseline because of the RCEP. Over the period 2019–2028, the removal of import tariffs, the reduction of ad valorem equivalents of services trade barriers, and logistics improvements are implemented gradually. Investment commitment has a lagged effect and pushes the growth rate after 2020. The annual growth rate of ASEAN peaks in 2028 at 5.6 percent, of which 0.4 percent is due to RCEP on top of the baseline growth rate of 5.2 percent. The effect of RCEP tapers off once its implementation period

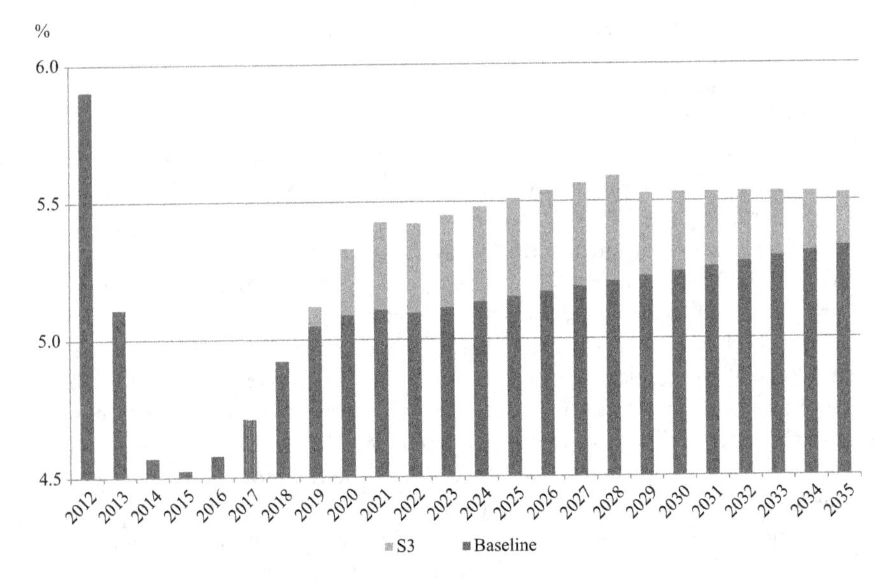

Figure 3.2 Annual Growth Rate of ASEAN's Real GDP (in percent), 2011–2035.
Note: S3 is for the RCEP Scenario 3, which implements removal of tariffs, logistics improvement, reduction in services trade barriers, and investment commitment.
Source: Author's simulation results.

is passed after 2028. Increased investment and capital stock contribute to the persistent effect of RCEP on real GDP growth rate for 2029–2035.

The differences in annual growth rates between the baseline and the RCEP policy scenarios accumulate over time, as shown in Figure 3.3. Each scenario deviates from the baseline after 2019. If tariff elimination is the sole component of RCEP (S1: Scenario 1), then the deviation from the baseline is 0.2 percent by 2035. Under Scenario 2 (S2), in addition to the tariff removal, reduction in services trade barriers and logistic improvements result in the cumulative increase in ASEAN's real GDP by 2.2 percent in 2035. For Scenario 3, all the liberalisation components of Scenario 2 plus the investment commitments culminate in a significant rise in real GDP by 4.7 percent in 2035 relative to the baseline.

The impacts of tariff removal observed in Figure 3.3 are rather small compared to the reductions in services trade barriers and logistics improvement. This can be understood by the fact that ASEAN has been lowering tariffs by the existing FTAs within ASEAN as well as with the RCEP partner countries. More potential gains from the RCEP can be found in services trade liberalisation and the seamless movement of merchandise goods. Attracting more investment may contribute further to the potential gains in real GDP. In Figure 3.4, each ASEAN Member State confirms these observations. For example, Brunei's real GDP becomes 1.3 percent larger than the baseline by 2035, by eliminating tariffs, lowering barriers in services trade, improving logistics and drawing more investment (Scenario 3), shown in Figure 3.4 panel (a).

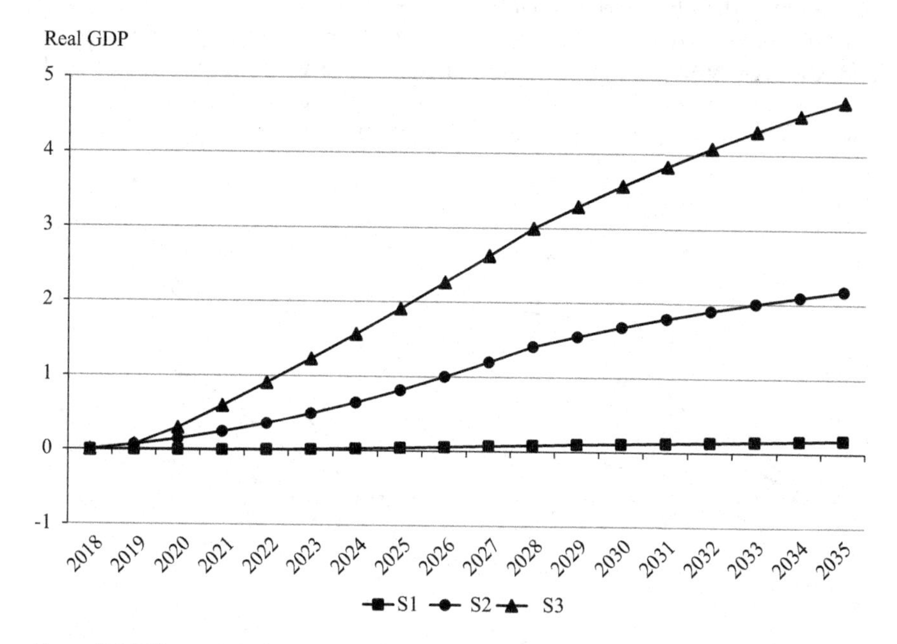

Figure 3.3 Effects of the RCEP on ASEAN's Real GDP (Cumulative Deviation from the Baseline, in percent).

Note: (S1) removal of tariffs, (S2) S1 + logistics improvement, reduction in services trade barriers, (S3) S2 + investment commitment.

Source: Author's simulation results.

The deviation from the baseline caused by tariff removal (S1) is positive but much smaller than the other two scenarios. This implies that services trade, logistics, and investment are relatively more important components in the RCEP for potential gains in GDP. Cambodia, Lao PDR, Malaysia, Singapore, Thailand and Viet Nam show a similar implication in their results. There are some cases for Indonesia and the Philippines where eliminating tariffs does not generate deviations from the baseline in any significant way, and their impacts are close to zero or very small negatives. RoSEAsia is assumed to be an aggregate of Myanmar and Timor-Leste because the GTAP database does not store detailed information for them. Partly because of this data deficiency, Scenarios 1 and 2 do not deviate much from the baseline for RoSEAsia.

Table 3.2 reports the cumulative effect of the RCEP on real GDP in 2035 for all countries and regions. The results in the left panel of the table are in terms of the percentage difference from the baseline in 2035. For example, the impacts on ASEAN's real GDP are 0.2 percent, 2.2 percent and 4.7 percent, respectively, for Scenarios 1, 2, and 3 (as shown in Figure 3.3 for 2035). From the results, we can see that all RCEP member countries gain in real GDP in all the scenarios, except for a few cases under S1 where small negatives are observed for Indonesia, the Philippines and RoSEAsia. It should be noted that the baseline growth rates are all positive. Thus, these small negative figures indicate that the policy simulation results are slightly below the baseline level. As we will see later, Indonesia's large import volume increase, the Philippines' slightly below baseline level investment, and RoSEAsia's subpar export volume change can be attributed to the real GDP changes observed under S1. However, we should keep in mind that the RCEP covers wider liberalisation items beyond the tariff reform.

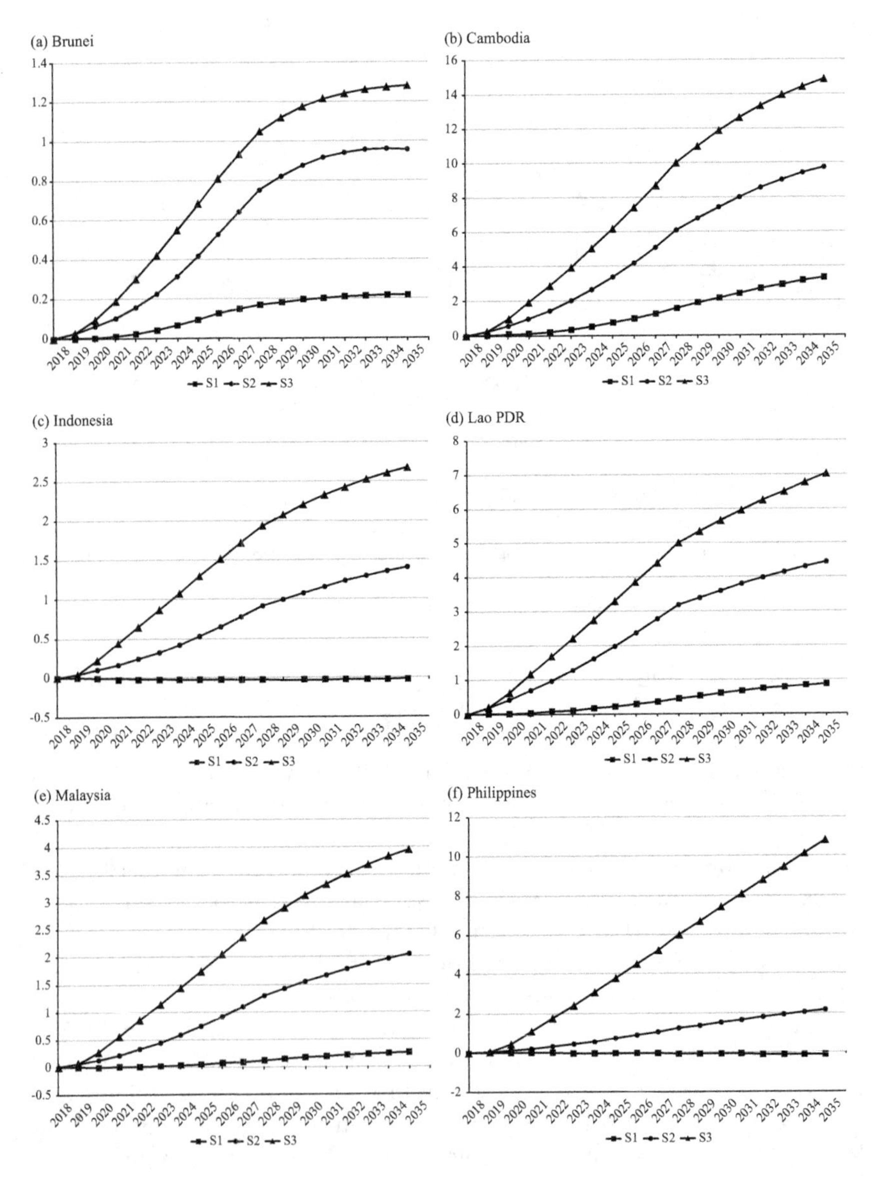

Figure 3.4 Effects of the RCEP on Real GDP for ASEAN Member States (Cumulative Deviation from the Baseline, in percent).

Note: (S1) removal of tariffs, (S2) S1 + logistics improvement, reduction in services trade barriers, (S3) S2 + investment commitment.

Source: Author's simulation results.

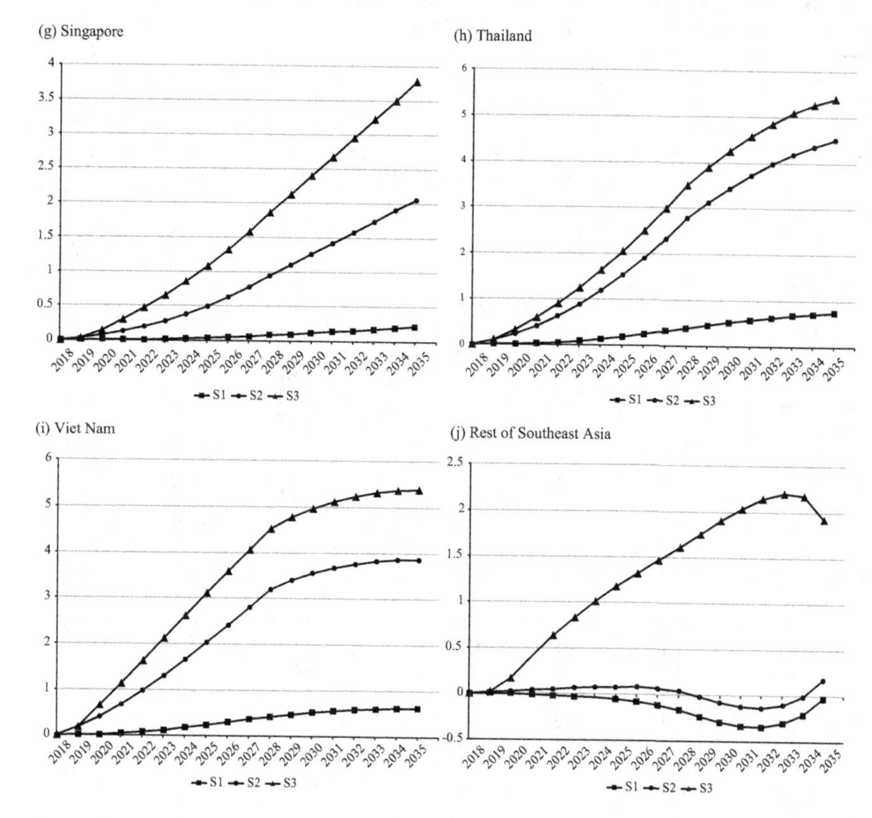

Figure 3.4 (Continued)

The gains in real GDP from the RCEP become larger as the liberalisation components are extended from the conventional tariff reform in S1 to cover non-tariff barriers in merchandise and services trade in S2, and further to promote investment in S3. Under Scenario 2, ad valorem equivalents of barriers in services trade are gradually cut by 20 percent over the period of 2019–2028 for services sectors such as utilities, construction, trade, transport and communication, financial businesses, and other services. These services sectors account for large shares in production, ranging from 29 percent (Brunei) to 74 percent (Australia), and the average of RCEP members is 48 percent in 2011. This average share of services sectors in production is projected to be 51 percent in 2035, indicating a structural shift towards a services economy. The increasing share of services amplifies the effect of reducing services trade barriers. On the other hand, for the rest of production, merchandise sectors still account for half of the production – 52 percent in 2011 and 49 percent in 2035 – on average. Thus, a 20 percent reduction in services trade costs to trade by logistics improvements is expected to substantially raise merchandise trade among the RCEP members. These two effects in Scenario 2 explain the large impact on real GDP in Table 3.2.

Table 3.2 Effects on Real GDP, 2035 (Cumulative Deviation from the Baseline (percent), Billion US Dollar, in Constant 2011 Price)

	S1	*S2*	*S3*	*S1*	*S2*	*S3*
		percent			*Billion US dollar*	
Brunei	0.2	1.0	1.3	0.1	0.4	0.5
Cambodia	3.3	9.8	14.9	2.0	5.8	8.8
Indonesia	-0.02	1.4	2.7	-0.6	42.2	80.3
Lao PDR	0.9	4.4	7.0	0.4	1.8	2.9
Malaysia	0.3	2.0	3.9	2.4	18.4	35.6
Philippines	-0.1	2.2	10.8	-1.2	24.1	120.2
Singapore	0.2	2.1	3.8	1.2	10.8	19.9
Thailand	0.7	4.5	5.4	5.4	32.5	39.1
Viet Nam	0.6	3.9	5.4	3.6	21.9	30.6
RoSEAsia	-0.03	0.2	1.9	-0.1	0.6	6.2
Japan	0.7	1.0	1.0	46.5	70.3	67.8
China	0.2	0.5	0.8	66.8	143.0	252.1
Korea	1.0	1.9	1.9	24.5	47.2	46.6
India	1.4	2.7	3.8	153.8	304.2	432.8
Australia	0.0	0.7	2.2	1.3	17.4	59.7
New Zealand	0.7	1.6	5.3	2.2	5.0	16.4
Hong Kong	-0.3	-1.1	-1.9	-1.5	-5.2	-9.4
Taiwan	-0.6	-1.0	-1.5	-4.8	-8.2	-12.1
US	-0.1	-0.1	-0.3	-14.6	-30.0	-78.3
Canada	-0.1	-0.1	-0.4	-1.6	-3.6	-11.1
Mexico	-0.3	-0.6	-1.9	-6.2	-13.6	-41.6
Chile	-0.3	-0.6	-1.2	-1.3	-2.9	-6.1
Peru	-0.1	-0.2	-0.4	-0.3	-0.7	-1.7
ROW	-0.2	-0.4	-1.0	-107.3	-229.4	-560.1
ASEAN	0.2	2.2	4.7	12.9	158.6	344.1
RCEP	0.5	1.2	2.0	307.9	745.7	1219.5
WLD	0.1	0.3	0.3	170.2	452.2	499.1

ROW = Rest of the world, WLD = World.
Source: Author's simulation results.

All RCEP members considerably increase GDP above the baseline. Small negatives observed in Scenario 1 for Indonesia, the Philippines, and RoSEAsia are overturned in Scenario 2. Investment commitment in the RCEP is expected to attract 20 percent more inward FDI in Scenario 3. The effect of additional investment contributes to raise GDP higher than in Scenario 2. Cambodia stands out in terms of percentage impact, 14.9 percent over the baseline, about 5 percentage points larger than Scenario 2. Under Scenario 3, of which all the 16 countries becoming more liberalised in terms of tariff rates on goods, reduced services trade costs as well as more liberalised investment, the Philippines shows a significant increase in its GDP of 10.8 percent.

To reflect each country's economic size, the impact in absolute values is also reported in the right-hand panel of the table in terms of billions of US dollar. India benefits most from RCEP by 433 billion US dollar in Scenario 3, followed by China (252 billion US dollar). When all RCEP members are combined, the increase in GDP amounts to 1.2 trillion US dollar, of which ASEAN accounts for one-third. Although non-member countries are unfavourably affected by RCEP as trade and investment are diverted, the world total clearly registers substantial gains.

Higher rates of return caused by RCEP liberalisation raise investment volumes above the baseline. Table 3.3 reports the investment volume simulation results, measured by the cumulative deviation from the baseline. RCEP gives rise to ASEAN's investment by 11.2 percent higher than the baseline under Scenario 3, whereas the increase in investment for the RCEP members is 5.0 percent. All the RCEP member countries, except RoSEAsia, experience increased investment, especially, and unsurprisingly, under Scenario 3. Higher rental rates on capital lead to higher rates of return, thereby boosting investment volume more than the baseline, as shown in Table 3.3. For example, India, the Philippines and China obtain significantly larger expansions of investment volume, respectively, 218 billion US dollar, 169 billion US dollar and 143 billion US dollar, in Scenario 3.

Table 3.3 Effect on Investment, 2035 (Cumulative Deviation from the Baseline (percent), Billion US Dollar, in Constant 2011 Price)

	S1	*S2*	*S3*	*S1*	*S2*	*S3*
		percent			*Billion US dollar*	
Brunei	0.9	1.6	2.9	0.3	0.5	0.9
Cambodia	7.7	20.6	35.4	0.9	2.5	4.2
Indonesia	0.1	2.9	6.2	1.4	41.5	88.0
Lao PDR	3.0	9.3	18.7	0.6	1.8	3.5
Malaysia	0.9	5.2	11.2	3.0	18.3	39.6
Philippines	-0.2	4.2	27.1	-1.5	26.5	169.1
Singapore	0.6	5.2	10.2	2.0	16.7	32.5
Thailand	2.1	10.6	11.7	4.6	22.9	25.4
Viet Nam	1.4	6.2	11.1	2.4	10.2	18.2
RoSEAsia	3.9	4.2	-2.5	7.9	8.6	-5.0
Japan	2.9	4.1	4.0	42.4	59.4	58.2
China	0.2	0.4	1.5	18.4	42.2	143.3
Korea	5.5	7.9	7.8	38.2	54.3	53.6
India	3.0	5.8	8.3	80.4	153.2	218.4
Australia	0.6	2.2	8.5	4.2	15.3	58.8
New Zealand	2.3	4.9	16.9	2.4	5.0	17.4
Hong Kong	-0.7	-2.7	-4.6	-1.9	-7.4	-12.6
Taiwan	-2.4	-4.2	-6.0	-4.9	-8.5	-12.1
US	-0.3	0.6	-1.6	-10.8	-22.9	-61.6
Canada	-0.1	-0.4	-1.4	-0.8	-2.2	-8.4
Mexico	-0.9	-1.8	-4.7	-9.7	-19.8	-51.2
Chile	-0.9	-1.8	-3.5	-2.0	-4.3	-8.3
Peru	-0.3	-0.5	-1.4	-0.3	-0.7	-1.7
ROW	-0.7	-1.4	-3.1	-115.8	-241.2	-546.1
ASEAN	0.6	4.4	11.2	21.5	149.4	376.4
RCEP	1.1	2.6	5.0	207.6	478.8	926.1
WLD	0.1	0.4	0.5	61.4	171.8	224.0

Source: Author's simulation results.

Table 3.4 reports the export volume simulation results, and Table 3.5 shows the import volume results in 2035. In general, the potential impact of RCEP on trade becomes larger as we extend Scenarios S1, S2, and S3; the wider the coverage of the liberalisation components the higher the trade volume for the RCEP members. For Scenario 3, the export volume growth of ASEAN is 3.9 percent while that of the RCEP is 4.3 percent. In a few cases, the results for the export volume fall below the baseline, indicated by negative figures, for Lao PDR, the Philippines and RoSEAsia in Scenario 3. Large investment increase in 2020 can explain the export volume changes in Lao PDR and the Philippines. Because of the data limitations, we put aside RoSEAsia here. In 2020, one year after the RCEP implementation begins, investment shoots up in Lao PDR by 7.3 percent and in the Philippines by 8.3 percent. Investment is a fixed capital formation which assembles industrial outputs into physical capital. As the large investment requires more sectoral outputs, these output prices are pushed up by the increased demand.

The rise in output prices is passed onto export prices, thereby lowering export volumes below the baseline. This descent of export volumes happens in 2020,

Table 3.4 Effects on Export Value, 2035 (Cumulative Deviation from the Baseline (percent), Billion US Dollar, in Constant 2011 Price)

	S1	*S2*	*S3*	*S1*	*S2*	*S3*
		percent			*Billion US dollar*	
Brunei	0.1	0.6	0.4	0.0	0.1	0.0
Cambodia	5.7	10.2	15.4	3.5	6.3	9.5
Indonesia	0.4	1.2	0.6	2.2	6.2	3.2
Lao PDR	2.2	0.2	-0.7	0.4	0.0	-0.1
Malaysia	1.0	3.1	5.5	6.5	21.1	36.7
Philippines	1.0	2.6	-1.3	4.8	11.9	-6.2
Singapore	0.2	1.3	1.9	1.3	9.2	13.6
Thailand	2.3	6.5	8.4	15.3	42.9	55.2
Viet Nam	2.3	5.4	6.5	7.9	18.8	22.6
RoSEAsia	-1.7	-1.7	1.5	-0.4	-0.4	0.4
Japan	3.1	4.3	4.8	45.3	62.9	70.2
China	1.9	2.9	3.2	161.3	241.9	270.2
Korea	2.6	4.0	4.5	42.7	65.3	72.6
India	4.0	5.5	6.9	162.3	221.6	277.7
Australia	0.1	1.9	1.3	0.6	8.4	5.7
New Zealand	2.0	2.8	3.1	1.8	2.5	2.7
Hong Kong	-0.3	-0.9	-1.2	-1.2	-3.7	-4.9
Taiwan	-0.8	-1.5	-1.6	-5.1	-9.2	-9.7
US	-0.3	-0.5	-0.6	-10.5	-20.4	-21.7
Canada	-0.3	-0.6	-0.9	-2.1	-3.7	-5.4
Mexico	0.0	0.0	-0.8	0.4	-0.1	-7.2
Chile	0.3	0.5	0.7	0.6	0.9	1.3
Peru	-0.2	-0.4	-0.3	-0.2	-0.3	-0.3
ROW	-0.4	-0.7	-1.2	-64.2	-123.2	-209.8
ASEAN	1.2	3.4	3.9	41.6	116.1	134.9
RCEP	2.3	3.7	4.3	455.5	718.7	834.0
WLD	0.9	1.3	1.3	373.2	559.0	576.2

Source: Author's simulation results.

when RCEP's investment commitment takes effect under Scenario 3. However, export volumes start growing after 2020 and eventually surpass the baseline. Figure 3.5 clearly shows this time path for Indonesia: fall then pass beyond the baseline. Lao PDR and the Philippines exhibit similar time paths but stop short before reaching the baseline by 2035. This is the reason why the two countries result in the negative figures.

Table 3.5 illustrates that the potential impacts of the establishment of the RCEP on import volumes are all positive for the member countries, except for RoSAsia. In percentage terms, the largest change is observed in the Philippines (16.4 percent), followed by Cambodia (16.3 percent) under Scenario 3. ASEAN and RCEP expand import volume almost 7 percent larger than the baseline. As for absolute value, China and India show bigger impacts: of 171 billion US dollar and 157 billion US dollar, respectively. Aggregated for ASEAN and the RCEP, import value will increase by 256 billion US dollar for ASEAN and 819 billion US dollar for the RCEP countries (Figure 3.5).

Table 3.5 Effects on Import Value, 2035 (Cumulative Deviation from the Baseline (percent), Billion US Dollar, in Constant 2011 Price)

	S1	*S2*	*S3*	*S1*	*S2*	*S3*
	percent			*Billion US dollar*		
Brunei	0.8	1.1	2.1	0.2	0.3	0.6
Cambodia	5.0	9.8	16.3	2.1	4.2	6.9
Indonesia	0.6	3.2	5.4	4.6	24.7	41.2
Lao PDR	2.5	4.1	9.2	0.6	0.9	2.1
Malaysia	1.0	3.8	6.8	6.9	26.8	48.5
Philippines	0.2	3.7	16.4	0.9	17.6	77.4
Singapore	0.4	3.0	4.8	2.8	20.4	33.4
Thailand	2.1	6.9	8.3	11.4	37.5	45.3
Viet Nam	1.8	4.6	6.8	7.4	18.9	27.8
RoSEAsia	10.2	11.2	-9.9	18.1	19.9	-17.6
Japan	5.5	7.5	7.5	69.5	94.7	95.2
China	2.8	4.2	4.7	102.2	154.0	171.2
Korea	4.0	6.1	6.3	49.3	74.9	77.4
India	5.1	7.2	8.6	93.7	131.1	157.0
Australia	1.6	4.3	7.4	9.4	24.9	42.9
New Zealand	3.5	5.6	11.3	3.0	4.9	9.7
Hong Kong	-0.6	-1.9	-2.9	-2.4	-8.1	-12.2
Taiwan	-1.5	-2.6	-3.0	-7.5	-13.3	-15.4
US	-0.4	-0.8	-1.3	-17.4	-34.1	-51.9
Canada	-0.1	-0.3	-0.6	-1.0	-2.2	-4.8
Mexico	-0.6	-1.2	-3.0	-4.9	-9.9	-25.3
Chile	-0.6	-1.3	-2.2	-1.2	-2.4	-4.1
Peru	-0.5	-0.8	-1.3	-0.5	-0.8	-1.2
ROW	-0.4	-0.9	-1.6	-96.6	-198.9	-350.9
ASEAN	1.4	4.4	6.9	55.0	171.3	265.6
RCEP	3.1	5.2	6.6	382.2	655.8	819.1
WLD	0.6	0.9	0.9	250.7	385.9	353.3

Source: Author's simulation results.

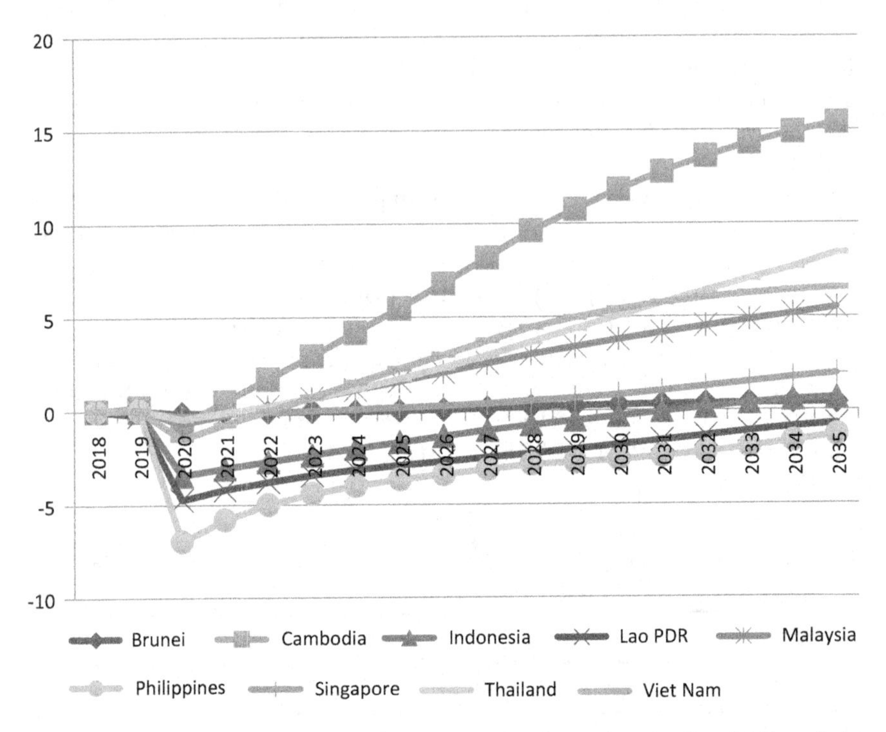

Figure 3.5 Effects of the RCEP on Export Volume for Indonesia, Lao PDR and the Philippines, Scenario 3 (Cumulative Deviation from the Baseline, in percent).

Source: Author's simulation results.

Sectoral output volume changes under Scenario 3 are reported in Table 3.6 for the ASEAN Member States. RCEP brings about a shift in Brunei's sectoral outputs towards primary, energy, minerals and services industries, while many manufacturing sectors slightly contract in absolute values. Cambodia results in growth in apparel (4.5 billion US dollar) and textile (2.4 billion US dollar). Construction in Indonesia and the Philippines expands by 66 billion US dollar and 74 billion US dollar, respectively, corresponding to the large investment increases. Primary and construction sectors in Lao PDR become larger by more than 10 billion US dollar. The biggest change in sectoral output in Malaysia is Trade (19 billion US dollar), followed by electronic equipment (12 billion US dollar). Singapore's chemical sector increases by 9 billion US dollar, second to construction (19 billion US dollar). Expansion of the machinery sector in Thailand amounts to 19 billion US dollar, and the motor vehicle industry also grows by 14 billion US dollar. Primary (7 billion US dollar) and chemical sectors in Viet Nam lead the increase in sectoral outputs there.

Table 3.6 Effects on Sectoral Output Volume for ASEAN Member State under Scenario 3, 2035

Cumulative Deviation from the Baseline (percent)

	Brunei	*Cambodia*	*Indonesia*	*LaoPDR*	*Malaysia*	*Philippines*	*Singapore*	*Thailand*	*Viet Nam*	*RoSEAsia*
Primary	1.8	2.9	0.9	3.2	1.8	2.4	−6.4	1.3	2.7	1.8
Energy	0.1	−1.1	0.1	−1.3	0.1	−1.5	0.6	0.1	0.3	2.8
BvrgTbcc	−10.1	5.2	1.0	7.3	−0.2	6.3	9.8	−0.1	1.3	0.2
Textile	−0.7	20.9	−0.6	−9.7	1.7	−1.6	−7.9	1.2	6.9	39.8
Apparel	0.0	18.2	−2.3	−5.8	0.4	−0.3	−3.9	−0.2	10.0	12.2
Leather	−2.0	6.8	−3.0	−27.3	1.0	1.7	−7.4	0.6	8.7	39.3
Wood	−1.7	10.3	3.0	−27.2	2.8	10.3	3.3	5.7	3.1	25.4
Paper	−0.1	13.3	1.4	−5.1	4.0	6.4	−2.1	6.2	3.0	31.3
PetCoProduct	0.1	16.6	−1.3	3.0	2.3	8.7	4.9	3.8	1.8	1.8
Chemical	−9.9	9.3	0.3	22.3	6.0	2.5	3.1	5.7	7.5	42.1
Minerals	1.9	28.4	4.7	15.4	5.1	20.9	6.4	5.5	6.0	14.4
FerrousMetal	−1.5	27.1	2.8	−2.6	4.6	7.3	−5.0	6.6	10.2	38.3
OtherMetal	−5.1	29.7	1.2	5.2	26.4	8.6	34.6	18.5	11.8	53.0
MetalProduct	−0.9	12.3	5.1	0.7	8.1	10.6	0.1	9.6	8.3	36.7
Motorvehicle	−8.6	17.1	2.1	20.5	3.1	21.6	−1.0	10.6	9.1	17.2
TrnsprtEquip	−3.0	34.0	1.1	134.5	8.1	9.1	−3.2	12.2	7.7	26.7
ElecEquip	−1.3	24.0	3.0	7.9	5.2	3.4	−2.6	10.8	15.8	35.7
Machinery	0.8	27.3	2.2	14.5	7.8	9.6	−0.8	12.4	15.9	43.3
OthMnfct	−7.9	13.1	2.5	7.4	9.0	6.3	−1.2	4.6	1.6	18.3
Utilities	0.2	15.9	2.0	5.7	4.7	8.9	3.3	4.6	5.2	3.4
Construction	2.7	34.4	6.0	18.3	5.7	26.7	9.8	11.2	10.7	−2.2
Trade	2.2	14.2	2.8	8.7	5.3	11.0	4.5	5.1	5.0	1.5
TransComm	1.4	19.5	2.0	6.7	4.0	13.1	2.0	3.6	5.7	1.7
FinsBusi	2.2	13.6	1.8	7.0	2.9	8.9	3.4	3.7	2.8	9.2
OthSrvc	0.8	11.8	2.0	9.7	1.0	8.0	2.1	0.6	4.7	2.1

(*Continued*)

In Million US Dollar, in Constant 2011 Price

	Brunei	*Cambodia*	*Indonesia*	*LaoPDR*	*Malaysia*	*Philippines*	*Singapore*	*Thailand*	*Viet Nam*	*RoSEAsia*
Primary	29	1,084	6,117	1,025	4,794	6,903	-41	2,653	6,670	4,027
Energy	10	-0	265	-15	138	-82	0	42	233	633
BvrgTbcc	-4	23	302	234	-16	889	141	-9	245	66
Textile	-0	2,357	-424	-48	102	-194	-8	351	1,357	75
Apparel	0	4,516	-304	-53	12	-64	-9	-32	1,940	207
Leather	-0	235	-537	-30	8	76	-2	63	1,467	29
Wood	-1	144	1,953	-255	665	2,232	17	1,032	417	19
Paper	-0	91	1,106	-2	1,363	1,350	-67	1,254	406	30
PetCoProduct	3	37	-1,485	134	1,240	2,409	7,429	3,180	470	57
Chemical	-1	1,005	1,351	69	10,916	3,054	8,609	6,376	5,362	52
Minerals	14	224	4,942	134	1,803	7,778	489	1,257	1,753	1,045
FerrousMetal	-0	58	1,619	-1	1,998	1,822	-130	1,247	146	38
OtherMetal	-0	40	557	483	9,971	6,493	1,251	7,398	668	12
MetalProduct	-1	27	13,682	1	3,977	3,580	7	2,257	354	94
Motorvehicle	-0	297	1,432	17	2,061	17,162	-5	13,566	790	96
TrnsprtEquip	-0	212	628	100	860	3,572	-214	2,045	1,668	37
ElecEquip	-1	174	1,028	5	11,808	8,387	-5,102	12,690	4,179	54
Machinery	0	119	1,903	46	10,595	20,768	-549	18,962	3,608	151
OthMnfct	-1	157	851	44	1,387	1,275	-13	974	174	679
Utilities	3	187	1,538	254	2,461	3,666	506	1,979	3,340	305
Construction	216	1,885	65,654	1,112	9,331	73,377	19,286	7,440	9,856	-1,642
Trade	175	1,498	18,658	578	18,740	24,380	5,939	11,244	5,352	850
TransComm	96	1,158	5,861	266	6,770	17,264	4,647	3,036	1,509	421
FinsBusi	426	491	4,956	46	6,980	12,423	7,127	2,862	1,097	430
OthSrvc	101	1,828	20,267	816	2,433	13,804	1,856	759	6,094	2,118

Source: Author's simulation results.

3.4 Summary

By applying a dynamic GTAP model with a recent database, we conducted a set of policy simulations for the RCEP focussing on the ASEAN Member States. In our simulation experiments, we use a set of economic databases and empirical estimates to explore the potential economic gains from the RCEP through liberalising goods and services trade, improving the logistics for merchandise goods trade, and fostering investment in the region. The simulation results reveal that all participating countries in the RCEP gain in terms of real GDP by liberalising their trade and promoting investment. Our simulation results show that the RCEP raises ASEAN's real GDP by 4.7 percent above the baseline in 2035. The impact of the RCEP varies for the individual ASEAN Member States, reflecting the differences in economic size and the depth of liberalisation. If the RCEP commits to promoting investment, then the increase in real GDP is bolstered further. Investment in all member countries rises as the RCEP is implemented; more foreign capital is likely to be attracted to the RCEP region by the higher rates of return. Trade volumes expand for the participating countries.

This study has some limitations that can be addressed with additional information and updated data. We assume full utilisation of the RCEP but, in reality, many producers and consumers have not used the preferential treatments made available by the existing FTAs. The utilisation rates can be incorporated into the simulation setting to reflect the under-utilisation of FTAs. We do not incorporate either the cost-reducing effect of consolidating existing FTAs or the cost-incurring effect of complying with different rules of origin. The movement of labour across the participating countries is not considered because of limitations with the current model. Although it is not easy, the model can be extended to capture the aforementioned limitations.

Note

1 Due to data limitation, GTAP Database does not have capital tax information. The model is absent from capital tax.

References

Aguiar, Angel, Badri Narayanan, and Robert McDougall (2016), 'An Overview of the GTAP 9 Data Base', *Journal of Global Economic Analysis*, 1(1), pp. 181–208.

Armington, Paul S. (1969), 'A Theory of Demand for Products Distinguished by Place of Production', *IMF Staff Papers*, 16, pp. 159–176, Washington, DC: IMF.

Brown, Drusilla K., Kozo Kiyota, and Robert M. Stern (2010), 'Computational Analysis of the Menu of U.S.-Japan Trade Policies', *RSIE Discussion Paper*, No. 611, Ford School of Public Policy, University of Michigan.

Busse, Matthias, Jens Köninger, and Peter Nunnenkamp (2010), 'FDI Promotion through Bilateral Investment Treaties: More Than a Bit?' *Review of World Economics*, 146(1), pp. 147–177.

Cheong, Inkyo, and Jose Tongzon (2013), 'Comparing the Economic Impact of the Trans-Pacific Partnership and the Regional Comprehensive Economic Partnership', *Asian Economic Papers*, 12(2), pp. 144–164.

Hertel, Thomas W. (Ed.) (1997), *Global Trade Analysis: Modeling and Applications*, New York: Cambridge University Press.

Honda, Kotomi, Takayuki Sugiura, Yasunari Morita, and Chunun Fong (2015), 'Effect of Bilateral Investment Treaties on Foreign Direct Investment: Need for International Investment Treaties', ISFJ Conference Paper (in Japanese), pp. 1–48.

Hummels, David L., and Georg Schaur (2013), 'Time as a Trade Barrier', *American Economic Review*, 103(7), pp. 2935–2959.

Ianchovichina, Elena, and Robert McDougall (2001), 'Theoretical Structure of Dynamic GTAP', *GTAP Technical Paper*, West Lafayette, IN: Purdue University, pp. 1–74.

International Monetary Fund (2017), *World Economic Outlook Database: April 2017*, Washington, DC: International Monetary Fund.

Itakura, Ken (2014), 'Impact of Liberalization and Improved Connectivity and Facilitation in ASEAN', *Journal of Asian Economics*, 35, pp. 2–11.

Itakura, Ken (2015), 'Chapter 1: Assessing the Economic Effects of the Regional Comprehensive Economic Partnership on ASEAN Member States', in Lili Yan Ing (ed.), *East Asian Integration*, Economic Research Institute for ASEAN and East Asia, pp. 1–23.

Kawai, Masahiro, and Ganeshan Wignaraja (2008), 'EAFTA or CEPEA: Which Way Forward?' *ASEAN Economic Bulletin*, 25(2), pp. 113–139.

Lee, Hiro, and Ken Itakura (2017), 'The Welfare and Sectoral Adjustment Effects of Mega-Regional Trade Agreements on ASEAN Countries', Conference on Trade, Industrialization and Structural Reforms in ASEAN, Ho Chi Minh City.

Lee, Hiro, Robert F. Owen, and Dominique van der Mensbrugghe (2009), 'Regional Integration in Asia and its effects on the EU and North America', *Journal of Asian Economics*, 20, pp. 240–254.

McDougall, Robert (2003), 'A New Regional Household Demand System for GTAP', *GTAP Technical Paper*, 20, pp. 1–57, West Lafayette, IN: Purdue University.

Minor, Peter (2013), *Time as a Barrier to Trade: A GTAP Database of Ad Valorem Trade Time Costs*. ImpactEcon, Second Edition.

Pichot, Xavier, Mondher Mimouni, Badri Narayanan, and Janine Pelikan (2014), 'Construction of ITC MACMAP Tariff Dataset', *GTAP Conference Paper*, #4419.

United Nations (2015), *World Population Prospects: The 2015 Revision*, New York: United Nations.

Urata, Shujiro (2014), 'Japan's Trade Policy with Asia', *Public Policy Review*, 10(1), pp. 1–31.

Urata, Shujiro (2015), 'Impacts of FTAs and BITs on the Locational Choice of Foreign Direct Investment: The Case of Japanese Firms', *RIETI Discussion Paper Series*, 15-E-066, pp. 1–28.

Walmsley, Terrie L., and Elena Ianchovichina (Eds.) (2012), *Dynamic Modeling and Applications for Global Economic Analysis*, New York: Cambridge University Press.

Wang, Zhi, Sushil Mohan, and Daniel Rosen (2009), 'Methodology for Estimating Services Trade Barriers', Rhodium Group and Peterson Institute for International Economics.

Appendix A

Table 3.A1 List of Countries and Regions

	Country/Region		*Country/Region*
1	Brunei	13	Korea
2	Cambodia	14	India
3	Indonesia	15	Australia
4	Lao PDR	16	New Zealand
5	Malaysia	17	Hong Kong
6	Philippines	18	Taiwan
7	Singapore	19	US
8	Thailand	20	Canada
9	Viet Nam	21	Mexico
10	RoSEAsia	22	Chile
11	Japan	23	Peru
12	China	24	ROW

Note: Lao PDR = Lao People's Democratic Republic, RoSEAsia = rest of Southeast Asia, which includes Myanmar and Timor-Leste. ROW = rest of the world. ASEAN is defined as an aggregate from Brunei to RoSEAsia.

Source: Author's aggregation based on Aguiar et al. (2016).

Appendix B

Table 3.A2 List of Sectors

No.	*Name*	*GTAP 57 Sectors*
1	Primary	Paddy rice; Wheat; Cereal grains nec; Vegetables, fruit, nuts; Oilseeds; Sugar cane, sugar beet; Plant-based fibres; Crops nec; Cattle, sheep, goats, horses; Animal products nec; Raw milk; Wool, silkworm cocoons; Forestry; Fishing; Minerals nec; Meat: cattle, sheep, goats, horse; Meat products nec; Vegetable oils and fats; Dairy products; Processed rice; Sugar; Food products nec.
2	Energy	Coal; Oil; Gas
3	BvrgTbcc	Beverages and tobacco products
4	Textile	Textiles
5	Apparel	Wearing apparel
6	Leather	Leather products
7	Wood	Wood products
8	Paper	Paper products, publishing
9	PetCoProduct	Petroleum, coal products
10	Chemical	Chemical, rubber, plastic products
11	Minerals	Mineral products nec
12	FerrousMetal	Ferrous metals
13	OtherMetal	Metals nec
14	MetalProduct	Metal products
15	Motorvehicle	Motor vehicles and parts
16	TrnsprtEquip	Transport equipment nec
17	ElecEquip	Electronic equipment
18	Machinery	Machinery and equipment nec
19	OthMnfct	Manufactures nec
20	Utilities	Electricity; Gas manufacture, distribution; Water
21	Construction	Construction
22	Trade	Trade
23	TransComm	Transport nec; Sea transport; Air transport; Communication
24	FinsBusi	Financial services nec; Insurance; Business services nec
25	OthSrvc	Recreation and other services; PubAdmin/Defence/Health/ Educat; Dwellings

Source: Author's aggregation based on Aguiar et al. (2016).

Note: "nec" stands for not elsewhere specified

4 The evolving structure of Southeast Asia-China trade

Zhihong Yu

4.1 Introduction

During the past 20 years the world has witnessed remarkable changes in economic integration in Asian economies. The first major advance is the rise of China as a trade powerhouse and manufacturing hub in the world economy; the second is the rapid growth of the Association of Southeast Asian Nations (ASEAN) economies into an important integrated regional market. Consequently, trade between ASEAN and China has increased enormously. In 2014, in constant dollar (deflated by US CPI 1997 as base year) ASEAN's exports to (imports from) China reached 184 (141) billion US dollar, which is about 15 times those in 1997 (12.6 billion US dollar for exports, 12.3 billion US dollar for imports). Such astonishing trade expansion, however, is not only about total amounts but also about dynamic changes in structure.

It is well known that during the last two decades the Chinese economy has emerged as the "The World's Factory" heavily relying on export-promotion policies and low-cost labour. However, now China is undertaking to promote structural transformation away from the investment-led low-efficiency growth model towards an innovation-based high-productivity model. In the meantime, ASEAN as a whole has also been well advanced on the way towards industrial upgrading and productivity improvement, by diversifying its economies and actively engaging in global and regional supply chains, rather than relying on commodity prices. Such an intriguing evolution of economic structure in both economies begs the following important questions. What are the dynamics of ASEAN-China integration via trade linkages? Over the last two decades what are the major changes in bilateral trade structure and why? Are these changes consequences, or causes, of the more fundamental structural transformations taking place in both economies?

To shed light on these issues, in this chapter we use detailed Chinese customs data at the product-country-year level to analyse the evolution of China's trade with ASEAN. One of the most interesting features of our data is that we can identify the customs regime (processing trade[1] versus ordinary trade) and ownership (foreign versus domestic) of each trade transaction. This enables us to examine the role of processing trade and foreign ownership in the dynamic structural change of China-ASEAN trade, features not explored fully in previous

DOI: 10.4324/9780429433603-4

literature due to data constraints. At the aggregate level, it is well known that around 30–40 percent of China's imports are processing trade, of which a substantial share is sourced from ASEAN countries. However, China's transformation towards a "new normal"[2] growth model has already led to a substantial decline in its processing trade share in the last decade. Does this trend also affect the China-ASEAN trade structure, and how does it vary across products and ownership? In this chapter we make an attempt to fully explore this important question using the unique feature of our data set, which identifies customs regime and foreign ownership at the product-country-year level.

In the first part of our analysis, we examine the special features of the compositional changes of China-ASEAN trade across sectors, products, ownership and regime over the last two decades, with comparison to China's trade with the rest of world as a benchmark. The most striking findings can be summarised as the following. Note that ASEAN as a whole has been running a trade surplus against China since the late 1990s, but this trend has been *reversed* in recent years, especially after the global financial crisis, leading to a sizeable trade deficit of ASEAN against China. We reveal that the reason for this dramatic change in the trade imbalance is to a large extent, due to the changing structure of the bilateral trade pattern.

First, at the ownership-regime level, the share of foreign-owned and processing trade in China's trade with ASEAN, as well as with the rest of the world (ROW), increased substantially between 1997 and 2006, and then sharply declined between 2006 and 2014. By contrast, the share of ordinary trade by domestic firms in China's exports to ASEAN has increased dramatically from 38 percent to 61 percent between 2006 and 2014.

Second, at the sectoral level, since the late 1990s China's trade with ASEAN has shifted away from agriculture and raw materials (A&R) with low processing trade intensity, towards machinery sectors characterised by high processing trade shares. However, since 2006 there has been a decrease in the share of machinery goods and intermediate inputs in China's imports from ASEAN, accompanied by a substantial decline in processing trade intensity. In other words, in the late 1990s, ASEAN's exports to China were heavily reliant on processing trade by China's foreign owned firms and intermediate goods, especially in machinery sectors, which was the main driving force of ASEAN's trade surplus with China. This was the well-known "triangular trade relationship" between China, ASEAN and US/Europe, where China is the centre of the production network importing intermediate inputs from ASEAN, processing them to be re-exported to the US or Europe. As a result, ASEAN ran a trade surplus with China, whilst the US and Europe ran a trade deficit against China.

However, our analysis shows that the previous pattern may also "hurt" ASEAN countries in recent years, especially after the global financial crisis, contributing to a widening trade deficit of ASEAN against China. This is because China's recent structural transformation towards a "new normal" trade model has already inevitably led to decreasing shares of low-value added assembly trade dominated by foreign firms, especially in machinery sectors. As a result, China's relative demand for processing imports in intermediate sectors (especially in electrical equipment and mechanical appliances products) from ASEAN has been falling over time. On the other hand, ordinary exports by domestic Chinese firms have grown dramatically in the last ten years, especially to ASEAN countries. Taken together, these two forces have already turned ASEAN's trade surplus to China into a trade deficit in recent years. When the structural transformation of the Chinese economy accelerates in future towards an innovation-driven and consumption-based new model of growth, we expect such bilateral trade imbalances are likely to continue and even be exacerbated in the years to come.

Having revealed the evolving cross-sectoral changes of China-ASEAN trade as described earlier, in the second half of our paper we analyse the degree of two-way trade in China's trade with ASEAN. Perhaps not surprisingly, we find a high degree of two-way trade captured by an intra-industry trade index (IIT index) in ASEAN's top traded products with China, such as electronics and machinery (E&M) products. Interestingly, this pattern holds even if we exclude processing trade, implying the importance of non-processing (NP) trade undertaken by domestic Chinese firms as a driving force of two-way trade between China and ASEAN. Furthermore, in terms of ASEAN exporters' main competitors in the Chinese market, we find that, compared to the US or Japan, the product basket of ASEAN's exports to China is most similar to that of Korea's exports to China, and the overlap has been rising overtime, implying an increasing degree of competition between ASEAN and Korea. By contrast, the similarity of ASEAN's exports to those of the US or Japan has slightly decreased in the last ten years. Finally, within ASEAN we find very different dynamics of trade patterns between China and ASEAN as a whole versus that of China-BCLM (Brunei, Cambodia, Lao, Myanmar). More specifically, in stark contrast to ASEAN's other major economies, BCLM's trade with China is characterised by low processing trade intensity, a low degree of IIT, a declining share of the machinery sector since 1997 and a low degree of similarity between BCLM and Korea or Japan in their exports to China.

Our paper is complementary to the existing literature examining the evolving China-ASEAN bilateral trade and investment relationship (Holst and Weiss, 2004; Lall and Albaladejo, 2004; Ravenhill, 2006; Salidjanova et al., 2015; Yu and Cui, 2016). A common finding from these analyses is that China's fast trade expansion is a "double-edged sword" to ASEAN countries. On one hand, ASEAN's exports benefit greatly from China's increasing demand for components and intermediate inputs, which are processed and re-exported to the US and Europe. On the other hand, however, ASEAN firms face fiercer competition from surging Chinese exports in both domestic and third markets. One limitation of this literature, however, is that their data often do not cover the most recent periods since the financial crisis (except Yu and Cui, 2016) and do not break down trade by regime and ownership. Our analysis fills this gap and shows that the heavy reliance of ASEAN's exports to China on processing trade and intermediate inputs (especially the high concentration in E&M products) could actually become a weakness in their exports structure as a result of China's recent structural transformation towards a new growth model. Furthermore, our paper is related to the very recent but burgeoning literature measuring the domestic value added of China's trade (Koopman et al., 2012; Kee and Tang, 2016). Both of these papers found a rising share of domestic content/value added in China's exports since China's entry into WTO. These results are perfectly consistent with our findings on the evolving structure of China's trade with ASEAN. When Chinese firms increasingly substitute for imported inputs with domestic inputs, we might expect China's relative demand for foreign intermediate goods to continue to fall in future, which could impose a serious challenge to ASEAN's major economies specialising in intermediate exports, especially in electronic devices.

The rest of the paper is organised as follows. The next section describes the data and some basic facts about China-ASEAN trade over the last two decades. Then in Section 4.3 we provide detailed analysis of the evolution of the structure of China's exports to and imports from ASEAN at the sector, product, regime and ownership level. Section 4.4 explores the degree of IIT for the top traded products. Section 4.5 examines the overlap of ASEAN's export basket to China with that to other Asia countries such as Korea and Japan. Section 4.6 concludes.

4.2 Data and basic facts

4.2.1 Data

The primary dataset for our analysis is from Chinese Customs Statistics, available at Harmonized System (HS) 8-digit level (about 7,500 product categories) by trade partner (around 200 countries and economies), ownership (foreign-owned, state-owned and domestically-owned private) and trade regime[3] (processing trade or NP trade) from 1997 to 2014.[4] All trade transactions are in current US dollars. We deflate trade values by US CPI data with base year 1997 to obtain constant dollar values.

4.2.2 The fluctuating growth of China-ASEAN trade

Figure 4.1 shows the value of China's trade with ASEAN-10 countries during our sample period and their annual growth rates. Between 1997 and 2014, China-ASEAN exports (imports) increased by 1460 percent (1146 percent) with an annual growth rate of around 17.9 percent (16.5 percent), whilst China's total exports (imports) with the world increased by 770 percent (800 percent) with an annual growth rate of around 14.3 percent (14.6 percent). However, as can be seen from the figure, there exists large variation in the growth rates over time. Most strikingly, China's exports to ASEAN continue to grow at 2-digit level after the recovery from the financial crisis (15.6 percent from 2012 to 2014), but China's import growth from ASEAN has slowed down substantially since 2011 (around 1 percent between 2012 and 2014), leading to a non-trivial trade *deficit* for ASEAN's trade with China in 2014. Note that the growth of China's total trade with the whole world became sluggish and fell to single digit growth rates, with exports growing at 4–6 percent and imports only growing at

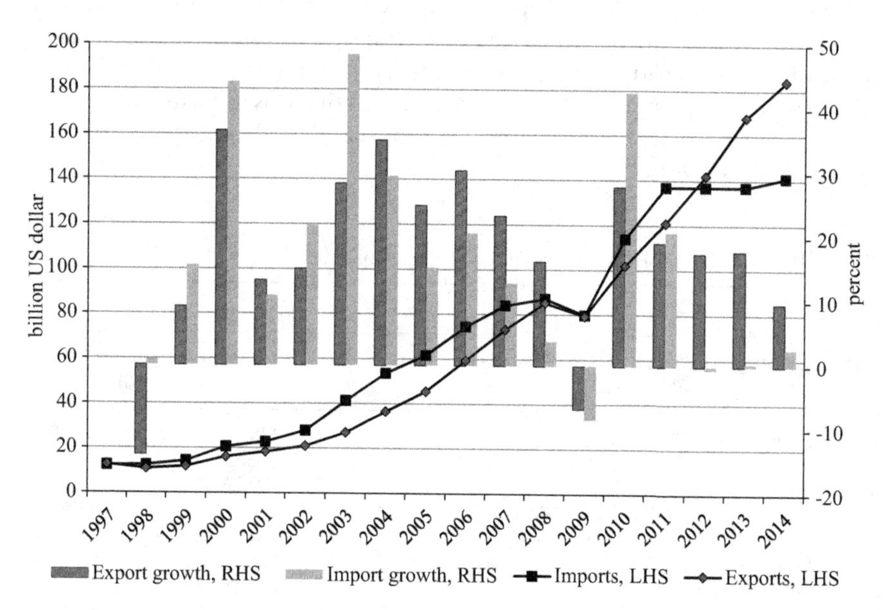

Figure 4.1 China's Exports to and Imports from ASEAN.

0–4 percent between 2012 and 2014. In other words, despite the recent slowing down of China's total trade growth after the financial crisis, China's exports to ASEAN kept growing strongly, whilst the growth of China's imports from ASEAN fell dramatically, turning ASEAN's trade imbalance with China from surplus to deficit.

4.2.3 The rise of ASEAN as China's main trade partner

Whilst China's total trade has been growing rapidly over the last two decades, the list of China's major trade partners has remained relatively stable over time. As can be seen in Table 4.1a and Table 4.1b, China's exports have been dominated by the "Big Four", namely the US, Hong Kong, Japan and ASEAN, whilst the US, Taiwan (China), Japan, ASEAN and Korea are China's top import source countries. Several patterns merit noting. First, ASEAN's share in China's imports rose from 8.9 percent in 1997 to 11.1 percent in 2014, placing ASEAN as a whole as China's largest source of imports. By contrast, all China's other major import source countries experienced a decline in their shares, implying a unique role played by ASEAN in China's imports basket. Second, the processing trade intensity of China's trade with ASEAN declined substantially during our sample period. In 2006, nearly 50 percent of China's imports from ASEAN was processing trade, but this share declined to only 30 percent in 2014. This is consistent with the trend of China's trade with other Asian countries (except Korea). It is often argued that ASEAN countries are heavily engaged in regional supply chains, serving as a major supplier of industrial intermediate inputs to China for further processing and re-export to Western countries. However, the previous pattern, especially the sharply declining processing share of China's imports from ASEAN countries, suggests that this particular link might be weakening rather than strengthening in recent periods, especially after the global financial crisis.

Table 4.1a China's Export Destinations and Processing Trade Shares

	1997			2006			2014		
Rank	*Country*	*Share (%)*	*PT (%)*	*Country*	*Share (%)*	*PT (%)*	*Country*	*Share (%)*	*PT (%)*
1	Hong Kong	24.2	56.0	US	20.8	63.2	US	16.9	49.2
2	US	17.6	70.8	Hong Kong	16.6	74.0	Hong Kong	15.4	59.4
3	Japan	17.5	57.3	Japan	9.5	57.7	ASEAN[a]	11.6	24.9
4	ASEAN[a]	6.9	43.9	ASEAN[a]	7.3	47.1	Japan	6.4	49.2
5	Korea	4.9	49.4	Korea	4.6	45.2	Korea	4.3	47.6
6	Germany	3.6	56.2	Germany	4.2	61.9	Germany	3.1	37.9
7	Netherlands	2.4	51.0	Netherlands	3.2	68.4	Netherlands	2.8	54.2
8	UK	2.1	60.7	UK	2.5	52.5	UK	2.4	33.3
9	Taiwan	1.9	61.6	Taiwan	2.1	53.7	India	2.3	18.7
10	France	1.3	56.1	Italy	1.6	28.4	Russia	2.3	16.0
Total		82.39			72.36			67.57	

Note: PT (percent) represents China's processing exports to Country *i*/China's total exports to Country *i*.
[a]ASEAN as a group of the 10 Southeast Asian countries and the focus in this study (ASEAN & China trade)

Table 4.1b China's Top Import Sources and Processing Trade Shares

	1997			2006			2014		
Rank	*Country*	*Share (%)*	*PT (%)*	*Country*	*Share (%)*	*PT (%)*	*Country*	*Share (%)*	*PT (%)*
1	Japan	20.0	60.7	Japan	14.4	43.7	ASEAN[a]	11.1	30.1
2	US	11.6	30.6	Korea	11.2	53.8	Korea	10.1	51.9
3	Taiwan	11.5	77.8	ASEAN[a]	11.1	47.3	Japan	8.7	34.0
4	Korea	10.6	65.5	Taiwan	10.7	70.1	US	8.1	16.0
5	ASEAN[a]	8.9	48.8	US	7.4	28.2	Taiwan	8.1	50.1
6	Hong Kong	4.8	78.5	Germany	4.7	13.2	Germany	5.6	7.6
7	Germany	4.3	17.3	Hong Kong	3.5	66.2	Australia	4.8	3.0
8	Russia	2.9	11.5	Australia	2.4	11.7	Brazil	2.8	4.8
9	Australia	2.4	53.6	Russia	2.2	10.9	Saudi Arabia	2.6	23.8
10	France	2.3	9.1	Saudi Arabia	1.9	12.7	Russia	2.2	5.4
Total		79.3			69.5				64.0

Note: PT (percent): China's processing imports from Country *i*/China's total imports from Country *i*.
[a]ASEAN as a group of the 10 Southeast Asian countries and the focus in this study

Next, we break down ASEAN's trade with China by country to investigate the heterogeneity in ASEAN member countries' bilateral trade flows and trade imbalances with China. As can be seen in Table 4.2, in the year 2014 ASEAN's trade with China was dominated by six countries, namely Singapore, Malaysia, Indonesia, Thailand, the Philippines and Viet Nam (ASEAN-6 henceforth), whilst the share of the remaining four countries (Myanmar, Brunei, Cambodia and Lao) is relatively small. It is important to note that Viet Nam's total trade with China rose dramatically (about 40-fold) during our sample period, from 1.4 billion US dollar in 1997 to 57 billion US dollar in 2014, whilst China's total trade with ASEAN has grown by 13 times during the same time period. So, it is important that we group Viet Nam with the other major trading countries with China such as Singapore, Malaysia, Indonesia, Thailand and the Philippines in the rest of our analysis. Most interestingly, there is a large variation in ASEAN members' trade imbalances with China across countries and over time. In 1997, although Singapore, Malaysia, Indonesia and Thailand each ran a trade surplus with China, the other six countries all incurred trade deficits, notably the Philippines, whose trade imbalance with China was around one billion US dollar. More interestingly, when we exclude processing trade and only look at trade imbalances in NP trade, the trade surpluses of Thailand, Malaysia and Indonesia shrink substantially, implying that these countries' trade surpluses with China are largely driven by their exports to China for further processing and then re-exporting to other Western countries. In the year 2006, consistent with Figure 4.1, ASEAN as a whole ran a large surplus with China, mainly due to three countries, namely the Philippines, Malaysia and Thailand, whilst Singapore and Viet Nam had large trade deficits with China. As we have noted before, however, in 2014 all ASEAN countries ran trade deficits with China, except Malaysia and Thailand, both of which continued to run a trade surplus even if processing trade is excluded. Very interestingly, Viet Nam emerged as the largest contributor to ASEAN's overall trade deficit, running a trade deficit of 30 billion US dollar due to its massive imports from China of 43 billion US dollar in 2014. It is also noteworthy that, in contrast to previous years, excluding processing trade has little effect on countries' trade imbalances, a result consistent with the declining role of processing trade in China-ASEAN trade in recent years. To summarise, the last two decades have witnessed the rapid rise of ASEAN's role in China's foreign trade, but there exists large heterogeneity across member countries. In particular, with respect to trade imbalance, among ASEAN's top trading nations with China, Thailand and Malaysia consistently maintained a trade surplus with China, whilst Singapore and Viet Nam incurred substantial trade deficits that increased over time. Note that although processing trade has played an important role in ASEAN countries' trade imbalances with China since 1997, its significance has declined substantially in recent years. In the following analysis, we will frequently split ASEAN countries into the two groups, namely ASEAN-6 and BCLM, due to their distinctive role in China-ASEAN trade.

Table 4.2 China's Trade Imbalance with ASEAN Countries and Processing Trade

	1997				*2006*				*2014*			
Country	*Exports*	*Imports*	*Imbalance*	*Imb_NP*	*Exports*	*Imports*	*Imbalance*	*Imb_NP*	*Exports*	*Imports*	*Imbalance*	*Imb_NP*
Philippines	322	1,310	-988	-660	14,400	4,800	9,570	3,130	14,200	15,900	-1,680	-3,250
Viet Nam	357	1,050	-693	-470	2,120	6,230	-4,110	-2,930	13,500	43,200	-29,700	-25,400
Myanmar	73	487	-413	-344	212	1,020	-806	-709	10,600	6,350	4,230	-3,020
Brunei	0	33	-33	-26	205	83	122	131	129	1,180	-1,060	-984
Cambodia	45	70	-25	-24	28	576	-548	-465	327	2,220	-1,890	-1,640
Lao	6	22	-16	-18	39	143	-104	-102	1,200	1,250	-49	-99
Singapore	4,250	4,150	97	573	15,500	19,300	-3,780	1,500	20,700	33,000	-12,300	-3,880
Thailand	1,960	1,440	520	-46	14,700	8,140	6,600	2,630	26,000	23,300	2,760	1,040
Malaysia	2,440	1,860	575	110	19,200	11,300	7,890	5,020	37,800	31,400	6,380	4,160
Indonesia	2,660	1,770	893	267	8,000	7,840	155	-418	16,600	26,500	-9,870	-6,700
Total	12,113	12,192	-83	-638	74,405	59,432	14,989	7,787	1,41,056	1,84,300	-43,179	-39,773

Notes: Exports= Country *i*'s exports to China, Imports = Country i's imports from China, Imbalance = Exports-Imports, Imb_PT = Trade Imbalance excluding processing trade, Units = USD million.

4.3 The structural change of ASEAN-China trade: products and trade regimes

The phenomenal growth of China-ASEAN trade is not only about increasing volume and value, but has also been accompanied by fundamental changes in the structure and composition of the trade basket. In the next analysis we break down the total trade value by sector, regime and ownership, and then provide a thorough investigation of the dynamics of China-ASEAN trade along different dimensions.

4.3.1 The compositional change of China-ASEAN trade: products, regime and ownership

4.3.1.1 Relocation across ownership and regime

It is very well known that China's rapid expansion in world trade is to a large extent driven by its firms' heavy engagement in processing trade and foreign ownership. As we have shown in the last section, processing trade accounts for a substantial share in China-ASEAN trade, especially before the financial crisis. In order to examine the specific roles of foreign ownership and processing trade, in Table 4.3 we break down China's trade with ASEAN (Panel A) and with the rest of the world (Panel B), respectively, by both trade regime and ownership. The most striking pattern revealed for China's exports to ASEAN, as can be seen from Panel A, is the U shape of the share of domestic NP trade over time. More specifically, the share of domestic NP trade in total exports decreased from nearly 50 percent in 1997 to 38 percent in 2006, but dramatically rose to 60 percent in 2014. By contrast, the share of processing trade by foreign-owned firms in total exports rose from 26 percent in 1997 to 40 percent in 2006 but declined to only 19 percent in 2014. Similar patterns hold for China's imports from ASEAN. For example, in 2006 processing imports by foreign firms accounted for 41 percent of China's total imports from ASEAN. However, this share declined dramatically to 24 percent in 2014. Needless to say, such substantial reallocation of trade shares away from foreign firms towards domestic firms, and from processing trade towards NP trade merits special attention. Actually, as can be seen from Panel B, this trend is not unique to ASEAN but holds for China's other destinations overall: clearly there is a rise of the share of domestic NP trade at the cost of a declining share of foreign-processing trade over the last ten years. What is unique about China-ASEAN trade is the very important role of Chinese domestic firms' NP exports which account for nearly 60 percent of China's exports to ASEAN in 2014, whilst for China's total exports to the world this share is only 45 percent. Hence, the sharp rise of indigenous Chinese firms' NP exports to ASEAN is likely the key to understand the driving force behind the widening ASEAN-China trade deficit in recent years.

Table 4.3 China's Exports to and Imports from ASEAN by Ownership and Trade Regime

Year		*1997*	*2006*	*2014*	*1997*	*2006*	*2014*
		Exports			*Imports*		
Panel A: China's Trade with ASEAN							
Domestic NP	share, %	49.6	38.0	60.8	33.5	26.1	42.4
	(value, USD Billion)	(6.05)	(22.6)	(112)	(4.06)	(19.4)	(59.9)
Foreign NP	share, %	6.4	14.8	14.3	17.7	26.5	27.4
	(value, USD Billion)	(0.783)	(8.81)	(26.3)	(2.14)	(19.7)	(38.7)
Domestic PT	share, %	18.2	7.1	6.3	13.5	5.9	6.5
	(value, USD Billion)	(2.22)	(4.22)	(11.7)	(1.63)	(4.4)	(9.21)
Foreign PT	share, %	25.8	40.0	18.6	35.3	41.4	23.6
	(value, USD Billion)	(3.14)	(23.8)	(34.3)	(4.28)	(30.8)	(33.3)
Panel B: China's Trade with the Rest of the World (except ASEAN)							
Domestic NP	share, %	39.2	33.1	45.4	29.6	35.4	46.9
	(value, USD Billion)	(64.5)	(250)	(637)	(36.8)	(210)	(530)
Foreign NP	share, %	6.1	13.6	15.2	21.1	24.8	27.3
	(value, USD Billion)	(10.1)	(102)	(214)	(26.1)	(147)	(309)
Domestic PT	share, %	19.4	8.3	7.0	15.9	5.9	5.0
	(value, USD Billion)	(31.9)	(62.3)	(97.9)	(19.7)	(35.1)	(57)
Foreign PT	share, %	35.2	45.1	32.4	33.4	33.9	20.8
	(value, USD Billion)	(57.9)	(340)	(454)	(41.4)	(201)	(236)

4.3.1.2 *Cross-sectoral relocation of trade shares*

4.3.1.2.1 BY SITC SECTOR

As was shown in Section 4.2, the fast growth of China-ASEAN trade outpaced that of China's total trade with the world, but a further question is whether this vast trade expansion is also accompanied by changes in trade structures in terms of the compositional shifts across sectors, products, customs regime and ownership. Previous studies (Amiti and Freund, 2010) show that for China's exports to the world there is a clear reallocation of the share towards the machinery sector away from light industrial products and A&R. But do we observe the same trend for China-ASEAN trade, especially in recent years? More interestingly, what is the role played by processing trade and foreign ownership in the cross-sectoral restructuring of China-ASEAN trade?

To investigate these important issues, we examine the distribution of China's trade across Standard International Trade Classification (SITC) sectors with ASEAN countries (Table 4.4, Panel A) by processing trade status and foreign ownership for the three key years 1997, 2006 and 2014. For comparison, we also show China's trade structure with the ROW excluding ASEAN in Panel B. The following interesting patterns emerge. First, in terms of China's exports to ASEAN, during the period of 1997–2006, clearly there is a relocation of the shares away from the A&R sector towards the machinery sector. The share of machinery (SITC7) in total exports rose from 33 percent in 1997 to around 52 percent in 2006, whilst the share of the A&R sector (SITC0-4) declined from 18 percent in 1997 to around 7 percent in 2006. This is perfectly consistent with the changing pattern of the composition of China's total exports to other parts of the world shown in Panel B, which was also shown in previous studies (Amiti and Freund, 2010). However, it is important to note that this trend did not continue in the more recent period 2006–2014, and, if anything, it reversed. In particular, the share of the machinery sector in China-ASEAN exports declined from around 52 percent in 2006 to 40 percent in 2014, whilst for China's other export destinations this share remains stable at around 48 percent.

Second, note that the share of the miscellaneous sector (mainly including light industries such as textiles, shoes, toys, etc.) in China's exports to ASEAN sharply increased from around 12 percent (between 1997 and 2006) to nearly 20 percent (in 2014), whilst during the same period for China's exports to ROW this share substantially declined from around 40 percent (in 1997) to nearly 27 percent (between 2006 and 2014). In other words, taken together, it is clear that during the more recent period up to 2014, China's exports to ASEAN became, to some extent, less concentrated in the machinery sector (high processing trade intensity) and more diversified towards light industry products and manufacturing materials (low processing trade intensity).

Third, on the import side, similar reallocation patterns emerge. In 1997, China's imports from ASEAN were mainly dominated by A&R (38 percent), but its share had almost halved by 2006 (20 percent), whilst the share of the machinery sector almost doubled (from 30 percent in 1997 to 58 percent in 2006). However, similar to that of exports, this trend reversed between 2006 and 2014, during which period the share of the machinery sector declined substantially from 58 percent to 44 percent, whilst the share of A&R sector increased from 20 percent to 27 percent. This is different from China's import structure with the ROW, as was shown in Panel B, where between 2006 and 2014 the share of the machinery sector declined only slightly from 42 percent to 39 percent whilst the share of A&R increased more substantially from 24 percent to 35 percent.

Fourth, note that, in almost all sectors, the shares of processing trade and foreign firms in China's exports to ASEAN are smaller than those in China's exports to ROW. For example, in the year 2014 foreign firms account for 50 percent of China's machinery exports to ASEAN, whilst for China's exports to the ROW this share is 66 percent. This is perhaps not very surprising since most of the foreign-invested enterprises (FIEs) in China are owned by multinationals either from North America/Europe or from Hong Kong/Taiwan, and their clients are mainly located in advanced economies outside ASEAN.

Last, it is noteworthy that, in all sectors except A&R, China's imports from ASEAN are dominated by foreign-owned firms, which usually account for 50 percent or more, and particularly in the machinery sector where these shares are above 70 percent. This is, however, a global pattern rather than something unique to regional China-ASEAN trade, as similar patterns can be observed for China's imports from the ROW as shown in Panel B. Hence, when China's total imports become less reliant on foreign firms and processing trade, we might expect a further decline of ASEAN's exports to China, particularly in machinery sector.

Table 4.4 Reallocation of China's Foreign Trade across SITC Sector: ASEAN versus Rest of the World

Product Category		*Exports (percent)*			*Imports (percent)*		
		1997	*2006*	*2014*	*1997*	*2006*	*2014*
Panel A: ASEAN							
SITC 0-4 Agriculture and Raw Materials	**Total Share**	**17.6**	**6.6**	**6.1**	**38.1**	**20.2**	**27.2**
	PT	7.4	5.7	6.7	32.6	21.4	7.6
	Foreign	13.9	41.8	23.1	30.2	29.4	20.3
SITC 5 Chemicals	**Total Share**	**8.7**	**8.0**	**7.9**	**12.3**	**12.4**	**11.4**
	PT	15.7	21.0	17.3	67.4	37.6	15.8
	Foreign	25.7	35.5	31.0	51.6	49.7	49.6
SITC 6 Manufacturing Materials	**Total Share**	**27.7**	**20.9**	**26.1**	**17.6**	**5.5**	**12.0**
	PT	41.4	18.0	11.0	60.6	53.7	63.5
	Foreign	18.7	27.2	20.0	60.2	62.0	41.5
SITC 7 Machinery	**Total Share**	**33.2**	**52.5**	**40.4**	**30.3**	**58.4**	**43.8**
	PT	67.3	68.8	39.2	77.0	57.2	41.2
	Foreign	54.8	75.6	50.0	83.4	87.4	72.9
SITC Miscellaneous Manufacturing	**Total Share**	**12.7**	**12.0**	**19.5**	**1.8**	**3.5**	**5.6**
	PT	54.7	38.7	13.6	54.9	58.6	28.5
	Foreign	40.6	46.7	20.4	71.3	77.2	67.6

Product Category		*Exports (percent)*			*Imports (percent)*		
		1997	*2006*	*2014*	*1997*	*2006*	*2014*
Panel B: Rest of the World (excluding ASEAN)							
SITC 0-4 Agriculture and Raw Materials	**Total Share**	**12.8**	**4.9**	**3.5**	**17.6**	**24.2**	**34.6**
	PT	14.7	18.4	16.9	40.2	12.0	9.2
	Foreign	23.9	38.6	31.0	29.6	21.3	17.6
SITC 5 Chemicals	**Total Share**	**5.3**	**4.6**	**5.6**	**15.1**	**12.2**	**10.3**
	PT	19.9	24.8	17.9	55.6	34.0	23.2
	Foreign	22.4	36.8	32.5	47.8	54.6	54.8
SITC 6 Manufacturing Materials	**Total Share**	**17.9**	**16.2**	**15.7**	**21.2**	**11.1**	**8.7**
	PT	45.3	28.2	17.5	79.3	59.9	41.8
	Foreign	31.7	37.7	28.1	64.5	66.9	55.8
SITC 7 Machinery	**Total Share**	**23.0**	**47.8**	**47.3**	**39.7**	**42.2**	**38.6**
	PT	83.4	77.4	55.9	34.1	44.5	35.6
	Foreign	64.1	78.0	66.1	63.9	73.2	68.0
SITC Miscellaneous Manufacturing	**Total Share**	**41.1**	**26.5**	**27.9**	**6.4**	**10.3**	**7.9**
	PT	59.6	40.4	31.3	64.1	64.0	39.7
	Foreign	41.5	46.6	33.4	57.7	78.9	69.2

Next, in Table 4.5, we replicate the previous analysis on the BCLM countries, and expect substantial differences in the sectoral distribution of their trade with China from that with ASEAN as a whole, due to fundamental differences in their stages of economic development, economic size and resource endowments. This is exactly what we observe. First, in terms of China's exports to the BCLM countries, unlike those to ASEAN as a whole, we did ***not*** observe a relocation of trade shares from agriculture and light industry sectors to the machinery sector over time. In contrast, the share of the machinery sector ***declined*** slightly from 43 percent in 1997 to below 40 percent during 2006 and 2014, whilst the light industry sector (miscellaneous manufacturing) saw an increase of its share from 6.6 percent in 2006 to 16 percent in 2014. It is also noteworthy that the share of processing trade and foreign ownership in China's exports to BCLM in the machinery sector is quite low, which is, again, in contrast to those to other ASEAN countries. Second, even more interesting patterns were found in China's imports from the BCLM countries, which were dominated by either the A&R sector or manufacturing materials, and the shares of the machinery sector and miscellaneous manufacturing sector were negligible (with shares consistently below 1 percent and 5 percent, respectively). Overall, this difference might reflect the fundamental differences between the BCLM group and other ASEAN countries in their local comparative advantage versus China.

Table 4.5 Reallocation of China's Foreign Trade with BCLM Countries across SITC Sector

Product Category		*Exports (percent)*			*Imports (percent)*		
		1997	*2006*	*2014*	*1997*	*2006*	*2014*
SITC 0-4 Agriculture and Raw Materials	**Total Share**	**10.6**	**8.5**	**3.9**	**46.6**	**93.7**	**27.2**
	PT	8.6	1.2	7.2	32.3	4.4	2.6
	Foreign	3.9	10.7	18.8	25.9	6.7	2.3
SITC 5 Chemicals	**Total Share**	**7.6**	**6.4**	**4.0**	**0.0**	**0.7**	**0.5**
	PT	8.4	4.6	10.8	59.2	7.1	1.6
	Foreign	19.2	9.7	13.2	19.5	6.8	26.1
SITC 6 Manufacturing Materials	**Total Share**	**33.9**	**49.0**	**38.5**	**52.6**	**4.3**	**67.9**
	PT	18.7	13.7	15.9	59.0	50.9	96.8
	Foreign	6.5	28.0	17.0	62.8	26.4	31.3
SITC 7 Machinery	**Total Share**	**43.0**	**29.3**	**37.9**	**0.0**	**0.3**	**0.3**
	PT	26.8	7.2	6.8	0.0	99.4	73.3
	Foreign	6.6	15.2	12.9	0.0	3.0	86.8
SITC Miscellaneous Manufacturing	**Total Share**	**4.9**	**6.6**	**15.7**	**0.7**	**1.1**	**4.0**
	PT	13.2	27.2	7.0	69.1	17.2	19.6
	Foreign	9.4	30.1	12.5	66.7	44.2	24.1

Notes: BCLM=Brunei, Cambodia, Lao Myanmar.

4.3.1.2.2 BY END USE – CONSUMPTION VERSUS INTERMEDIATE GOODS

An alternative way to examine the cross-sectoral relocation of China-ASEAN trade structures is to break down trade flows by classification of each sector's end use; namely, consumption goods versus intermediates or capital or raw materials, according to the Broad Economic Categories (BEC) introduced by United Nations. Similar to the previous analysis at SITC, in Table 4.6 we show the distribution of China's trade with ASEAN (Panel A) and with the ROW (Panel B) across the end-use sectors. First, it is clear that China-ASEAN trade is dominated by intermediate goods, which account for around 60 percent (65–70 percent) of China's exports to (imports from) ASEAN, and these shares are greater than those for China's trade with the ROW. For example, in 2014 56 percent (65 percent) of China's exports to (imports from) ASEAN were in intermediate sectors; this is substantially higher than that of China's exports to (imports from) the ROW at around 40 percent (52 percent). Second, note, however, that the share of intermediate goods in China's imports from ASEAN has declined since 2006, from 74 percent to 65 percent in 2014. This has been accompanied by a decreasing share of foreign-owned firms and processing trade in this sector between 2006 and 2014, which declined from 70 percent to 60 percent, and from 50 percent to 30 percent, respectively. Similar trends took place for China's imports from the ROW. Taken together, this may reflect China's shrinking relative demand for processing imports in intermediate inputs, as a result of China's structural transformation towards a "new normal" trade model with decreasing reliance on low-value added assembly trade dominated by foreign owned firms. Third, the share of consumption goods in China's exports to ASEAN follows a U shape when plotted over the period 1997–2014. This share declined from 22 percent in 1997 to 14 percent in 2006, and then returned to 21 percent in 2014. This pattern is in contrast to that for China's exports to the ROW, where we observe this share declining steadily from 50 percent in 1997 to 30 percent in 2014. Also note that the consumption good sector has very low shares of processing trade and foreign firms, particularly for China's exports to ASEAN, where 93 percent of its trade value is NP trade, which is much greater than that of China's exports to the ROW (70 percent). In other words, NP trade by domestic firms in China in the consumption goods sector has become more important in China's exports to ASEAN countries, which may become more important still as a contributor to China's trade surplus against ASEAN countries in future. Finally, we break down China's trade with the BCLM group by end-use sectors in Table 4.7. It is important to note that in terms of China's imports from the BCLM countries there is a dramatic relocation of trade shares away from intermediate goods to raw materials between 1997 and 2014. This is in stark contrast with the pattern for China's imports from ASEAN as a whole, where the shares across sectors are relatively stable over time (Panel A). On the other hand, in terms of China's exports to these countries, the distribution of shares across sectors is stable over time and very similar to that of ASEAN as a whole.

Table 4.6 Reallocation of China's Foreign Trade across End-Use Sectors: ASEAN versus Rest of the World

Product Category		*Exports (percent)*			*Imports (percent)*		
		1997	*2006*	*2014*	*1997*	*2006*	*2014*
Panel A: ASEAN							
Raw Materials	**Total Share**	**3.2**	**1.3**	**0.4**	**12.6**	**5.6**	**16.9**
	PT	0.6	0.3	47.9	28.1	12.3	36.3
	Foreign	5.6	85.7	10.8	17.9	8.7	17.8
Capital Goods	**Total Share**	**17.3**	**24.9**	**22.6**	**6.3**	**16.3**	**10.6**
	PT	62.1	67.9	41.1	45.2	38.3	25.7
	Foreign	41.6	71.9	46.7	76.1	83.2	61.9
Intermediates	**Total Share**	**57.3**	**59.8**	**56.1**	**76.9**	**73.5**	**64.6**
	PT	43.3	46.4	25.1	53.5	50.3	30.6
	Foreign	30.3	52.1	34.1	58.0	69.3	58.4
Consumption Goods	**Total Share**	**22.1**	**13.9**	**20.9**	**4.2**	**4.6**	**7.9**
	PT	37.7	18.4	6.5	30.6	32.2	19.6
	Foreign	33.7	32.1	15.1	32.3	46.9	47.1
Panel B: Rest of the World (excluding ASEAN)							
Raw Materials	**Total Share**	**3.2**	**1.2**	**0.4**	**5.7**	**15.5**	**25.0**
	PT	4.4	18.9	28.6	36.0	9.8	13.3
	Foreign	11.4	38.2	44.2	13.1	11.7	12.3
Capital Goods	**Total Share**	**12.7**	**27.3**	**28.3**	**19.6**	**20.3**	**14.5**
	PT	84.0	81.5	64.6	10.4	32.6	23.8
	Foreign	62.3	79.1	69.6	57.0	65.6	56.3
Intermediates	**Total Share**	**33.7**	**38.6**	**40.3**	**70.6**	**60.0**	**52.0**
	PT	48.0	45.3	29.3	60.1	48.3	35.1
	Foreign	37.9	55.0	43.6	57.0	66.1	60.7
Consumption Goods	**Total Share**	**50.5**	**32.9**	**31.0**	**4.2**	**4.2**	**8.5**
	PT	54.8	41.5	29.6	66.5	32.5	9.6
	Foreign	40.2	46.9	32.7	56.0	60.6	62.4

4.3.2 Econometric analysis

In this descriptive analysis, we revealed interesting patterns in the structural changes of China's trade with ASEAN countries. In particular, it appears that trade in intermediate inputs and processing trade have played important roles in China-ASEAN trade. In this section, we implement some econometric analysis to complement the exercises in previous sections, with the purpose of seeing if the roles of intermediate and processing trade are statistically significant. Specifically, we run the following regressions:

$$X_{jpr} = \beta \text{ASEAN}_j * \text{Intermediate}_p + \mu_j + \mu_p + \mu_r + C + \varepsilon_{jpr} \quad [1]$$
$$X_{jpr} = \gamma \text{ASEAN}_j * \text{Processing}_r + \mu_j + \mu_p + \mu_r + C + \varepsilon_{jpr} \quad [2]$$

where X_{jpr} represents exports from Country j to China in product (HS6) p in regime r (processing trade or NP trade), Intermediate_p is a dummy for

Table 4.7 Reallocation of China's Foreign Trade with BCLM Countries across End-Use Sectors

Product Category		*Exports (percent)*			*Imports (percent)*		
		1997	*2006*	*2014*	*1997*	*2006*	*2014*
Raw Materials	**Total Share**	**0.0**	**0.2**	**4.3**	**29.3**	**47.4**	**79.2**
	PT	0.4	0.1	73.9	77.7	1.8	81.9
	Foreign	38.3	1.2	0.2	75.4	1.6	26.5
Capital Goods	**Total Share**	**30.5**	**16.2**	**22.7**	**0.0**	**0.0**	**0.2**
	PT	33.6	8.5	6.7	0.0	0.8	65.5
	Foreign	7.3	18.7	12.9	0.0	47.4	80.7
Intermediates	**Total Share**	**49.4**	**66.6**	**53.1**	**66.1**	**48.5**	**15.9**
	PT	19.5	14.0	10.3	33.6	9.9	11.6
	Foreign	6.3	22.3	16.7	34.1	12.0	7.4
Consumption Goods	**Total Share**	**20.1**	**17.0**	**19.9**	**4.6**	**4.1**	**4.8**
	PT	9.4	12.2	7.0	35.9	26.2	14.1
	Foreign	7.8	18.2	13.4	21.3	32.3	19.5

Notes: BCLM=Brunei, Cambodia, Lao and Myanmar.

intermediate products, $ASEAN_j$ is a dummy for ASEAN countries, $Processing_r$ is a dummy for processing trade regime and μ_p, μ_j and μ_r are fixed effects for product, country and trade regime, respectively. We further run [1] and [2] for country *j*'s imports from China, for the three years 1997, 2006 and 2014. Our focus is on coefficients β and γ, which would be significantly positive if ASEAN countries trade with China more in intermediate products or processing trade relative to other countries. The results are presented in Table 4.8. First, in terms of trade in intermediate inputs, as is shown in Column 1, β is positive for ASEAN countries' exports and imports to China in all years although insignificant in year 1997 for imports and year 2014 for exports. In other words, ASEAN's trade with China is more biased towards intermediate good sectors compared to other countries' trade with China. These results are consistent with the descriptive results in Table 4.6, where the shares of intermediate goods in China's trade with ASEAN are greater than those of China's trade with other countries in other sectors. In Column 2, we repeat this exercise for the BCLM countries. Very interestingly, in stark contrast, β is insignificant in all years for their exports to China but significant and positive for their imports from China in year 2006 and year 2014. Second, in terms of the role of processing trade, as is shown in Column 3, γ is positive and significant for countries' exports to China, but negative and significant for their imports from China. This pattern is robust across all years, and the magnitudes of the coefficients increase over time. For example, for countries' imports from China, γ is –0.36 in 1997 but decreased to –1.08 in 2014. By contrast, for countries' exports to China, γ increased sharply from 0.60 in 1997 to 1.42 in 2014. We interpret these results as evidence that, compared to China's other trade partners, China's imports from ASEAN are more biased towards processing trade inputs that are assembled and re-exported to the world, whilst China's exports to ASEAN are more biased towards NP trade, mostly from indigenous Chinese firms. More interestingly, such biases actually increase substantially over time, which may have important implications for China's bilateral trade balance with ASEAN countries. Last, in Column 4 we report the results for the BCLM countries. Perhaps as expected, the coefficients are not very robust and are mostly insignificant. In other words, there is "nothing special" about China's trade with the BCLM countries in terms of the relative importance of processing trade, compared with China's other trade partners. Again, this might be a result of differences in production structures and stages of industrial development between the BCLM countries and ASEAN-6.

Table 4.8 The Importance of ASEAN in China's Exports and Imports: The Role of Intermediate and Processing Trade

Country Group Dummy =	*ASEAN*	*BCLM*		*ASEAN*	*BCLM*
	(1)	(2)		(3)	(4)
The role of intermediate good			The role of processing trade		
Panel A: 1997					
Dep Var. = Country *I*'s exports to China					
Country group × *Intermediate good*	0.676***	0.546	*Country group* × *Processing trade*	0.604***	-0.511
	(0.151)	(1.207)		(0.175)	(0.763)
Dep Var. = Country *I*'s imports from China					
Country group × *Intermediate good*	0.160	0.010	*Country group* × *Processing trade*	-0.362***	0.690**
	(0.116)	(0.117)		(0.131)	(0.334)
No. of observations	253,089	253,089		253,089	253,089
Panel B: 2006					
Dep Var. = Country *I*'s exports to China					
Country group × *Intermediate good*	0.685***	1.170	*Country group* × *Processing trade*	1.343***	0.395
	(0.102)	(0.222)		(0.226)	(0.653)
Dep Var. = Country *I*'s imports from China					
Country group × *Intermediate good*	0.343***	0.290***	*Country group* × *Processing trade*	-0.674***	-0.076
	(0.122)	(0.091)		(0.106)	(0.325)
No. of observations	503,142	503,142		503,142	503,142
Panel C: 2014					
Dep Var. = Country *I*'s exports to China					
Country group × *Intermediate good*	0.324	-0.680	*Country group* × *Processing trade*	1.417***	0.138
	(0.199)	(0.593)		(0.109)	(0.298)
Dep Var. = Country *I*'s imports from China					
Country group × *Intermediate good*	0.441***	0.486***	*Country group* × *Processing trade*	-1.075***	-0.610**
	(0.103)	(0.177)		(0.129)	(0.300)
No. of observations	565,649	565,649		565,649	565,649

Notes: The regression sample is China's bilateral exports or imports with all countries of the world; the level of the data is at country-HS6 product-regime level (regime = processing trade or non-processing). Each regression includes the following fixed effects/dummies: country FE, Product HS6 FE, Regime dummy. In Columns 1–2, country group (ASEAN or BCLM) dummy is interacted with the intermediate good dummy; in Columns 3–4 the country group dummies are interacted with processing dummy; cluster standard error at country level reported in the bracket; and *, **and ***represent significance level at 10 percent, 5 percent and 1 percent, respectively.

4.4 Intra-industry trade versus inter-industry trade between China and ASEAN

4.4.1 *Top traded products and the role of electronics and machinery (E&M) trade*

4.4.1.1 The dynamics of top traded products

In the previous sections, we have provided a detailed description of the dynamic reallocation of China-ASEAN trade across broadly defined sectors and the role of processing trade or foreign ownership. However, one further question is whether China-ASEAN trade is mainly concentrated within a small range of narrowly defined products, or more evenly spread/diversified across a larger number of goods. To answer this question, we calculate China-ASEAN's trade shares across 2-digit HS products (about 100 categories), which is more disaggregated than 1-digit SITC classification (nine categories). We focus on China's top traded products to ASEAN, where a "top product" is defined as one of the main five products in terms of trade shares during 1997–2014. In Figure 4.2a, we show the dynamics of these shares for ASEAN's exports to China. The following pattern merits special attention. First, two HS categories, namely 84 (recording, electrical machinery and equipment) and 85 (machinery and mechanical appliances), stand out as the most important exports from ASEAN to China. In 1997, they account for 25 percent of ASEAN's exports, but this share rose sharply to around 60 percent in 2006 and then declined to nearly 50 percent in 2014. Substantial shares of trade in both products are under the processing trade regime, which is expected given ASEAN's important role as a parts and components supplier in China's global production network in these products. Second, note that, in 1997, neither 85 nor 84 is the top exported product. The No. 1 product is actually fuel and oil (HS code 27), accounting for around 30 percent of ASEAN's exports to China. However, this share fell dramatically to around 10–15 percent subsequently, with a reshuffling of trade shares away from fuel and oil towards electronic equipment and mechanical appliances during 1997–2014. Note that this trend is in contrast to China's imports from the whole world, where the share of product 27 (fuel and oil) increases from 5 percent in 1997 to above 14 percent in 2014. This may reflect the diversion of China's imports in the fuel and oil category away from ASEAN towards other resource rich countries such as Russia, Brazil, and so on. Overall, the top-five products account for 60–80 percent of ASEAN's total exports to China, implying a relatively high degree of concentration at the HS 2-digit product level.

We now turn to ASEAN's imports from China, in Figure 4.2b. Interestingly, again, products 84 and 85 are the top two products, with a combined share of 28 percent in 1997, rising steadily to peak at nearly 45 percent in 2006, and then falling to 33 percent in year 2014. In both product categories processing trade shares are quite high, above 50 percent in 1997 and 2006, but they fell substantially in 2014. Second, iron and steel (72) and fuel and oil (27) are consistently ranked as the third- and fourth-largest exported products from China to ASEAN, but their shares are quite low (around 5 percent for each product). Third, note that whilst textile and clothing products are among China's top exported products to the world, its share in China's exports to ASEAN is very small (product HS-61's share is only 2–3 percent), and it falls out of the list of top five exported products. This may reflect China's local comparative disadvantage against ASEAN countries in these sectors. Finally, there is a sharp increase in the share of precision, medical or surgical instruments (90) from 1.4 percent in 1997 to around 3–4.5 percent between 2006 and 2014.

Next, we again replicate the previous analysis on the BCLM countries and report the results in Figures 4.3a and 4.3b. First, in terms of BCLM's exports to China (Figure 4.3a), in contrast to that of the ASEAN (Figure 4.2a), E&M

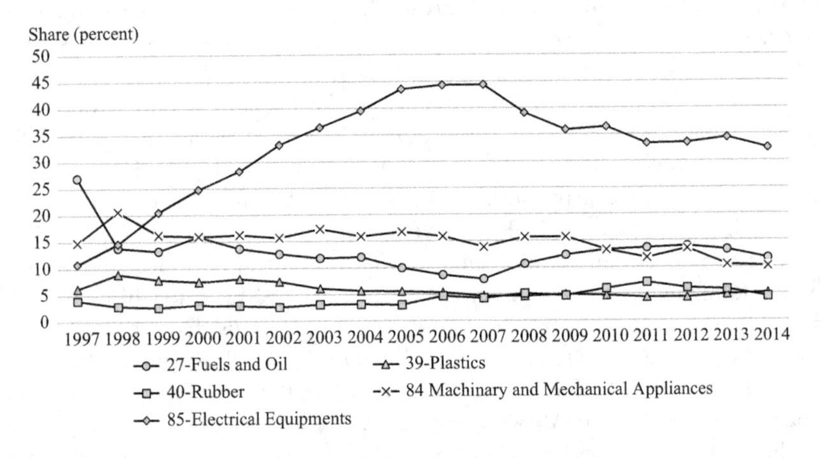

Figure 4.2a Shares of the Top Five HS Products in ASEAN's Exports to China.
Notes: Top five products defined as 1997–2014 exports in total.

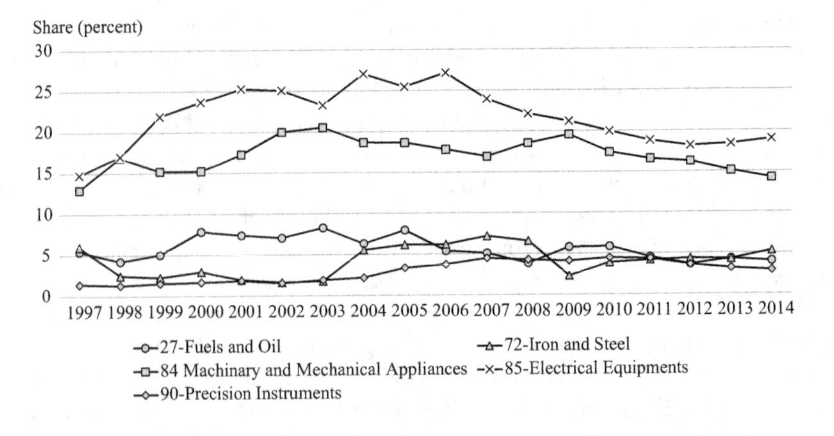

Figure 4.2b Shares of the Top Five Products in ASEAN's Imports from China.
Notes: Top five products defined as 1997–2014 imports in total.

products (HS 84–85) disappear from the list of top exported products. Instead, the top five products are mainly raw materials, including Ores, slag and ash (HS 26); Mineral fuels and oils (HS 27); Rubber (HS 40); Wood (HS 44); and Natural or cultured pearls (HS 71). Second, note that the shares of these products are very volatile over time. For example, there is an enormous increase in the share of pearls (HS 71) from nearly zero in 1997–2008 to 30 percent in 2013 to 70 percent in 2014. In stark contrast, the share of wood (HS 44) declined sharply from 60 percent in 1997 to only 10 percent in 2014. Finally, in terms of BCLM's imports from China shown in Figure 4.3b, similar to Figure 4.2b,

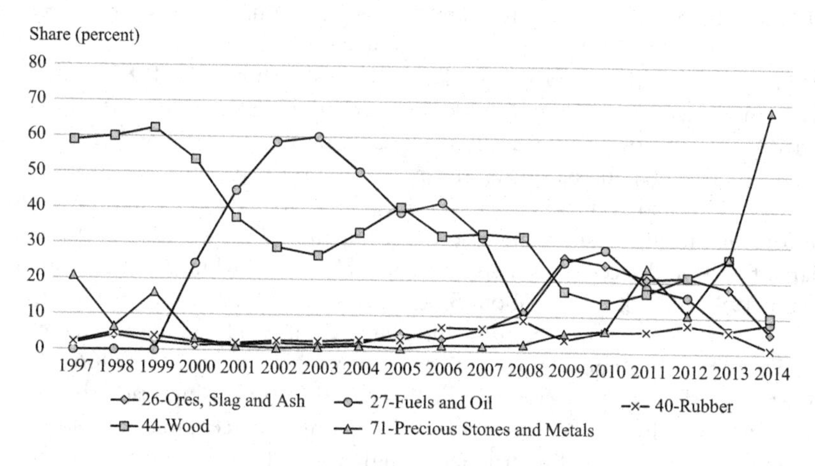

Figure 4.3a Share of the Top Five Products in BCLM's Exports to China.

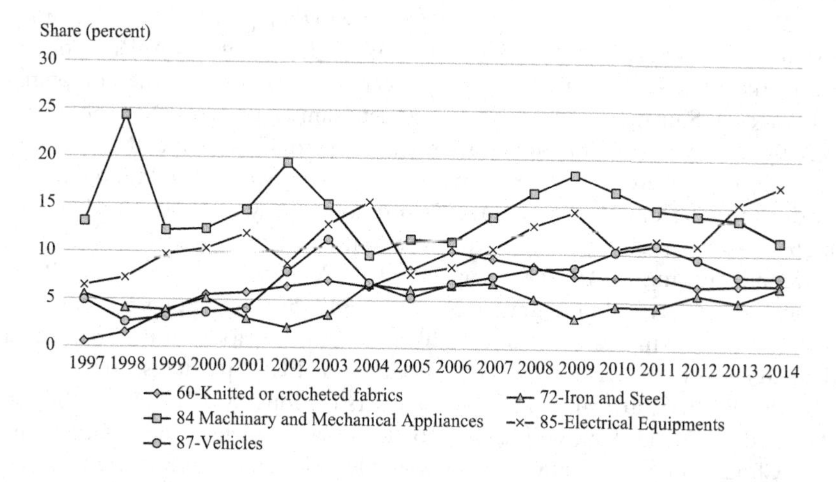

Figure 4.3b Share of the Top Five Products in BCLM's Imports to China.

E&M products (HS 84–85) are the largest product groups, but with a relatively smaller combined share of 20–30 percent. Overall, the top five imports are mainly industrial products and altogether account for around 50 percent of China's exports to BCLM.

4.4.1.2 *Trade of electrical equipment and mechanical appliance products (HS 84 and 85)*

The dominant role of Electrical and machinery products (E&M, HS chapter 84 and 85) in China-ASEAN trade merits special attention. These are relatively broad product categories, including around 130 4-digit HS categories and nearly 800 6-digit HS codes. Hence, to examine whether China-ASEAN trade in E&M is concentrated in a few even more narrowly defined products, in Table 4.9 we present the top five traded 4-digit HS products within HS 84–85, and their shares in China-ASEAN E&M trade, by year and by exports/imports. First, in Panel A, in terms of ASEAN's exports to China, category HS 8542 (Electronic integrated circuits) stands out as the most important product, accounting for around half of trade values in E&M products in 2006 and 2014, but only around 11 percent in 1997. This sharp rise is accompanied by a substantial declining share of parts and accessories with machines (HS 8473), which is around 36 percent in 1997 but fell to only about 5 percent since 2006. Most interestingly, the processing trade share in Electronic integrated circuits (HS 8542) also increased sharply from only 12 percent in 1997 to 60 percent (50 percent) in 2006 (2014), whilst in the parts and accessories category (8473) processing trade shares declined dramatically from 46 percent in 1997 to only 8 percent in 2014. Note that the total share of the top five products is high, around 75 percent (83 percent) in year 2014 (2006), implying a high degree of concentration. A further question is which countries among ASEAN members are the main exporters in "Electronic integrated circuits" to China. In Table 4.10, we further break down exports of 8,542 by country, and show each country's share in this specific product category. Strikingly, Malaysia alone accounts for around 58 percent of ASEAN's exports in Electronic integrated circuits to China in year 2014, followed by the Philippines (14 percent), Singapore (13 percent) and Viet Nam (7 percent). Note that back in 2006, Malaysia and Philippines' shares are around 37 percent and 38 percent, respectively, so there is a clear relocation of shares away from the Philippines towards Malaysia from 2006 to 2014. It is also noteworthy that Viet Nam's export in 8542 is zero in 2006, but it sharply rose to nearly 7 percent in 2014.

Second, turning to ASEAN's imports of E&M products as shown in Panel B, note that electronic integrated circuits (8542) is also among the top two traded products in years 2006 and 2014, accounting for around 15 percent (10 percent) of ASEAN's imports from China in E&M products. More interestingly, however, in year 2014, telephone sets (product 8517) become the top imported E&M product, with a share of 14.5 percent, which might be mainly from China's booming mobile phone assembly industry by both foreign-owned assembly plants such as Foxconn and indigenous domestic Chinese firms with their own brands such as Huawei.

Table 4.9 China-ASEAN's Top Traded Products within Electrical Equipment and Machinery Category (HS 84 and 85)

	1997			*2006*			*2014*		
Rank	*Product*	*Share*	*PT Share*	*Product*	*Share*	*PT Share*	*Product*	*Share*	*PT Share*
Panel A: ASEAN's Exports to China									
1	8473	36.33	45.90	8542	53.88	59.20	**8542**	48.54	45.30
2	8542	11.26	12.34	8471	16.21	9.69	8471	10.93	4.09
3	8471	6.21	5.16	8473	5.97	7.33	8541	6.23	7.18
4	8522	5.14	5.87	8541	4.16	4.71	8473	5.52	7.90
5	8540	3.88	4.90	8529	2.80	2.89	8517	3.42	3.53
Total		62.82	74.17		83.01	83.82		74.63	67.99
Panel B: ASEAN's Imports from China									
1	8473	10.09	14.33	8542	14.50	18.31	8517	14.47	18.57
2	8471	8.89	12.01	8473	13.03	17.64	8542	9.66	19.44
3	8522	5.72	8.21	8525	12.47	14.05	8471	8.37	16.34
4	8542	5.26	7.59	8471	9.60	12.62	8541	3.27	3.16
5	8527	4.29	5.93	8529	7.22	8.34	8504	2.99	2.49
Total		34.24	48.07		56.81	70.96		38.75	60.00

Notes: Share = products' share in total exports or imports within HS 84–85. PT share= product's processing trade share in total processing exports or imports within 84–85 category. HS codes are 4-digit HS codes, HS1997 version for year 1997, HS2002 version for year 2006 and HS2012 version for year 2014.

List of Product Codes and Names: 8471 – Automatic data processing machines and units; 8473 – Parts and accessories (other than covers, carrying cases and the like) suitable for machines of headings Nos. 84.69–84.72; 8504 – Electrical transformers, static converters and inductors; 8517 – Telephone sets, including telephones for cellular networks or for other wireless networks; other apparatus for the transmission or reception of voice, images or other data; 8522 – Parts and accessories suitable for use solely or principally with the apparatus of headings Nos. 85.19–85.21; 8525 – Transmission apparatus for radio-telephony, radio-telegraphy, radio-broadcasting or television, television cameras and other video cam; 8527 – Reception apparatus for radio-telephony, radio-telegraphy or radio-broadcasting; 8529 – Parts suitable for use for the apparatus of headings 85.25–85.28; 8540 – Thermionic, cold cathode or photo-cathode valves and tubes; 8541 – Diodes, transistors and similar semiconductor devices; photosensitive semiconductor devices; 8542 – Electronic integrated circuits.

Table 4.10 Shares of Each Country's Exports of Electronic Integrated Circuits (8542) in ASEAN

	2006		*2014*	
Country	*Share* (%)	*PT Share* (%)	*Share* (%)	*PT Share* (%)
Singapore	17.5	18.4	13.0	20.2
Thailand	7.1	8.5	8.1	8.9
Malaysia	36.7	33.5	57.8	49.1
Indonesia	0.7	0.7	0.2	0.3
Brunei	0.0	0.0	0.0	0.0
Philippines	38.0	38.9	13.9	17.1
Cambodia	0.0	0.0	0.0	0.0
Viet Nam	0.0	0.0	7.2	4.5
Lao	0.0	0.0	0.0	0.0
Myanmar	0.0	0.0	0.0	0.0

Notes: This table shows each ASEAN country's share in their exports in electronic integrated circuits to China in 2006 and 2014, both for total exports (Share) and for processing exports (PT Share), respectively.

4.4.2 IIT index

A very interesting pattern emerging from the last section is that China-ASEAN's top traded products (E&M products) clearly exhibit features of two-way trade. For example, HS product 85 is China's top export to ASEAN but it is also ASEAN's No. 1 export to China. Hence, in this section, we conduct a more rigorous IIT analysis distinguishing between processing and NP trade. Specifically, we calculate the Grubel-Lloyd IIT index (Grubel and Llyod, 1975) for China-ASEAN/BCLM, China-US, China-Japan and China-Korea for 2006 and 2014, with and without processing trade.[5] The IIT index is calculated for each 6-digit HS product and then aggregated to 2-digit HS codes.

The results are presented in Table 4.11, where we show the bilateral IIT index for top ten HS 2-digit products (by value of exports plus imports) between China and ASEAN countries. The following important points are worth noting. First, comparing across products, clearly product HS 85 (Electrical equipment) or HS 84 (mechanical appliances) has the highest IIT index. In particular, for China-ASEAN trade, in year 2014 the overall IIT index for HS 85 and HS 84 are 0.41 and 0.38, respectively, which are similar to that of product 90 precision instruments (0.39). This may not be very surprising, since E&M products are often characterised by a high degree of fragmentation or outsourcing by firms heavily engaged in the global production network. As a result, two-way trade in components and assembled final products within the same product category frequently takes place between China and its main Asian trade partners, which leads to high measures of IIT. Second, comparing across years (Panel A and Panel B), the IIT indices for most top products remain similar for China-ASEAN trade. However, note that for products HS 84 and 85, between 2006 and 2014 the IIT index for *NP trade* increased for China-ASEAN trade. This implies the rising importance of indigenous Chinese firms' NP trade in the two-way flow between China and its main Asian trade partners, with the declining role of processing trade. Finally, we investigate whether there is any significant difference between China-ASEAN-6 trade and China-BCLM trade in terms of their IIT intensity. As shown in Table 4.11, Columns 13–15, interestingly, the IIT indices of China-BCLM trade are almost all zero for their top ten products, indicating a very clear pattern of one way/inter-industry trade. In particular, this even holds for products 84 and 85, which are identified as the top two products with a high degree of two-way trade (big IIT index) for China-ASEAN. However, this may not be surprising since the BCLM countries' exports are mainly natural resource rich products, and thus they produce/export little in electrical equipment and machinery (E&M) products. Note that, however, the only exception for China-BCLM's IIT index is product 71 (precious stones), which accounts for around 40 percent of China-BCLM trade in 2006 with IIT index of 0.17. Overall, China-BCLM trade exhibits clear features of inter-industry trade, even in E&M products that exhibit a high IIT index for China's trade with ASEAN as a whole.

Table 4.11 Intra-Industry Trade between China and ASEAN

China-ASEAN				*China-BCLM*			
	(1)	(2)	(3)		(13)	(14)	(15)
Panel A: 2006							
HS2	Share in Total Bilateral Trade (%)	*IIT*	*IIT_NP*	*HS2*	Share in Bilateral Trade (%)	*IIT*	*IIT_NP*
85	36.7	0.368	0.251	27	13.5	0.002	0.002
84	16.7	0.431	0.240	84	8.9	0.000	0.000
27	7.2	0.278	0.275	60	8.0	0.002	0.001
39	3.7	0.177	0.207	44	6.9	0.002	0.002
72	3.0	0.054	0.046	85	6.8	0.001	0.000
29	2.9	0.071	0.056	52	6.5	0.040	0.005
40	2.9	0.062	0.074	87	5.4	0.000	0.000
90	2.4	0.323	0.522	72	5.3	0.000	0.000
15	1.7	0.004	0.004	55	4.7	0.000	0.000
73	1.4	0.200	0.141	73	4.2	0.000	0.000
Total share	78.6	0.285	0.210		70.1	0.006	0.004
Panel B: 2014							
85	24.8	0.407	0.308	71	39.2	0.169	0.160
84	12.4	0.380	0.274	85	8.3	0.019	0.008
27	7.3	0.311	0.183	44	5.5	0.002	0.002
39	3.9	0.210	0.175	84	5.4	0.003	0.000
72	3.1	0.012	0.009	27	5.4	0.035	0.035
71	3.1	0.167	0.900	72	4.0	0.000	0.000
90	2.7	0.391	0.436	87	3.7	0.003	0.003
29	2.6	0.094	0.087	60	3.3	0.001	0.000
94	2.3	0.074	0.066	26	3.0	0.000	0.000
40	2.3	0.110	0.087	94	2.1	0.022	0.021
Total share	64.6	0.247	0.216		79.8	0.078	0.073

Notes: IIT is the IIT index, IIT_NP is the IIT index calculated excluding processing trade.

List of 2-digit HS2002 products: 12 – Oilseeds and oleaginous fruits, miscellaneous grains, seeds and fruit, industrial or medicinal plants, straw and fodder; 15 – Animal or vegetable fats and oils and their cleavage products; prepared edible fats; animal or vegetable waxes; 26 – Ores, slag and ash; 27 – Mineral fuels, mineral oils and products of their distillation, bituminous substances, mineral waxes; 29 – Organic chemicals; 39 – Plastics and articles thereof; 40 – Rubber and articles thereof; 44 – Wood and articles of wood; wood charcoal; 52 – Cotton; 55 – Man-made staple fibres; 60 – Knitted or crocheted fabrics; 61 – Articles of apparel and clothing accessories, knitted or crocheted; 62 – Articles of apparel and clothing accessories, not knitted or crocheted; 64 – Footwear, gaiters and the like; parts of such articles; 71 – Natural or cultured pearls, precious or semi-precious stones, precious metals, metals clad with precious metal and articles thereof; imitation, jewellery; coin; 72 – Iron and steel; 73 – Articles of iron or steel; 74 – Copper and articles thereof; 76 – Aluminium and articles thereof; 84 – Nuclear reactors, boilers, machinery and mechanical appliances; parts thereof; 85 – Electrical machinery and equipment and parts thereof; sound recorders and reproducers, television image and sound recorders and reproducers, and parts and accessories of such articles; 87 – Vehicles other than railway or tramway rolling-stock, and parts and accessories thereof; 88 – Aircraft, spacecraft and parts thereof; 90 – Optical, photographic, cinematographic, measuring, checking, precision, medical or surgical instruments and apparatus; parts and accessories thereof; 94 – Furniture; bedding, mattresses, mattress supports, cushions and similar stuffed furnishings; lamps and lighting fittings, not elsewhere specified or included; 95 – Toys, games and sports requisites; parts and accessories thereof.

4.5 Competing in China: ASEAN versus other countries

The rapidly growing Chinese economy and its surging demand for foreign products provide a great export opportunity to firms from ASEAN countries, but they may also face fierce competition from other Asian countries such as Korea and Japan. To investigate this question, we use China's import data to calculate the Finger-Kreinin (1979) export similarity index (ESI) to examine the product level overlap between ASEAN, Japan, the US and Korea's exports to China, with and without processing trade, where ESI is defined as the following:

$$ESI^i = \sum_k \min\left(S_k^{ic}, S_k^{ac}\right)$$

where *i* is Country *i*, *a* denotes ASEAN countries, *c* is China, *k* is product k and S^{ic}_k is the share of exports of product *k* in Country *i*'s total exports to China. The value is between 0 and 1. A higher ESI indicates a greater degree of the overlap of product baskets exported by ASEAN countries and Country *i*, in terms of their exports to the Chinese market.

The results are reported in Table 4.12, where the row "NP" shows results using only NP trade data. First, comparing across countries, we can see that the ESI is highest for ASEAN-Korea (0.524), followed by ASEAN-Japan (0.315) and ASEAN-US (0.251). This indicates that, in terms of their exports to China, the product basket of ASEAN is most similar to that of Korea, but has a smaller overlap with that of the US. Second, comparing over time, there is a large increase of the ESI of ASEAN-Korea between 1997 and 2006, from 0.352 to 0.492, and it keeps rising to 0.524 in 2014. Since around 70 percent of China's imports from ASEAN are intermediate goods, this trend may reflect an increasingly important role of ASEAN firms as a source of industrial supply to Chinese firms versus that of Korean firms. By contrast, the export similarity of ASEAN and Japan and of ASEAN and the US both increased from 1997 to 2006, but then both declined since 2006. The decreasing export similarity between ASEAN and Japan/US in recent periods is worth noting as it implies a divergence of ASEAN's exports profiles from those of Japan and the US in the Chinese market, and thus less direct competition with firms from the US and Japan. Last, when we exclude processing trade, ESI declined irrespective of the comparison country or year. In other words, there is a higher degree of overlap between ASEAN and other countries in processing trade than NP trade. This, however, is not surprising, as processing trade is more concentrated in intermediate goods and materials as inputs to export processing, which may be more similar across ASEAN and other countries from which Chinese firms import for further assembly and processing.

Next, as in the previous analysis, in Panel B we further compare the BCLM countries' ESI against Korea, Japan and the US separately. First, note that the ESIs for the BCLM countries are very low, with the highest being only 0.066 against Korea in 2014. This might simply reflect BCLM's very different local comparative advantages (against China) relative to industrialised countries, which leads to a lower degree of overlap between their exports and those from

Table 4.12 Export Similarity between ASEAN or BCLM Group and Other Countries' Exports to China

		1997	*2006*	*2014*
Panel A: ASEAN				
ASEAN vs Korea	*All*	0.3524	0.4922	0.5242
	NP	0.3527	0.3942	0.4530
ASEAN vs Japan	*All*	0.2931	0.3373	0.3154
	NP	0.1974	0.2535	0.2480
ASEAN vs US	*All*	0.2390	0.3096	0.2506
	NP	0.1723	0.2119	0.2064
Panel B: BCLM				
BCLM vs Korea	*All*	0.0029	0.0144	0.0656
	NP	0.0017	0.0103	0.0147
BCLM vs Japan	*All*	0.0029	0.0155	0.0154
	NP	0.0021	0.0052	0.0162
BCLM vs US	*All*	0.0125	0.0211	0.0238
	NP	0.0056	0.0153	0.0282

Notes: All is the ESI calculated using all trade, NP is the ESI calculated excluding processing trade.

Korea, Japan and the US. Second, however, over time the ESIs for the BCLM countries have increased substantially. For example, their ESI against Korea rose from nearly zero in 1997 to 0.014 in 2006 and then shot up to 0.066 in 2014. Third, as a result of the sharp rise of ESI against Korea, in 2014 BCLM's exports to China are the most similar to those from Korea, followed by those from the US (0.024) and those from Japan (0.015).

4.6 Conclusions

In the last two decades ASEAN's trade with China has not only grown dramatically in total amount, but also transformed substantially in structure. In this paper, using detailed Chinese Customs data from 1997 to 2014, we analyse the rapidly evolving trade pattern between China and ASEAN and its relation to the structural changes taken place in both economies. Most interestingly, we find that since the late 1990s China's active engagement in the global production network has led to increasing import demand for ASEAN countries, especially in intermediate goods and machinery sectors, which are characterised with high processing trade intensity and dominated by foreign-owned firms located in China. As a result, ASEAN's exports to China surged, leading to sizeable trade surpluses. However, this trend did not continue in recent years, and, if anything, reversed. This is due to China's structural change towards a "new normal" model of growth relying on domestic demand and innovation rather than processing trade by foreign firms. Consequently, the growth of China's imports from ASEAN firms slowed down, accompanied by decreasing shares of processing trade, particularly in machinery and intermediate good sectors. On the other hand, NP exports from indigenous Chinese firms to ASEAN rose sharply. Taken together, these turned ASEAN's trade surplus against China into a trade deficit, which might even be widening in the years to come.

These findings may generate important implications for policymakers and planners in the ASEAN region. In order to maintain a more balanced trade relation with China in future, ASEAN countries may need to take appropriate policy adjustments to cope with China's structural transformation towards a new growth model. In particular, for those countries whose current exports to China heavily concentrate in machinery/intermediate sector and processing trade, it might be necessary to make an effort to establish a more diversified export portfolio, especially expanding into those sectors with booming domestic consumption demand in China to reap the opportunities resulting from a more liberalised Chinese market. In the meantime, whilst NP exports by domestic Chinese firms became the driving force of the recent surge of China's trade surplus, the ASEAN governments may need to design and implement industrial policies that encourage firms to invest more in technological upgrading in key manufacturing sectors to establish competitive advantage against the fiercer competition from indigenous Chinese firms that increasingly penetrate the ASEAN market. Overall, a closer integration between China and ASEAN means both opportunities and competition for ASEAN firms, and it is those who are "well prepared" can fully reap the gains and avoid the potential losses from an ongoing structural transformation of China-ASEAN relation in the new era of globalisation.

Acknowledgements

The author would like to thank Kyung Hwang for excellent research assistance and Miaojie Yu for comments.

Notes

1 Processing trade is the import of intermediates for assembly and transformation in China and their subsequent re-exporting to foreign markets, rather than for sale in the Chinese market. Imported products under the processing trade regime are often exempt from tariffs and import-related taxes. See Yu (2015) and Manova and Yu (2016), for example, for further details on the determinants and consequences of processing trade at the firm level.

2 The phrase "new normal" is used by President Xi Jinping in 2014 to define China's new model of economic growth. The main characteristics of the new normal model are the following. First, the growth rate has declined from high speed to a medium-to-high speed. Second, there has been upgrading of the economic structure. Third, economic growth will be mainly driven by innovation rather than accumulation of capital or material inputs.

3 We can precisely identify the processing trade status of the trade data for years 1997–2006, and 2014 but, unfortunately, cannot separately identify processing trade status for 2007–2013 in our data.

4 Please see Manova and Yu (2016), Wang and Yu (2012) and Brandt and Morrow (2012) for more detailed discussions on the processing trade regime and firm level determinants.

5 The IIT index is defined as $IIT_i = 1 - |X_i - M_i| / |X_i + M_i|$, where i is six-digit HS products and we then aggregate it to HS2 digit level using trade weights in 2006 and 2014, correspondingly.

References

Amiti, M., and Freund, C. (2010), "The Anatomy of China's Export Growth". In *China's Growing Role in World Trade*, edited by Robert C. Feenstra and Shang-Jin Wei, 35–62. Chicago, IL: University of Chicago Press.

Brandt, L., and Morrow, P. (2012), "Tariffs and the Organization of Trade in China". *mimeo.*

Grubel, H. G., and Lloyd, P. J. (1975), *Intra-industry Trade: The Theory and Measurement of International Trade in Differentiated Products.* New York: John Wiley.

Holst, D., and Weiss, J. (2004), "ASEAN and China: Export Rivals or Partners in Regional Growth?" *World Economy*, 27, 1255–1274.

Kee, H. L., and Tang, H. (2016), "Domestic Value Added in Exports: Theory and Firm Evidence from China". *American Economic Review*, 106, 1402–1436.

Koopman R., Wang, Z., and Wei, S. (2012), "How Much of Chinese Exports in Really Made in China? Assessing Domestic Value-Added When Processing Trade is Pervasive". *Journal of Development Economics*, 99, 178–189.

Lall, S., and Albaladejo, M. (2004), "China's Competitive Performance: A Threat to East Asian Manufactured Exports?" *World Development*, 2004, 32, 1441–1466.

Manova, K., and Yu, Z. (2016), "How Firms Export: Processing vs. Ordinary Trade with Financial Frictions". *Journal of International Economics*, 100, 120–137.

Ravenhill, J. (2006), Is China an Economic Threat to Southeast Asia? *Asian Survey*, 46, 653–674.

Salidjanova, N., Koch-Weser, I., and Klanderman, J. (2015), "China's Economic Ties with ASEAN: A Country-by-Country Analysis". US-China Economic and Security Review Commission, Staff Research Paper.

Wang, Z., and Yu, Z. (2012), "Trade Partners, Products, and Firm Performance of China's Exporter-Importers: Does Processing Trade Make a Difference?" *The World Economy*, 35, 1795–1824.

Yu, M. (2015), "Processing Trade, Tariff Reductions and Firm Productivity: Evidence from Chinese Firms". *Economic Journal*, 125, 943–988.

Yu, M., and Cui, X. (2016), "The Impact of China's Trade on ASEAN's Trade". In Production Networks in Southeast Asia, edited by Lili Yan Ing and Fukunari Kimura, 26–88. London: Routledge.

5 The impacts of ASEAN FTAs on trade in goods

Misa Okabe

5.1 Introduction

According to the regional trade agreement (RTA) database of the World Trade Organization (WTO), the number of cumulative notifications of RTAs in force has rapidly increased nearly tenfold in the last thirty years since 1990. One reason for the surge in RTAs is that global trade liberalisation under the WTO system has not proceeded smoothly with the increasing number of member countries. Many countries have pursued trade liberalisation by forming bilateral or plurilateral trade agreements to gain from the various economic benefits that come from trade creation and market expansion through the elimination of trade barriers. They also hope to gain from the various dynamic effects, such as capital accumulation and productivity improvement, brought about by the liberalisation of foreign direct investment (FDI) and technology transfer among member countries. With regard to free trade agreements (FTAs) in East Asia, as illustrated in Figure 5.1, bilateral and regional FTAs have increased rapidly since the 2000s along with the world trend of FTAs. Table 5.1 is a chronological list of FTAs among East Asian countries. Until the 2000s, only a few countries had joined regional or interregional agreements on trade preferences in this region, such as the Asia Pacific Trade Agreement and the Global System of Trade Preferences among Developing Countries. Although the first regional FTA in this region, the ASEAN Free Trade Area (AFTA), was established in 1992, the formation of regional FTAs lagged behind other regions in the world, leading to East Asia being called an 'FTA vacuum' until the beginning of the 2000s. However, the number of bilateral FTAs in this region has since rapidly increased, and five ASEAN+1 FTAs – namely the ASEAN-China FTA (hereafter ACFTA), the ASEAN-Korea FTA (hereafter AKFTA), the ASEAN-Japan FTA (hereafter AJFTA), the ASEAN-Australia-New Zealand FTA (hereafter AANZFTA), and the ASEAN-India FTA (hereafter AIFTA) – have been established one after the other since the latter half of the 2000s. At this point, more than 40 FTAs have been formed by East Asian countries. In addition, a wider regional FTA, the Regional Comprehensive Economic Partnership (RCEP), has been under negotiation since 2010.

DOI: 10.4324/9780429433603-5

Table 5.1 FTAs in East Asian Countries

1976–2000	*2001–2002*	*2003–2004*	*2005–2006*
Asia Pacific Trade Agreement (1976) Australia-Papua New Guinea (1977) Australia-New Zealand (1983) Global System of Trade Preference (1989) Lao PDR-Thailand (1991) ASEAN Free Trade Area (1992)	India-Sri Lanka (2001) New Zealand-Singapore (2001) Japan-Singapore (2002)	China-Hong Kong (2003) China-Macao (2003) Singapore-Australia (2003) Republic of Korea-Chile (2004)	ASEAN-China (2005) India-Singapore (2005) Japan-Mexico (2005) Thailand-Australia (2005) Thailand-New Zealand (2005) Japan-Malaysia (2006) Korea-Singapore (2006) TPSEP (2006)
2007–2008	*2009–2010*	*2011–2012*	*2013–2015*
ASEAN-Korea (2007) Japan-Thailand (2007) ASEAN-Japan (2008) Brunei-Japan (2008) China-New Zealand (2008) Japan-Indonesia (2008) Japan-Philippines (2008)	China-Singapore (2009) Japan-Viet Nam (2009) ASEAN-AUS-NZ (2010) ASEAN-India (2010) Korea-India (2010) New Zealand-Malaysia (2010)	Hong Kong-New Zealand (2011) India-Japan (2011) India-Malaysia (2011)	Malaysia-Australia (2013) New Zealand-Taiwan (2013) Singapore-Taiwan (2014) Korea-Australia (2014) Japan-Australia (2015) China-Republic of Korea (2015) Republic of Korea-Viet Nam (2015) Republic of Korea-New Zealand (2015) Australia-China (2015)

	Number of New FTAs	*Cumulative Number of FTAs*
1976	1	1
1977	1	2
1978	0	2
1979	0	2
1980	0	2
1981	0	2
1982	0	2
1983	1	3
1984	0	3
1985	0	3
1986	0	3
1987	0	3
1988	0	3

(*Continued*)

	Number of New FTAs	*Cumulative Number of FTAs*
1989	1	4
1990	0	4
1991	1	5
1992	1	6
1993	0	6
1994	0	6
1995	0	6
1996	0	6
1997	0	6
1998	0	6
1999	0	6
2000	0	6
2001	1	7
2002	1	8
2003	3	11
2004	0	11
2005	4	15
2006	3	18
2007	1	19
2008	5	24
2009	2	26
2010	5	31
2011	3	34
2012	0	34
2013	2	36
2014	2	38
2015	5	43

Source: Author's tabulation based on data from the RTA Information System of WTO.

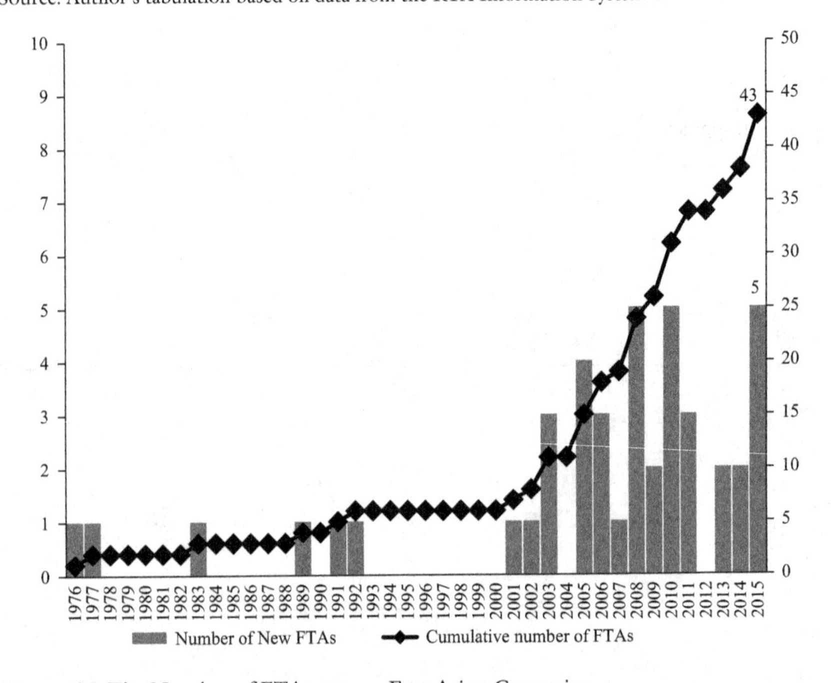

Figure 5.1 The Number of FTAs among East Asian Countries.

Note: Calculated based on WTO RTA database. Figures represent the number of FTAs established by ASEAN members, Australia, China, India, Japan, Korea, and New Zealand.

Source: Author's calculations based on data from the RTA Information System of WTO.

With the increase of FTAs in East Asia, intra-regional trade has increased since the 2000s. Figure 5.2 shows the total regional shares of intra-regional trade of ASEAN members with Australia, China, India, Japan, Korea and New Zealand. Intra-regional trade shares have been slowly increasing in intermediate goods,

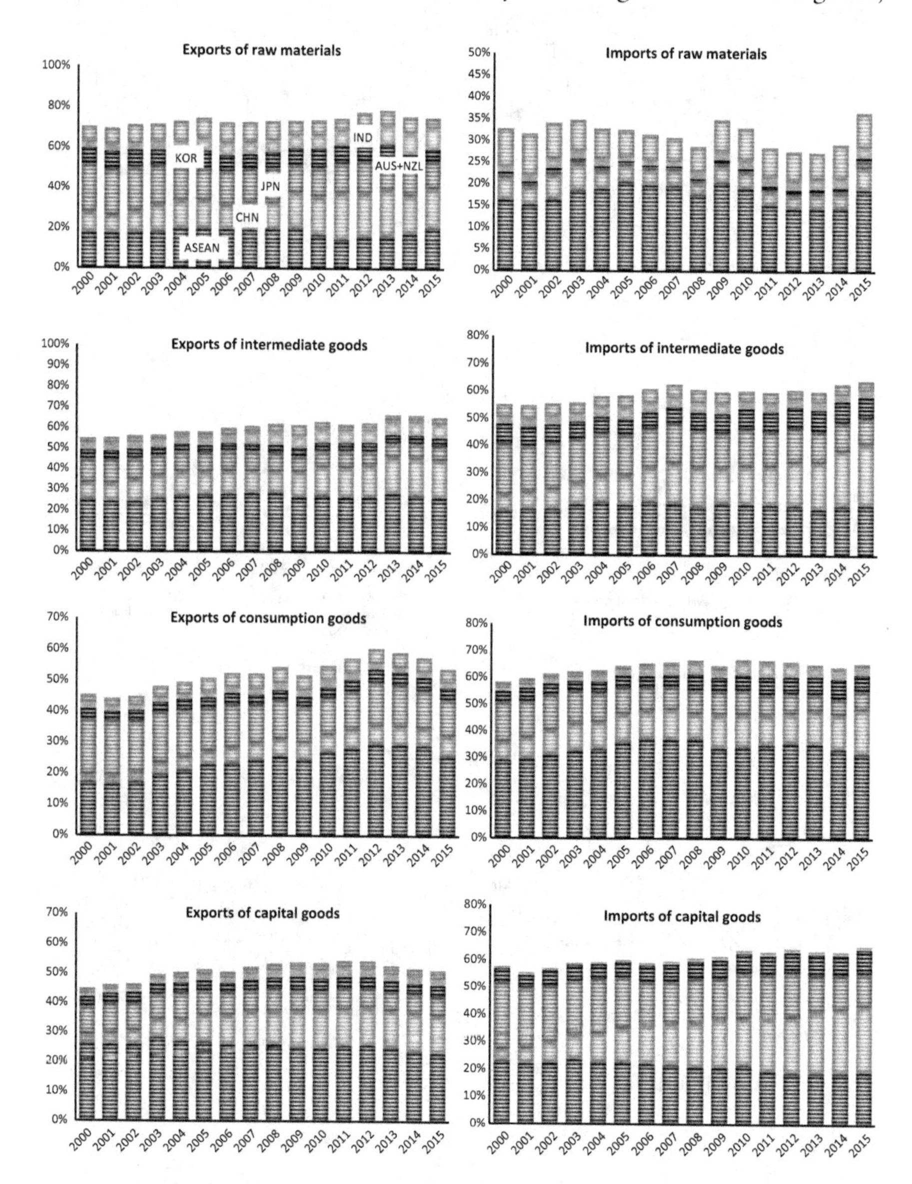

Figure 5.2 Shares of Exports and Imports of ASEAN with Australia, China, Japan, Korea and New Zealand.

Note: The share is a ratio of ASEAN's exports or imports with Australia (AUS), China (CHN), India (IND), Japan (JPN), Korea (KOR) and New Zealand (NZL) to the total exports or imports of ASEAN to the world.

Source: United Nations COMTRADE statistics, 2000–2015.

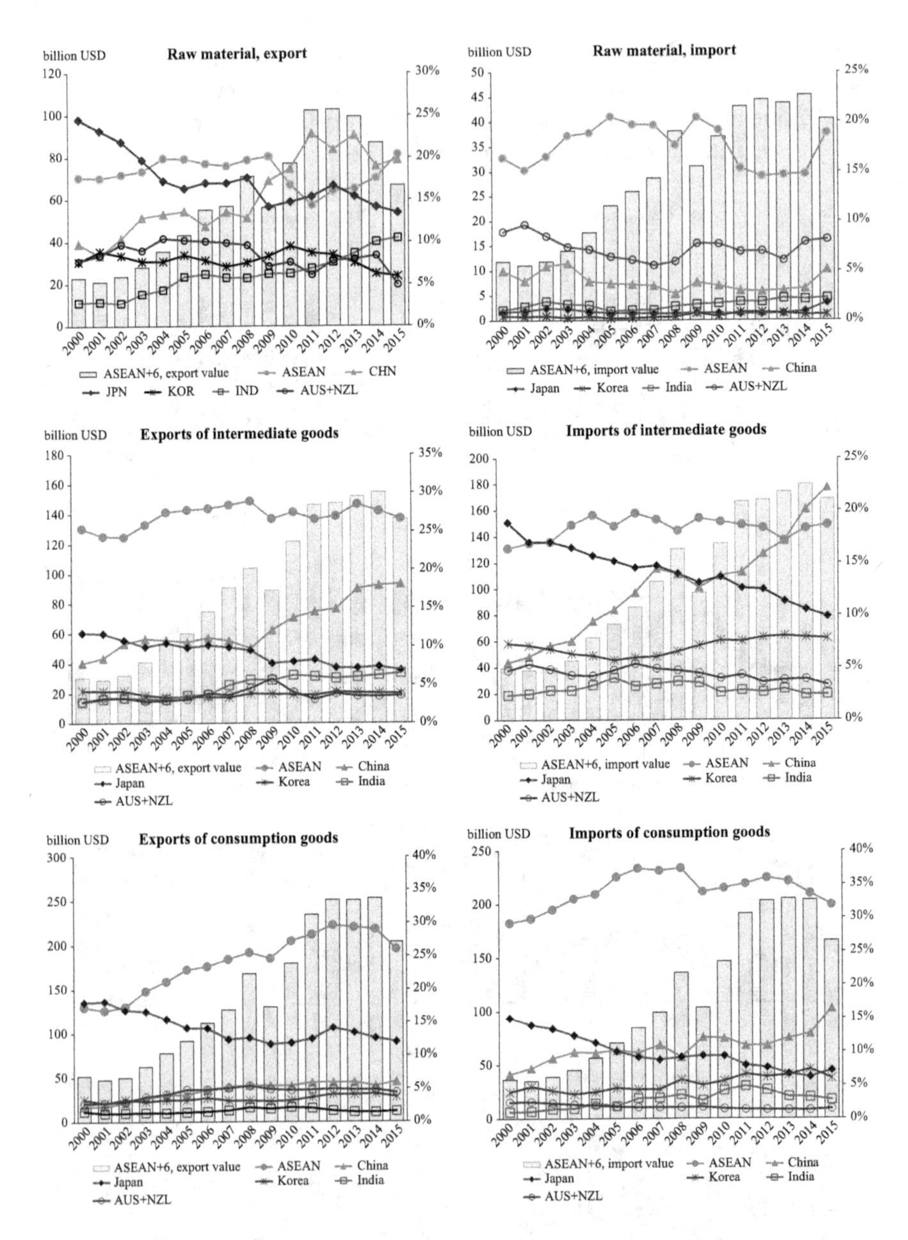

Figure 5.2 (Continued)

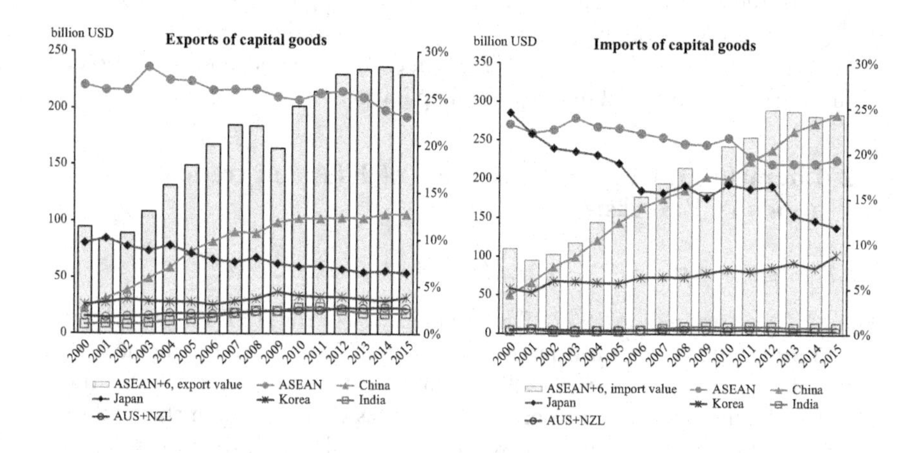

consumption goods and capital goods sectors in the past 15 years, and the sum of the trade shares of ASEAN with these six countries has consistently exceeded 40 percent in these sectors. The gradual upward trend of regional trade reflects an expanding regional production in the manufacturing sectors supported by active FDI from around the world. The fact of the expansion of regional trade synchronised with the increase of the number of regional FTAs implies that the upsurge of regional FTAs in the region is an important factor in facilitating and expanding regional trade involving inward FDI and productivity improvement in the region.

Each of the existing regional FTAs led by ASEAN, known as the ASEAN+1 FTAs, was established with the aim of developing regional production and sales networks in the region. The next challenge is the merging of these existing ASEAN+1 FTAs to form a wider regional FTA. In this context, not only the impact of coexisting regional FTAs on regional trade but also the mutual effects among regional FTAs are issues to be solved. Furthermore, it is important to examine the costs and benefits of merging the existing regional FTAs. This chapter aims to examine the impact of the existing regional FTAs on trade flows in East Asia. At the same time, we investigate the mutual effects of concurrent regional FTAs to deduce the implications for a region-wide FTA.

The remainder of this chapter is organised as follows. Section 5.2 reviews the ex post studies on the impact of regional FTAs on trade in goods in East Asia. Focusing on empirical analyses of the tariff reductions of FTAs on trade in goods, Sections 5.2.1–5.2.3 review studies related to AFTA, ASEAN FTAs, and bilateral FTAs in East Asia. Subsequently, we conduct an empirical analysis on the impact of ASEAN FTAs on trade in goods by using a gravity model in Sections 5.3 and 5.4. Ex post evaluation of these recent regional FTAs is important to predict the impacts of the RCEP under negotiation and to design policies to facilitate economic development under the region-wide FTA. Despite the importance of ex post investigation on these ASEAN+1 FTAs, there are still few studies on the ex post analysis of the ASEAN FTAs. Based on recent developments in empirical methodology, we apply gravity equations with all FTA dummies and preferential tariff margins under each FTA to the trade flows in each sector and county. Section 5.5 summarises the results and draws policy implications.

5.2 Literature review on the impact of FTAs on trade in goods in East Asia

5.2.1 Impacts of the AFTA on trade in goods in East Asia

The AFTA was signed in 1992. The key objective of the AFTA is trade liberalisation under the Common Effective Preferential Tariff (CEPT) scheme, which has been in effect since January 1993, to eliminate tariffs on intra-ASEAN trade. The AFTA initially planned to reduce tariff rates on products in the 'inclusion list' to between 0 percent and 5 percent by 2008, although the target date was later changed to 2002. The ASEAN-CEPT agreement was also revised significantly by the ASEAN Trade in Goods Agreement in 2008. The tariff rates on the products in the inclusion list were to be 0 percent by the year 2010 for six ASEAN members and by 2015 for the remaining four members. By 2010, the share of tariff lines with 0 percent tariff rates was about 99 percent for the six members, and the share of tariff lines with 0 to 5 percent tariff rates was more than 95 percent for the other four members. Tariff elimination under AFTA has almost been completed in the last 20 years.

At the start of the AFTA, according to Frankel (1997), many studies presumed that trade creation by the AFTA would be small. For example, DeRosa (1995) used a computable general equilibrium (CGE) model to find that the most-favoured-nation (MFN) treatment of WTO rule would increase trade among ASEAN members more than trade liberalisation by the AFTA. Frankel and Wei (1996) examined the impact of ASEAN's regional trading bloc by using a gravity model with ASEAN dummies. Although the coefficient of their ASEAN dummy was significant and had positive values, they found that this ASEAN bloc effect disappeared completely when the East Asian bloc effect dummy was added to the estimated equation simultaneously with the ASEAN dummy. They concluded that ASEAN's trade relations with outside industrialised countries were more important than intra-ASEAN trade relations. Endoh (1999) introduced two types of RTA dummies for capturing trade creation and diversion effects in a gravity model. Based on the estimated results, he found that ASEAN had no effect on boosting trade among its member countries during the sample period 1960–1994. He presumed that this result reflected the fact that the share of intra-ASEAN trade for each ASEAN country was still low.

As described in the previous section, the methodology for estimating the gravity model has developed since the 2000s, and data coverage has also expanded. Solaga and Winters (2001) use a Tobit model for estimation with consideration of zero trade flows. They quantify the impact of major preferential trade agreements on trade. Their coefficient for the intra-bloc trade of ASEAN is negative but insignificant. Given that country-pair effects are unobservable, Carrère (2006) applies an instrumental variable method proposed by Hausman and Taylor (1981). Comparing the estimation results by panel and cross-sectional data, she finds that most RTAs resulted in an increase in intra-regional trade while reducing imports from the rest of the world. As for ASEAN, a trade creation effect is seen over the examined periods.

With increased interest in the growing intra-regional trade of ASEAN members since the 1990s, the number of studies focusing on the impacts of the AFTA has gradually increased. Major studies are summarised in Table 5.2. For example, Elliot and Ikemoto (2004) apply a modified gravity model to examine the trade creation and diversion effects of the AFTA. Comparing the estimated

Table 5.2 Studies on the Impacts FTAs in ASEAN on Its Trade

Authors (year)	*Methodology*		*Data*	*Increased Trade: Estimated Coefficient (Elasticity)*
Endoh (1999)	ASEAN dummy	Cross-sectional analysis by pooled data	80 countries, 1960–1994	0.589–0.778 (80%–117%)
Carrère (2006)	ASEAN dummy	GL and Hausman-Taylor estimation, panel data	130 countries, 1962–1996	0.64–2.02 (90%–653%)
Elliot and Ikemoto (2004)	AFTA dummy	Cross-sectional analysis by pooled data	34 countries, 1983–1999	0.35–2.03 (42%–661%)
Kien (2009)	AFTA dummy	Hausman-Taylor estimation with two-way components	39 countries, 1988–2002	0.626 (87%)
Bun et al. (2009)	AFTA dummy *time trend	Panel data approach with country-pair specific time trends	217 countries, 1948–1997	0%–9% annually in average
Manchin and Pelkmans-Balaoing (2007)	AFTA tariff margin	Panel data with time-varying country fixed effects	217 countries, 2001–2003	0.19%–0.96% change when preferential margins are from 25% to 60%
Cheong (2008)	AFTA tariff margin	Panel data with the fixed effects PQML estimator	HS 6-digit level, 2001–2003	Intra-regional ASEAN imports are increased at 2% in average
Okabe and Urata (2014)	AFTA tariff margin	Hausman Taylor estimation	52 sectors, 193 countries 1980–2010	0.36% for export 0.38% for import

Note: The elasticity of the AFTA dummy with trade is calculated by (EXP (estimated value) –1)*100.
Source: Author's tabulation based on the result of each study.

coefficient of AFTA dummies before and after the AFTA process started, they find that both effects are significantly positive. Their findings indicate that the AFTA increased not only intra-regional trade among its members but also trade with non-members. Kien (2009) employed the Hausman-Taylor estimation for panel data from 1988 to 2002 to estimate several RTAs. By using the dynamic method of an AFTA dummy that takes the value of one for only effective years, he investigates the effects of the AFTA as an institutional framework rather than a regional trading bloc. Similar to Elliot and Ikemoto (2004), the result indicates that the AFTA has a trade creation effect; at the same time, the effects of the AFTA on trade between members and non-members was positive. Controlling for unobserved heterogeneity, by using a country-pair specific time trend, Bun et al. (2009) apply two types of AFTA dummies, that is, an AFTA dummy that takes the value of one for members after the year 1992 and an AFTA dummy multiplied by the time trend, which captures the effects of gradual tariff reductions under the AFTA. They find that the AFTA positively affected trade during the sample periods and suggest that careful controls for the unobserved explanatory variables of the trend in trade are necessary for testing the impacts of the AFTA.

Although many studies conclude that ASEAN regional trade blocs had little impact at the beginning of the AFTA, several recent studies have found that the AFTA made a significant and positive impact on trade as regional trade liberalisation progressed under the AFTA framework. This transition in the research findings is also caused by improved data availability and estimation methodologies. These studies lead us to the temporary finding that the institutional framework of the AFTA has facilitated intra-regional trade to a varying degree. In addition, trade liberalisation under RTAs is usually implemented through several measures along with tariff elimination. To understand the impacts of the FTAs more comprehensively, it is necessary to investigate the effects of these measures directly.

On the impact of the tariff elimination process under the CEPT scheme of the AFTA, a few studies have attempted to estimate the impact by using tariff data. Manchin and Pelkmans-Balaoing (2008) apply a gravity model with time-varying country fixed effects as multilateral trade resistance terms for aggregated and disaggregated trade data to estimate the effects of preferential AFTA tariffs on the trade flows of the AFTA members. Although their data set is limited to four ASEAN members, that are, Indonesia, Malaysia, Philippines and Thailand, for 2001–2003, they carefully investigate the impact of different preferential margins on trade. The result shows that the tariff reduction in the AFTA had no or little impact on intra-ASEAN trade. However, they find that positive tariff reduction effects of AFTA are significant in a limited range of products where the preferential margin is higher than 25 percent. Interestingly, their result implies that the cost of using AFTA is higher than the benefit from obtaining the preferential treatment when the difference between the MFN tariff rate and the preferential AFTA tariff rate is small. Similar to Manchin and Pelkmans-Balaoing (2008), Cheong (2008) applies a gravity model with preference tariff margins to HS 6-digit level disaggregated data, by using the Poisson quasi-maximum likelihood estimator. He finds that ASEAN's intra-regional trade, particularly in metals, machinery, electrical products and transportation equipment, is facilitated by ASEAN preferential tariffs. He concludes that the AFTA had a positive significant welfare effect since these sectors, which have complex production networks and a high level of product differentiation, account for the majority share of total ASEAN imports. Likewise, Okabe and Urata (2014) utilise preferential margins, defined as the difference between the MFN rates and the preferential tariff rate under the CEPT scheme, as an explanatory variable in their gravity model. They investigate the effects of tariff reductions under the CEPT scheme for each ASEAN member during 1980–2010. They find positive and significant trade creation effects from the tariff reductions for a wide range of products, while the elasticity of the tariff reductions on imports tends to be much larger than that for exports.

Although very few studies on the impact of tariff reductions under the AFTA exist, it could be argued that tariff reduction under the AFTA has a positive impact on regional trade in products where the difference between the MFN and preferential tariff rate is large, and on regional trade between countries trading in relatively large volumes. However, the impact on trade flows does not appear to be strong. Also, the effect of tariff reductions under the AFTA on newer members is limited. Based on these results, tariff reductions under the AFTA are not necessarily the most important measures for promoting region-wide trade. To promote region-wide trade in ASEAN and to make the AFTA contribute to raising the economic welfare of all member countries, other measures, such as trade facilitation, the reduction of non-tariff measures (NTMs), and the coordination of rules of origin (RoOs), as well as the improvement of AFTA utilisation, should be examined carefully. We review studies on other measures in the following sections.

5.2.2 Impacts of ASEAN+1FTAs on trade in goods in East Asia

More recently, several studies have attempted to examine the impacts of the ASEAN+1 FTAs by using trade indices or by estimation using trade data. Sheng, Tang and Xu (2014) estimate a gravity model using intra-industry trade flow data in parts and components for 1980–2008, and the predicted trade creation effect on intra-industry trade under the ACFTA, based on actual 2008 data. They find that the ACFTA will have a substantially large impact on trade flows between members, particularly those flows based on close international production linkages, while the positive impact will be spread unevenly among ASEAN countries. Likewise, Yang and Martinez-Zarzoso (2014) examine the impact of the ACFTA by applying a gravity model using aggregated and disaggregated data. They find that the ACFTA has a trade creation effect in total trade and trade in manufacturing and chemical products. By using trade indices, such as trade intensities and trade potential indices, several studies have attempted to estimate the predicted impact by sector. Bano, Takahashi and Scrimgeour (2013) calculate the trade intensities between ASEAN members and New Zealand and the trade potential of the members of the AANZFTA using trade data from 1980. They show that the trade intensities between members of the AANZFTA have increased continuously, and the significant potential for future growth in specific export sectors by estimating the potential trade between New Zealand and ASEAN across industries. Chandran (2012) discusses the impact of the AIFTA, focusing on India's fishery sector by using trade indices and a comparative advantage index. Based on sectoral analysis, he concludes that India could improve trade by tariff elimination under the AIFTA with some ASEAN countries, particularly less-developed members.

Regarding the ex post evaluation of ASEAN+1 FTAs, studies are still limited due to the small sample periods because most of these FTAs started recently. Considering the results of previous ex ante studies, conducting ex post analysis will hopefully investigate the impacts of various measures along with tariff elimination under the existing ASEAN+1 FTAs. In addition, as Sheng, Tang and Xu (2014) and Chandran (2012) demonstrate, examining the impacts of the existing ASEAN+1 FTAs on the growth gaps, among member countries and on industrial sector trade flows in the long term is an interesting research topic.

5.2.3 Impact of FTAs on trade in goods in East Asia: bilateral FTAs in East Asia

Ex post studies on bilateral FTAs in East Asia are scarce because of limited data. Ando (2007) examines the impacts of the Japan-Singapore Economic Partnership Agreement (EPA) and the Japan-Mexico EPA by applying a gravity model using trade data at the commodity level. Comparing actual values to fitted values before and after the EPA's implementation, she finds that the Japan-Singapore EPA has had little impact on trade, while the Japan-Mexico EPA has had a positive impact on trade, particularly on exports. She points out that one of the reasons for the limited impact of the Japan-Singapore EPA is the quite limited actual reduction of tariffs by the Japan-Singapore EPA. This result is consistent with an ex ante study by Lee (2002) that found a negligible impact of the Japan-Singapore EPA in the absence of positive spillovers to productivity. Besides, an ex ante study by Hertel, Walmsley and Itakura (2005) using a modified version of the dynamic GTAP model found that customs automisation under the Japan-Singapore EPA plays the most important role in increases in trade. As Ando (2007) concludes, the conditions beyond tariff elimination, such as trade liberalisation in services, various trade facilitation measures, improvement of business environment, and FTA utilisation, are important factors for designing effective FTAs. These ex ante and ex post studies suggest that further ex post study will need to capture both direct and indirect effects of FTAs.

As an ex post study which focuses on the indirect effects of a bilateral FTA, for example, Athukorala and Kohpaiboon (2011) examine the impact of the Thailand-Australia FTA (hereafter TAFTA), paying attention to the implications of the RoOs and the utilisation of tariff preferences. By linking a data set of the utilisation of tariff preferences by traders to bilateral trade volumes between Australia and Thailand, they find that trade expanded faster after the TAFTA came into effect, but the impact was heavily concentrated on a few product lines in Australian imports from Thailand. They point out that the reason for this limited impact can be attributed to the rate of FTA utilisation. Hence, their result suggests that enhancing FTA utilisation is also necessary for strengthening the positive impacts of the existing FTAs. To sum up, similar to the results of studies on the AFTA and other FTAs in East Asia, ex post studies on bilateral FTAs also show that bilateral FTAs positively affect trade. To some extent, however, the positive impact is brought about by tariff elimination under FTAs and by other necessary conditions for trade liberalisation, such as improvement of the utilisation rate of preferential tariffs.

5.3 Empirical investigation of the impact of ASEAN FTAs

ASEAN's six dialogue partners – Australia, China, India, Japan, Korea and New Zealand – have formed bilateral FTAs with ASEAN members since the mid-2000s. For example, Japan has formed seven bilateral FTAs with other ASEAN members, starting with Singapore in 2002. Singapore has actively arranged bilateral FTAs with all the dialogue partners. Thailand and Malaysia also have arranged bilateral FTAs with Australia, New Zealand, and India since the late 2000s. As the active FTA proponent in the region, ASEAN, through which regional efforts for economic integration among its members started in the 1990s, has taken on the role of a hub for the regional FTA network in East Asia. After the ACFTA came into force in 2005, four other ASEAN+1 plurilateral FTAs – namely the AKFTA, AJFTA, AANZFTA, and AIFTA – have sequentially been formed in this region.

Regional production and sales networks accompanied by industrial agglomeration revolving around ASEAN have developed in East Asia since the 1990s. Regional FTAs in the region are more important than bilateral FTAs since region-wide FTAs enable multinational enterprises (MNEs) to effectively use the expanding regional production and sales networks as a means to increase their productivity by reducing transport and transaction costs across countries. As a natural response from the MNEs, the aforementioned five ASEAN+1 FTAs have been formed one after another. Furthermore, a wider regional FTA, the RCEP, covering AFTA and five ASEAN+1 FTAs, is under negotiation. The RCEP is expected to play the role of a regional FTA to coordinate the five segmented ASEAN+1 FTAs.

In order to examine the effects of these concurrent regional ASEAN+1 FTAs on the trade flows for each FTA member, we conduct an ex post evaluation of the existing ASEAN FTAs by using the gravity model. By using all regional FTAs as explanatory variables, we attempt to identify the effects of each regional FTA on trade among the members.

5.3.1 Estimation methodology and data

We apply the gravity model to estimate the impact of ASEAN FTAs, namely the AFTA and the five ASEAN+1 FTAs on ASEAN's trade in goods by sector. To examine the impact of each FTA on trade in each sector and individual ASEAN member, we use both the export and import flows of the ASEAN members with 188 countries in the world at the 2-digit level of International Standard Industrial Classification of All Economic Activities (ISIC) revision 3. The sample periods are from 2000 to 2015. We apply the most-often-formulated gravity model as follows:

$$E\left(x_{ijkt}|A_0,\ Y_{jt},\ y_{jt},\ D_{ij},\ C_{it},\ \tau_{ijkt},\ FTA_{ijt},\ BFTA_{M,ijt},\ I_i,\ J_j,\ T_t\ \right)=$$
$$\exp\left(A_0+\beta_1\ \ln\left(Y_{\text{it}}\ \right)+\beta_2\ln\left(Y_{jt}\right)+\beta_3\ln\left(y_{it}\right)+\beta_4\ln\left(y_{jt}\right)+\beta_5\ln\left(D_{ij}\right)+\beta_6 C_{ij}\right.$$
$$+\sum\nolimits_N \gamma_N\tau_{ijkt}+\sum\nolimits_N \Gamma_N FTA_{ijt}+\sum\nolimits_M \theta_M\tau_{M,ijkt}+\sum\nolimits_M \Theta_M BFTA_{M,ijt}$$
$$\left.+\sum\nolimits_{i=1}^{13}\lambda_i I_i+\sum\nolimits_{j=1}^{188}\mu_i J_j+\sum\nolimits_{t=2000}^{2015} v_t T_t\right)$$

where A_0 is a constant, and Y and y are the real GDP and GDP per capita, respectively. GDP and GDP per capita represent the economic scale and income level, which are thought to be factors affecting bilateral trade volumes. D_{ij} and C_{ij} are proxies of trade cost. D_{ij} is the geographical distance between the largest city of Country i and of Country j, and C_{ij} is the contiguity of countries i and j. Trade costs are assumed to be smaller when the geographical distance is closer and countries i and j share a border. I_i and J_j are country dummies, and T_t is year dummy.

In order to estimate the impact of FTAs, we use two variables capturing the effects of implementation of each FTA. One is a tariff margin, τ_{ijt}, which is the difference between the MFN tariff rate and the preferential tariff rate under the FTA, to capture the impact of the tariff reduction under the FTA on trade flows. The other variable, FTA_{ijt}, is a binary dummy that equals one when a trade partner is a member of an FTA after the effective year. This dummy variable captures the overall impacts of the FTA on trade flows, including both static and dynamic effects, such as increases in trade caused by a reduction in non-tariff barriers, the implementation of various trade facilitation measures, market enlargement, and competition promotion effects. The effective dates for each ASEAN+1 FTA differ by country-pair, as shown in Table 5.A2. In addition to the six ASEAN FTAs (N=6), we add all 49 bilateral and regional FTAs (M=49) other than the ASEAN+1 FTAs to the previous estimation equation. Subscripts i, j, k, and t denote the reporter, partner, sector, and year, respectively.

To use all the bilateral trade flow data, which include many zero trade flows, as an independent variable, the Poisson pseudo-maximum likelihood (PPML) estimator is used to estimate the equation. The list of countries for estimation is shown in Table 5.A1.

For data for the estimation, we use the trade values of nine ASEAN members. Import and export values in US dollar at the 2-digit level of ISIC revision 3 are from the Commodity Trade Statistics (COMTRADE) of the United Nations. Real GDP and real GDP per capita are from the World Development Indicators of the World Bank. Geographical distance is from the GeoDist database provided by the French Research Center in International Economics (CEPII). The MFN tariff rates and the preferential tariff rates under each FTA are from the United Nations Conference on Trade and Development (UNCTAD)'s Trade Analysis Information System (TRAINS). Information on the date when the tariff elimination starts under the bilateral and plurilateral FTAs is from the WTO's RTA database.

5.4 Results

5.4.1 Estimation by sector

We estimate the gravity equation explained earlier by using pooled bilateral trade data for nine ASEAN members with 188 countries in 26 sectors. Based on the estimated coefficients, Table 5.3 summarises the estimated marginal effect of the enforcement and tariff reduction of the ASEAN FTAs on exports and imports.

5.4.1.1 Impacts of the AFTA

The results show that the AFTA has had both positive and negative effects on exports and imports between ASEAN members. In particular, in contrast to previous studies, manufacturing sectors that have already formed regional production and sales networks around ASEAN, involving China, Korea and Japan, reduce their exports and imports between ASEAN members under AFTA. These sectors include textiles (ISIC 17), wearing apparels (ISIC 18), office and computing machinery (ISIC 30), electrical machinery (ISIC 31), medical and optical instruments (ISIC 33), and motor vehicles (ISIC 34). Meanwhile, both exports and imports in these sectors are facilitated by the ACFTA and AKFTA. Based on the estimated marginal effects of AFTA as well as five other ASEAN FTAs, it is conceivable that regional trade between the ASEAN members under AFTA transformed into increased trade between ASEAN and China after the ACFTA started, and between ASEAN and Korea after the AKFTA started.

On the other hand, the AFTA promotes trade among ASEAN members in natural resources and industrial materials and consumption goods, such as mining, petroleum, chemical products, basic metals, and foods. This result suggests that the existing ASEAN+1 FTAs mainly and gradually promote regional trade, particularly in the manufacturing sector supported by regional production networks, while AFTA, the first regional FTA in this region, facilitates regional trade in materials and consumption goods.

Tariff reduction under the AFTA promotes mainly imports from members in a wide range of manufacturing sectors, although the effect is much smaller than the overall impacts of FTAs. The increased regional imports of materials and intermediate and capital goods, such as petroleum, chemical plastics and rubber products, fabricated metals, machinery, office equipment and motor vehicles, suggest that the development of regional production in ASEAN is supported by tariff reduction under the AFTA.

Table 5.3 The Marginal Effects of Tariff Reductions under FTAs on ASEAN's Exports and Imports in 26 Selected Sectors

			ASEAN	
			FTA into effect (0/1)	*Tariff reduction (%)*
ISIC 01	Agriculture, hunting and related service activities	Export		0.011
		Import		
ISIC 02	Forestry, logging and related service activities	Export	6.222	
		Import		
ISIC 05	Fishing, operation of fish hatcheries and fish farms	Export		
		Import		
ISIC 10–15	Mining and quarrying	Export	8.981	-0.422
		Import	7.069	-0.288
ISIC 15	Manufacture of food products and beverages	Export		
		Import	4.52	
ISIC 16	Manufacture of tobacco products	Export	1.706	0.00951
		Import		
ISIC 17	Manufacture of textiles	Export	-2.123	
		Import	-7.183	
ISIC 18	Manufacture of wearing apparel; dressing and dyeing of fur	Export	-2.667	
		Import	-7.406	-0.0262
ISIC 19	Tanning and dressing of leather; manufacture of luggage, footwear	Export	-2.809	0.0157
		Import		
ISIC 20	Manufacture of wood and of products of wood and cork	Export		
		Import	-11.15	
ISIC 21	Manufacture of paper and paper products	Export	4.616	
		Import		0.0247
ISIC 22	Publishing, printing and reproduction of recorded media	Export		
		Import		
ISIC 23	Manufacture of coke, refined petroleum products and nuclear fuel	Export	16.65	
		Import	3.085	0.0349

ASEAN–China		*ASEAN–Korea*		*ASEAN–Japan*	
FTA into effect (1/0)	*Tariff reduction (%)*	*FTA into effect (1/0)*	*Tariff reduction (%)*	*FTA into effect (1/0)*	*Tariff reduction (%)*
−0.4			−0.0233	0.685	
		−0.398	−0.0288	−1.504	0.733
1.002	0.0757	0.438			−0.166
		−1.426		−1.17	0.49
		0.869	0.197		
−0.62		1.508	−0.84		1.556
		0.213			
				−0.212	
		1.283		2.552	
−0.672		1.5	0.0325		
		0.533			
	0.014	0.567			−0.886
1.151	0.0345	1.536	0.0495		
0.587					−4.28
		0.388			0.153
0.418					−2.297
−0.489				0.832	
0.525		0.409		−0.191	
−0.512			−2.578	0.347	
0.374				−0.302	0.0485
	−0.586	−1.306		−0.848	
0.382				−0.326	−5.341
		1.022		−0.867	
0.0676		0.952		1.217	

(*Continued*)

			ASEAN	
			FTA into effect (1/0)	*Tariff reduction (%)*
ISIC 24	Manufacture of chemicals and chemical products	Export		
		Import	4.011	0.0532
ISIC 25	Manufacture of rubber and plastics products	Export		
		Import	-10.19	0.00917
ISIC 26	Manufacture of other non-metallic mineral products	Export		
		Import		
ISIC 27	Manufacture of basic metals	Export	2.59	
		Import	6.794	
ISIC 28	Manufacture of fabricated metal products	Export	4.659	
		Import	-5.746	0.0171
ISIC 29	Manufacture of machinery and equipment n.e.c.	Export	2.963	
		Import	-3.905	0.0388
ISIC 30	Manufacture of office, accounting and computing machinery	Export		
		Import	-2.46	0.087
ISIC 31	Manufacture of electrical machinery and apparatus n.e.c.	Export	-2.925	0.0146
		Import		
ISIC 32	Manufacture of radio, TV and communication equipment and apparatus	Export	4.379	0.0268
		Import		
ISIC 33	Manufacture of medical, precision and optical instruments	Export	-2.568	
		Import		0.0844
ISIC 34	Manufacture of motor vehicles, trailers and semi-trailers	Export	-3.859	
		Import	-4.558	0.0179
ISIC 35	Manufacture of other transport equipment	Export	4.876	
		Import		
ISIC 36	Manufacture of furniture; manufacturing n.e.c.	Export	1.05	
		Import	4.535	

ASEAN–China		*ASEAN–Korea*		*ASEAN–Japan*	
FTA into effect (1/0)	*Tariff reduction (%)*	*FTA into effect (1/0)*	*Tariff reduction (%)*	*FTA into effect (1/0)*	*Tariff reduction (%)*
		0.212		0.271	
0.324		0.423	−0.0373	−0.218	−1.751
0.856	−0.0308		0.0389		
		0.392		−0.149	−0.481
−1.211	0.0585			1.63	−1.408
		0.244			0.719
−0.351					
0.549		0.467			
	0.0142	0.286	0.0548		
0.426	0.0332	0.355			−0.202
0.434		−0.345	−0.418		
	0.232			−0.414	−3.567
0.357				−0.521	1.735
0.358	0.0427	0.642		−0.152	−0.179
0.725				0.218	
0.307	0.108	0.329			
				−0.22	
0.344	0.0498	0.883		−0.111	−0.56
−0.68				0.343	
				−0.125	
		0.658			
	0.0389			−0.523	−0.169
				0.532	−0.257
0.453		0.722		0.379	−0.74

(*Continued*)

			ASEAN–Australia–New Zealand	
			FTA into effect (0/1)	*Tariff reduction (%)*
ISIC 01	Agriculture, hunting and related service activities	Export		0.85
		Import		
ISIC 02	Forestry, logging and related service activities	Export		
		Import	-0.976	0.612
ISIC 05	Fishing, operation of fish hatcheries and fish farms	Export		-0.803
		Import		
ISIC 10–15	Mining and quarrying	Export		-14.05
		Import		
ISIC 15	Manufacture of food products and beverages	Export		0.143
		Import	-0.266	-0.108
ISIC 16	Manufacture of tobacco products	Export	2.511	0.338
		Import		
ISIC 17	Manufacture of textiles	Export		
		Import		0.233
ISIC 18	Manufacture of wearing apparel; dressing and dyeing of fur	Export	0.588	
		Import		-0.336
ISIC 19	Tanning and dressing of leather; manufacture of luggage, footwear	Export		
		Import	-0.304	0.0986
ISIC 20	Manufacture of wood and of products of wood and cork	Export		
		Import	0.302	
ISIC 21	Manufacture of paper and paper products	Export		
		Import		
ISIC 22	Publishing, printing and reproduction of recorded media	Export		
		Import		
ISIC 23	Manufacture of coke, refined petroleum products and nuclear fuel	Export		
		Import	-0.266	

ASEAN–India			
FTA into effect (0/1)	*Tariff reduction (%)*	*Observations*	*R-squared*
0.576		11,898	0.819
0.325	-0.0267	10,264	0.722
		6,179	0.87
0.77		5,067	0.631
		7,299	0.687
		4,238	0.886
		9,808	0.348
		12,731	0.358
		15,056	0.757
-0.327		11,000	0.718
-0.619		4,614	0.606
	-0.243	3,284	0.618
		14,628	0.753
		10,418	0.936
		14,015	0.949
		9,014	0.837
		12,531	0.923
		7,877	0.831
0.61		11,616	0.902
	0.0659	7,756	0.7
		11,610	0.842
		8,125	0.719
-1.511		11,435	0.562
-0.552	-0.265	8,639	0.69
-0.714		5,745	0.94
		5,557	0.91

(*Continued*)

			ASEAN–Australia–New Zealand	
			FTA into effect (0/1)	*Tariff reduction (%)*
ISIC 24	Manufacture of chemicals and chemical products	Export	0.212	
		Import	-0.21	
ISIC 25	Manufacture of rubber and plastics products	Export		
		Import		
ISIC 26	Manufacture of other non-metallic mineral products	Export		
		Import	-0.501	-0.105
ISIC 27	Manufacture of basic metals	Export		
		Import	-0.209	0.199
ISIC 28	Manufacture of fabricated metal products	Export		0.211
		Import		-0.13
ISIC 29	Manufacture of machinery and equipment n.e.c.	Export		
		Import	-0.176	
ISIC 30	Manufacture of office, accounting and computing machinery	Export	0.246	
		Import	0.45	-12.74
ISIC 31	Manufacture of electrical machinery and apparatus n.e.c.	Export		
		Import		-0.0801
ISIC 32	Manufacture of radio, TV and communication equipment and apparatus	Export		
		Import		
ISIC 33	Manufacture of medical, precision and optical instruments	Export	0.263	
		Import		
ISIC 34	Manufacture of motor vehicles, trailers and semi-trailers	Export		
		Import	-0.883	
ISIC 35	Manufacture of other transport equipment	Export	-0.357	
		Import	-0.258	-0.249
ISIC 36	Manufacture of furniture; manufacturing n.e.c.	Export		
		Import	-0.2	-0.0676

ASEAN–India			
FTA into effect (0/1)	*Tariff reduction (%)*	*Observations*	*R-squared*
0.119		14,326	0.922
		11,936	0.914
0.256		14,678	0.94
0.171	0.0319	10,358	0.911
-0.271		12,506	0.644
		8,230	0.89
		9,615	0.673
-0.7	-0.192	8,882	0.863
0.381		13,221	0.9
-0.257	0.0284	10,272	0.929
		13,821	0.935
		11,765	0.944
		10,960	0.84
-0.614	-1.032	8,697	0.864
0.49		12,963	0.876
0.352		10,558	0.929
0.368		12,956	0.884
	-0.309	9,984	0.875
-0.238		11,424	0.91
		9,734	0.95
		10,713	0.913
0.626		8,062	0.915
		9,876	0.797
		6,868	0.866
		14,817	0.708
-0.738		9,711	0.868

Notes: The values are based on the estimated coefficient of the estimated gravity model. Each value denotes the percentage change in export value due to FTA enforcement or tariff reduction by 1% point. Blank cells are omitted values due to statistically insignificance or zero tariff margins. All figures are estimated values statistically significant at 1%, 5%, or 10% level.
Source: Author's estimates.

5.4.1.2 Impacts of the ACFTA, AKFTA, and AJFTA on Trade in East Asia

Positive signs for the marginal effect of the AKFTA are found in most sectors. Likewise, a trade facilitation effect of the overall measures of the ACFTA on trade between members is found in a wide range of manufacturing sectors. In particular, both imports and exports in the manufacturing sectors for textiles, coke and refined petroleum products, and chemical products increase concurrently under the AKFTA. Also, both exports and imports in the manufacturing sectors for wearing apparel and electrical and communication equipment are facilitated by the ACFTA. This result suggests that the FTAs promote regional intra-industry trade between ASEAN and Korea or China in these sectors. In fact, regional trade in industrial intermediate goods between ASEAN members and China or Korea has been increasing rapidly since the mid-2000s. A region-wide FTA has the potential to actualise efficient production through the regional division of labour by strengthening regional networks. This implies that the AKFTA and ACFTA take on the role of developing regional production networks in the aforementioned sectors by promoting regional intra-industry trade. The value of the marginal effect also indicates that trade facilitation by overall measures under FTA, such as various trade liberalisation and facilitation measures as well as the dynamic effects caused by FDI facilitation and technology transfers, is more effective than tariff reduction under these FTAs.

In contrast, there are fewer sectors in which regional trade is promoted under the AJFTA. Moreover, the marginal effects of ASEAN-FTA on a wide range of manufacturing sectors, including electrical and communication equipment, are negative. As Figure 5.2 shows, ASEAN's export and import share with Japan for all types of goods decreased before the enforcement of the AJFTA, in contrast with the increased trade share with China.

The negative effects of the AJFTA seem to reflect the replacement of regional trade between ASEAN and Japan with increased regional trade between ASEAN and China. Regional trade between ASEAN and Japan is supported by regional value chains in the manufacturing sectors as with the ACFTA and AKFTA. The negative marginal effects under the AJFTA may reflect that the trade facilitation effects of the ACFTA and AKFTA are stronger than those of the AJFTA. Another possible reason for the insignificant or negative marginal effects under the AJFTA is that the overcrowded existing regional FTAs. If most exporters and importers use the existing bilateral FTAs, newer FTAs will have no effect or a negative effect, reflected in the decreasing trade share of ASEAN with Japan. This result suggests that a newer regional FTA should set more liberalised measures than existing FTAs in terms of the liberalisation schedule when concurrent FTAs have already been formed between the same members, otherwise there will be no impacts on trade at all.

5.4.1.3 Impacts of the AANZFTA and AIFTA on Trade in East Asia

There are fewer sectors with increased trade between members under the AANZFTA and AIFTA. Negative marginal effects under these FTAs are found in a wide range of sectors. ASEAN's trade shares with Australia and New Zealand have been on a downward trend since the mid-2000s, while ASEAN's trade shares with China have increased rapidly. ASEAN's export shares in consumption goods and import shares in intermediate goods with India have also been on declining trend since the mid-2000s. As in the case of the AJFTA, a possible reason for the negative marginal effect of the AANZFTA and the AIFTA could be that the rapid increase of ASEAN's trade with China replaced ASEAN's trade shares with Australia, New Zealand and India. Moreover, it is conceivable that the length of time since these FTAs started is too short to reveal their effects. Some trade liberalisation and facilitation measures are implemented gradually rather than immediately, and dynamic effects usually need more time before the effects can be seen.

However, the effect of the tariff reductions in the materials and natural resources sectors under the AANZFTA seems to be larger than for the other ASEAN FTAs. For example, ASEAN's exports to Australia and New Zealand for agriculture and food manufacturing increased by 0.85 percent and 0.14 percent, respectively, with respect to a 1 percent tariff rate reduction. Moreover, the AANZFTA and AIFTA facilitate both exports and imports for the manufacturing of office and computing machinery and electrical machinery. These results suggest that newer ASEAN FTAs have the potential to increase trade between members and expand the production and sales networks that have already developed in the region.

5.4.1.4 Comparative advantage in East Asia

ASEAN members increased their exports in the manufacturing sectors for electrical and communication equipment (ISIC 31–32) under the ACFTA and AIFTA. Likewise, ASEAN's exports for the manufacturing of chemical products (ISIC 24) grew under the AKFTA, AJFTA, AANZFTA, and AIFTA. If a country or region is revealed to have a comparative advantage in a sector which increases its exports under a trade liberalisation regime, then ASEAN as a region has a comparative advantage in the manufacturing of electrical and communication equipment and chemical products in the East Asian region.

For the manufacturing sectors for electrical and communication equipment, ASEAN members have developed region-wide production and sales networks and experienced a rapid increase of inward FDI. As a result of the well-developed production and sales networks involving industrial agglomerations in ASEAN, we can consider the fact that ASEAN members use their competitive advantage to further expand regional production under a region-wide FTA. Moreover, in the manufacturing sectors for chemical products, such as basic chemicals (ISIC 2411), plastic products in primary (ISIC 2413), and cosmetics products (ISIC 2424), the export shares from ASEAN to Korea, Japan, and India have increased since the mid-2000s. An increase of ASEAN's exports through liberalisation under the ASEAN+1 FTAs including not only tariff reduction and elimination but also various NTMs, such as regulations and technical barriers, implies that ASEAN has the potential to be a larger exporter in these sectors in the East Asian region.

Table 5.4 The Marginal Effects of Tariff Reductions under FTAs by Country and Sector

		ASEAN FTA		*ASEAN-China*		*ASEAN-Korea*		*ASEAN-Japan*		*ASEAN-AUS-NZL*		*ASEAN-India*	
		FTA into effect (0/1)	*Tariff reduction (%)*	*FTA into effect (0/1)*	*Tariff reduction (%)*	*FTA into effect (0/1)*	*Tariff reduction (%)*	*FTA into effect (0/1)*	*Tariff reduction (%)*	*FTA into effect (0/1)*	*Tariff reduction (%)*	*FTA into effect (0/1)*	*Tariff reduction (%)*
ISIC 01–05: Agriculture, Forestry, and Fishing													
Cambodia	Export					1.097		2.636	−1.356	−2.559		1.070	
	Import	−10.67										−0.803	
Indonesia	Export	−8.896	0.027	0.984		0.324						0.436	
	Import		0.041	−0.378	0.036	−0.558						0.357	0.389
Malaysia	Export	−0.962				0.324		1.226	−1.248	−1.804			
	Import	2.225				−1.614			−0.506	2.200		0.411	−1.925
Philippines	Export	−2.363		−1.198		−0.393	0.009						
	Import	5.606			0.074					0.967			
Singapore	Export	6.164				−0.396						−0.472	
	Import	−2.905		0.334		0.883						0.252	
Thailand	Export			−0.387			−0.005					0.243	
	Import	−39.07					−0.038			0.410		0.666	−0.009
Viet Nam	Export		0.009	0.567		−0.248			0.608	−0.302	0.292	1.101	
	Import	8.195				−1.476	−0.168		−0.152			0.674	
ISIC 10–14: Mining and Quarrying													
Cambodia	Export												
	Import				−0.398			−3.455				−4.052	
Indonesia	Export	−2.063		−0.669		1.133				−0.497	−7.132	0.862	
	Import			−1.107								−2.290	
Malaysia	Export	17.67	−0.273	−0.754				0.887		0.930	−12.950	−0.438	
	Import		−0.384	−1.030		−3.074	1.339		4.049	0.915	−0.975	−2.732	1.720
Philippines	Export	23.11				1.626					3.268		
	Import			−1.276		−1.047		−2.682				−2.638	
Singapore	Export			2.297				−2.122		−4.278	4.122	3.219	
	Import	−1.333		−0.890		0.843				−0.518			
Thailand	Export		0.127	0.860	−0.505	1.311	−0.566		14.050	−2.532	9.789		
	Import				2.720					0.336			0.805
Viet Nam	Export		0.009	0.562		−0.248		−0.617		−0.300	0.292	1.101	

ISIC 15–16: Manufacture of Food Products, Beverages, and Tobacco Products													
Cambodia	Export	1.594						–5.056	0.241	–2.077			
	Import				–0.398			–3.455				–4.052	
Indonesia	Export	3.576		0.394		0.195					0.168		
	Import	3.027	0.066							2.622		0.753	
Malaysia	Export	1.688				0.248							
	Import		–0.053			0.463	0.058			–0.569		–0.396	
Philippines	Export	–2.669		0.482								1.120	
	Import	2.539	0.043	0.632				–0.402		–0.419		–0.437	
Singapore	Export	3.987			0.080	2.502	–0.117			0.503		0.784	
	Import	1.706				0.475							
Thailand	Export	2.719		–0.441		0.241		1.293	–0.383				
	Import	2.459	0.012	1.203		1.231	–0.013					1.608	–0.011
Viet Nam	Export	5.728	0.018			0.180	0.006	–0.386			0.105	0.809	
	Import	–5.950	–0.006	0.550			0.017	–0.357		–0.493		–0.406	
ISIC 17–19: Manufacture of Textiles, Wearing Apparels, and Tanning and Dressing of Leather													
Cambodia	Export	2.443		1.203		0.986				–0.694			
	Import	–0.711			0.140	–0.774		–3.015		–0.998		–2.634	
Indonesia	Export	5.022		0.621						0.310			
	Import				0.015						–0.916		
Malaysia	Export	5.913	–0.022				–0.044	0.902		1.329			
	Import		0.019	1.319						0.623	0.120		–0.089
Philippines	Export	2.835				1.905		0.822					
	Import	–0.508		0.469		0.670				–5.093		–0.819	
Singapore	Export					1.460	0.104	1.561		1.391			
	Import	–12.20		0.804						0.613		0.407	
Thailand	Export		–0.023					0.765		0.334			
	Import	8.436				–0.455				–0.619		0.326	
Viet Nam	Export	28.01		0.703		0.510					–0.049		
	Import	5.321		0.487	–0.031		–0.051		–0.047		0.165		

(Continued)

ISIC 20–22: Manufacture of Wood, Paper, Publishing, and Printing Media

Cambodia	Export	-3.421		4.242		-5.470	0.505	-1.883		-3.435	0.691	-4.111	
	Import				0.105								
Indonesia	Export	-3.771		-0.614		-0.251							
	Import					0.258							
Malaysia	Export	4.909	-0.016	-0.736	-0.079					0.442		0.757	
	Import	2.802	0.023	1.266		1.260				0.944			
Philippines	Export	6.233			0.145		-0.240	1.746	-0.398	-5.093	2.061		
	Import		0.061		-0.150							-0.512	
Singapore	Export	4.485		0.668		-0.680		-0.989		-0.290		-1.095	
	Import												
Thailand	Export	-1.466	0.085				0.135					-1.692	
	Import			1.187	0.048							0.504	
Viet Nam	Export			0.727		0.503	0.072						
	Import	6.148	-0.026	0.570							-0.436		0.190

ISIC 23–26: Manufacture of Coke, Petroleum Products, Chemical Products, Rubber, Plastics Products, and Other Non-Metallic Mineral Products

Cambodia	Export	-76.91		2.464							1.139		
	Import						0.775					-0.510	
Indonesia	Export		-0.039							0.246			
	Import	1.693	0.086	2.278	0.110	2.039			-1.214		2.554		
Malaysia	Export		-0.034										
	Import	11.97	-0.029		0.051	0.551		0.032				-0.259	
Philippines	Export												
	Import	2.336		1.366		1.734			-0.315		1.800		
Singapore	Export												
	Import					0.786			-0.322				
Thailand	Export	6.914	-0.021				-0.826	0.455	0.360				
	Import	1.700	0.040	1.692	0.055	1.358					1.474		
Viet Nam	Export	3.786						0.544	-1.162	0.275	0.823		
	Import	-3.038		0.565	0.099	0.273							0.190

ISIC 27–28: Manufacture of Basic Metals and Fabricated Metal Products													
Cambodia	Export												
	Import	0.871		2.577	0.146	2.079				−1.437		−1.250	0.504
Indonesia	Export	−6.529	0.012							0.727			
	Import					0.240				−0.502		−0.667	
Malaysia	Export	3.909	−0.031			0.398		−5.477	4.039	0.739		0.560	
	Import	−0.821	0.033	0.764		1.293				1.634			
Philippines	Export		−0.062				−0.247						
	Import			0.649		0.644						−0.760	
Singapore	Export	19.38	0.091				0.070	−0.371		−0.707			
	Import	5.145		0.423								−0.943	
Thailand	Export	6.726		−1.570						−1.159	0.244		
	Import		0.054	0.778	0.126			−0.233	0.048	−0.376	−0.075	−0.486	0.078
Viet Nam	Export		−0.050	2.001	0.052		0.147	−2.299	9.272		−0.099	1.258	
	Import		0.028	0.715	0.069	0.941			0.049		−0.352		−0.360
29–33: Manufacture of Machinery, Computing, Electrical Machinery, Communication Equipment, and Precision Instruments													
Cambodia	Export	−1.633								−1.479		−2.563	
	Import	−39.78										0.688	
Indonesia	Export	0.983		−0.776							0.269		
	Import	4.674		0.293							−0.486		
Malaysia	Export			0.349				0.273			0.161		
	Import		−0.057										0.254
Philippines	Export	2.874		0.689	−0.171				2.153		0.718	0.634	
	Import	−8.769											
Singapore	Export	3.788		0.398			0.040	0.265					
	Import	−9.664		0.645				−0.285					
Thailand	Export	−6.311	0.052		−0.084	0.420			1.387				
	Import	13.49											
Viet Nam	Export	8.598	−0.042	1.695	0.058		0.116	−1.063	4.655			1.272	
	Import	1.889		1.230		2.466		0.620		−1.310	−0.238	0.681	

(Continued)

ISIC 34–35: Manufacture of Motor Vehicles and Other Transport Equipment

Cambodia	Export			2.345	0.062						2.814	
	Import								−1.745			−0.189
Indonesia	Export									−0.265		
	Import	−21.44				−0.843			−0.576		0.963	
Malaysia	Export	1.705										
	Import					0.793			−1.265		−1.538	
Philippines	Export			0.941			0.095		−1.808			
	Import	2.816	0.080						−1.400			
Singapore	Export	1.954	0.054	0.818				−0.369			−0.430	
	Import			1.163		1.007			−0.356			
Thailand	Export			−0.578				0.166				
	Import			1.254			−0.041		−0.940		0.645	
Viet Nam	Export					2.848	−0.178		1.143		1.074	
	Import	−8.971	−0.016		0.045				−0.927		1.330	

Cambodia	Export												
	Import	−28.77		−0.448			−0.045	0.763					
Indonesia	Export				−0.023		−0.044				−0.098	1.548	
	Import		0.163	2.329	0.039	1.307	0.035			−1.688			
Malaysia	Export	−2.183	−0.014				0.044	0.170	0.102	−0.200			
	Import	−1.259	0.103	0.916				1.250		−1.666	0.121		
Philippines	Export					0.536	−0.047	1.032		0.319	−0.126		
	Import	0.693		0.927		−0.603				0.854		−1.009	
Singapore	Export	5.392	0.016							−1.817	0.590	0.577	
	Import	−5.676		0.837		−0.694		−0.443				−0.709	
Thailand	Export	5.717	0.020		0.023								
	Import	3.984			0.017	0.303		0.230		0.411	0.080	−0.264	−0.052
Viet Nam	Export	−8.842		−2.097		−1.063	0.050						
	Import	−6.935		0.649		0.179			−0.034			0.787	0.268

Notes: The values are based on the estimated coefficient of the estimated gravity model. Each value denotes the percentage change in export value due to FTA enforcement or tariff reduction by 1% point. Blanc cells are omitted values due to statistically insignificance or zero tariff margins. All figures are estimated values statistically significant at 1%, 5%, or 10% level.
Source: Author's estimates.

5.4.2 Results by country

Next, we estimate the gravity model by country and sector. Table 5.4 shows the estimation results for seven ASEAN members and nine semi-aggregated sectors at the ISIC 2-digit level.

Taking a look at the impact of the ASEAN+1 FTAs, the estimated marginal effect of the ACFTA, AKFTA, and AIFTA on Indonesia's exports for agriculture, forestry, and fishing (ISIC 01–05) shows that the enforcement of these FTAs caused an increase in the export value from Indonesia to China, Korea and India by 0.98 percent, 0.32 percent and 0.43 percent, respectively. This result suggests that Indonesia has a revealed comparative advantage in agriculture, forestry, and fishing products against its FTA partners. Likewise, Malaysia has a revealed comparative advantage in basic and fabricated metals in the region since Malaysia's exports in the manufacturing sector for basic and fabricated metals (ISIC 27–28) have been facilitated under the AKFTA, AANZFTA and AIFTA as well as the tariff reduction under the AIFTA.

Thailand already formed the international division of labour in several sectors with its ASEAN+1 FTAs partners before the ASEAN+1 FTAs were in force. Thailand's imports from China, Korea and India in the manufacturing sectors for food products and beverages (ISIC 15–16) increased with the enactment of the ACFTA and AKFTA and tariff reduction under the AIFTA. Meanwhile, the enactment of the AKFTA and AJFTA at the same time facilitated Thailand's exports in these sectors to Japan, Australia, and Korea. Both exports and imports with ASEAN have also increased under AFTA in these sectors. Examining the aforementioned results together, Thailand has developed a production base in food and beverage products involving ASEAN members and China, Korea, and India under the ASEAN+1 FTAs. As for the Philippines, exports in general and electrical machinery (ISIC 29–33) increased with the enactment of the ACFTA and AIFTA and tariff reduction under the AJFTA and AANZFTA. Additionally, the enactment of the ACFTA and tariff reduction under the AKFTA facilitated exports to China and Korea of motor vehicles and other transport equipment (ISIC 34–35). The level of involvement of the Philippines in the regional production networks for the manufacturing of electrical machinery and motor vehicles has been relatively small compared with other original ASEAN members, such as Malaysia and Thailand. Trade liberalisation measures under the ASEAN+1 FTAs could encourage the Philippines to further participate in the regional production networks in these sectors.

Viet Nam has increased both exports and imports under ASEAN FTAs in a wide range of sectors, such as the agricultural sectors (ISIC 01–05); the manufacturing of food (ISIC 15–16), petroleum, chemical, and other non-metallic products (ISIC 23–26); basic and fabricated metals (ISIC 27–28) and general and electrical machinery (ISIC 29–33). The ACFTA strongly promotes Viet Nam's exports and imports with China in all sectors. For example, imports of industrial supplies to Viet Nam from China have grown 20-fold since the mid-2000s, while Viet Nam's total imports increased 17-fold. The estimated marginal effects show that the enforcement of the ACFTA raised Viet Nam's exports and imports by 2.0 percent and 0.72 percent, respectively, for basic and fabricated metal, and by 1.7 percent and 1.2 percent, respectively, for general and electrical machinery. The enforcement and tariff reduction under the AKFTA, AJFTA, and AIFTA also facilitated Viet Nam's trade with these FTA partners. As such, trade liberalisation and facilitation under the ASEAN FTAs seem to have supported the rapid growth in Viet Nam's regional trade. The country has actively developed the regional trade relationship between the ASEAN FTA members under the FTAs and formed a production base in manufacturing sectors with the support of inward FDI.

Likewise, Cambodia's exports in the textile and wearing apparel industry (ISIC 17–19) to the ASEAN members, China, and Korea have increased under each ASEAN FTA. The textile and apparel sectors in Cambodia are the leading industries and are rapidly growing with the increase in inward FDI from the FTA partners. The positive marginal effects show that the AFTA, the ACFTA and the AKFTA facilitated Cambodia's exports in the textile and apparel sectors along with the formation of division of labour among the member countries. Moreover, the ACFTA and AIFTA increase Cambodia's exports in the manufacturing sectors of motor vehicles and other transport equipment. Increased exports from Cambodia under the ACFTA and AIFTA reflect the increase in production of motor vehicle parts as an enlargement of regional production networks in this sector. The results suggest that there is an opportunity for enhancing the competitive advantage of the region in manufacturing sectors by utilising the newly developing production and sales networks under the ASEAN FTAs. Regional FTAs that promote the enlargement of regional production and sales networks have the potential to support Cambodia's catching-up process. The results for the newer members of ASEAN, such as Cambodia and Viet Nam, suggest that a region-wide FTA has the potential to promote the participation of the newer members in regional production and sales networks and to increase their competitive advantage in order to catch up with the original members of ASEAN. The regional FTAs take the role of facilitating trade to allow emerging countries to find new market opportunities in the region.

5.5 Conclusion

Although the AFTA increases regional trade in natural resources, industrial materials, and consumption goods between its members, ASEAN's regional trade in manufacturing sectors that have well-developed regional production networks is replaced by trade between ASEAN and China, and ASEAN and Korea under the ACFTA and the AKFTA. In other words, the ACFTA and AKFTA could have a trade diversion effect against trade among ASEAN members. This result suggests that the diversion effects could be caused by the fact that the intensity of the trade linkages between the ASEAN members and their FTA partners is stronger than the regional trade among the ASEAN members, in particular in manufacturing sectors that have developed an international inter-process division of labour. In addition, ASEAN's intra-regional production networks in the manufacturing sectors still remain in some members, such as Singapore,

Malaysia and Thailand. To remain a central part of a region-wide FTA in this region, ASEAN should engage in further developing its own regional production and sales networks in the manufacturing sectors. Further industrial agglomerations in the other original members, such as Indonesia and the Philippines, are necessary to increase ASEAN's intra-regional trade in these sectors. Moreover, the expansion of intra-regional division of labour to the catching-up members, such as Viet Nam and Cambodia, is also an important issue for the further development of intra-regional trade in ASEAN.

On the other hand, ASEAN has a revealed comparative advantage in manufacturing sectors such as electrical and communication equipment and chemical products in East Asia. ASEAN members can take advantage of well-developed production and sales networks with its FTA partners to strengthen the networks under the existing ASEAN+1 FTAs. The estimation results suggest that ASEAN has the potential to become an even larger exporter in these manufacturing sectors by utilising regional FTA regimes.

Moreover, the estimation results show that various trade liberalisation measures under the ASEAN+1 FTAs support the rapid growth of regional trade for Viet Nam and Cambodia. One of the most important objectives for ASEAN's economic integration is to narrow the gap between its members. The results show that the ASEAN+1 FTAs provide an opportunity to the newer members of ASEAN to catch up with the original members by joining the existing and also newly developing production and sales networks under the ASEAN FTAs. A region-wide FTA has the potential to narrow the gap among members by promoting the participation of the newer members in the regional production and sales networks.

Based on the estimated marginal effects for the ASEAN FTAs, we can see that the impact of the tariff reduction under each FTA is a small portion of the whole impact of the overall FTA. Liberalisation measures other than tariff reduction, such as the elimination or harmonisation of NTMs or various trade facilitation measures, have a much larger impact on trade among members. A region-wide FTA in this region should enhance such effective liberalisation and facilitation measures to promote regional trade. Moreover, as the results of the AANZFTA and AIFTA show, it can take several years for the effects of an FTA on trade to be revealed. A necessary condition for an effective region-wide FTA is the immediate or early implementation of trade liberalisation.

In addition, as in the case of the AJFTA, a newer FTA has no or little impact if the members already have an existing FTA among the same members. The cost of utilisation of an FTA is significant for exporters and importers. A reduction in the cost of utilisation, in particular the harmonisation of RoOs with the existing FTA, is a necessary factor to build an effective newer region-wide FTA. If a newer region-wide FTA is formed between the same members as an existing FTA, it should have a greater degree of liberalisation or should have a lower utilisation cost than the existing FTA.

RCEP, which will be formed by coordinating AFTA and five ASEAN+1 FTAs, needs to enhance the strengths and eliminate the weaknesses of the existing regional FTAs. The necessary conditions for RCEP to be a substantially effective region-wide FTA are a higher level of liberalisation, a lower cost of utilisation compared to existing bilateral and plurilateral FTAs in the region, earlier tariff reduction or elimination on sectors already liberalised under the existing ASEAN+1 FTAs, and more comprehensive liberalisation in order to develop productivity and narrow development gaps in the region. As the estimation results indicate, the concurrent ASEAN+1 FTAs have trade diversion effects in several sectors. RCEP is expected to be a facilitator to extend the existing production and sales networks between ASEAN and its FTA partners to region-wide networks. At the same time, in order to avoid trade diversion, RCEP needs to be an accelerator for ASEAN members to be able to increase their productivity and extend and deepen industrial agglomeration in the regional production and sales networks.

References

Ando, Mitsuyo (2007), 'Impacts of Japanese FTAs/EPAs: Preliminary Post Evaluation', *The International Economy*, 11, pp. 57–83.

Athukorala, Prema-chandra and Archanun Kohpaiboon (2011), 'Australia-Thai Trade: Has the Free Trade Agreement Made a Difference?' *Australian Economic Review*, 44(4), pp. 457–467.

Balassa, Bela (1961), *The Theory of Economic Integration*, Richard D. Irwin, Homewood, IL.

Bano, Sayeeda, Yoshiaki Takahashi and Frank Scrimgeour (2013), 'ASEAN-New Zealand Trade Relations and Trade Potential: Evidence and Analysis', *Journal of Economic Integration*, 28(1), pp. 144–182.

Bun, Maurice. J. G., Franc, J. G. M. Klaassen and G. K. Randolph Tan (2009), 'Free Trade Areas and Intra-Regional Trade: The Case of ASEAN', *The Singapore Economic Review*, 54(3), pp. 319–334.

Carrère, Cèline (2006), 'Revisiting the Effects of Regional Trade Agreements on Trade Flows with Proper Specification of the Gravity Model', *European Economic Review*, 50(2), pp. 223–247.

Chandran, B. P. Sarath (2012), 'Implications of India-ASEAN FTA on India's Fisheries Sector', *MPRA Paper* No. 38712.

Cheong, David (2008), 'The Effects of AFTA: A Disaggregated Analysis', Paper submitted to the John Hopkins University SAIS, Bologna Center, Italy.

DeRosa, Dean A. (1995), 'Regional Trading Arrangements among Developing Countries: The ASEAN Example', *International Food Policy Research Institute, Research Report* No.103, Washington, DC.

Elliot, Robert J. R. and Kengo Ikemoto (2004), 'AFTA and the Asian Crisis: Help or Hindrance to ASEAN Intra-Regional Trade?' *Asian Economic Journal*, 1, pp. 1–23.

Endoh, Masahiro (1999), 'The Transition of Post-war Asia-Pacific Trade Relations', *Journal of Asian Economics*, 10, pp. 571–589.

Frankel, Jaffrey A. (1997), 'Chapter 5: Estimated Effects of Trading Blocs', in *Regional Trading Blocs in the World Economic System*, Institute for International Economics.

Frankel, Jaffrey A. and Shang-Jin Wei (1996), 'ASEAN in a Regional Perspective', *Center for International and Development Economic Research Working Paper* No. C96-074.

Hertel, Thomas, Terrie Walmsley and Ken Itakura (2005), 'Chapter 18: Dynamic Effects of the "New Age" Free Trade Agreement between Japan and Singapore', in *Quantitative Methods for Assessing the Effects of Non-Tariff Measures and Trade Facilitation*, World Scientific, Singapore, pp. 483–523.

Hausman, Jerry A. and William E. Taylor (1981), 'Panel Data and Unobservable Individual Effects', *Econometrica*, 49(6), pp. 1377–1398.

Kien, Nguyen Trung (2009), 'Gravity Model by Panel Data Approach: An Empirical Application with Implications for the ASEAN Free Trade Area', *ASEAN Economic Bulletin*, 26(3), pp. 266–277.

Lee, Hiro (2002), 'General Equilibrium Evaluation of Japan-Singapore Free Trade Agreement', in P. Drysdale and K. Ishigaki (eds.), *East Asian Trade and Financial Integration: New Issues*, pp. 110–126.

Mayer, Thierry and Soledad Zignago (2011), 'Notes on CEPII's DISTANCE MEASURES: The GeoDist DATABASE', *CEPII Working Paper 2011–25*, December 2011, CEPII.

Manchin, Miriam and Annette O. Pelkmans-Balaoing (2008), 'Clothes without an Emperor: Analysis of the Preferential Tariffs in ASEAN', *Journal of Asian Economics*, 19 (3), pp. 213–223.

Okabe, Misa and Shujiro Urata (2014), 'The Impact of AFTA on Intra-AFTA Trade', *Journal of Asian Economics*, 35, pp. 12–31.

Sheng, Yu, Hsiao Chink Tang and Xinpeng Xu (2014), 'The Impact of the ACFTA on ASEAN-PRC Trade: Estimates Based on an Extended Gravity Model for Component Trade', *Applied Economics*, 46(19), pp. 2251–2263.

Solaga, Isidro and L. Alan Winters (2001), 'Regionalism in the Nineties: What Effect on Trade?' *The North American Journal of Economics and Finance*, 12(1), pp. 1–29.

Viner, Jacob (1950), 'The Customs Union Issue', *Carnegie Endowment for International Peace*, New York, pp. 41–56.

Yang, Shanping and Inmaculada Martinez-Zarzoso (2014), 'A Panel Data Analysis of Trade Creation and Trade Diversion Effects: The Case of ASEAN-China Free Trade Area', *China Economic Review*, 29(C), pp. 138–151.

Appendix

Table 5.A1 The List of Countries/Regions

Afghanistan	Djibouti	Lebanon	Rwanda
Albania	Dominica	Lesotho	Saint Kitts and Nevis
Algeria	Dominican Republic	Liberia	Saint Lucia
Angola	Ecuador	Libyan Arab Jamahiriya	Saint Vincent and the Grenadines
Antigua and Barbuda	Egypt	Lithuania	Samoa
Argentina	El Salvador	Luxembourg	Sao Tome and Principe
Armenia	Equatorial Guinea	Macao	Saudi Arabia
Australia	Eritrea	Macedonia	Senegal
Austria	Estonia	Madagascar	Serbia
Azerbaijan	Ethiopia	Malawi	Seychelles
Bahamas	Fiji	Malaysia	Sierra Leone
Bahrain	Finland	Maldives	Singapore
Bangladesh	France	Mali	Slovakia
Barbados	Gabon	Malta	Slovenia
Belarus	Gambia	Marshall Islands	Solomon Islands
Belgium	Georgia	Mauritania	South Africa
Belize	Germany	Mauritius	South Sudan
Benin	Ghana	Mexico	Spain
Bermuda	Greece	Micronesia, Federated States of	Sri Lanka
Bhutan	Grenada	Republic of Moldova	Sudan
Plurinational State of Bolivia	Guatemala	Mongolia	Suriname
Bosnia and Herzegovina	Guinea	Montenegro	Swaziland
Botswana	Guinea-Bissau	Morocco	Sweden
Brazil	Guyana	Mozambique	Switzerland
Brunei Darussalam	Haiti	Myanmar	Tajikistan
Bulgaria	Honduras	Namibia	United Republic of Tanzania
Burkina Faso	Hong Kong	Nauru	Thailand
Burundi	Hungary	Nepal	Togo
Cambodia	Iceland	Netherlands	Tonga

Cameroon	India	New Zealand	Trinidad and Tobago
Canada	Indonesia	Nicaragua	Tunisia
Cape Verde	Islamic Republic of Iran	Niger	Turkey
Central African Republic	Iraq	Nigeria	Turkmenistan
Chad	Ireland	Norway	Tuvalu
Chile	Israel	Oman	Uganda
China	Italy	Pakistan	Ukraine
Colombia	Jamaica	Palau	United Arab Emirates
Comoros	Japan	Panama	United Kingdom
Republic of Congo	Jordan	Papua New Guinea	United States
Democratic Republic of Congo	Kazakhstan	Paraguay	Uruguay
Costa Rica	Kenya	Peru	Uzbekistan
Côte d'Ivoire	Kiribati	Philippines	Vanuatu
Croatia	Republic of Korea	Poland	Venezuela
Cuba	Kuwait	Portugal	Viet Nam
Cyprus	Kyrgyzstan	Qatar	Yemen
Czech Republic	Lao People's Democratic Republic	Romania	Zambia
Denmark	Latvia	Russian Federation	Zimbabwe

Table 5.A2 ASEAN+1 FTAs: FTA In Effect Date for Each Member

ASEAN-China FTA			*ASEAN-Korea FTA*		*ASEAN-Japan EPA*		*ASEAN-Australia-New Zealand FTA*		*ASEAN-India FTA*	
	Normal track	*Early harvest*		*Normal track*		*Normal track*		*Normal track*		*Normal track*
China	Jul., 2005	Jan., 2004	Korea	Jun., 2007	Japan	Dec., 2008	Australia	Jan., 2010	India	Jan., 2010
Brunei	Jul., 2005	Jan., 2004	Brunei	Jun., 2007	Brunei	Jan., 2009	New Zealand	Jan., 2010	Brunei	Jan., 2010
Cambodia	Jul., 2005	Jan., 2006	Cambodia	Jun., 2007	Cambodia	Jan., 2010	Brunei	Jan., 2010	Cambodia	Jul., 2011
Indonesia	Jul., 2005	Jan., 2004	Indonesia	Jun., 2007	Indonesia	Still pending	Cambodia	Jan., 2011	Indonesia	Jan., 2010
Lao PDR	Jul., 2005	Jan., 2006	Lao PDR	Jun., 2007	Lao PDR	Dec., 2008	Indonesia	Jan., 2012	Lao PDR	Jan., 2010
Malaysia	Jul., 2005	Jan., 2004	Malaysia	Jun., 2007	Malaysia	Feb., 2009	Lao PDR	Jan., 2011	Malaysia	Jan., 2010
Myanmar	Jul., 2005	Jan., 2006	Myanmar	Jun., 2007	Myanmar	Dec., 2008	Malaysia	Jan., 2010	Myanmar	Jan., 2010
Philippines	Jul., 2005	Jan., 2006	Philippines	Jun., 2007	Philippines	Jul., 2010	Myanmar	Jan., 2010	Philippines	May., 2011
Singapore	Jul., 2005	Jan., 2004	Singapore	Jun., 2007	Singapore	Dec., 2008	Philippines	Jan., 2010	Singapore	Jan., 2010
Thailand	Jul., 2005	Jan., 2003	Thailand	Jan., 2010	Thailand	Jun., 2009	Singapore	Jan., 2010	Thailand	Jan., 2010
Viet Nam	Jul., 2005	Jan., 2004	Viet Nam	Jun., 2007	Viet Nam	Dec., 2008	Thailand	Mar., 2010	Viet Nam	Jan., 2010
							Viet Nam	Jan., 2010		

Source: Author's tabulation based on information of FTAs/EPAs by Japan External Trade Organization.

Table 5.A3 Estimated FTAs Included in the Estimation Equation

FTAs among ASEAN members	
ASEAN Free Trade Area	
Lao People's Democratic Republic-Thailand	
ASEAN and Australia, China, India, Japan, Korea and New Zealand	
ASEAN FTAs	
ASEAN-Australia-New Zealand	ASEAN-China
ASEAN-India	ASEAN-Japan
ASEAN-Korea	
Bilateral FTAs	
Brunei Darussalam-Japan	Indonesia-Japan
Malaysia-India	Malaysia-Japan
Malaysia-New Zealand	Philippines-Japan
Singapore-Australia	Singapore-China
Singapore-India	Singapore-Japan
Singapore-Republic of Korea	Singapore-New Zealand
Thailand-Australia	Thailand-New Zealand
Thailand-Japan	Viet Nam-Japan
FTAs among Australia, China, India, Japan, Korea and New Zealand	
China-Hong Kong	China-New Zealand
Australia-New Zealand	India-Japan
India-Republic of Korea	
FTAs between ASEAN+6 and other countries/regions	
Malaysia-Chile	Malaysia-Pakistan
Singapore-EFTA	Singapore-Jordan
Singapore-Panama	Singapore-Peru
Singapore-US	Australia-Chile
Australia-US	China-Chile
China-Costa Rica	China-India
China-Pakistan	China-Peru
India-Afghanistan	India-Bhutan
India-MERCOSUR	Japan-Mexico
Japan-Peru	Japan-Switzerland
Republic of Korea-Chile	Republic of Korea-EFTA
Republic of Korea-EU	Republic of Korea-Peru
Republic of Korea-US	New Zealand-Hong Kong
South Asian Preferential Trade Arrangement (SAPTA)	

6 The use of FTAs

The Thai experience

Archanun Kohpaiboon and Juthathip Jongwanich

6.1 Introduction

The flood of bilateral and regional free trade agreements (FTAs) is reshaping the architecture of the world trading system. Worldwide, the number of FTAs involving reciprocal tariff reductions jumped from 124 in 1994 to 625 by February 2016, nearly 70 percent of which are currently in force.[1] FTAs are expected to proliferate further. The newly launched agreements tend to be over and above existing FTAs with the hope of consolidating and overcoming the problems of the existing agreements. A clear example here is the ongoing negotiation of an FTA among the Association of Southeast Asian Nations (ASEAN) members – Japan, the Republic of Korea (hereafter, Korea), China, India, Australia and New Zealand – known as the Regional Economic Comprehensive Partnership (RCEP).

Nonetheless, the extent to which the signed FTAs are utilised and firms' perceptions of the business opportunities that emerge from these FTAs are important for designing these new agreements. The expected effect on trade induced by a signed FTA is conditional on various factors, such as the complexity of the rules of origin (RoOs) (criteria to prove product originality) that are imposed and implemented, tariff margins, and pre-trading volumes. The trade-enhancing effect of FTAs, therefore, varies across products but also across FTAs (Figure 6.1). This points to the need for a comprehensive study of how firms actually utilise signed FTAs and the problems encountered so far in using preferential trade schemes.[2]

In general, this can be done in two ways.[3] The first way is through questionnaire surveys, and the other is by analysing the flow of transactions applied for FTA tariff preferential schemes. While the main advantage of a questionnaire survey is that all questions central to the policy circle can be addressed explicitly, information from the returned questionnaires is likely to be subjective and biased, and respondents tend to answer in a manner that will be favourable to their firms. In some cases, doing so can provide contradictory outcomes.[4]

Against this backdrop, this chapter examines the official records of preferential trade (both exports and imports) for Thai firms. The analysis includes primary and secondary relevant information from previous studies in order to shed light

DOI: 10.4324/9780429433603-6

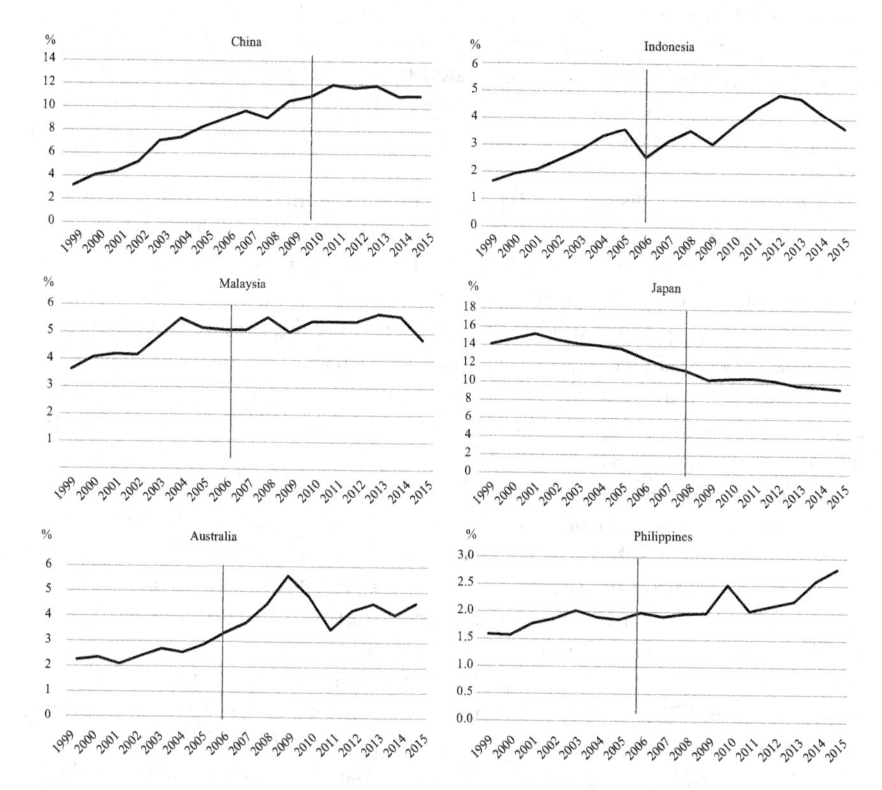

Figure 6.1 Export Performance of Thailand vis-à-vis Major FTA Partners between Pre- and Post-Signing of FTAs (as a share of Thai's total imports).

Note: a vertical line in each diagram indicates a year where the signed FTA between Thailand and the country in question was in effect, i.e. 2006 is for Australia, the Philippines, Indonesia, and Malaysia; 2008 is for Japan; and 2010 is for China.

Source: UN Comtrade database.

on designing the ongoing negotiations for RCEP. Our study mainly emphasises the effect on trade. Analysis of investment requires a different analytical framework that is far from the current scope of this chapter.

We choose Thailand as the case study as data on the customs official (c/o) record are available from 2006 onwards. This allows a systematic analysis to be performed. In addition, we supplement the firm interviews performed by Kohpaiboon and Jongwanich (2015) to address some of the implementing issues experienced by the firms.

6.2 Development of FTAs in Thailand

Until 2001, Thailand benefited from unilateral tariff reductions and the success of multilateral agreements in the context of the General Agreement on Tariffs and Trade and the World Trade Organization (WTO). The slowdown in WTO liberalisation negotiations resulted in a switch of political attention and negotiating resources in Thailand towards preferential trade agreements and bilateral FTAs in particular. It was also accelerated by a significant change in the political situation in Thailand (Sally, 2007). In particular, between 2001 and 2006, Prime Minister Thaksin's Thai Rak Thai party came to power with a strong mandate.

One of the government mandates was to sign as many FTAs as possible to secure preferential market access. The government initiated 15 FTAs during the Thaksin administration period (2001–2006). This was done without the consultation of government officials in charge of trade policy. FTA commitments made during this period largely involved tariff liberalisation and market access for goods. Many signed FTAs were concluded in a rush and without careful study or public consultation. Indeed, some were signed before the advantages and disadvantages could be studied, and consultation with the interested parties outside government was inadequate.

Between 2006 and May 2011, FTA enthusiasm in Thailand stalled. Following the new constitution promulgated in 2007, the execution of international trade agreements is subject to parliamentary approval (Article 190) to prevent the rushed conclusion of agreements. Article 190 requires that all international trade agreements must be carefully studied and subject to countrywide public hearings, and more time is now needed to enact international trade agreements compared with the Thaksin period. The constitutional amendment had a significant impact on FTAs, and the government became much less active in initiating bilateral FTAs. Indeed, not a single bilateral FTA was ratified between 2006 and May 2011. During this period, new FTA negotiations were only in the ASEAN 'plus' format.[5]

In May 2011, Prime Minister Yingluck Shinawatra, the younger sister of former Prime Minister Thaksin Shinawatra, started to pay attention to FTA negotiations again. The negotiations for several FTAs, such as the Thailand–EFTA, Thailand–Chile, and Thailand–Peru FTAs, which had stalled between 2006 and May 2011, were resumed and progressed. Moreover, the current administration also launched several new FTA talks, including negotiations with Canada in March 2012, and expressed an interest in becoming a member of the Trans-Pacific Partnership (TPP) during the US president's visit to Thailand in November 2012.

6.2.1 Signed FTAs in Thailand and their coverage

Table 6.1 presents details of all the FTAs in which Thailand has been involved since the 1990s, some of which comprise ongoing negotiations. These amount to a total of 18 FTAs, of which 12 have come into force. Regarding the coverage of the tariff cuts, there are only eight FTAs in which tariff cuts have been substantial, covering more than 80 percent of tariff lines and having been offered since 2010. They comprise the ASEAN Free Trade Area (AFTA), the ASEAN–China FTA (ACFTA), the Thailand–Australia FTA (TAFTA), the Thailand–New

Table 6.1 FTAs Where Thailand Is a Signatory (1990 – present)

FTA	*Signed*	*Effective*	*Remarks*
ASEAN	1990	2006	Tariff reduction completed in 2010 for original ASEAN members; 2015 for new members
Australia	July 2004	January 2005	Australia's tariff reduction: 83 percent (2005), 96.1 percent (2010), and 100 percent (2015)
			Thailand's tariff reduction: 49.5 percent (2005), 93.3 percent (2010), and 100 percent (2025)
New Zealand	April 2005	July 2005	New Zealand's tariff reduction: 79.1 percent (2005), 88.5 percent (2010), and 100 percent (2015)
			Thailand's tariff reduction: 54.1 percent (2005), 89.7 percent (2010), and 100 percent (2025)
China	2003	2003	China's tariff reduction: 60 percent in 2006 and 90 percent in 2010
			Thailand's tariff reduction: 33.3 percent in 2009, 90 percent in 2010, and more than 90 percent in 2012
India	October 2003	n.a.	82 items under Early Harvest Programme; the rest under negotiation
Japan	April 2007	November 2007	Japan's tariff reduction: 86.1 percent (2007) and 91.2 percent (2017)
			Thailand's tariff reduction: 31.1 percent (2007) and 97.6 percent (2017)
Peru	November 2005	December 2011	Tariff reduction between Thailand and Peru: 50 percent (2011) and 70 percent (2015)
Chile	2006		Under negotiation and expected to be implemented in 2014
BIMSTEC	July 2010	2013	Tariff reduction programme for India, Sri Lanka, and Thailand: 10 percent (2013) and 60 percent (2016)
			Tariff reduction programme for Bangladesh, Bhutan, Nepal, and Myanmar: 10 percent (2011) and 60 percent (2014)
ASEAN–Japan	April 2008	June 2008	Japan's tariff reduction: 85.51 percent in December 2008 and 90.16 percent in April 2018
			Thailand's tariff reduction: 30.94 percent in June 2009 and 86.17 percent in April 2018

(*Continued*)

FTA	*Signed*	*Effective*	*Remarks*
ASEAN–Korea	February 2009	January 2010	Korea's tariff reduction: 90 percent (2010) Thailand's tariff reduction: 83 percent (2010), 84 percent (2012), 89 percent (2016), and 90 percent (2017)
ASEAN–Australia–New Zealand FTA	February 2009	January 2010	Australia's tariff reduction: 95.96 percent in 2010 and 100 percent in 2020 New Zealand's tariff reduction: 90.13 percent in 2010 and 100 percent in 2020 Thailand's tariff reduction: 89.5 percent in 2015 and 98.8 percent in 2020
ASEAN–India	August 2009	January 2010	Tariff reduction for Thailand, Malaysia, Indonesia, Singapore, Brunei Darussalam, and India: 71 percent in 2013 and 80 percent in 2016
ASEAN+3*	Under negotiation		Initiated by November 1999 in Manila (3rd Informal Asian Summit)
Regional Comprehensive Economic Partnership	Under negotiation		Initiated by August 2006, known as ASEAN+6; changed to RCEP in 2011; targeted for the substantial conclusion in 2018 was postponed to 2019
Thailand–EU	Under negotiation/stalled		Initiated by November 2007 under ASEAN–EU; shift to bilateral agreement with individual ASEAN members in 2009; targeted for implementation in 2015, but talks have been stalled due to the 2014 coup
Thailand–Canada	Under negotiation/stalled		Initiated by March 2012, but stalled due to the 2014 coup
Thailand–EFTA (European Free Trade Association)	Under negotiation/stalled		Initiated by October 2005, but talks have been stalled due to the 2014 coup
Trans-Pacific Partnership (TPP)	Uncertain		The Thai Prime Minister expressed interest in the TPP during the US President's visit to Thailand in November 2012
Thailand–Turkey FTA	Just launched		Launched the negotiation in July 2016
ASEAN	1990	2006	Tariff reduction completed in 2010 for original ASEAN members; 2015 for new members.
Australia	July 2004	January 2005	Australia's tariff reduction: 83 percent (2005), 96.1 percent (2010), and 100 percent (2015) Thailand's tariff reduction: 49.5 percent (2005), 93.3 percent (2010), and 100 percent (2025)

New Zealand	April 2005	July 2005	New Zealand's tariff reduction: 79.1 percent (2005), 88.5 percent (2010), and 100 percent (2015)
			Thailand's tariff reduction: 54.1 percent (2005), 89.7 percent (2010), and 100 percent (2025)
China	2003	2003	China's tariff reduction: 60 percent in 2006; and 90 percent in 2010
			Thailand's tariff reduction: 33.3 percent in 2009; 90 percent in 2010; and more than 90 percent in 2012
India	October 2003	n.a.	82 items under Early Harvest Program; the rest under negotiation
Japan	April 2007	November 2007	Japan's tariff reduction: 86.1 percent (2007) and 91.2 percent (2017)
			Thailand's tariff reduction: 31.1 percent (2007) and 97.6 percent (2017)
Peru	November 2005	December 2011	Tariff reduction between Thailand and Peru: 50 percent (2011) and 70 percent (2015)
Chile	2006		Under negotiation and expected to be implemented in 2014
BIMSTEC	July 2010	2013	Tariff reduction programme for India, Sri Lanka, and Thailand: 10 percent (2013) and 60 percent (2016)
			Tariff reduction programme for Bangladesh, Bhutan, Nepal, and Myanmar: 10 percent (2011) and 60 percent (2014)
ASEAN–Japan	April 2008	June 2008	Japan's tariff reduction: 85.51 percent in December 2008; 90.16 percent in April 2018
			Thailand's tariff reduction: 30.94 percent in June 2009; 86.17 percent in Apr 2018
ASEAN–Korea	February 2009	January 2010	Korea's tariff reduction: 90 percent (2010)
			Thailand's tariff reduction: 83 percent (2010); 84 percent (2012); 89 percent (2016); 90 percent (2017)
ASEAN–Australia–New Zealand FTA	February 2009	January 2010	Australia's tariff reduction: 95.96 percent in 2010; 100 percent in 2020
			New Zealand's tariff reduction: 90.13 percent in 2010; 100 percent in 2020
			Thailand's tariff reduction: 89.5 percent in 2015; 98.8 percent in 2020
ASEAN–India	August 2009	January 2010	Tariff reduction for Thailand, Malaysia, Indonesia, Singapore, Brunei Darussalam, and India: 71 percent in 2013; 80 percent in 2016

(*Continued*)

FTA	*Signed*	*Effective*	*Remarks*
ASEAN+3*	Under negotiation		Initiated by November 1999 in Manila (3rd Informal Asian Summit)
Regional Comprehensive Economic Partnership	Under negotiation		Initiated by August 2006, known as the ASEAN+6; changed to the RCEP in 2011; targeted for the substantial conclusion in 2018 was postponed to 2019
Thailand–EU	Under negotiation/ Stalled		Initiated by November 2007 under the ASEAN–EU; shift to bilateral agreement with individual ASEAN members in 2009; targeted for implementation in 2015, but talks have been stalled due to the 2014 coup
Thai–Canada	Under negotiation/ Stalled		Initiated by March 2012, but stalled due to the 2014 coup
Thai–EFTA (European Free Trade Association)	Under negotiation / Stalled		Initiated by October 2005, but talks have been stalled due to the 2014 coup
Trans-Pacific Partnership (TPP)	Uncertain		The Thai Prime Minister expressed interest in the TPP during the US President's visit to Thailand in November 2012
Thailand-Turkey FTA	Just launched		Launched the negotiation in July 2016

Note: *= Japan, South Korea and China

Source: Author's compilation from official data source. Available at http://www.thaifta.com/thaifta/Home/FTAbyCountry/tabid/53/Default.asp

Zealand FTA (TNFTA), the Japan–Thailand Economic Partnership Agreement (JTEPA), the ASEAN–Japan FTA (AJFTA), the ASEAN–Korea FTA (AKFTA) and the ASEAN–Australia–New Zealand FTA (AANZFTA).

For another three FTAs (the Thailand–Peru FTA, the Thailand–Chile FTA, and the ASEAN–India FTA), substantial tariff cuts have taken place only in recent years, i.e. in 2015 and 2016. FTA negotiations between Thailand and India continued over a prolonged period. However, they culminated with bleak prospects. Out of six ongoing FTA talks that had yet to reach satisfactory conclusions, four stalled due to the 2014 coup. Henceforth, our discussion emphasises the eight aforementioned FTAs.

Table 6.1 shows FTAs which mainly describe liberalisation in trade in goods. The commitments that Thailand made on other issues under these FTAs, except in the case of the AEC, were rather weak and at most in line with WTO commitments (Kohpaiboon et al., 2015). These issues include government procurement, service liberalisation (for air transport, professionals, education, health, tourism, marine transport, financial services, and the movement of natural persons), environmental standards, competition policy, sanitary and phytosanitary measures, technical barriers to trade, intellectual property protection, labour standards, environmental obligations, agricultural export subsidies, import licensing and customs procedures. This is especially true for FTAs that Thailand has with developing country FTA partners.

6.2.2 *Tariff cuts in the FTAs*

Table 6.2 presents data on the simple (unweighted) averages of the most-favoured-nation (MFN) rates and preferential tariff rates received by Thailand from the eight FTAs in 2014. It also presents information on the distribution of the tariff margins and the differences between the MFN and preferential tariff rates. First, the average MFN tariffs of the developed countries (i.e. Australia, New Zealand and Japan) were generally lower than those of the developing countries. This implies that the magnitude of the tariff margin received from developed countries tends to be smaller. Korea seems to be an outlier as the average MFN tariff was relatively high by high-income-country standards at 11.9 percent.

Second, the preferential tariffs offered in these agreements vary across FTAs, so the tariff margins also vary considerably, from 0.1 percent to 10.7 percent. As expected, when analysing the MFN averages, the tariff margins for the developed countries are smaller – ranging from 0.1 percent to 5.7 percent. The corresponding range for the developing countries is between 2 percent and 10.7 percent.

Third, in all FTAs, except those with China and India, more than half of the product lines had tariff margins less than or equal to 5 percent. The proportion of such product lines reaches more than 80 percent for developed countries. On the other hand, the proportion of product lines whose tariff margin exceeded 20 percent is rather small in all cases. Hence, FTA preferential schemes tend to be highly concentrated within certain product lines whose tariff margins are substantial. As seen later, this is supported by the analysis of product concentration. In addition,

Table 6.2 Distribution of the Margin between General and Preferential Tariff Rates (in percent)

	Indonesia	*Malaysia*	*Philippines*	*Viet Nam*	*Australia*	*Japan*	*China*	*Korea*
MFN Tariff								
1995	19.4*	13.0*	20	12.8	5.5**	4.1	23.6**	19. 4*
2006	6.9	7.2	6.2	16.8	3.4	3.1	9.9***	6.3***
Preferential Tariffs in 2006	2	2	2.1	2.5***	1.1	2.4	1.9***	3.9***
Distribution of the margin between general and preferential tariffs (percent of total tariff lines)								
$\Delta t = 0$****	34.1 (10.4)	59.4 (53.6)	9.5 (2.3)	33.4 (30.7)	85 (83.7)	53.9 (49.6)	21.7 (5.7)	65.5 (59)
$0 < \Delta t \leq 5$****	41.9	12.7	70.7	18.7	15	27.8	23.4	20.6
$5 < \Delta t \leq 10$****	15.2	6.8	16.9	6.3	0	15.5	40.4	10.8
$10 < \Delta t \leq 20$****	8.3	15.4	1.7	10.1	0	3	12.6	0.5
$20 < \Delta t \leq 30$****	0.2	4.4	0.7	9.6	0	0	1.7	2.4
$30 < \Delta t$****	0.3	1.2	0.6	21.9	0	0	0.1	0.0
# tariff lines (percent of total tariff lines)	5,391	5,222	5,390	5,224	5,218	5,039	5,051	5,036

Notes: *and **denote data for 1994 and 1996, respectively; ***indicates data for 2010; ****represents percent of total tariff lines; and a number in parenthesis indicates the percentage of tariff lines whose MFN tariff is zero.

Sources: Data for 1994–1995 are from Jongwanich and Kohpaiboon (2007), whereas the others are based on the author's calculations using official documents.

items with MFN tariffs greater than 20 percent (tariff peak items) are less likely to be included in FTA tariff cuts. This is especially true for developing countries whose tariffs, on average, are generally high compared to developed countries.

Fourth, China and India seem to be outliers, as both had numerous product lines with tariff margins between 5 percent and 20 percent. In the case of China, 66 percent of product lines had tariff margins between 5 percent and 20 percent. Similarly, between 5 and 20 tariff margin categories for India accounted for nearly 65 percent of the total figure. This points to the fact that high-potential FTAs can be implemented intensively.

Last, there were many product lines with zero tariff margins. These zero tariff margins could be due to two reasons. The MFN tariffs could have been already zero and others were excluded from tariff cuts. Hence, the difference between the items with zero tariff margins and those with zero MFN tariffs indicates the size of the exclusion list for each FTA. The difference is huge for many developing countries. In the case of Indonesia, 34.6 percent of product lines had zero tariff margins; about half of which were from already zero tariffs. There was another 17 percent whose MFN tariffs were not zero. By contrast, product lines with zero tariff margins with regard to Australia accounted for 46.75 percent, wherein the tariffs of most of these products were already zero.

On the other hand, tariff cuts offered by Thailand in each FTA were in the narrow range, between 6.3 percent and 10.2 percent, compared to the MFN rate (Table 6.3). The highest tariff margin was for AFTA (10.2 percent), and the least was for the JTEPA (6.3 percent). The distribution of the five tariff margin

Table 6.3 Margin between General and Preferential Tariff Rates Offered by Thailand and Their Distribution in 2010 (in percent)

	AFTA	*ASEAN–China*	*Thailand–Australia*	*Thailand–New Zealand*	*Japan–Thailand*	*ASEAN–Korea*
Tariff Margin	10.2	9.3	9.7	9.5	6.3	8.6
Distribution of the margin between general and preferential tariffs (percent of total tariff lines)						
$\Delta t = 0$	20.1	25.3	21.2	20.7	30.7	26.7
$0 < \Delta t \leq 5$	39.9	38.3	39.3	39.6	42.5	37.9
$5 < \Delta t \leq 10$	15.3	13.3	15.6	15.6	13.1	13.8
$10 < \Delta t \leq 20$	6.6	6.3	6.6	6.7	4.5	7.9
$20 < \Delta t \leq 30$	14.8	13.6	14.4	14.4	8.0	11.0
$30 < \Delta t$	3.4	3.1	3.0	3.1	1.3	2.7
#tariff lines	4,995	4,996	4,996	4,996	4,985	4,996

Notes: The average MFN rate of Thailand in 2010 was 10.7 percent. There are 993 items whose MFN tariff is zero.

Sources: Data based on the author's calculations using official documents.

categories offered by Thailand is not different among the FTAs. In general, about half of the product lines were subject to tariff margins of less than 5 percent. Given that Thailand has the highest average MFN rate among the original ASEAN members, more than 20 percent of its tariff lines were subject to 10 percent or higher preferential tariffs.

6.3 FTA use in Thailand

To illustrate the use of FTAs in Thailand, we analyse the records of the certificate of origin (c/o). In Thailand, Trade Preference Division, Department of Foreign Trade, Ministry of Commerce, is the government office in charge of collecting information on the export side. On the import side the Customs Department, Ministry of Finance, is responsible. In general, the c/o record is classified according to the HS classification.

6.3.1 The use of FTAs by Thai exporters

Table 6.4 reports the c/o record for exports between 2006 and 2015. We choose the year 2006 as many comprehensive FTAs were in effect. The dollar value of preferential exports increased over the period, from 10 billion US dollar in 2006 to 50.6 billion US dollar in 2015. Its corresponding annual growth was slow, averaging at 18 percent. The rapid growth observed between 2006 and 2010 was a result of the increased number of FTAs in effect. Since 2013, its value has been predominately stagnant, hovering at around 50 billion US dollar.

The AFTA and its successor, the ASEAN Economic Community (AEC), accounted for about 29.5 percent of total preferential exports on average between 2006 and 2015, as described in Table 6.4. Although the export value through the AEC continued to grow from 5.5 billion US dollar in 2006 to 19.2 billion US dollar in 2015, its share of total preferential export dropped from 55 percent to 37.9 percent during the period due to newly signed FTAs after 2006.

Generally, the firms applying for AEC preferential schemes were seeking market access to the original ASEAN members. Of the total AEC preferential export figure, 64 percent was for market access to the original ASEAN Member States. Among the original members, Indonesia accounted for the largest share, i.e. 26 percent of total AEC preferential exports, followed by the Philippines (18.8 percent) and Malaysia (16.1 percent). Nonetheless, their relative importance declined over the period due to the rapid growth of preferential exports to new ASEAN member markets, i.e. Cambodia, Lao PDR, Myanmar and Viet Nam (henceforth referred to as CLMV). The dollar value of preferential exports to CLMV increased to 6.9 billion US dollar in 2015, from 1.3 billion US dollar in 2006. Hence, the share was 36 percent in 2015. The most important export destination among CLMV was Viet Nam.

Despite having the largest share among ASEAN members, Indonesia experienced not only a declining relative importance but also a decline in terms of dollar values. This could be explained by increasing protectionism sentiments in Indonesia (Pantunru and Rahardja, 2015).

By 2015, China had become the most important non-ASEAN FTA partner in terms of the c/o records. Such a pronounced surge in preferential exports to China was due to the progress of trade liberalisation through the ACFTA as well as substantial tariff margins of more than 5 percent (Table 6.3). This was particularly due to significant growth performance of the Chinese economy over the past two decades. Until 2013, Japan was the second after China in terms of the value of its preferential exports. After 2013, Australia has become the second.

There has been a growing number of new FTAs, namely with AANZFTA, AJFTA and Thailand-India FTA (TIFTA). Interestingly, firms are unlikely to apply the new FTAs. For example, in the case of Australia, the TAFTA and AANZFTA were in effect from 2006 and 2010, respectively. Hence, from 2010 onwards, firms were free to choose either the TAFTA or AANZFTA. Table 6.3 shows that almost all preferential exports from Thailand to Australia took place under TAFTA. Similar pattern is also found with preferential exports to Japan. Such a pattern inevitably raises policy attention.

In principle, the regional wider FTAs, such as the AJFTA and AANZFTA, allow for members to count imported inputs from other members as original content to compile with rules of origins. This matters amid the increasing importance of global production sharing in which a production process is fragmented and straddle borders. In practice, they fail to function effectively as suggested in our analysis earlier. It is arguable that the ineffective function of accumulation clauses might be specific to Thailand but it indicates the need for supporting evidence for the relative importance of accumulation clauses.

The pattern observed in India is the opposite. There are two preferential FTA schemes available, the TIFTA and the ASEAN–India FTA (AIFTA), both were in effect in 2005 and 2010, respectively. As the former offered the limited tariff cuts as opposed to the latter, nearly 75 percent of transactions were concluded under the banner of the AIFTA.

The c/o records of the AKFTA grew remarkably after the agreement's signing in 2008. The value increased from 0.9 billion US dollar in 2010 to 2.2 billion US dollar in 2011 and then has remained roughly constant since then. Data captured concerning New Zealand were very low as the records accounted for only transactions under the AANZFTA preferential schemes. There are no records for the TNZFTA signed in 2005 due to the paperless system adopted under the TNZFTA. Hence, the figures reported in Table 6.3 are likely to underestimate the actual transactions.

Table 6.5 presents an overall assessment of how firms utilised FTA preferential schemes between 2006 and 2015. To illustrate the use of FTAs, we calculate the ratio of preferential exports to the actual export value. The total actual exports are used in the denominator when calculating the utilisation rates.[6] When all partners are combined, the utilisation rate is rather low, averaging 32.6 percent from 2006 to 2015 with an increasing trend.[7]

Table 6.4 Preferential Export Value (in billion US dollar)

	2006	*2007*	*2008*	*2009*	*2010*	*2011*	*2012*	*2013*	*2014*	*2015*
AEC	**5.5**	**7.9**	**10.7**	**9.7**	**14.1**	**15.3**	**14.9**	**19.5**	**18.9**	**19.2**
Original AEC Member	4.2	6.0	8.3	6.9	10.7	11.8	11.7	15.2	13.7	12.3
Brunei	0.0	0.0	0.0	0.0	0.0	0.0	0.0	0.0	0.0	0.0
Indonesia	1.7	2.6	3.8	2.7	4.5	6.0	6.1	7.4	6.2	5.0
Malaysia	1.4	1.8	2.5	2.2	3.0	3.1	2.9	3.5	3.8	3.1
Philippines	1.0	1.3	1.6	1.7	2.7	2.2	2.4	4.0	3.4	3.6
Singapore	0.2	0.3	0.4	0.3	0.4	0.5	0.4	0.4	0.4	0.7
New Member	1.3	1.9	2.4	2.8	3.3	3.5	3.2	4.3	5.2	6.9
Cambodia	0.0	0.0	0.0	0.0	0.1	0.1	0.1	0.2	0.4	0.4
Lao PDR	0.0	0.0	0.0	0.1	0.1	0.1	0.1	0.1	0.2	0.2
Myanmar	0.0	0.0	0.0	0.0	0.0	0.0	0.1	0.3	0.4	0.7
Viet Nam	1.2	1.8	2.3	2.7	3.1	3.2	2.8	3.7	4.3	5.7
Non-ASEAN	**4.5**	**6.9**	**11.6**	**12.9**	**20.1**	**24.7**	**26.9**	**32.6**	**33.3**	**31.4**
Australia	2.7	4.1	4.9	4.3	5.6	5.0	5.1	7.8	7.4	8.2
TAFTA	2.7	4.1	4.9	4.3	5.6	5.0	4.9	7.5	7.0	7.8
AANZFTA	0.0	0.0	0.0	0.0	0.0	0.0	0.2	0.3	0.4	0.4
New Zealand	0.0	0.0	0.0	0.0	0.0	0.0	0.0	0.0	0.1	0.1
TNZFTA	n.a.	n.a.	n.a.	n.a.	n.a.	n.a.	n.a.	n.a.	n.a.	n.a.
AANZFTA	0.0	0.0	0.0	0.0	0.0	0.0	0.0	0.0	0.1	0.1
China	1.5	1.8	1.7	4.0	7.4	9.4	11.3	13.8	13.9	11.5
India	0.3	0.4	0.4	0.4	1.4	2.0	2.1	2.2	2.9	3.0
Japan	0.0	0.6	4.5	4.2	4.8	6.1	6.3	6.5	6.8	6.7
JTEPA	0.0	0.6	4.5	4.2	4.8	6.0	6.3	6.5	6.8	6.7
ASEAN–Japan	0.0	0.0	0.0	0.0	0.0	0.0	0.0	0.0	0.0	0.0
Korea	0.0	0.0	0.0	0.0	0.9	2.2	2.1	2.3	2.2	1.9
Total	10.0	14.8	22.3	22.6	34.2	40.0	41.8	52.1	52.2	50.6
% of total preferential export										
AEC	55.0	53.4	48.0	42.9	41.2	38.3	35.6	37.4	36.2	37.9
Original AEC Member	42.0	40.5	37.2	30.5	31.3	29.5	28.0	29.2	26.2	24.3
Brunei	0.0	0.0	0.0	0.0	0.0	0.0	0.0	0.0	0.0	0.0
Indonesia	17.0	17.6	17.0	11.9	13.2	15.0	14.6	14.2	11.9	9.9
Malaysia	14.0	12.2	11.2	9.7	8.8	7.8	6.9	6.7	7.3	6.1
Philippines	10.0	8.8	7.2	7.5	7.9	5.5	5.7	7.7	6.5	7.1
Singapore	2.0	2.0	1.8	1.3	1.2	1.3	1.0	0.8	0.8	1.4
New Member	13.0	12.8	10.8	12.4	9.6	8.8	7.7	8.3	10.0	13.6
Cambodia	0.0	0.0	0.0	0.0	0.3	0.3	0.2	0.4	0.8	0.8
Lao PDR	0.0	0.0	0.0	0.4	0.3	0.3	0.2	0.2	0.4	0.4
Myanmar	0.0	0.0	0.0	0.0	0.0	0.0	0.2	0.6	0.8	1.4
Viet Nam	12.0	12.2	10.3	11.9	9.1	8.0	6.7	7.1	8.2	11.3
Non-ASEAN	45.0	46.6	52.0	57.1	58.8	61.8	64.4	62.6	63.8	62.1
Australia	27.0	27.7	22.0	19.0	16.4	12.5	12.2	15.0	14.2	16.2
TAFTA	27.0	27.7	22.0	19.0	16.4	12.5	11.7	14.4	13.4	15.4
AANZFTA	0.0	0.0	0.0	0.0	0.0	0.0	0.5	0.6	0.8	0.8
New Zealand	0.0	0.0	0.0	0.0	0.0	0.0	0.0	0.0	0.2	0.2
TNZFTA	n.a.	n.a.	n.a.	n.a.	n.a.	n.a.	n.a.	n.a.	n.a.	n.a.
AANZFTA	0.0	0.0	0.0	0.0	0.0	0.0	0.0	0.0	0.2	0.2
China	15.0	12.2	7.6	17.7	21.6	23.5	27.0	26.5	26.6	22.7
India	3.0	2.7	1.8	1.8	4.1	5.0	5.0	4.2	5.6	5.9

	2006	2007	2008	2009	2010	2011	2012	2013	2014	2015
Japan	0.0	4.1	20.2	18.6	14.0	15.3	15.1	12.5	13.0	13.2
JTEPA	0.0	4.1	20.2	18.6	14.0	15.0	15.1	12.5	13.0	13.2
ASEAN–Japan	0.0	0.0	0.0	0.0	0.0	0.0	0.0	0.0	0.0	0.0
Korea	0.0	0.0	0.0	0.0	2.6	5.5	5.0	4.4	4.2	3.8
Total	100.0	100.0	100.0	100.0	100.0	100.0	100.0	100.0	100.0	100.0

Note: n.a. found in TNZFTA is replaced by 0 in the summation.

Sources: Authors' calculations from official data sources: preferential exports from Bureau of Preferential Trade, Ministry of Commerce.

Table 6.5 FTA Utilisation Rate on Exports (Share of Thai's Export Value to FTA Partners)

	2006	2007	2008	2009	2010	2011	2012	2013	2014	2015	2006–2015
AEC	20.5	24.0	27.1	29.8	31.8	28.1	26.3	32.9	31.8	35.4	29.5
Original AEC Member	20.4	23.8	28.2	29.9	33.6	30.4	29.7	37.7	35.4	38.1	31.4
Brunei	8.3	10.0	9.7	6.9	10.9	20.9	13.5	11.4	17.2	16.4	11.5
Indonesia	50.9	53.6	61.5	57.9	61.5	59.5	54.1	67.9	64.8	65.2	60.6
Malaysia	20.6	23.7	25.2	28.7	28.7	24.9	23.1	26.5	29.9	30.6	24.3
Philippines	38.1	43.4	46.9	56.1	55.9	46.6	48.6	78.6	58.6	61.8	55.2
Singapore	2.5	2.7	3.9	3.7	5.0	4.5	4.0	3.7	4.1	8.3	3.9
New Member	20.8	24.9	23.8	29.6	27.0	22.3	18.4	22.6	25.1	31.5	24.9
Cambodia	0.0	0.0	0.5	2.2	3.9	3.9	3.6	5.3	7.9	8.1	4.7
Lao PDR	2.3	2.3	2.6	4.0	4.3	3.9	3.6	3.8	4.1	4.4	3.7
Myanmar	0.4	1.0	1.7	1.3	1.0	0.9	2.7	6.7	9.8	16.0	6.0
Viet Nam	40.1	46.6	46.6	57.3	53.8	45.7	42.1	51.2	54.0	64.9	46.6
Non-ASEAN	12.1	15.3	22.4	27.4	33.5	35.2	37.6	46.1	49.3	49.7	35.0
Australia	63.0	70.9	62.5	50.3	60.2	63.1	51.9	72.1	75.6	81.2	64.9
New Zealand	*	*	*	*	0.4	0.9	1.7	4.1	6.3	5.6	3.5
China	12.4	11.9	10.6	24.7	34.3	34.2	42.0	50.7	55.3	49.3	36.2
India	18.2	14.1	12.4	10.9	32.8	38.0	38.0	42.7	51.4	58.0	35.7
Japan	0.0	3.6	22.7	26.9	23.5	25.3	26.9	29.2	31.2	33.8	25.0
Korea	0.0	0.0	0.0	0.1	24.4	48.4	44.6	50.4	48.6	47.5	40.3
Total	15.4	18.9	24.5	28.4	32.8	32.2	32.6	40.1	41.1	43.7	32.6

Note: *indicates the effect of a paperless system adopted under TNZFTA so that official records are not available.

Sources: Author's calculations from official data source; preferential exports from Bureau of Preferential Trade, Ministry of Commerce; trade data from UNComtrade.

The utilisation rates vary across FTA partners. Among the ASEAN members, Indonesia had the highest utilisation rate. From 2006 to 2015, it stood between 50.9 percent and 67.9 percent. The Philippines and Viet Nam were the first and second runners-up in applying for AEC preferential schemes, respectively.

The averages of their utilisation rates during the period of 2006–2015 were 55.2 percent and 46.6 percent, respectively. There is no clear pattern among these ASEAN top-three nations in FTA utilisation over the period considered. Malaysia, another major economy in ASEAN, recorded rather low utilisation rates at around 24.3 percent between 2006 and 2015. The low utilisation rate for Singapore is not surprising given the fact that the country is tariff-free. Hence, most transactions reflect the increasingly important role of Singapore as the location of many multinational enterprises' regional headquarters (Channel News Asia, 2016). Turning to Cambodia, Lao PDR and Myanmar, utilisation rates registered at less than 10 percent, on average, between 2006 and 2015. This was due to their gradual adjustment to tariff reduction.

Utilisation rates were slightly lower for the non-ASEAN partners. The average figure during the period 2006–2015 was 35 percent, with an accompanying increasing trend. Utilisation rates were the highest for Australia, fluctuating between 51.9 percent and 81.2 percent. This was largely driven by product with high tariffs such as vehicles that were actually liberalised under the TAFTA. For other non-ASEAN FTA partners, utilisation rates exhibited a continuously upward trend. This was especially true for China and India.

6.3.2 The FTA use of Thai importers

Table 6.6 presents the pattern of c/o records on the import side between 2006 and 2015. The dollar value of preferential imports grew rapidly, from 3.9 billion US dollar in 2006 to 51.2 billion US dollar in 2015. Imports from ASEAN accounted for the largest share, in spite of the declining relative importance. The share of ASEAN was 38.5 percent of total preferential imports in 2015, dropping from 79.8 percent in 2006, as many FTAs were signed and came into effect after 2007. Among the ASEAN members, Indonesia, the Philippines, and

Table 6.6 Preferential Import Value (in billion US dollar)

	2006	*2007*	*2008*	*2009*	*2010*	*2011*	*2012*	*2013*	*2014*	*2015*
AEC	3.07	3.05	3.64	4.06	7.18	9.65	10.74	19.91	19.47	19.70
Original AEC Member	2.91	2.81	3.22	3.55	6.27	8.14	8.90	15.52	14.12	12.66
Brunei Darussalam	0.00	0.00	0.00	0.00	0.00	0.00	0.00	0.02	0.03	0.02
Indonesia	0.98	1.08	1.53	1.52	2.47	3.35	3.78	7.39	6.16	5.02
Malaysia	0.83	0.84	0.81	0.88	1.79	2.42	2.77	3.46	3.82	3.08
Philippines	0.48	0.45	0.51	0.70	1.12	1.14	1.08	3.96	3.44	3.64
Singapore	0.61	0.45	0.36	0.46	0.90	1.23	1.28	0.68	0.66	0.90
New Member	0.16	0.24	0.42	0.51	0.90	1.50	1.83	4.40	5.35	7.04
Cambodia	0.00	0.00	0.00	0.03	0.04	0.04	0.11	0.22	0.36	0.40
Lao PDR	0.00	0.01	0.15	0.17	0.34	0.55	0.51	0.14	0.17	0.18
Myanmar	0.01	0.01	0.01	0.03	0.04	0.04	0.05	0.26	0.41	0.66
Viet Nam	0.15	0.22	0.26	0.28	0.49	0.87	1.16	3.78	4.41	5.80

	2006	2007	2008	2009	2010	2011	2012	2013	2014	2015
Non-ASEAN	0.78	1.10	2.80	2.73	5.34	13.91	19.46	32.84	33.51	31.50
Australia	0.47	0.44	0.38	0.41	0.61	0.90	1.12	7.81	7.45	8.16
Thailand–Australia	0.45	0.44	0.38	0.41	0.61	0.89	1.10	7.46	7.03	7.81
AANZ	0.02	0.00	0.00	0.00	0.00	0.01	0.02	0.35	0.42	0.36
New Zealand	0.12	0.16	0.17	0.14	0.22	0.28	0.34	0.09	0.16	0.07
AANZ	0.04	0.00	0.00	0.00	0.00	0.00	0.01	0.00	0.00	0.00
Thailand–New Zealand	0.08	0.16	0.17	0.14	0.22	0.28	0.33	0.09	0.16	0.07
China	0.14	0.46	0.10	0.00	0.00	6.54	9.16	13.81	13.87	11.49
India	0.04	0.03	0.04	0.04	0.02	0.12	0.32	2.21	2.89	3.02
Japan	0.00	0.05	2.12	2.14	3.97	5.06	7.03	6.60	6.95	6.84
JTEPA	0.00	0.05	2.12	2.13	3.93	5.01	6.92	6.50	6.80	6.68
ASEAN–Japan	0.00	0.00	0.00	0.01	0.04	0.06	0.11	0.10	0.14	0.16
Korea	0.00	0.00	0.00	0.00	0.51	1.00	1.50	2.31	2.20	1.91
Total	3.9	4.2	6.4	6.8	12.5	23.6	30.2	52.75	52.99	51.20
% of total preferential import										
AEC	79.8	73.5	56.5	59.7	57.4	41.0	35.6	37.7	36.8	38.5
Original AEC Member	75.5	67.7	49.9	52.3	50.1	34.6	29.5	29.4	26.6	24.7
Brunei Darussalam	0.0	0.0	0.0	0.0	0.0	0.0	0.0	0.0	0.1	0.4
Indonesia	25.5	26.0	23.8	22.4	19.7	14.2	12.5	14.0	11.6	9.8
Malaysia	21.7	20.2	12.5	12.9	14.3	10.3	9.2	6.6	7.2	6.0
Philippines	12.5	10.8	8.0	10.2	8.9	4.9	3.6	7.5	605	7.1
Singapore	15.9	10.8	5.7	6.7	7.2	5.2	4.2	1.3	1.2	1.8
New Member	4.3	5.8	6.6	7.5	7.2	6.4	6.1	8.3	10.1	13.7
Cambodia	0.0	0.0	0.1	0.4	0.3	0.2	0.4	0.4	0.7	0.8
Lao PDR	0.1	0.2	2.3	2.5	2.7	2.3	1.7	0.3	0.3	0.4
Myanmar	0.1	0.2	0.2	0.4	0.3	0.2	0.2	0.5	0.8	1.3
Viet Nam	4.0	5.3	4.0	4.2	3.9	3.7	3.9	7.2	8.3	11.3
Non-ASEAN	20.2	26.5	43.5	40.3	42.6	59.0	64.4	62.3	63.2	61.5
Australia	12.3	10.6	5.9	6.0	4.9	3.8	3.7	14.8	14.1	15.9
Thailand–Australia	11.8	10.6	5.9	6.0	4.9	3.8	3.6	14.1	13.3	15.2
AANZ	0.5	0.0	0.0	0.0	0.0	0.0	0.1	0.7	0.8	0.7
New Zealand	3.1	3.9	2.6	2.1	1.8	1.2	1.1	0.2	0.3	0.1
AANZ	1.1	0.0	0.0	0.0	0.0	0.0	0.0	0.0	0.0	0.0
Thailand–New Zealand	2.0	3.8	2.6	2.1	1.8	1.2	1.1	0.2	0.3	0.1
China	3.7	11.1	1.6	0.0	0.0	27.8	30.3	26.2	26.2	22.4
India	1.1	0.7	0.6	0.6	0.2	0.5	1.1	4.2	5.5	5.9
Japan	0.0	1.2	32.8	31.5	31.7	21.5	23.3	12.5	13.1	13.4
JTEPA	0.0	1.1	32.8	31.4	31.4	21.3	22.9	12.3	12.8	13.0
ASEAN–Japan	0.0	0.0	0.0	0.1	0.3	0.3	0.4	0.2	0.3	0.3
Korea	0.0	0.0	0.0	0.0	4.1	4.2	5.0	4.4	4.1	3.7
Total	100.0	100.0	100.0	100.0	100.0	100.0	100.0	100.0	100.0	100.0

Source: Authors' calculation from official data; preferential import from the Customs Department, Ministry of Commerce.

Malaysia were the most important sources of preferential imports, accounting, respectively, for 9.8 percent, 7.1 percent, and 6.0 percent of total preferential imports in 2015.

The dollar value of preferential imports from non-ASEAN partners grew noticeably and reached 31.5 billion US dollar in 2015 from 0.8 billion US dollar in 2006. The largest non-ASEAN FTA partner from the import side was China, accounting for 22.4 percent of total preferential imports in 2015. The second and third were Australia and Japan, with 15.9 percent and 13.4 percent of total preferential imports, respectively. Preferential imports from the other FTA partners to Thailand remained small despite its steady growth.

Table 6.7 presents the FTA utilisation for imports from 2006 to 2015. Utilisation increased gradually from 5.2 percent in 2006 to 19.7 percent in 2015. The ratios on the import side were much lower than those on the export side. The ASEAN utilisation rate on imports fluctuated. It was 13.0 percent in 2006, increased to 26.6 percent in 2012 and then dropped to 17.4 percent in 2015. Indonesia, the Philippines, Viet Nam, and Lao PDR were top in terms of utilisation for imports. Cambodia's utilisation reached 42.8 percent in 2012 due to the increasing importance of cassava imports to Thailand in recent years. For the Philippines and Indonesia, the high utilisation was due to the operation of the global production network of automotives, where each country is assigned to

Table 6.7 FTA Utilisation Rate on Imports (Share of Thai's Imports from FTA Partners)

	2006	*2007*	*2008*	*2009*	*2010*	*2011*	*2012*	*2013*	*2014*	*2015*	*2006–2015*
AEC	13	12.1	12.1	16.4	23.7	26.1	26.6	14.7	16.4	17.4	17.9
Original AEC Member	14.7	13.3	13.1	17.7	24.9	26.9	27.7	19.1	19.2	19.6	19.6
Brunei Darussalam	0	0	0	0	0	0	0	10.2	9.2	12.5	3.2
Indonesia	28.3	27.1	28.4	40	43.5	45.5	46.7	27.5	29.1	29.2	34.5
Malaysia	9.9	9.7	8.3	10.2	16.7	19.6	21.1	23.9	24.3	22.2	16.6
Philippines	22.6	21	22.6	39	47.1	42.3	39.8	18.5	18.5	18.7	29.0
Singapore	10.8	7.2	5.2	8	14.3	15.8	16.3	15.2	14.8	15.4	12.3
New Member	4.4	6.1	7.6	10.8	17.5	22.8	22.5	10.4	13.6	15.2	13.1
Cambodia	1.1	0	3.8	32.5	19.3	22.5	42.8	6.7	11.8	10.6	15.1
Lao PDR	0.8	2.1	23.9	37.4	45.2	48.9	41.2	6.4	9.9	13.3	22.9
Myanmar	0.2	0.4	0.4	1	1.3	1.1	1.5	4.3	7.2	10.7	2.8
Viet Nam	17.1	19.8	18	20.4	35	43.1	39	24.2	25.6	26.2	26.8
Non-ASEAN	1.6	1.9	4.1	5.1	6.8	14.9	18.6	18.3	20.5	22.1	11.4
Australia	13.8	11.2	7.3	10.8	10.4	11.3	20.5	23.2	24.3	22.3	15.5
New Zealand	37.9	38.8	26	46.4	43	47.8	55.8	14.2	14.1	16.9	34.1
China	1	2.7	0.5	0	0	21.4	24.8	13.7	14.9	15.7	9.5
India	2.7	1.4	1.4	2.2	0.9	4.1	10.1	22.4	28.5	31.5	10.5
Japan	0	0.2	6.3	8.6	10.5	12	14.2	18.6	18.5	20.5	10.9
Korea	0	0	0	0	6.4	10.9	16.7	17.6	22.4	25.4	10.0
Total	5.2	4.9	6.5	8.7	11.5	18.1	20.8	16.5	18.4	19.7	13.0

Sources: Authors' calculation from official data; preferential imports from Customs Department, Ministry of Commerce; trade data from UN Comtrade.

specialise in a certain vehicle segment (e.g. pickup trucks or passenger vehicles) and then export to the rest of the region. Indonesia has been positioned as a production base for multipurpose vehicles (e.g., Toyota Innova, Toyota Avanza and Honda HRV). Indonesia produces these vehicles and sells them to other countries in Southeast Asia and Oceania.

The utilisation rate was slightly higher for non-ASEAN members than it was for ASEAN members. In 2015, the utilisation rate for non-ASEAN members was 22.1 percent, compared to 17.4 percent for ASEAN members. Interestingly, the rate varied significantly across individual partners. New Zealand was top in terms of FTA utilisation. Its utilisation rate in the more recent years exceeded 40 percent, dominated by milk and dairy products. Nonetheless, its dollar value was rather small, around 1 billion US dollar a year. For other FTA partners, the utilisation rate was less than 20 percent, despite the gradually increasing trend.

6.4 Which countries and products apply for FTA preferential trade schemes

Table 6.8 presents the cumulative share of preferential trade of the top-10 and top-15 products in two periods (i.e. 2011–2012 and 2014–2015) to indicate the extent of concentration of the products traded under FTA preferential trade schemes. Note that the calculations were undertaken at the 6-digit HS level, which consists of more than 5,000 product items. Both exports from and imports into Thailand are reported in the table.

On the export side, products from Thailand that applied for FTA schemes were highly concentrated with noticeably increasing trends. The top-10 and top-15 export items of Thailand to other ASEAN members through the AEC scheme in 2011–2012 accounted for 26.8 percent and 33.2 percent, respectively. The cumulative shares of the top-10 and top-15 export items virtually doubled to 54.7 percent and 62.2 percent in 2014–2015, respectively. The members for which the preferential export value from Thailand was relatively low —Brunei Darussalam, Cambodia, Lao PDR, and Myanmar– registered a far higher degree of product concentration. Their cumulative share of the top-15 products approached 80 percent during 2011–2012. By contrast, the cumulative shares for Indonesia, Malaysia, Viet Nam and the Philippines were lower.

For non-ASEAN members, the degree of product concentration was higher in the cases of Australia and New Zealand. The top-15 products for Australia were 71.6 percent in 2014–2015, dominated by complete built-up (CBU) vehicles, electrical appliances (air conditioning, washing machines) and primary petrochemical products whose MFN tariff remains high as opposed to other products. In contrast, the degree of product concentration of the other non-ASEAN partners declined slightly over the considering period. More new products were traded under the FTA preferential schemes.

Jongwanich and Kohpaiboon (2015) detail that the top-15 preferential exports in 2012 were not much different from each FTA partner, largely dominated by automotive products (both vehicles and auto parts), electrical appliances,

Table 6.8 Cumulative Shares of Top-10 and Top-15 Preferential Trade in 2011–2015

	Top 10		*Top 15*	
	2011–2012	*2014–2015*	*2011–2012*	*2014–2015*
Export				
AEC	26.8	54.7	33.2	62.2
Original AEC	33.2	52.8	40.7	59.9
Brunei Darussalam	58.2	70.5	66.1	77.2
Indonesia	41.6	38.2	48.4	46.0
Malaysia	29.1	38.3	36.3	45.3
Philippines	45.9	52.6	53.3	59.0
Singapore	50.0	64.1	56.4	71.8
New AEC	21.8	56.6	28.5	64.5
Cambodia	79.6	62.5	88.8	71.3
Lao PDR	71.1	55.7	82.8	64.5
Myanmar	88.8	71.0	92.3	77.4
Viet Nam	22.6	37.3	29.6	44.8
Australia	50.1	66.2	57.5	71.6
New Zealand	73.3	61.1	78.4	67.3
China	59.3	48.8	68.8	56.7
India	49.5	36.3	55.9	43.2
Japan	50.9	42.4	58.2	50.4
Korea	41.4	29.5	48.4	36.4
Import				
AEC	34.9	53.7	40.1	61.3
Original AEC	35.9	51.2	42.2	58.5
Brunei Darussalam	100.0	62.2	100.0	69.6
Indonesia	52.4	37.2	60.3	45.5
Malaysia	32.6	37.7	39.5	44.7
Philippines	71.7	52.6	77.5	58.9
Singapore	65.1	66.5	76.3	74.0
New AEC	51.2	56.3	57.7	64.1
Cambodia	76.0	62.4	76.6	71.2
Lao PDR	100	55.6	99.1	64.3
Myanmar	97.6	71.0	98.6	77.4
Viet Nam	36.7	36.1	45.1	43.4
Australia	67.7	67.8	72.0	74.2
New Zealand	79.3	61.1	85.4	67.3
China	12.8	48.8	16.8	56.7
India	24.2	36.3	29.2	43.2
Japan	40.6	51.8	47.7	61.6
Korea	26.5	29.5	30.4	36.5

Sources: Authors' calculations from official data sources; preferential export from the Bureau of Preferential Trade, Ministry of Commerce, preferential import from the Customs Department, Ministry of Commerce.

petrochemical products, and processed foods. Hence, large firms are in a better position than smaller firms. This finding is in line with previous studies (JETRO, 2007; Takahashi and Urata, 2008; Kawai and Wignaraja, 2011; Hayakawa et al., 2013) that show that large firms are more likely to apply for an FTA preferential trade scheme.

Second, products from these sectors have a high level of local content. As shown in previous studies (Athukorala and Kohpaiboon, 2012; Kohpaiboon and Jongwanich, 2013), CBU vehicle exports from Thailand rely heavily on locally manufactured parts, and local content for some models is approaching 100 percent. While the import content for electrical appliances varies from product to product, air conditioning and washing machines exhibit high local content. In particular, major components – in compressors and cases, for example – are locally sourced. This is especially so for petrochemical products, which are wholly obtained from Thailand's petrochemical complex, one of the leading petrochemical complexes in the region. Similarly, a complete supply chain of processed shrimp has been long developed in Thailand so that processed shrimp exports exhibit remarkably high local content (Kohpaiboon, 2006). The high local content makes complying with existing RoOs much easier.

Third, tariff margins (margins of preference) matter for firms' use of FTA preferential export schemes. As argued by Kohpaiboon and Jongwanich (2015: Table 12), the top-15 preferential export products usually have a relatively high tariff margin. The margins averaged at 15.5 percent, 18.3 percent, 4.7 percent, 3.2 percent, 7.4 percent, and 7.9 percent for Indonesia, Malaysia, Australia, Japan, China, and Korea, respectively. All were far higher than the average tariff margin as outlined in Table 6.5. The observed pattern of high tariff margins is consistent with the finding that complying with the RoO incurs fixed costs.

On the import side, non-ASEAN members generally had a higher degree of product concentration than the ASEAN members. Within the ASEAN members, the top-ten cumulative shares in 2014–2015 were ranged from 36.1 percent to 71 percent. Myanmar registered the highest cumulative share, whereas Viet Nam had the lowest. For Indonesia, Malaysia, and the Philippines, the cumulative share was moderate, within a rather narrow range of 37.2 percent–52.6 percent. The cumulative share of the other newer ASEAN members was higher than the original members. Another interesting pattern is that the cumulative share increased between 2011–2012 and 2014–2015, indicating that the range of products applying for the FTA preferential schemes became narrower.

As revealed by Kohpaiboon and Jongwanich (2015), product detail in the top-15 preferential imports in 2012 varied across partners. The most important product among the top 15 was coal, accounting for 22.4 percent of the total preferential imports of Thailand from Indonesia. The others were CBU vehicles, certain auto parts, shovels, and excavators. The structure of the top-15 preferential imports of Thailand from Malaysia was much more diverse compared to that of Indonesia. The imports include electronics (other colour reception apparatus for television, automatic controlling equipment), petrochemical products, CBU vehicles, air conditioning units, foods, lumber, and plastic products. In the Philippines, auto parts and transmissions for motor vehicles, as well as CBU vehicles, were among the top-15 preferential imports.

Despite the observed high degree of product diversification, preferential imports from Cambodia to Thailand were dominated by garment products (HS 61 and HS 62) and primary agricultural products, such as cassava, maize, and sesame seeds. The latter is likely to be traded at the border. Viet Nam's preferential imports covered a wide range of products – from primary agricultural products (such as coffee, cuttlefish, cashew nuts, and wheat) to steel, textiles, and motorcycles. The high product concentration for Myanmar and Lao PDR was driven by the import of copper cathodes, which accounted for 39 percent and 79 percent of total preferential imports with Thailand, respectively.

For non-ASEAN members, the degree of product concentration also varied. It was highly concentrated for Australia and New Zealand, where the cumulative shares of the top-10 preferential imports were 71.6 percent and 80.2 percent, respectively. The cumulative shares of their top-15 preferential imports slightly increased to 75.1 percent for Australia and 86.1 percent for New Zealand. The former was dominated by primary products, such as copper, bituminous, aluminium, and zinc. In the latter, milk and cream powder alone accounted for 34.1 percent of total preferential imports between the two countries.

Similar to Viet Nam, Thailand's preferential imports from China covered a wide range of products – from fresh fruits (mandarin oranges and apples) to steel, textiles, electrical appliances (DVD players), and auto parts. Despite the relatively low product concentration, preferential imports from Japan to Thailand were dominated by two main product groups – steel (HS 72) mainly used in the automotive sector and auto parts. Preferential imports from Korea were the most highly concentrated, dominated by steel, petroleum products, petrochemical products, textiles, and auto parts.

Analysis of Thailand's top-15 preferential imports from its major FTA partners suggests that the nature of the country's preferential imports is fresh agricultural products and raw materials/intermediates for further uses. The former is usually traded across borders due to the perishable nature of the products, so business transactions tend to be small and perhaps seasonal. This perhaps explains the limited impact of FTAs on overall bilateral trade. The latter is mainly primary manufactured intermediates, such as chemical and mining products. For both product groups, RoOs are unlikely to be a significant barrier in using FTA preferential import schemes.

Interestingly, the relative importance of raw materials/intermediates in preferential imports might explain to a certain extent why the utilisation rate on the import side is generally lower than on the export side. Raw materials/intermediates are eligible for the tariff exemption schemes that have long been available for export businesses. Hence, firms have many options to bypass tariffs in addition to applying for FTA preferential trade schemes. This is different from preferential exports from Thailand, which are largely finished products for direct consumption. Figure 6.2 illustrates the shares of the total tariff exemption scheme as well

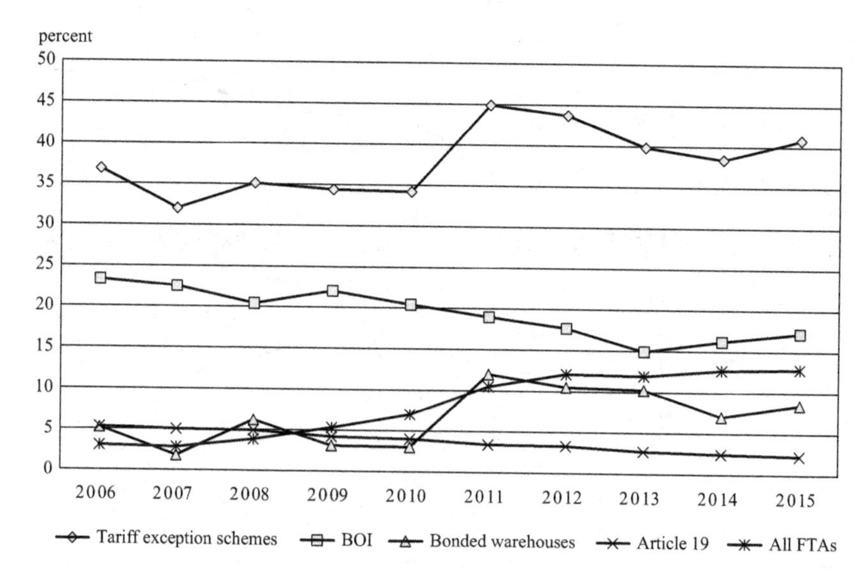

Figure 6.2 Relative Importance of Tariff Exemption Schemes in Thailand between 2006 and 2015.

Source: Authors' calculation from data from the Customs Department, Ministry of Commerce, 2006–2015.

as its three compositions (Board of Investment, bonded warehouses, and Article 19 tax rebates) in total imports, together with the share of preferential imports to total imports from 2006 to 2012. While the share of preferential imports increased steadily, the share of total tariff exemption schemes grew at a faster rate with composition changes. The relative importance of the Board of Investment scheme decreased from 2006.

Another important trend found by Kohpaiboon and Jongwanich (2015) is that the top-15 preferential imports from major FTA partners exhibited a relatively high tariff margin. This finding confirms our earlier finding based on preferential export analysis that complying with the RoO is costly. Interestingly, for most FTA partners, the cumulative share of the top-15 preferential imports was much larger than that calculated from the actual import share, indicating the limited role of FTAs on overall imports. The only exception was China, whose cumulative share of the top-15 preferential imports was slightly higher than that for the actual import share. This reflects the nature of preferential imports, which were largely border trade and handled by small- and micro-enterprises.

Figure 6.3 shows the import shares of major FTA partners vis-à-vis Thailand's total imports to illustrate the effect of FTAs on bilateral imports. As shown in Figure 6.3, there was no major change between the pre- and post-signing of the FTAs. In many cases, import shares declined. This

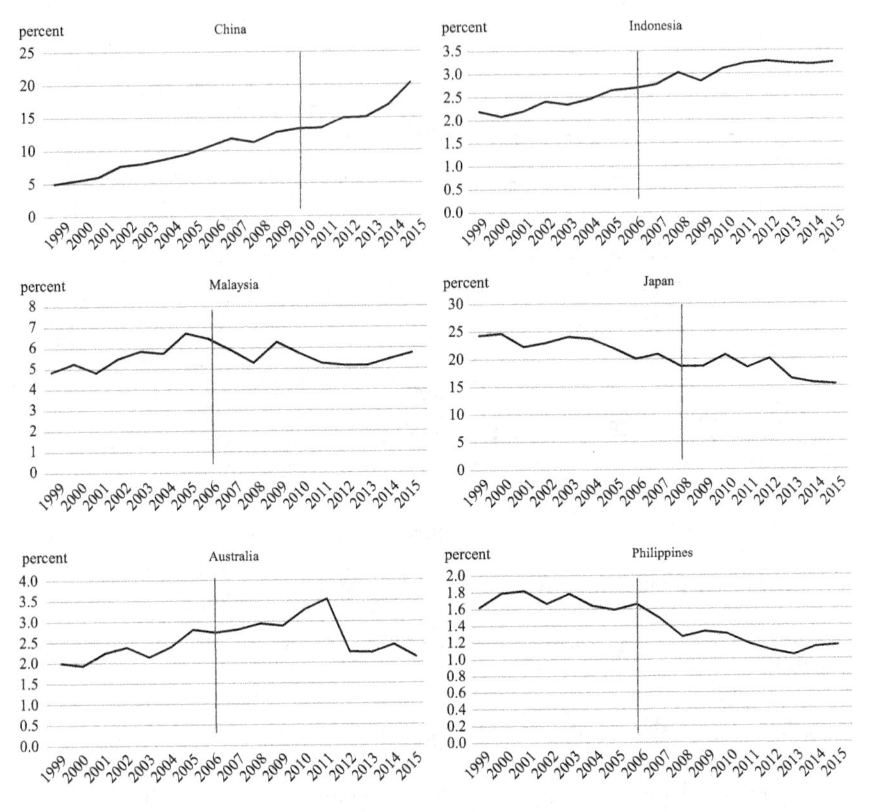

Figure 6.3 Import Share of Major FTA Partners between Pre-and Post-Signing of FTAs (Share of Thai's Total Imports).

Note: a vertical line in each diagram indicates a year where the signed FTA between Thailand and the country in question was in effect, i.e. 2006 is for Australia, the Philippines, Indonesia, and Malaysia; 2008 is for Japan; and 2010 is for China.

Source: UN Comtrade database.

confirms the finding on the export side of the limited effect of FTAs on overall trade.

6.5 Other problems of using FTA preferential schemes

The firm interviews documented in Kohpaiboon and Jongwanich (2015)[8] point to problems occurring from a business viewpoint when using FTAs. Due to the fact that firms must apply for c/o in order to receive preferential tariffs, the main burden for firms is about request by the official to fill in information about their production process. While there are fees on c/o application, its dollar cost is rather small.[9] This can act as a deterrent for firms. Firms in industries like the automotive sector, which have long experience in sharing their production process details with government officials to comply with local content requirement schemes, consider this usual business. The requirements are less likely to discourage these types of firms from using the FTA schemes. In contrast, details of the production process are highly sensitive for some businesses, such as for the production of chemical compounds, where input composition matters for business competition. This would explain the high product concentration nature found in preferential trade patterns and would also be a big obstacle for others and small and medium enterprises (SMEs). Although their production process is straightforward, sharing such information might be new to them. To a certain extent, this might also be related to issues of income tax bases, i.e. some firms underreport their true income to pay less corporate tax.

Second, another cumbersome process in obtaining c/o is receiving a reference number. In general, firms receive a reference number after the process of identifying the product origin is complete. The number can be used for a certain period. For firms whose production technology is mature and input structure stable, there is no problem. Applying to another FTA is costless. This is applicable for products that have their own niche market. But for firms for which the production technology is subject to rapid change and the input structure evolves over time, such a process can be costly. In addition, new products require separate documents of goods' origin as proof. How to define the new products is still subject to discretion. For example, when there are changes in input structure, are the products regarded as new products? If so, firms must resubmit all the required documents.

Third, firms may encounter difficulty in identifying the HS code at a very disaggregate level, that is at the HS 6-digit level. The difficulty becomes more serious for firms with limited experience of international trade and/or new products. The problem can become even more severe because of the fast changes in HS versions (from 2002 to 2007 and now 2012). Mismatching can cause delays in port clearance.

Last, there is no guarantee that the c/o issued by an exporting country's government will be fully recognised by customs officials in the importing FTA counterpart. In some cases, the customs officials of the FTA counterpart might request for additional information to ensure that products comply with the RoO. This can make firms reluctant to share information, especially on the local-content RoO type, and be further burdened by documentation.

Jongwanich and Kohpaiboon (2017) analyse the determinants of FTA utilisation using administrative records of FTA implementation at the product level from Thai exporters. Their results show that the cost of complying with RoO averages out at around 8.6 percent of tariff equivalence. The cost varies across countries. The lowest figure is close to zero and found among developed countries. The cost is substantially higher for developing countries. In some cases, such as Viet Nam and China, the cost estimate reaches double digits at 12.6 percent and 14.1 percent, respectively.[10]

Box A

Determinants of the FTA utilisation of Thai exporting firms

Jongwanich and Kohpaiboon (2017) examine how exporters actually responded to the FTA preferential schemes, analysing administrative records of FTA implementation at the product level from Thai exporters. Interestingly, the inter-product, cross-country econometric analysis is performed in this study with FTA utilisation as the dependent variable. It is calculated at the HS 4-digit level. The key determinants for firms for applying preferential schemes are tariff margins, the ability to comply with RoOs, and the economic fundamentals driving trade, such as those measured by prior-actual export values and trade under the production networks of multinationals. The econometric analysis covers the period 2006–2015. The analysis covers eight major partners as tariff cuts under the corresponding FTAs covered more than 80 percent for the period before 2010. The partners are Australia (2006), Indonesia (2006), Malaysia (2006), the Philippines (2006), Viet Nam (2006), Japan (2007), China (2010) and Korea (2010).

As the dependent variable is censored, i.e. we do not observe values of less than zero (the left censoring) and greater than 100 percent (the right censoring), random-effect Tobit (weighted maximum likelihood) estimator is used to obtain unbiased, consistent, and efficient estimates. The statistical significance of the tariff margins suggests that applying for such tariff concessions is costly to a certain extent. Companies whose products have a high local content are likely to apply for FTA preferential schemes. The statistical significance of prior-actual export values points to the fact that products must be traded substantially before applying to become involved in an FTA, i.e. in the pre-signing FTA period, to ensure that FTA export creation is considerable. It is relatively unlikely that joining an FTA will open up significant, new export opportunities for companies whose products either are previously untraded or involve relatively low sales volumes. While tariff margins could influence a firm's decision to employ FTAs, their influence is more likely to come into play once sound economic fundamentals underlying trade have already been established. There is no statistical difference between products traded under MNE production networks and other manufacturing products in terms of the decision to apply for entry into FTA preferential schemes. As long as there are adequate tariff margins to cover the costs incurred by the RoOs, and the economic fundamentals are supportive, these products can be traded through preferential schemes like FTAs.

In this study, the estimated cost of complying with RoOs averages around 8.6 percent of tariff equivalence. The lowest figure is close to zero and found among developed countries. The cost is substantially high for developing countries. In some cases, such as Viet Nam and China, the cost estimate reaches double digits, at 12.6 percent and 14.1 percent, respectively.

Source: Jongwanich and Kohpaiboon (2017)

6.6 Conclusions and policy recommendations

This chapter presented analysis on the use of FTAs in Thailand between 2006 and 2015 in order to shed light on the ongoing negotiations of the RCEP. It examined the official records of the preferential trade (both exports and imports) of Thai firms, together with other primary and secondary relevant information. The analysis focussed solely on the impact of FTA preferential tariffs on trade.

The key finding is that while c/o records significantly increased over the period in consideration, their value remained less than one-third of total trade. The AFTA and its successor, the AEC, accounted for the largest share. Nonetheless, the relative importance of ASEAN declined noticeably due to the faster growth of Japan and China. Newer FTAs on the top of existing ones have not been much utilised. Firms prefer to apply preferential trade through the TAFTA, TNZFTA and JTEPA to the AANZFTA and ASEAN–Japan FTAs.

The products often traded under an FTA preferential trade scheme are highly concentrated in a few product categories. On the export side (Thailand's exports to FTA partners), automotive products (both vehicles and auto parts), electrical appliances, petrochemical products, and processed foods are the top products. Firms in these sectors are generally large in size and their products have a high level of local content. In contrast, Thailand's preferential imports from its FTA partners are usually perishable/unprocessed agricultural products and basic manufacturing intermediates. Preferential trade of such products is unlikely to be constrained by any form of RoO. In addition, the relative importance of raw materials/intermediates found in the top-15 preferential import items explain why the utilisation rate on the import side is generally lower than that on the export side. Raw materials/intermediates are eligible for tariff exemption schemes that have long been available for export businesses, so business persons have many options for bypassing tariffs in addition to applying for FTA preferential trade schemes.

Another interesting finding, in both export and import analyses, is that the top-15 items usually record a high tariff margin (the gap between the MFN and FTA preferential tariff rates). This indicates the presence of costs incurred by firms when applying for a c/o. The procedure for obtaining a c/o is rather long and cumbersome for newcomers in the international trade business. In many cases, requests to declare detailed information on the production process discourage firms from using FTAs. Other problems also discourage firms – these include policy discretion, which occurs in many steps for obtaining a c/o; difficulty in identifying the HS code at the highly disaggregate level; and uncertainty that the c/o issued by the exporting countries' government will be fully recognised by customs officials in the importing FTA counterpart country.

At least two policy inferences can be drawn from this study. First, while the use of FTAs by Thai firms suggests that the RCEP has the potential to promote trade among members, the negotiations must focus on the problems of the already existing agreements, such as sizeable exclusion lists in which trade liberalisation has yet to begin, deterrents as a result of RoO, and protectionism practices at the border. Enhancement of coordination among customs officers to minimise any protectionism practices at the border is another example of what to be focussed in an FTA, such as the RCEP.

Second, the scope of the negotiations of the RCEP should go beyond opening up trade in goods. This is derived from the finding that many of the RCEP members already signed FTAs with each other with emphasis on trade liberalisation in goods. More importantly, these signed FTAs were in place for a certain period though there are remaining challenges to be resolved as mentioned earlier. Hence, additional gains in terms of goods market liberalisation in RCEP negotiation over the existing FTAs would be negligible. It is several areas of services liberalisation that yet discussed but could bring in mutual benefits for all members and indirectly facilitate trade and investment among the RCEP members.

Acknowledgements

The authors benefited greatly from the research work, entitled *FTAs and Thai Manufacturing*, financed by the Thailand Research Fund.

Notes

1 Further details are available at www.wto.org/english/tratop_e/region_e/region_e.htm.
2 Arguably, utilisation might not be an appropriate indicator for the success of FTAs if the signed FTAs are expected to be a catalyst for unilateral liberalisation. The more FTAs are signed, the less the need for cross-border trade barriers. This would induce a country to eventually remove barriers. In this case, FTA utilisation would be zero. This would be the ultimate target. In the meantime, however, FTA utilisation remains relevant as an indicator of whether a signed FTA is effective for policymakers.
3 There are also many empirical studies examining the effect of FTAs on trade through quantitative analyses like computable general equilibrium (CGEs) and the gravity equation. Their analyses use aggregate trade data under the assumption that all trade transactions applied for FTA tariff preferential schemes.
4 For example, Hayakawa et al. (2013) argue that Japanese affiliates in Singapore are the most active in using FTAs. Kawai and Wignaraja (2011) find the opposite. The contradictory results are also found in other studies undertaking the questionnaire survey. Other examples by JETRO (2007) and Kawai and Wignaraja (2011) *show* that about 30 percent of their samples thought that multiple ROOs in East Asian FTAs complicated procedures for proving the country of origin, which led to increased business costs. The corresponding percentage in Takahashi and Urata (2008) is only 5 percent.
5 The possible exception would be the Thailand–European Union (EU) FTA, which replaced the ASEAN–EU FTA as a consequence of unresolved issues about Myanmar during the negotiations. Since May 2014 the Thailand–EU FTA has been stalled as the EU has expressed reluctance to have further negotiations with the junta.
6 There is an ongoing debate on what the appropriate denominator in calculating the ratio should be when the overall assessment of FTAs is concerned. See Appendix 1 for a full discussion.
7 Note that there was a significant drop in 2015. This development should be noted for further investigation in the future.

8 The firm interview performed in this study was based on a rather small sample as the main purpose of the interview was to document problems firms actually face.
9 The cost is about B1,500–B2,000 (US$50–US$75) per FTA for the new users and B300–B500 (10–17 US dollar) per FTA for returned users. This is regardless of the shipment's dollar value.
10 See more details about this study in Box A.
11 This is based on the interview with the Department of Foreign Affairs and Trade, Australia conducted by the authors on 5 June 2013 in Canberra.
12 See details at http://europa.eu/rapid/press-release_MEMO-13-179_en.htm.

References

Athukorala, P. and A. Kohpaiboon (2012), 'Australian-Thai Trade: Has the FTA Made a Difference?', *Australian Economic Review* 44(4): 457–67.

Channel New Asia (2016), 'More Firms Setting Up Regional Headquarters in Singapore Even as Others Relocate', available at www.channelnewsasia.com/news/singapore/more-firms-setting-up/2566738.html.

Hayakawa, K., D. Hiratsuka, K. Shiino and S. Sukegawa (2013), 'Who Uses Free Trade Agreements?', *Asian Economic Journal*, 27(3): 245–64.

JETRO (2007), *FY 2006 Survey of Japanese Firms' International Operations*, Japan External Trade Organization (JETRO), Tokyo.

Jongwanich, J. and A. Kohpaiboon (2007), 'Determinants of Protection in Thai Manufacturing', *Economic Papers*, 26(3): 276–94.

Jongwanich, J. and A. Kohpaiboon (2017), 'Exporter Responses to FTA Tariff Preferences: Evidence from Thailand', *Asia Pacific Economic Literature*, 31(1): 21–38.

Jongwanich, J. and A. Kohpaiboon (2010) 'Determinants of Protection in Thai Manufacturing', *Economic Papers: A journal of applied economics and policy*, 26(3), 276–294.

Kawai, M. and G. Wignaraja (2011), *Asia's Free Trade Agreements: How is Business Responding?* Cheltenham: Edward Elgar.

Kohpaiboon, A. (2006), *Multinational Enterprises and Industrial Transformation: Evidence from Thailand*. Cheltenham: Edward Elgar.

Kohpaiboon, A. and J. Jongwanich (2013), 'International Production Network, Clusters and Industrial Upgrading: Evidence from Automotive and Hard Disk Drive Industries', *Review of Policy Research* 30(2): 211–239.

Kohpaiboon, A. and J. Jongwanich (2015), 'Use of FTAs from Thai Experience', *ERIA Discussion Paper*, 2015-02, Economic Research Institute of ASEAN and East Asia (ERIA), Jakarta.

Kohpaiboon, A., A. Tanasritunyakul, and P. Jongwattanakul (2015), 'Thailand and FTAs', Research Paper submitted to Thailand Research Fund, Bangkok (in Thai).

Patunru, A. and S. Rahardja (2015), 'Trade Protectionism in Indonesia: Bad Times and Bad Policy', Lowy Institute for International Policy, available at www.lowyinstitute.org/files/patunru_and_rahardja_trade_protectionism_in_indonesia_0.pdf.

Plummer, M., D. Cheong and S. Hamanaka (2010), *Methodology for Impact Assessment of Free Trade Agreements*. Manila: Asian Development Bank (ADB).

Sally, R. (2007), 'Thai Trade Policy: From Non-discriminatory Liberalisation to FTAs', *World Economy*, 30(10): 1594–1620.

Takahashi, K. and S. Urata (2008), 'On the Use of FTAs by Japanese Firms', *RIETI Discussion Paper* No. 08-E-002.

Appendix 1

How to measure FTA utilisation

Calculating FTA utilisation at the product level (HS 2, 4, or 6-digits) is rather straightforward. It becomes controversial when the overall assessment of an FTA is concerned. There is disagreement whether the denominator when calculating the FTA utilisation should be the total value or the value of non-zero tariff items only. Consider the assessment on the export side. On the one hand, there are many items with tariffs that are already zero. For these items, firms have no incentive to use FTAs. Including them in the denominator would underestimate the FTA utilisation. Hence, it would be more appropriate to use non-zero tariff item values in the denominator. This method is popular among many policy-makers[11] and referred to as the FTA utility rate by Plummer et al. (2010).

On the other hand, there are at least three reasons against the use of non-zero tariff items in the denominator. First, in every FTA negotiation, the potential trade highlighted in the press is based on the total trade. An example is the European Union–Thailand FTA press release, which refers to total trade between the two partners worth 32 billion Euro.[12] If non-zero tariff trade were to be considered, the trade value would be much lower because the external tariffs of European countries are already low. Second, negotiation in designing RoOs is done in all HS items regardless of their existing MFN tariff. If zero-tariff items are not relevant for FTA use, RoO negotiations should focus on non-zero-tariff items only. Finally, the appropriate definition of non-zero-tariff items remains unclear when other tariff exemption schemes exist. A clear example is an export processing zone, where tariffs of inputs used for export can be exempted. As the argument in favour of using only non-zero-tariff items goes, such exempted items should be excluded from the denominator. However, it is very difficult to exclude them in practice as it is not clear how much import values are subject to tariff exemption schemes. All in all, in this study, the denominator used in calculating the FTA utilisation is the total value where zero tariff items values are included.

7 How restrictive are ASEAN's Rules of Origin?

Olivier Cadot and Lili Yan Ing

7.1 Introduction

Two major trends characterise the world trading system today. On the one hand, it is increasingly structured by preferential trade agreements (PTAs), of which there are close to having a new one almost every month (Calvo-Pardo et al., 2009). On the other hand, international trade has increasingly involved 'trade in tasks' within global value chains (GVCs). Rules of origin (RoOs) stand in the middle of these two major trends and have the potential to make them incompatible because they constrain the sourcing choices of multinational firms along regional patterns dictated by existing PTAs, whereas GVC optimisation may call for different choices. One of the challenges of multilateralising regionalism – an expression coined by Baldwin (2006) – is to prevent RoOs from working at cross purposes with the rise of GVCs.

The issues are salient in East Asia and the Pacific, where regionalism is a relatively recent phenomenon (Kimura, 2010) but is spreading rapidly. Since the creation of the Association of Southeast Asian Nations (ASEAN) Free Trade Area (AFTA) in 1992, the drive for regional trade liberalisation has accelerated, in particular after the Asian currency crisis of the late 1990s. Although the tariff-elimination schedule was more progressive in ASEAN than, for instance, in the North American Free Trade Agreement (NAFTA), it proceeded largely on time, and tariff elimination between the six founding members[1] was largely completed by 2010, only two years after the scheduled date, and covered over 90 percent of intra-bloc trade (Calvo-Pardo et al., 2009). ASEAN+3 and ASEAN+6 initiatives have gained momentum with their upgrading to the so-called 'track-1' level (government-to-government). Last, the Trans-Pacific Partnership (TPP), initiated in 2006 by Brunei Darussalam, Chile New Zealand and Singapore as the 'Pacific-4', gained considerable momentum and visibility with President Obama's 2011 announcement that the US would join (in September 2008, the US first announced it would join the negotiations in early 2009) before President Trump reversed the US's position. Given that most-favoured-nation (MFN) tariffs are still substantial in at least some of the member countries, tariff preference margins can make a difference.

DOI: 10.4324/9780429433603-7

Compared to other regional blocs, particularly in the South, East Asian and trans-Pacific regionalism have several distinguishing features. NAFTA and the European Union (EU) association/partnership agreements have been arguably of a hegemonic nature; for instance, the EU's Association Agreements with some of its Mediterranean partners mandate the harmonisation of non-tariff measures (NTMs) on EU standards; similarly, RoOs in both NAFTA and the EU's Paneuro system have been largely dictated by the Northern partner (the US and EU, respectively). They were also characterised by strong hub-and-spoke trade structures. In contrast, East Asian/Pacific regionalism brings together a multipolar region with several economic and political heavyweights, including Japan, China and the US, and a number of midsize but politically sophisticated partners like the Republic of Korea (henceforth, Korea), Australia and New Zealand. Second, and perhaps most important, a large chunk of the region's trade is in manufactured products (particularly electronics) characterised by economies of scale and the prevalence of large firms organised in cross-border value chains. Together, these features imply that the political economy of RoOs is likely to be quite different from that in NAFTA or EU partnerships.

A voluminous literature (for recent surveys, see Cadot et al. (2006a, 2006b), Medalla and Balboa (2009), Kelleher (2013) and the references therein) has looked into the drivers and effects of RoOs in PTAs. In principle, their objective is to prevent 'trade deflection' in the absence of external-tariff harmonisation – imports entering a bloc through the lowest-tariff member and then moving tariff-free within the bloc. However, the literature has also highlighted their power to depress preference uptake by forcing inefficient sourcing and by imposing fixed compliance costs – paperwork and bureaucratic hassle – explaining the low utilisation rates of FTAs, in spite of high tariff-preference margins, as for textiles in the NAFTA. Essentially, the political-economy mechanism behind restrictive RoOs in North-South agreements is twofold. First, costly RoOs are a way of 'denying preferences' granted to Southern producers and hence of relieving the competitive pressures generated within the bloc by tariff phase-outs. That is, when Moroccan shirt producers are forced to procure relatively expensive fabric in the EU preferential zone instead of more price-competitive Asian fabric, one source of their competitiveness is eliminated and they become less of a competitive threat for Portuguese or Italian shirt producers. Second, when a Northern country has a comparative advantage in upstream, capital-intensive sectors – such as weaving in the textiles and apparel sector, or the making of engines in the automobile sector – RoOs create a captive market for those intermediates in the Southern partner where, under bilateral cumulation, assemblers have no choice but to source those intermediates from the Northern (hegemonic) country. While these considerations have no doubt receded in importance over the last decade, they were very much behind the initially complex and restrictive design of product-specific RoOs in both NAFTA and Paneuro.

Given the different patterns of economic and political fundamentals in the East Asia and Pacific region, these political-economy drivers are likely to be weaker, although not necessarily absent. First, as noted by Kimura (2010), neither Japan nor China, the region's heavyweights, has acted as engines of regional integration, as the US and EU did in their respective spheres of influence. Japan, in particular, has not sought to create a Japan-centred hub-and-spoke regional trade bloc. In part, this is because part of the motivation for the US and EU trade preferences with Southern partners – Mexico for the US, and Central Europe and the Mediterranean countries for the EU – was to create 'mini-worlds' where the gains from specialisation could be reaped while at the same time maintaining some degree of trade protection vis-à-vis efficient Asian countries, in particular in the textiles and apparel sector where high MFN tariffs made preferential liberalisation highly relevant.[2] This motivation was much weaker, although not necessarily absent in at least some sectors, for Japan.

Second, although there are no systematic data on firm-level control over GVCs,[3] many of the GVCs in the electronics sector are dominated by large firms that internalise all complementarities in the sector. Such firms have no interest in forcing inefficient sourcing at any stage of processing. Even in the absence of vertical integration, subcontracting relationships are rarely arms-length, and economies of scale are so strong that many components are produced in a handful of establishments serving the entire world market. In such conditions, throwing in RoOs to hurt the competitiveness of some of the downstream assemblers in order to favour others makes little sense.

Thus, there is a prima facie reason to believe that RoOs in the Asia-Pacific region are less susceptible to distortion by special-interest capture than their equivalents in the NAFTA or Paneuro. However, they could still be trade-restricting because they are unnecessarily complex or cumbersome to satisfy, and they can vary across agreements, even for a single country. This is essentially an empirical question that should be settled by statistical analysis. This is what we set out to do in this chapter, using the variation in trade flows across country pairs and products as the identification mechanism to detect any trade-inhibiting effect of RoOs. Our exploration is guided by the gravity equation, the workhorse of much empirical work in international trade. We run a disaggregated gravity equation at the product level (HS 6-digit), controlling for the gravity model's usual determinants as well as tariffs and a vector of dummies marking the presence of each type of product-specific RoOs.

To preview our results, we find that ASEAN's RoOs have significant and quantitatively substantial trade-inhibiting effects. The simple average of the ad valorem equivalent (AVE) of ASEAN's RoOs across instruments and products is 3.40 percent, in line with the estimates in the literature. This means that RoOs inhibit ASEAN's trade by an amount roughly equivalent to a quarter of its MFN tariffs. Put differently, RoOs seem to nullify a quarter of the effect of tariff-preference margins. The trade-weighted average is substantially lower, at 2.09 percent. However, the effect is heterogeneous. While it is small in sectors like electronics or capital equipment, where MFN tariffs are low, so trade is only weakly affected by preferences, it peaks in sectors that matter for the development of ASEAN's poorest Member States, such as fats (6.7 percent), leather products (9 percent), textiles and apparel (8.3 percent), footwear (12.7 percent), and automobiles (6.9 percent). Thus, the streamlining of ASEAN's RoOs should be viewed as part of its own development agenda.

The chapter is organised as follows. Section 7.2 summarises the existing literature on the analysis of RoOs (7.2.1), stylised facts about ASEAN's RoOs (7.2.2) and trade in East Asia and the Pacific (7.2.3), highlighting in particular the prevalence of GVCs in light of recent data on trade in value added. Section 7.3 details the econometric analysis and includes an explanation on the data, estimation strategy and results. Section 7.4 concludes.

7.2 Stylised facts

7.2.1 Rules of origin: how do they work?

While the legal form of RoOs varies, they are essentially local-content requirements imposed on exporters of final goods who want to claim the benefit of preferential tariffs within a trade bloc. In principle, their objective is twofold. First, it is to prevent arbitraging of external tariff differences in free trade agreements (FTAs). This makes them redundant in customs unions, where members share a common external tariff, although even some of these, like the Southern Common Market (Mercosur), have RoOs. Second, it is to prevent superficial assembly operations with little or no value added that would, de facto, extend the benefit of preferential access to non-eligible intermediate producers upstream of those assembly operations.

There are two broad types of RoOs: product-specific rules and regime-wide rules. Product-specific rules specify the minimum degree of local transformation needed to qualify for preferential treatment. They typically take a limited number of legal forms, each of which has advantages and disadvantages for exporters: changes in tariff classification (CTCs), regional value contents (RVCs), or technical requirements (Figure 7.1).

CTCs require that when a final good is produced using intermediates imported from outside the bloc, it may not belong to the same category as those intermediates. The tariff classification is typically the Harmonized System (HS), and the change can be specified at either the chapter level (HS 2-digit, with 99 categories), the heading level (HS 4-digit, with over 1,000 categories), or the subheading level (HS 6-digit, with over 5,000 categories). In principle, the lower the level (HS 2-digit being the highest and HS 6-digit the lowest), the less stringent is the rule, as a jump from a subheading to another may entail a relatively minor transformation compared to a jump from one chapter to another. However, the reality is more complex as the HS has narrower categories for, say, textiles and apparel than for machinery and equipment.

RVCs can take various forms, including a maximum share of imported intermediates in total intermediates or a minimum share of local value added in the product's price. The definition of local value added (inclusion or not of overheads, distribution, etc.) varies across agreements and is typically a subject of bargaining; so is the price definition (ex-works price, i.e. factory-door and wholesale price).

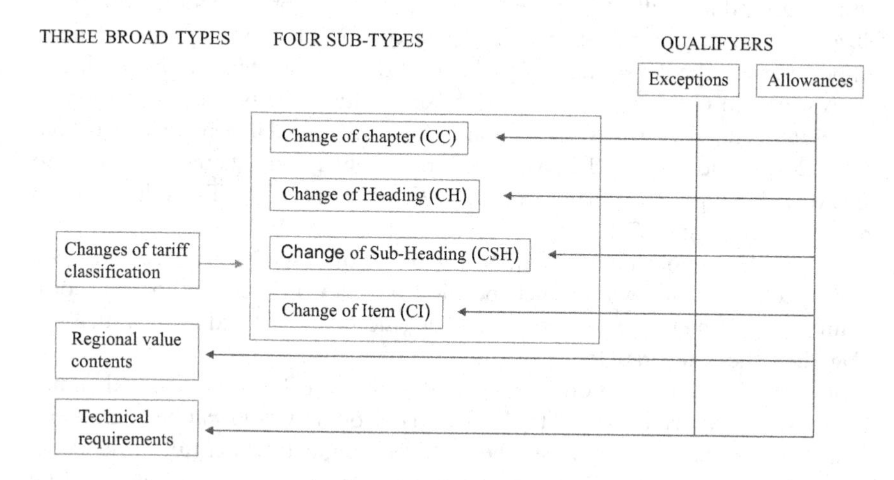

Figure 7.1 Types of Product-Specific RoOs.
Source: Authors' description.

Some rules even used weight as the criterion, although this led to so many distortions that weight-based criteria have largely been eliminated. One extreme case of value content is the 'Wholly Obtained' category, which allows no foreign content at all. Most agricultural products, vegetal or animal, are subject to the Wholly Obtained requirement. Finally, technical requirements can take as many forms as imagination allows, being sometimes tailor-made to benefit narrow interests, as explained in Hirsch (2002) and Chase (2007).[4]

Each product-specific RoO can be qualified by either an exception or an allowance. Exceptions make the rule more stringent. For instance, applied to a change of tariff subheading, an exception can specify that if a final product belonging to subheading *x* is assembled from imported intermediates, then those must come from any subheading other than *x*, except *z*. By contrast, allowances relax the stringency of RoOs.

Regime-wide rules – essentially cumulation rules, the other ones being of secondary importance – specify the treatment of intermediates imported from other countries in the same bloc or countries with special status in terms of cumulation. There are three broad types of cumulation: bilateral, diagonal, and full. Under bilateral cumulation (a clause that applies only to bilateral FTAs), if an exporter from Country *A* exports to Country *B*, only intermediates from *A* or *B* count as local. Under diagonal cumulation, in an FTA between *A*, *B*, and *C*, when exporting to *B*, *A* can count intermediates from *C* as local. Full cumulation is the most complicated, in particular in the case of a multistage production process. Consider an FTA between three countries, *A*, *B* and *C*, and the following production process. A firm in Country *A* imports 25 US dollar of intermediate products from the rest of the world (ROW) and does a first transformation involving 25 US dollar of local value added. The firm then exports the resulting product, still an intermediate one, to *B* for a price of 50 US dollar. In *B*, another firm again transforms it, adding 10 US dollar more of intermediates imported from the ROW and 40 US dollar of value added. Finally, the product is re-exported to *C* at a price of 100 US dollar. Assume that between the intermediates imported from the ROW to *A* and the transformed intermediate exported from *A* to *B*, there is no CTC, whereas between the intermediates imported into *B* and the final good exported from *B* to *C*, there is a CTC. The value chain is represented in Figure 7.2.

In order to understand the interplay of product-specific and regime-wide RoOs, consider now two product-specific RoOs, a CTC and a 60 percent local content requirement, and two regime-wide rules, diagonal and full cumulation. Together, these generate four cases.

Suppose first that the product-specific RoO is a CTC. Under diagonal cumulation, when exported from *B* to *C*, the final product would *not* be eligible because the first stage fails to satisfy the CTC requirement. Under full cumulation, in contrast, the entire value of intermediates imported from *A* to *B* would be counted as local; therefore, only the CTC at the second stage would count, and as it is satisfied, the final product exported to *C* would satisfy the RoO.

Suppose now that the product-specific RoO is a 60 percent local value content requirement. Under diagonal cumulation, the eligible local content would be 40 US dollar (the last transformation) out of a sales price of 100 US dollar, which does not pass the mark. Under full cumulation, in contrast, the eligible local content would be 40 US dollar + 25 US dollar, or 65 US dollar, which would pass the mark. The final product would then be eligible.

Thus, mechanically, full cumulation is less stringent than diagonal cumulation. However, in practice, proving compliance with full-cumulation rules

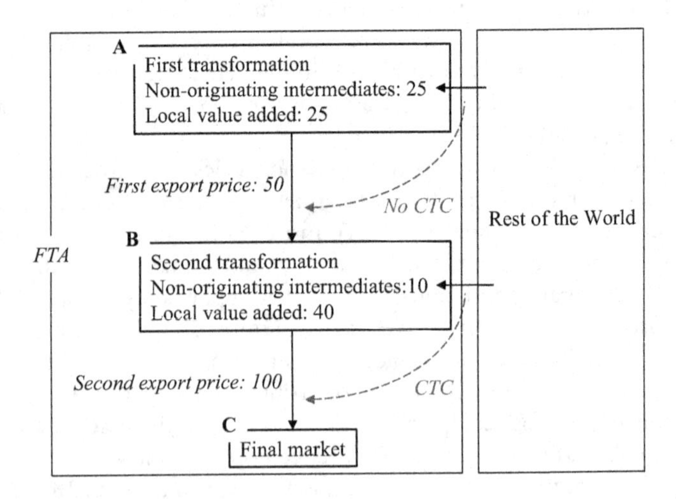

Figure 7.2 A Representative Value Chain with Cumulation.
Source: Authors' description.

implies complete traceability of the production process and sourcing of intermediates. This is a heavy burden for many companies, both in terms of paperwork and – more importantly – in terms of disclosure of sensitive price and supplier information. As such, some firms prefer not to use full cumulation, despite its advantages on paper.

RoOs also raise potentially difficult issues in terms of legal liability. If certificates of origin are issued by officials in the exporting country, there has to be mutual recognition of those certificates of origin, which is not always the case when customs administrations distrust each other. Alternatively, the ultimate importing country, in our example Country *C*, may take importer local-content declarations at face value, as they do with product valuation. But, if fraud is later uncovered, the importer will be held liable and will be expected to turn against his own suppliers at his own expense. As this would involve actioning foreign jurisdictions in the exporting country with uncertain prospects for redress, the importer will typically not pass on the preferential tariff reduction to his suppliers, either keeping it as 'legal insurance' or forsaking altogether the benefit of preferential treatment. In both cases, the objective of the preferential tariff reduction will be missed.

7.2.2 *The trade effects of RoOs: what do we know?*

Assessing the impact of RoOs means establishing a causal relationship between a measure of RoOs and a measure of trade performance. All three (measuring RoOs, measuring trade performance, and establishing causation) involve difficult issues.

The modern analysis of RoOs goes back to the measurement work of Estevadeordal (2000), who coded NAFTA's product-specific rules and aggregated them into a restrictiveness index. Index values were assigned on the basis of logic; for instance, CTCs were classified as increasingly stringent as one goes up the hierarchy of HS categories (that is, a change of heading had a higher index value than a change of subheading). Technical requirements were ranked highest in terms of restrictiveness because – as already argued – they are often deliberately cumbersome to satisfy. Similar indices have been constructed since then by Australia's Productivity Commission (2004), Anson et al. (2005) and Harris (2007), involving variants from Estevadeordal's method. Estevadeordal treats the Wholly Obtained requirement as the most stringent. However, it is typically applied to agricultural products, for which it is not binding. Anson et al. (2005), in contrast, code it as least stringent. This difference of treatment illustrates the notion that the stringency of a given RoO depends on which sector it applies to, an issue to which we will later return.

As for the dependent variable, ideally one would like to have data on shipments by regime (MFN versus preferential). However, preference-utilisation data are sometimes taken by governments – although without much rationale – as confidential and sensitive. Thus, the performance measure is often taken as the relative trade flows – the trade flows in a pair of countries affected by the

RoO versus those in a pair not affected, under the assumption that stiff RoOs will not just make the utilisation of preferences redundant but that they will also stifle trade itself by denying preferences. That is, ceteris paribus, a stringent RoO acts like a reduction in the tariff-preference margin and, thus, reduces trade flows.

Given the data constraints on the dependent variable, identification is often roundabout. One would want to equate RoOs with a 'treatment' and compare treated trade flows with untreated ones by using standard approaches like difference-in-differences. Part of the literature has taken that route. Other approaches, particularly when utilisation-rate data are available, have instead relied on a revealed preference argument. That is, suppose that firm compliance costs are distributed around some central value corresponding to the average firm. Suppose that the tariff preference margin for a certain product and country pair is 5 percent. If the rate of preference utilisation is 100 percent, it must be that all firms have RoO compliance costs below 5 percent; then 5 percent can be taken as an upper bound on the AVE of the average compliance cost. If the utilisation rate is 0 percent, it must be that all firms have compliance costs above 5 percent, so 5 percent gives a lower bound of the compliance cost's AVE. Finally, if the utilisation rate is somewhere between 0 and 100, it must be that some firms have more than 5 percent compliance costs, while others have less. One can then take 5 percent as the best approximation for the average compliance cost.

Using this revealed-preference approach, Herin (1986) estimates the compliance costs of EU RoOs for Central European countries at 5 percent; Cadot et al. (2005) find 2 percent for NAFTA. Manchin and Pelkmans-Balaoing (2007) note that the AFTA utilisation rate was on average only 5 percent and attribute this low uptake to RoO and other documentation requirements. They also find threshold effects in tariff-preference margins (only at high levels did they affect trade), again suggestive of compliance costs offsetting the benefit of tariff reductions. Brenton and Manchin (2003) and others note similarly low utilisation rates for EU preferences, but the issue was muddled in the case of the EU by the large number of overlapping schemes, which depressed the uptake for each one taken in isolation, while EU preferences, as a whole, had a high combined uptake (Candau and Jean, 2005).

Using econometric approaches instead, Francois et al. (2006) estimate compliance costs at 4 percent and Cadot et al. at 6.5 percent. Beyond averages, Cadot et al. (2006a), Estevadeordal (2000) and Estevadeordal and Suominen (2008) find that RoO restrictiveness is typically higher in sectors also characterised by tariff peaks. Portugal-Perez (2009) decomposes NAFTA's RoOs into a component reflecting traditional trade-deflection concerns (proxied by the tariff differential between the US and Mexico) and political-economy interference, and finds that the latter raised the compliance costs of RoOs on average by 4.5 percentage points. Most recently, Kelleher (2013) modifies Harris' restrictiveness index to take cumulation rules into account. She proxies the facilitation effect of cumulation rules by the economic size of the cumulation zone (the share of the zone's combined gross domestic products (GDPs) in world GDP) and finds a significant and sizeable trade-inhibiting effect associated with higher values of her modified restrictiveness index, in particular in the textiles and apparel sector.

7.2.3 ASEAN's tariffs and RoOs

7.2.3.1 MFN and preferential tariffs

RoOs can be binding only when tariff-preference margins are substantial, which in turn requires the presence of sufficiently large MFN tariffs. ASEAN has made rapid progress in the phasing out of preferential tariffs – except for Cambodia and, to a lesser extent, Viet Nam (Figure 7.3) – so the tariff-preference margins are essentially the MFN rates. These rates are not negligible, implying that tariff-preference margins are substantial and confer benefits to exporters, justifying the choice of the preferential regime even in the presence of compliance costs.

Decomposing MFN tariffs by sector, Table 7.1 shows, on the basis of the limited availability of tariffs from the multilateral TRAINS database, that ASEAN Member States have substantial MFN tariffs, in particular on sensitive sectors like food and beverages (HS 4), textiles and apparel (HS 11), footwear

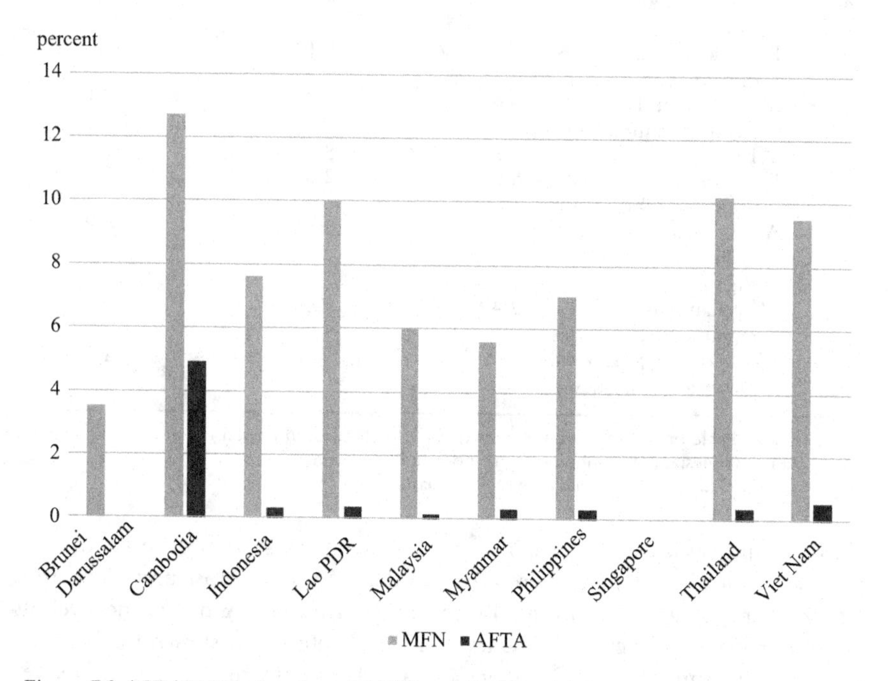

Figure 7.3 ASEAN Member States' MFN and Preferential Average Tariffs.

Note: Brunei Darussalam, Cambodia, Indonesia, Malaysia and the Philippines use 2015 data. The rest use 2017 data.

Source: Authors' calculations using TRAINS database.

Table 7.1 ASEAN's Average MFN Tariffs by HS Section

Section	*Summary Description*	*Brunei*	*Indonesia*	*Philippines*	*Singapore*	*Viet Nam*
1	Live animals; animal products	–	5.05	10.78	–	13.46
2	Vegetable products	–	5.08	9.41	–	15.94
3	Animal or vegetable fats	–	4.28	5.91	–	10.61
4	Food and beverages	0.08	6.76	11.57	–	28.78
5	Mineral products	–	3.79	2.53	–	4.47
6	Products of the chemical or allied industries	0.46	5.02	3.07	–	2.93
7	Plastic and articles thereof; rubber and articles thereof	1.71	8.3	7.26	–	9.09
8	Leather and leather products	1.22	5.25	6.53	–	11.33
9	Wood and articles of wood	12.09	3.49	7.72	–	7.98
10	Pulp and paper	–	4.0	5.14	–	12.2
11	Textiles and apparel	0.5	10.47	10.44	–	12
12	Footwear	5.31	14.61	10.86	–	28.51
13	Cement, glass, and stone	0.49	7.88	7.32	–	18.81
14	Precious metals and stones	2.26	6.13	4.91	–	8.79
15	Base metals and articles of base metal	0.05	6.87	5.19	–	7.07
16	Machinery and electrical equipment	9.6	5.45	2.74	–	5.15
17	Vehicles	3.32	9.16	8.92	–	17.57
18	Precision instruments, optics, watchmaking	8.22	5.77	2.85	–	6.2
19	Arms and ammunition; parts and accessories thereof	–	6.05	13.47	–	4.86
20	Miscellaneous manufactured articles	2.47	9.8	7.44	–	19.24
21	Works of art, collectors' pieces and antiques	–	6.19	7.86	–	4.29

Note: Data available on WITS from the TRAINS multilateral tariff databases include only Brunei Darussalam, Indonesia, the Philippines, Singapore and Viet Nam.
Source: Authors' calculations using TRAINS database.

(HS 12) and vehicles (HS 17). These are all sensitive sectors in terms of employment but also sectors where cross-border GVCs are most prevalent, and hence where RoOs can substantially constrain firms. Going down one level of disaggregation, the picture at the level of HS chapters (not shown for brevity) is largely the same. Except for Singapore and Brunei Darussalam, which have very low MFN tariffs, the number of zero-rated chapters is relatively low. Out of 98 chapters, Brunei has 68, Indonesia just one, the Philippines none, Singapore 96 and Viet Nam 6.

7.2.3.2 Rules of origin (RoOs)

ASEAN's RoOs have a relatively simple structure compared to, say, the NAFTA or Paneuro, as they are largely based on a 40 percent RVC requirement. Moreover, in many cases, the importer can choose which rule to use between two. However, behind the relatively simple logical structure, there is substantial variation at the product level.

The most prevalent combination of instruments at the product level is a choice between RVC at 40 percent and a change of tariff heading (HS at 4-digit level). This concerns 11,764 product lines in all of ASEAN's trade (internal and bilateral with preferential partners), or 37.74 percent of the product lines. Another 6 percent of the lines give the importer the choice between the same RVC and a change of tariff subheading (HS 6-digit level).

7.2.4 Trade patterns in the Asia-Pacific region

As background, in order to give a feel for the importance of ASEAN's preferential trade as a share of the region's overall imports, Figure 7.4 presents the value of ASEAN's imports from its main trading partners in 2000 and 2017.

The various main trading partners (with whom ASEAN has preferential agreements) thus represent a substantial chunk of ASEAN's imports, underscoring the potential impact of preferential rules. As already discussed, one of the key issues raised by the presence of RoOs in PTAs is that they mandate a minimum degree of local transformation in order to grant tariff preferences, while, in many sectors, the degree of local transformation of intermediate products is determined by multinational companies on the basis of technology and country fundamentals. This is a particularly serious issue for electronics value chains in the East Asia and Pacific region, where local content can sometimes represent a very thin slice of the overall value generated along the chain.

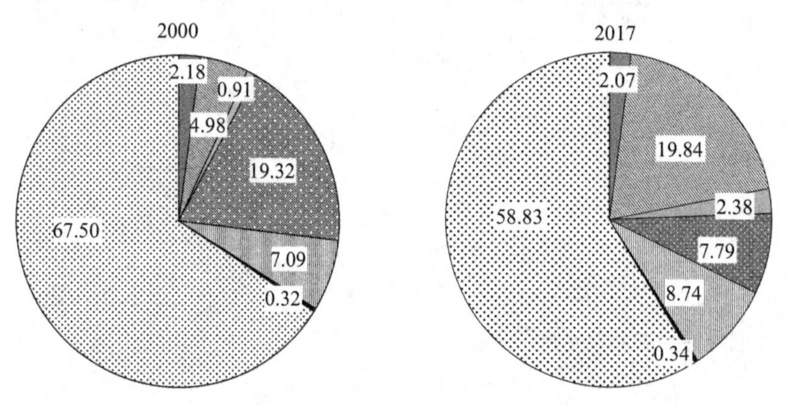

Figure 7.4 ASEAN's Total Imports from Its Main Trading Partners (in percent).
Source: Authors' calculations based on WITS-Comtrade database, 2000 and 2017.

In the case of the iPod's GVC, the trade-inhibiting potential of the RoOs is not as severe as one might expect. First, global electronics companies lobbied the governments of large industrial countries in the 1990s to lower tariffs to practically zero on most electronics products and, in particular, on components, precisely in order to make RoOs irrelevant, knowing that they would be incompatible with the organisation of production. This lobbying effort led to the signing of the World Trade Organization's Information Technology Agreement (ITA) by 29 countries at the Singapore Ministerial in 1996 and the subsequent phasing out of tariffs on the majority of electronics products.[5] In the case of ASEAN countries, MFN tariffs are zero-rated on computers and most electronics products, but some positive rates linger on. Figure 7.5 shows the distribution of MFN tariff rates for Chapters 84–86, which comprise all machinery and electronics products, both industrial and consumer, for the three ASEAN members with data for which MFN tariffs are substantially above zero: Indonesia, the Philippines and Viet Nam.

Second, a significant chunk of China's iPod exports goes to the US and EU, where ASEAN RoOs do not apply. Even those shipped to Japan are affected only by the ASEAN-Japan rules rather than AFTA's.

Beyond the special case of the electronics sector, what is the evidence on the importance of domestic versus foreign content in exports? The evidence can

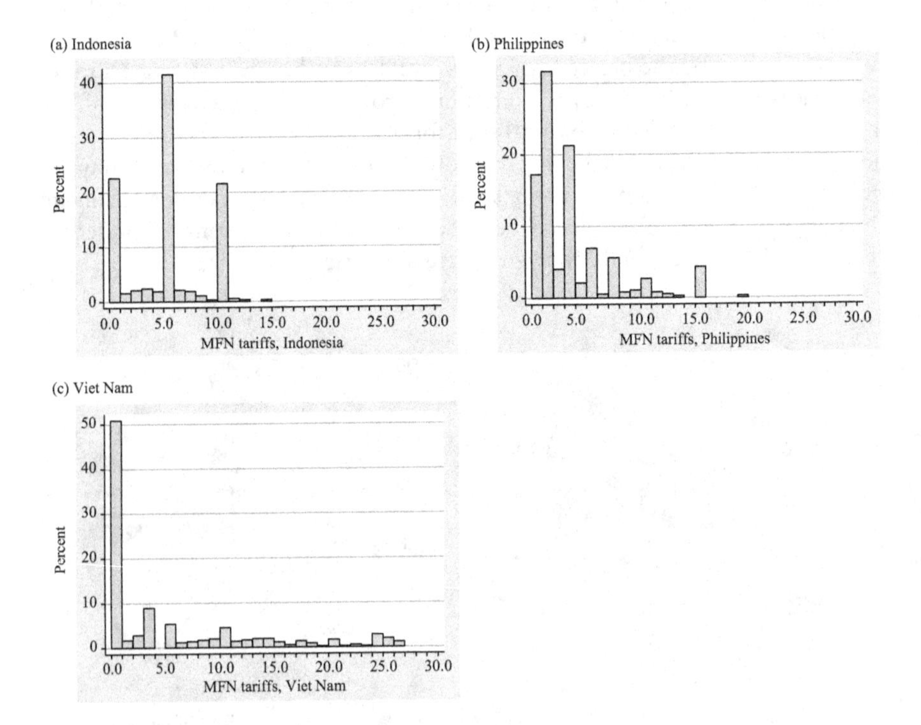

Figure 7.5 Distribution of MFN Tariffs in Chapters 84–86 (Machinery and Electronics Products).

Source: Authors' estimation.

only be fragmentary given that the calculation of foreign content requires the combination of trade data with detailed input-output data, which are currently not available. However, Johnson and Noguera (2010) and Koopman et al. (2011) have recently calculated the value-added content of exports using innovative methodologies. Intuitively, one would expect the share of domestic content in exports to rise with the level of economic development, as low-income and lower-middle-income countries tend to confine their participation in GVCs to superficial assembly. This conjecture has been used in policy debates about the reform of RoOs in the EU to justify relaxed RVC levels for least-developed countries. Johnson and Noguera's (2010) calculations for 56 countries show that this conjecture does not seem to stand to scrutiny for the sample of countries covered, as the average domestic content of exports shrinks instead of rises with the level of income.

However, this result should be interpreted very cautiously as it may change when the sample is enlarged to include least developed countries. Also, it may be a composition effect, with at least some lower-middle-income countries in the sample exporting relatively more agricultural products while upper-middle income countries export more electronics and other products in which assembly represents a very thin slice.

Figure 7.6, constructed using data from Koopman et al. (2011), gives prima facie evidence of how constraining ASEAN's RoOs (for example RVC) could be by plotting the average foreign content of exports for countries in Koopman et al.'s sample. With a 40 percent RVC, the foreign content of exports should be no more than 60 percent. Koopman et al. do not calculate the regional value added in gross exports, only the domestic versus foreign (all origins, including both regional and non-regional). So, only foreign content widely in excess of 60 percent

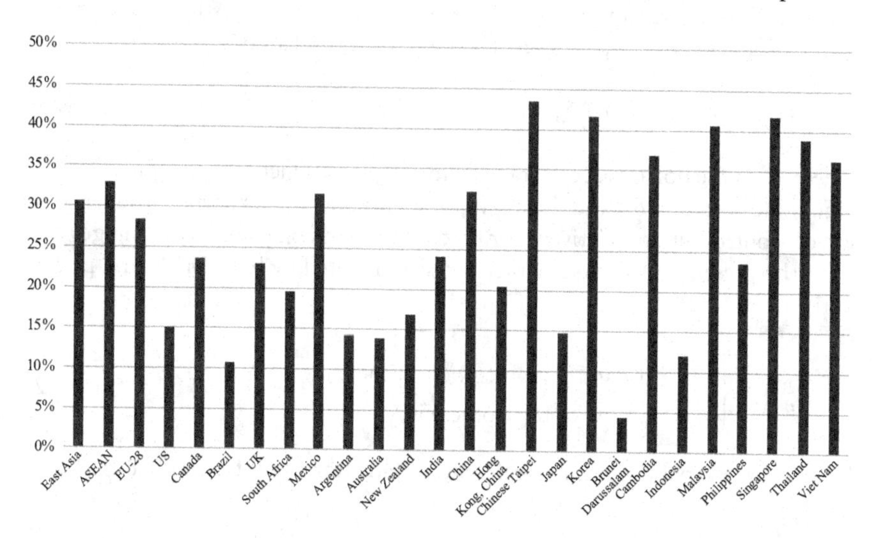

Figure 7.6 Foreign Content of Exports, by Exporting Country.
Source: Adapted from Koopman et al. (2011).

would put a country's exports at risk of violating the 40 percent RVC. Figure 7.6 shows that for most of ASEAN's Member States for which data are available, the foreign content of exports is less than 60 percent, suggesting that prima facie, ASEAN's RoOs should not be overly constraining.

Thus, prima facie evidence suggests that RoOs should be only moderately constraining of ASEAN's trade. But this evidence can hide substantial effects once the sectoral composition of trade is taken into account. Moreover, the bureaucratic hassle of proving compliance may be perceived by companies to be a burden. Only econometric analysis, controlling for various possible confounding influences, can give a response.

7.3 Econometric analysis

7.3.1 Data and estimation

RoO data in the form of precise requirements at the HS 6-digit level of product classification were provided to us by the ASEAN Secretariat. Trade data in thousand US dollars are from the Center for Prospective Studies and International Information (CEPII)'s International Trade database called BACI, which is based on COMTRADE then reconciling data of direct exports and mirrored—imports. The gravity variables are from the CEPII's free-access online database.

Our estimation strategy is based on the ubiquitous gravity equation, but we estimate it at a disaggregated (product) level, which requires some adjustment in the formulation of the estimation equation. Appendix 1 derives our estimation equation from the standard Anderson-van Wincoop (2004) framework after relaxing key symmetry assumptions about production costs and trade costs. That is, we allow for variation in those costs across products and estimate the gravity at the product-country-pair level. The baseline formulation is:

$$\ln v_{ijk} = \beta \ln \tau_{ijk} + \delta_{jk} + \delta_{ik} + u_{ijk} \tag{7.1}$$

where v_{ijk} is the dollar value of trade from i to j in product k; τ_{ijk} is a product-specific trade cost; and δ_{jk} and δ_{ik} are importer-product and exporter-product fixed effects controlling, respectively, for preferences and comparative advantage.

In the presence of RTAs, market access is affected by both MFN and preferential tariffs. Let

$$I_{ij}^{\text{RTA}} = \begin{cases} 1 & \text{if } i \text{ and } j \text{ are members of the same RTA} \\ 0 & \text{otherwise} \end{cases} \tag{7.2}$$

be a dummy variable marking preferential trade (for any RTA) and let

$$r_{ijk\ell} = \begin{cases} 1 & \text{if RoO } \ell \text{ applies to product } k \text{ in the agreement between } i \text{ and } j \\ 0 & \text{otherwise} \end{cases} \tag{7.3}$$

where ℓ indexes the various forms of RoOs (CTC, local content, and other forms of rules). Let t_{ijk}^{MFN} be the MFN tariff rate on product k applicable to trade between i and j and let $\mathbf{x}_{ij}$ be a vector of country-pair attributes, such as distance and common language. The trade-cost expression is then

$$\tau_{ijk} = \exp\left[\beta_1 t_{ijk}^{\mathrm{MFN}} + \beta_2\left(I_{ij}^{\mathrm{RTA}} \times t_{ijk}^{\mathrm{MFN}}\right) + \beta_3 I_{ij}^{\mathrm{RTA}} + \sum_{\ell} \beta_{4\ell}\left(I_{ij}^{\mathrm{RTA}} \times r_{ijk\ell}\right) + \mathbf{x}_{ij}\gamma\right]. \quad (7.4)$$

Expressions – represent an 'ideal' formulation that we need to adapt to data constraints. First, we have RoO data only for ASEAN countries and not for other preferential agreements in the world. Therefore, we can hope to disentangle the effects of tariffs from those of RoOs for ASEAN country pairs but not for others.

Accordingly, we mark all country pairs eligible for preferential rules with a single dummy variable defined as in equation (2). Because the value of preferences depends on MFN tariffs (for instance, when MFN tariffs are zero, preferences are non-existent), we include MFN tariffs in the estimation, both linearly and interacted with the RTA dummy. Given that for most RTAs, preferential tariffs are set to zero, the coefficient on the interaction term gives the effect of tariff preference margins in RTAs (and should therefore be positive).

For RTAs other than ASEAN's, the RTA dummy and interaction term together capture the average effect of trade-preference packages, including both tariff-preference margins and RoOs. For ASEAN pairs, however, we also include the applicable RoO in the form of a vector of dummies, one for each type of RoO, as in equation (3). Thus, for ASEAN country pairs, the RTA dummy and its interaction with the MFN tariff capture only the effect of tariff-preference margins, while the RoO dummies capture specifically the effect of RoOs.

Country-product fixed effects at HS 6-digit level, as in equation (1), imply the estimation of one million coefficients. Estimating a system with about 30 million observations and over one million coefficients is beyond the computational capabilities of most computers and would tie up too much costly time on a supercomputer. Therefore, we simplify the estimation in several ways. First, we replace country-product fixed effects with a vector of fixed effects by exporter, importer, and product, totalling about 5,000 instead of one million. This gives the following alternative formulation:

$$\begin{aligned} \ln v_{ijk} = {} & \beta_1 t_{ijk}^{\mathrm{MFN}} + \beta_2\left(I_{ij}^{\mathrm{RTA}} \times t_{ijk}^{\mathrm{MFN}}\right) + \beta_3 I_{ij}^{\mathrm{RTA}} + \sum_{\ell} \beta_{4\ell} I_{ij}^{\mathrm{ASEAN}} r_{ijk\ell} \\ & + \mathbf{x}_{ij}\gamma + \delta_i + \delta_j + \delta_{s(k)} + u_{ijk} \end{aligned} \quad (7.5)$$

where δ_i, δ_j, and $\delta_{s(k)}$ are, respectively, the exporter, importer, and sector (HS4) fixed effects, $s(k)$ being the HS 4-digit sector to which HS 6-digit product k belongs. Using HS 4-digit level instead of HS 6-digit fixed effects reduces the number of fixed effects from 5,000 to 1,000, substantially reducing the estimation's computational demands.

We also carry out the estimation by section, making sure that each section includes goods with different types of RoO. We then convert the estimates into AVEs of RoOs using a standard formula for semi-logarithmic equations, namely

$$\text{AVE}_{\ell} = e^{\beta_{4\ell}} - 1. \tag{7.6}$$

7.3.2 Aggregate results

The baseline results are presented in Table 7.2. In all regressions, commodities and oil products are excluded. Columns 1 and 2 present the estimates for the whole sample of non-commodity trade: in Column 1, the RoO variables are omitted, while in Column 2 they are included. Column 3 presents the results for manufactured products only. For readability, the table is split into two parts, the first with standard gravity control variables plus tariffs and RTA markers, and the second with RoO coefficients only. These two parts refer to the same regressions.

The parameter estimates of the standard gravity controls are as expected. Note that the trading countries' GDPs are not included because they are absorbed by the exporter and importer fixed effects. This formulation is superior to one with GDPs, as fixed effects control adequately for Anderson and van Wincoop's (2004) 'multilateral resistance terms'.

The elasticity of trade to distance is –0.442, implying that a doubling in bilateral distance reduces trade by 25 percent.[6] A common land border raises trade by 50 percent $\left(e^{0.420} - 1\right)$. Note by comparison between Columns 1 and 2 that the parameter estimates are not affected by the introduction of the RoO dummies, which confirms that the specification and baseline results are robust. The second part of the parameter estimates of the standard gravity controls is as expected.

Table 7.2 shows the parameter estimates for the effects of RoOs with different types consolidated into 14 main rules. Twelve out of the 14 are highly significant (at the 1 percent level), and all except two are negative. Of the two positive ones, only one, RVC or CTH, is strongly significant.

The parameter estimates are displayed graphically in Figure 7.7. We can see that the most trade-inhibiting instruments are Wholly Obtained (–36.81 percent) and the Textile Rule, even when offered on choice with either a change of tariff classification (CTC or TR) or regional value content (RVC or TR). This is somewhat of a puzzle since RVCs do not appear very restrictive when used alone (–6.01), while a change of chapter (CC), the most restrictive of CTCs, has an AVE of 18.54 percent, already high but much lower than when offered as a choice with the Textile Rule.

The apparent puzzle of the Textile Rule's very strong effect suggests that the restrictiveness of RoOs should be assessed by section in order to better filter out the heterogeneity of effects across sectors. Our estimation method with product fixed effects filters out the effect of product heterogeneity on trade values, but not on 'treatment effects' (the effects of RoOs on trade). Section-by-section estimates allow for different effects across sectors.

Across the board, RoOs appear heavily restrictive. However, estimation on the whole sample may capture confounding influences that artificially inflate their estimated effect on trade flows. We now turn to estimation section by section.

Table 7.2 Gravity Regression Results, Non-Commodity Trade: Control Variables

Estimator	*OLS (within)*	*OLS (within)*	*OLS (within)*
Sample	*All a/*	*All a/*	*Manufacturing*
Dependent Variable: ln(trade value)	*(1)*	*(2)*	*(3)*
Gravity controls			
ln(distance)	−0.442***	−0.448***	−0.477***
	(268.00)	(260.15)	(264.38)
Comm. border	0.420***	0.415***	0.407***
	(97.47)	(95.84)	(89.42)
Comm. language	0.189***	0.191***	0.227***
	(55.28)	(55.77)	(63.38)
Comm. colonizer	0.234***	0.235***	0.234***
	(38.24)	(38.18)	(36.33)
Trade policy variables			
MFN tariff	−0.005***	−0.005***	−0.009***
	(22.52)	(22.30)	(38.31)
RTA pair	0.223***	0.223***	0.231***
	(54.28)	(54.13)	(54.22)
MFN tariff × RTA	0.001***	0.001***	0.001***
	(3.59)	(2.96)	(2.56)
Rules of origin			
CC		−0.205***	−0.204***
		(5.35)	(3.97)
CTH		−0.101	−0.067
		−1.26	−0.75
RVC		−0.062***	−0.063***
		(4.02)	(3.89)
RVC at 35 percent (ASEAN-India)		−0.443***	−0.519***
		(19.69)	(22.17)
Wholly Obtained		−0.459***	−0.136
		(10.42)	(1.16)
CTC and exception		−0.177***	−0.193***
		(6.40)	(6.80)
CTC and RVC		0.542*	0.841*
		(1.71)	(1.69)
CTC or TR		−0.533***	−0.528***
		(8.33)	(8.19)
CTC or (TR and RVC)		−0.314	−0.340*
		(1.64)	(1.78)
RVC or CC		−0.149***	−0.036
		(6.08)	(1.16)
RVC or CTH		0.059***	0.047***
		(5.76)	(4.48)
RVC or CTSH		−0.170***	−0.222***
		(8.71)	(11.06)

(*Continued*)

Estimator	*OLS (within)*	*OLS (within)*	*OLS (within)*
Sample	*All a/*	*All a/*	*Manufacturing*
Dependent Variable: ln(trade value)	*(1)*	*(2)*	*(3)*
RVC or TR		−0.459***	−0.563***
		(11.19)	(13.76)
RVC or (CTC and exception)		−0.286***	−0.347***
		(15.94)	(19.07)
Constant	6.525***	6.600***	6.518***
	(138.18)	(138.45)	(128.62)
Observations	4,411,362	4,411,362	3,959,384
R-squared	0.26	0.26	0.28

Note: The parameter estimates of the standard gravity controls are as expected. Note that the trading countries' GDPs are not included because they are absorbed by the exporter and importer fixed effects. This formulation is superior to one with GDPs as fixed effects control adequately for 'multilateral resistance terms'.

*significant at 10 percent; **significant at 5 percent; ***significant at 1 percent.

Source: Authors' calculations.

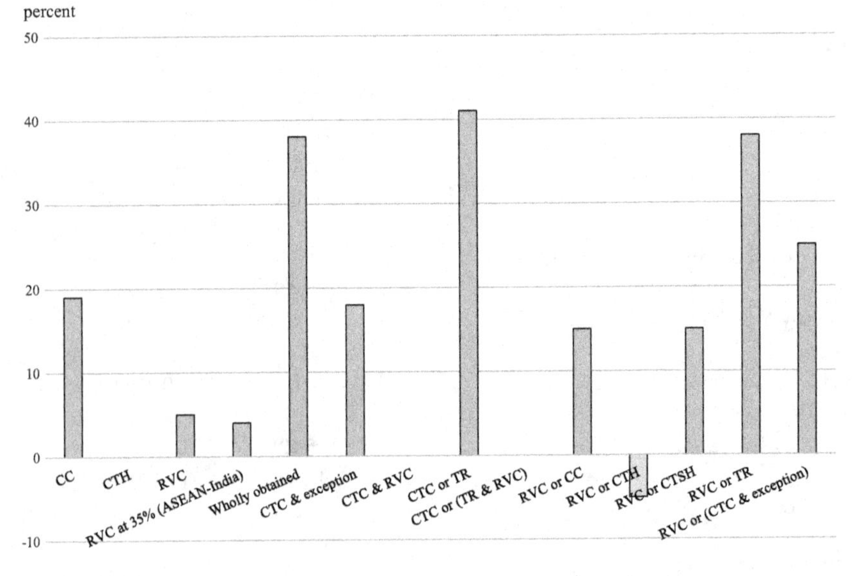

Figure 7.7 AVEs of RoOs, All Sample.

Source: Authors calculations using CEPII Database, BACI (2014).

7.3.3 Results by section

We now report the results of 21 regressions run on subsamples restricted to products within one section. The averages across all instruments are shown in Table 7.3 together with the weights used to calculate the trade-weighted average. Following Leamer (1974), in order to avoid the endogeneity of trade flows from biasing the weights used in calculated weighted averages, we use world trade weights rather than ASEAN trade weights.

Figure 7.8 further decomposes the AVEs of the RoOs by section and by instrument, keeping only the statistically significant estimates. For brevity, we display only a few sections selected for their importance in ASEAN trade. The results for other sections are available from the authors upon request.

Although the results are, unsurprisingly, less stable at the sector level than at the aggregate level, a few observations arise from the analysis. First, the Wholly Obtained criterion appears to have a restrictive effect on preferential trade in the food, beverage and tobacco sector, which is to be expected since it essentially prevents foreign sourcing of any sort. Chemicals (HS 06) is one of the few where the RVC seems to have a strong trade-inhibiting effect. In Textiles and Apparel (HS 11), unsurprisingly, the Textile Rule appears restrictive, while in Footwear (HS 12), all rules appear restrictive. This parallels the results obtained for NAFTA and Paneuro. In Machinery and Equipment, including Electronics (HS 16), the results are very unstable, which is to be expected given the presence of the World Trade Organization's Information Technology Agreement already discussed. Last, in

Table 7.3 Average AVEs for All RoO Instruments, by Section (HS code 2-digit)

Section	*Summary Description*	*Average AVE (percent)*	*Trade Weights a/*
1	Live animals; animal products	–	–
2	Vegetable products	1.91	2.61
3	Animal or vegetable fats	6.67	0.58
4	Food and beverages	1.73	3.05
5	Mineral products	1.52	19.59
6	Products of the chemical or allied industries	3.50	9.70
7	Plastic and articles thereof; rubber and articles thereof	1.87	4.63
8	Leather and leather products	9.05	0.60
9	Wood and articles of wood	-3.20	0.77
10	Pulp and paper	4.98	1.75
11	Textiles and apparel	8.29	4.06
12	Footwear	12.67	0.77
13	Cement, glass, and stone	2.42	0.93
14	Precious metals and stones	3.81	2.97
15	Base metals and articles of base metal	-0.46	7.77
16	Machinery and electrical equipment	-0.36	25.89
17	Vehicles	6.89	8.99
18	Precision instruments, optics, watchmaking	3.34	3.33
19	Arms and ammunition; parts and accessories thereof	–	–
20	Miscellaneous manufactured articles	-3.37	1.99
21	Works of art, collectors' pieces and antiques	–	–
Average (percent)			
Simple		3.40	
Trade-weighted			2.09

Note: Trade weights calculated using world trade, following Leamer (1974), averaged over 2010–2011. Only sections where RoO AVEs are significant were used in their calculations; Section 1 omitted because entirely covered by 'Wholly Obtained' rule.

Source: Authors' calculations using CEPII Database, BACI (2014).

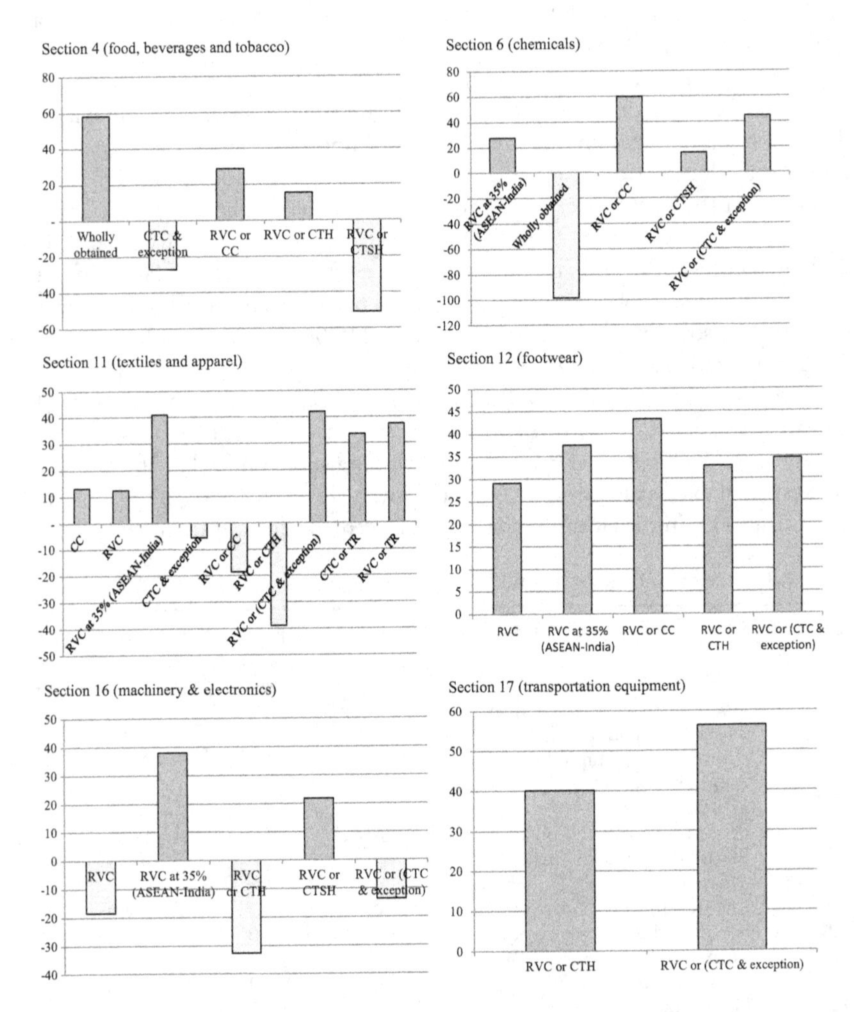

Figure 7.8 AVEs of RoOs, Selected Sectors (in percent).
Source: Authors' calculations.

the all-important Transportation Equipment (HS 17), strong trade-inhibiting effects are observed for RVCs, even when offered on choice with other rules (change of tariff heading or CTC other than heading, but with an exception). These rules appear tailor-made to stifle, to some extent, automobile trade in the region.

7.4 Concluding remarks

This chapter reviewed the evidence on the effect of ASEAN's RoOs on preferential trade. While the first-best approach for measuring the effect of RoOs would be to use preference utilisation rates as the dependent variable, in the absence of utilisation-rate data, we based our identification strategy on the variation in trade flows across country pairs, controlling for product and country heterogeneity with product, exporter, and importer fixed effects in a disaggregated HS 6-digit level cross-sectional gravity framework.

Prima facie, ASEAN's RoOs have a relatively simple and transparent structure, with a large chunk of trade flows subject to a 40 percent RVC requirement or a CTC rule. In many cases, the importers can choose which rule to claim, which makes the system less penalising.

However, the econometric analysis of trade flows uncovers evidence of moderately restrictive effects, with an average tariff equivalent across all measures and products of 3.40 percent (2.09 percent, if we weight by trade). That is, ASEAN's RoOs 'deny preferences' by an amount roughly comparable to one-fourth of the tariff-preference margins. Although moderate, this may contribute to the low take-up rates that have been observed on the basis of fragmentary evidence.

Overall, ASEAN's relatively restrictive RoOs may not have a huge impact on trade flows, as a large proportion of international trade in the Asia-Pacific region is in the electronics and capital equipment sector, where MFN tariffs are low and the attractiveness of preferences is (with or without RoOs) limited anyway. Thus, low take-up rates may simply reflect the fact that most trade is in product lines that do not stand to benefit very much from tariff reductions.

However, there may be gains to reap from the simplification of RoOs in sectors like textiles and apparel or footwear, which currently represent a low proportion of Asia-Pacific trade but may represent substantial opportunities for export-led growth and thus poverty reduction in some of the region's poorest countries. The same applies to prepared foods. Automobiles also stand out as a sector where the relaxation of RoOs might be considered, or at least carefully coordinated with plans to build up 'deep' value chains within the region.

Thus, the simplification and streamlining of RoOs should prioritise light industries like textiles and apparel, footwear and prepared foods (in particular fats), and this should be seen as part of ASEAN's internal development and poverty-reduction strategy. Future research should be carried out to assess the specific gains that ASEAN's poorer Member States might reap from less stringent RoOs.

Acknowledgements

The authors are grateful to the ASEAN Secretariat and Erlinda Medalla for sharing data on ASEAN's RoOs, and Cristian Ugarte for many useful conversations and suggestions.

Disclaimer

The work was conducted when Lili Yan Ing was with ERIA. The views expressed by her here are personal and do not represent the view of the Ministry of Trade of Indonesia.

Notes

1 Brunei Darussalam, Indonesia, Malaysia, the Philippines, Singapore and Thailand. ASEAN later expanded to include Viet Nam, Lao PDR, Myanmar and Cambodia.
2 The idea that trade-diverting PTAs are more appealing politically than trade-creating one was developed theoretically in Grossman and Helpman (1995). Empirical evidence, however, is mixed.
3 See Dedrick et al. (2008) for an in-depth study of two electronics value chains.
4 For instance, one of NAFTA's rules for certain textile products used to specify that intermediates had to be woven with a loom width of less than 76 cm, woven in the United Kingdom in accordance with the rules and regulations of the Harris Tweed Association, Ltd., and so certified by the association.
5 The ITA-1 was concluded in December 1996. Six out of ten ASEAN countries, Indonesia, Malaysia, the Philippines, Singapore, Thailand and Viet Nam, were members of the ITA-1, and almost all ASEAN's main trading partners, such as Australia, India, Japan, Korea and New Zealand, are also members of the ITA. China is in the process of accession. The ITA requires all members to completely eliminate duties on IT products covered by the Agreement. The ITA-2 was concluded in December 2015. In 2017, the ITA-1 had 82 member countries, which have trade of about 97 percent of world trade in information technology products.
6 Note that distance is a continuous variable not a binary one; so formula (6) does not apply. Instead, the coefficient can be read directly as an elasticity, as both the value and distance are in logs.

References

Anderson, J., and E. van Wincoop (2004), 'Trade Costs', *Journal of Economic Literature*, 42, pp. 691–751.

Anson, J., O. Cadot, A. Estevadeordal, J. de Melo, A. Suwa-Eisenmann, and B. Tumurchudur (2005), 'RoO in North-South Preferential Trading Arrangements with an Application to NAFTA', *Review of International Economics*, 13(3), pp. 501–517.

Australian Productivity Commission (2004), *Rules of Origin under the Australia-New Zealand Closer Economic Relation Trade Agreement*, Canberra: Research Report.

Baldwin, R. (2006), 'Multilateralising Regionalism: Spaghetti Bowls as Building Blocs on the Path to Global Free Trade', NBER Working Paper, No. 12545.

Brenton, P., and M. Manchin (2003), 'Making EU Trade Agreements Work: The Role of Rules of Origin', *World Economy*, 26(5), pp. 755–769.

Cadot, O., A. Estevadeordal, and A. Suwa-Eisenmann (2005), 'RoO as Export Subsidies', CEPR Discussion Paper, No. 4999.

Cadot, O., C. Carrère, J. de Melo, and B. Tumurchudur (2006a), 'Product Specific RoO in EU and US Preferential Trading Agreements: An Assessment', *World Trade Review*, 5(2), pp. 199–224.

Cadot, O., A. Estevadeordal, A. Suwa-Eisenmann, and T. Verdier (eds.) (2006b), *The Origin of Goods: Rules of Origin in Regional Trade Agreements*, London: CEPR.

Candau, F., and S. Jean (2005), 'What Are EU Trade Preferences Worth for Sub-Saharan Africa and Other Developing Countries?', CEPII Working Paper 2005–19, Paris: Centre d'Etudes Prospectives en Economie Internationale.

Chase, K. A. (2007), 'Industry Lobbying and RoO in Free Trade Agreements', Paper Presented at the International Studies Association 48th Annual Convention, Chicago, IL, February 28–March 3.

Calvo-Pardo, H., C. Freund, and E. Ornelas (2009), 'The ASEAN Free Trade Agreement: Impact on Trade Flows and External Trade Barriers', World Bank Policy Research Working Paper 4960, Washington, DC: The World Bank.

CEPII. (2014). BACI: International Trade Database at the Product Level. http://www.cepii.fr/CEPII/en/bdd_modele/presentation.asp?id=1

Dedrick, J., K. Kraemer, and G. Linden (2008), 'Who Profits from Innovation in Global Value Chains? A Study of the Ipod and Notebook PCs', Alfred P. Sloan Industry Studies 2008.

Estevadeordal, A. (2000), 'Negotiating Preferential Market Access – The Case of the North American Free Trade Agreement', *Journal of World Trade*, 34(1), pp. 141–166.

Estevadeordal, A., and K. Suominen (2008), *Gatekeepers of Global Commerce; Rules of Origin and International Economic Integration*, Washington, DC: Inter-American Development Bank.

Francois, J., B. Hoekman, and M. Manchin (2006), 'Preference Erosion and Multilateral Trade Liberalisation', *The World Bank Economic Review*, 20(2), pp. 197–216.

Grossman, G., and E. Helpman (1995), The Politics of Free-Trade Agreements', *The American Economic Review*, 85(4), pp. 667–690.

Harris, J. T. (2007), 'Measurement and Determination of RoO in Preferential Trade Agreements (PTAs)', PhD Thesis, University of Maryland.

Herin, J. (1986), 'Rules of Origin and Differences in Tariff Levels in EFTA and in the EC', European Free Trade Association Occasional Papers, No. 13, February.

Hirsch, M. (2002), 'International Trade Law, Political Economy and Rules of Origin – A Plea for a Reform of the WTO Regime on Rules of Origin', *Journal of World Trade*, 36(2), pp. 171–188.

Johnson, R., and G. Noguera (2010), 'Accounting for Intermediates: Production Sharing and Trade in Value Added', *mimeo*.

Kelleher, S. (2013), 'Playing By the Rules? The Development of an Amended Index to Measure the Impact of Rules of Origin on Intra-PTA Trade Flows', *The World Economy* (forthcoming).

Kimura, F. (2010), 'FTA Networking In East Asia And Asia-Pacific: Where Are We Going?', GEM Policy Brief 2010, Paris: Institut National des Sciences Politiques.

Koopman, R., W. Powers, Z. Wang, and S. J. Wei (2011), 'Give Credit Where Credit Is Due: Tracing Value Added in Global Production Chains', NBER Working Paper, No. 16426.

Leamer, E. (1974), 'The Commodity Composition of International Trade in Manufactures: An Empirical Analysis', *Oxford Economic Papers*, 26, pp. 350–374.

Manchin, M., and A. O. Pelkmans-Balaoing (2007), 'RoO and the Web of East Asian Free Trade Agreements', World Bank Policy Research Working Paper, No. 4273, July.

Medalla, E., and J. Balboa (2009), 'ASEAN Rules of Origin: Lessons and Recommendations for Best Practice', ERIA Discussion Paper, No. 2009–17, Jakarta: ERIA.

Portugal-Perez, A. (2009), 'Assessing the Impact of Political Economy Factors on Rules of Origin under NAFTA', World Bank Policy Research Working Paper, No. 4848.

Appendix 1

This appendix derives the estimation equation at the product level from the gravity equation using the Anderson-van Wincoop (2004) framework but relaxing key symmetry assumptions on production costs and trade costs. Suppose that Country i exports n_i varieties to Country j and let x_{ijk} be the quantity of variety k exported from i to j (in tons), p_{ijk} its CIF price, E_j the total expenditure in Country j, and s_{ijk} its share in Country j's expenditure. We have

$$p_{ijk}x_{ijk} = s_{ijk}E_j. \tag{7.7}$$

With CES preferences, P_j being composite price index in j and σ elasticity of substitution between varieties, it can be shown that

$$s_{ijk} = \left(\frac{p_{ijk}}{P_j}\right)^{1-\sigma}. \tag{7.8}$$

Let τ_{ijk} be the bilateral trade cost between i and j for variety k, including all of its components (tariffs, RoOs, and other barriers). Let p_{ik} be the producer price of variety k in Country i; we will assume that it is affected by an idiosyncratic shock φ_{ik} representing comparative advantage; i.e.

$$p_{ik} = \frac{p_i}{\varphi_{ik}}. \tag{7.9}$$

The consumer price of variety k in Country j is then

$$p_{ijk} = \tau_{ijk}p_{ik}. \tag{7.10}$$

Let V_{ij} be the total value of exports from i to j. Bilateral trade between i and j is given by

$$V_{ij} = \sum_k p_{ijk} x_{ijk} = \sum_k s_{ijk} E_j = \sum_k \left(\frac{p_{ijk}}{P_j} \right)^{1-\sigma} E_j$$
$$= \sum_k \left(\frac{\tau_{ijk} p_{ik}}{P_j} \right)^{1-\sigma} E_j. \quad (7.11)$$

Country i's GDP is the sum of its sales to all destinations, including itself:

$$Y_i = \sum_{j=1}^{m} V_{ij} = \sum_{j=1}^{m} \sum_k \left(\frac{\tau_{ijk} p_{ik}}{P_j} \right)^{1-\sigma} E_j = \sum_k \left[p_{ik}^{1-\sigma} \sum_{j=1}^{m} \left(\frac{\tau_{ijk}}{P_j} \right)^{1-\sigma} E_j \right]. \quad (7.12)$$

Let us define a product-specific remoteness term Ω_{ik} (the product-specificity comes here only from the fact that trade costs τ_{ijk} vary across products):

$$\Omega_{ik} = \sum_{j=1}^{m} \tau_{ijk}^{1-\sigma} \left(\frac{E_j}{P_j^{1-\sigma}} \right) \quad (7.13)$$

and write

$$Y_i = \sum_k p_{ik}^{1-\sigma} \Omega_{ik} = p_i \sum_k \left(\frac{1}{\varphi_{ik}} \right)^{1-\sigma} \Omega_{ik}. \quad (7.14)$$

Let

$$\tilde{\Omega}_i = \sum_k \left(\frac{1}{\varphi_{ik}} \right)^{1-\sigma} \Omega_{ik} \quad (7.15)$$

be a remoteness term adjusted for comparative advantage. Inverting gives

$$p_i = \frac{Y_i}{\tilde{\Omega}_i}. \quad (7.16)$$

Writing in terms of p_i gives

$$V_{ij} = p_i \sum_k \left(\frac{\tau_{ijk}}{\varphi_{ik} P_j} \right)^{1-\sigma} E_j = \frac{Y_i}{\tilde{\Omega}_i} \sum_k \tau_{ijk}^{1-\sigma} \frac{E_j}{P_j^{1-\sigma}} = \sum_k \tau_{ijk}^{1-\sigma} \frac{Y_i E_j}{\tilde{\Omega}_i P_j^{1-\sigma}}. \quad (7.17)$$

Noting finally that $E_j = Y_j$ (income equals expenditure) and letting $\bar{\tau}_{ij} = \sum_k \tau_{ijk}^{1-\sigma}$ be the average trade cost from i to j across all varieties gives a modified gravity equation holding at the aggregate level in the absence of symmetry:

$$V_{ij} = \bar{\tau}_{ij} \frac{Y_i Y_j}{\tilde{\Omega}_i P_j^{1-\sigma}}. \tag{7.18}$$

We are here interested in estimating this equation at the product level. Let v_{ijk} be the value of the flow of variety k from Country i to Country j. Using

$$\begin{aligned} v_{ijk} = s_{ijk} V_{ij} &= \left(\frac{p_{ijk}}{P_j} \right)^{1-\sigma} V_{ij} \\ &= \left(\frac{p_i \tau_{ijk}}{\varphi_{ik} P_j} \right)^{1-\sigma} \bar{\tau}_{ij} \frac{Y_i Y_j}{\tilde{\Omega}_i P_j^{1-\sigma}}. \end{aligned} \tag{7.19}$$

How does expression differ from an ordinary gravity expression? The two key differences are the presence of an exporter-product term φ_{ik} correcting for comparative advantage and of a dyad-product term τ_{ijk} correcting for product-specific trade costs, which are what we are interested here (product-specific tariffs and RoOs). Letting δ_j and δ_{ik} be respectively importer- and exporter-product fixed effects, we can write after log-linearisation as

$$\ln v_{ijk} = \beta_1 \ln \tau_{ijk} + \beta_2 \ln \tau_{ij} + \delta_{ik} + \delta_j + u_{ij} \tag{7.20}$$

where

$$\tau_{ijk} = e^{\gamma_1 t_{ijk} + \gamma_2 r_{ijk}}, \tag{7.21}$$

with t_{ijk} and r_{ijk} being, respectively, the tariff and RoO applying to good k between Countries i and j, and τ_{ij} is the usual array of gravity controls (distance, common border and common language).

Appendix 2

This appendix details the classification of the RoOs used in the regression analysis. The large number of instrument combinations used in the various trade agreements involving ASEAN required consolidation for regression analysis. We have consolidated all types into 15 broader types, preserving special categories for instruments combined with additional requirements and for cases of instrument choice. Frequency numbers shown in Table 7.A1 are the numbers of HS6 lines concerned by the instrument on all ASEAN trade. Thus, the numbers add up to substantially more than the notional number of HS6 lines (about 5,000). Consolidation choices were made on the basis of frequency ratios (the consolidation concerned instruments or combinations of instruments with low frequency).

Table 7.A1 RoO Types

Raw	*Consolidated*	*Frequency, All ASEAN Imports*	*Frequency Ratio, All ASEAN Imports*
RVC	rvc	5,149	16.52
RVC + CC	rvc+ctc	2	0.01
RVC + CTH	rvc+ctc	5	0.02
RVC + CTSH	rvc+ctc	3	0.01
RVC + Textile Rule or CC	(rvc+tr)_or_ctc	218	0.7
RVC + Textile Rule or CTH	(rvc+tr)_or_ctc	6	0.02
RVC or CC	rvc_or_cc	1,323	4.24
RVC or CC + Textile Rule	rvc_or_ctc+x	2	0.01
RVC or CC or SPR	rvc_or_ctc+x	89	0.29
RVC or CC or Textile Rule	rvc_or_ctc+x	463	1.49
RVC or CC with exception	rvc_or_ctc+x	86	0.28
RVC or CTH	rvc_or_cth	11,764	37.74
RVC or CTH + CTSH	rvc_or_ctc+x	195	0.63
RVC or CTH or CTSH	rvc_or_ctc+x	136	0.44
RVC or CTH or SPR	rvc_or_ctc+x	24	0.08
RVC or CTH or Textile Rule	rvc_or_ctc+x	347	1.11
RVC or CTH with exception	rvc_or_ctc+x	194	0.62
RVC or CTSH	rvc_or_ctsh	1,877	6.02
RVC or CTSH with additional reqt	rvc_or_ctsh	4	0.01

(*Continued*)

Raw	*Consolidated*	*Frequency, All ASEAN Imports*	*Frequency Ratio, All ASEAN Imports*
RVC or CTSH with exception	rvc_or_ctsh	41	0.13
RVC or Textile Rule	rvc_or_tr	428	1.37
RVC with additional reqt	rvc	5	0.02
RVC35+CTSH	rvc_35	5,224	16.76
CC	cc	987	3.17
CC + Textile Rule	cc+x	40	0.13
CC or Textile Rule	ctc_or_tr	15	0.05
CC with additional reqt	cc+x	348	1.12
CC with exception	cc+x	261	0.84
CTH	cth	230	0.74
CTH or Textile Rule	ctc_or_tr	91	0.29
CTH with additional reqt	cc+x	615	1.97
CTH with exception	cc+x	32	0.1
CTSH	cth	8	0.03
WO	wo	963	3.09

Source: Authors' estimation.

8 Non-tariff measures and harmonisation

Issues for East Asian Integration

Olivier Cadot and Lili Yan Ing

8.1 Introduction

The Regional Comprehensive Economic Partnership (RCEP) currently being negotiated has the potential to be a critical element of regional integration in East Asia and the Pacific and take initiatives on regional economic integration in East Asia to a higher level. For this, RCEP commitments would need to be substantially stronger than those under existing Association of Southeast Asian Nations (ASEAN)+1 FTAs, as mere consolidation would risk taking place on the lowest common denominator, delivering, in the end, less than some of the existing ASEAN+1 FTAs. Thus, to be viable (i.e. seen as worth the extended negotiation time and resources), RCEP would need to be more ambitious. Moreover, given that it effectively includes an implicit FTA agreement among China, Japan and the Republic of Korea (henceforth, Korea), resulting in trade and investment diversion from ASEAN, only deeper facilitation and liberalisation commitments would deliver additional benefits to ASEAN member states (AMSs) compared with the existing ASEAN+1 FTAs.

Yet the challenge of furthering integration in a bloc bringing together half the world's population and a third of its gross domestic product (GDP), with countries at widely different levels of development, is likely to be a formidable one, especially in the absence of the kind of deep-rooted political drive that characterised the European continent when it embarked on the process of integration after the Second World War. As the leader and facilitator of RCEP, ASEAN can play a central role in defining its agenda if it proves capable of formulating proposals that hold the promise of substantial and widely distributed welfare increases while at the same time being sufficiently flexible to accommodate the needs of very heterogeneous partners.

Deep integration in the form of regulatory convergence is a potential new frontier for RCEP that could fit these requirements, provided that it is approached in the right way. In the absence of strong regional disciplines, there is always a risk that regulations, which tend to proliferate everywhere, are 'instrumentalised' one way or another. For instance, they could be captured by special interests as surrogate trade-protection instruments. As manufacturing jobs are important and growing in many of RCEP's future partners, there is always a

DOI: 10.4324/9780429433603-8

risk of tit-for-tat regulations, although these have not yet materialised to the extent predicted by some observers (Evenett and Wermelinger, 2010). As wealthier consumers become more health-conscious, risk-averse regulatory systems may overreact to idiosyncratic and transient health crises with permanently stricter regulations, a ratchet effect that could lead to unnecessarily stringent regulations. Moreover, when triggering crises are local and uncorrelated, regulatory systems can end up diverging even though the underlying force – risk aversion – is the same everywhere.[1]

Thus, regulatory convergence could be a potentially useful and important item in the agenda of future ASEAN and RCEP negotiations. However, the issues involved are complex. The research summarised in this chapter suggests that the gains from harmonisation may not always be as large as sometimes expected. In particular, when poor countries harmonise their regulations with those of richer partners in a regional bloc, they may impose upon themselves 'over-stringent' regulations – regulations that rich countries have built to placate risk-averse consumers – and in so doing, subject their producers to disproportionate regulatory burdens, hampering their ability to make headway in other Southern markets where stringent standards confer no marketing advantage. By contrast, something as simple as the mutual recognition of conformity-assessment procedures seems to deliver solid gains, at least provided that weaker member states receive assistance to get their conformity-assessment infrastructure up to speed. This is an area where the ASEAN Secretariat could play a useful role, together with development partners, to improve market access for some of its weaker member states.

By this, we mean subjecting potentially important new regulations to a quality-control process based on consistency with the sanitary and phytosanitary (SPS) and technical barriers to trade (TBT) agreements of the World Trade Organization (WTO) and with international standards. Such a process would naturally promote regulatory convergence, even in the absence of formal coordination mechanisms, as best-practice regulations are, in many cases, similar (for instance, SPS regulations based on the *Codex Alimentarius* tend to look alike). Thus, it would not rely on the need for supranational institutions, which would be difficult to create in the ASEAN context. More importantly, it would contribute to 'multilateralising' RCEP from the outset by grounding deep integration on international standards, thus avoiding worsening the 'spaghetti bowl' phenomenon (see Baldwin and Kawai (2013)).

This chapter provides an analysis and practical suggestions to move forward with a deep-integration agenda in ASEAN focussed on 'soft' regulatory convergence. The essence of the approach proposed here is to move away from a trade-centred view of non-tariff barrier (NTB) elimination where each move is viewed through a negotiating lens as a 'concession' towards a country-centred view where national regulatory improvement efforts naturally lead to convergence.[2] Specifically, under our proposal, each AMS would put in place an institutional setup geared towards establishing what we call 'dynamic disciplines'.

The approach could deliver substantial welfare gains. Poorly designed trade-related regulations can fragment markets, create monopoly positions, and stifle regional trade; at the same time, they can fail to achieve consumer-protection objectives at the heart of the role of a modern state. For instance, in some AMSs, pharmaceutical regulations fail to contain the widespread traffic of hazardous counterfeits, with disastrous consequences for public health. In some cases, trade and non-trade objectives are congruent; in others, trade-offs must be made, and smart regulations must balance multiple objectives. Few governments have effective inter-ministerial coordination mechanisms to ensure that such trade-offs are made explicitly and rationally; our approach is to create one based on the same blueprint in each AMS.

One advantage of such an approach over existing NTB-elimination schemes is that it closes a potentially critical loophole, namely the replacement of eliminated NTBs with new ones. Another advantage is that it bypasses the traditional incentive problem that no country wants to move first in order not to burn future bargaining chips, making progress dependent on episodic and uncertain negotiation rounds. Instead, it makes regulatory convergence (on best practices) the natural by-product of national regulatory-improvement agendas, themselves embedded in trade-facilitation and doing-business agendas already in place.

The rest of this chapter is organised as follows. Section 8.2 analyses the effects of NTMs and standardisation on market structure and trade. Section 8.3 provides estimates of the costs involved. Section 8.4 proposes a new approach to measuring the 'regulatory distance' between countries to be bridged by convergence. Section 8.5 lays out our core proposal. Section 8.6 concludes.

8.2 NTMs and standardisation: sorting out the issues

This section disentangles various components of the cost-raising effect of NTMs and assesses conceptually their channels of influence using the heterogeneous-firms perspective of modern trade theory. Quantification approaches are discussed in the following section. NTMs affect regional trade through two broad types of effects: a stringency effect and a fragmentation effect. These effects are distinct conceptually, although they can interact. Conceptually, the key point is that the NTM compliance costs linked to their stringency are likely to matter most when they affect variable costs rather than fixed costs, whereas fragmentation effects linked to their non-harmonisation matter if they lead to reduced competition. In other words, NTMs and their non-harmonisation matter in as much as they affect firm pricing strategies.

8.2.1 Stringency effects

The stringency effect is the trade-reduction effect that is attributable to the increased cost of doing business due to the presence of NTMs. This effect can itself be conceptually separated into two components: a sourcing cost and an enforcement cost.

The *sourcing cost* is due to the possible forced switch of importers from low-grade foreign suppliers to high-grade ones meeting the NTM's requirements. For instance, Indonesia's steel standard mandates a minimum steel quality. The standard precludes the importation of the cheapest kind of steel. For some users, this makes no difference because they source high-quality steel anyway. For instance, Japanese automakers with production facilities in Indonesia procure their steel from Nippon steel, which produces some of the best steel in the world. However, other firms, e.g. in the construction sector, may have imported cheap, low-quality steel before the regulation. Those firms now find themselves forced to procure it with more expensive suppliers meeting the technical regulation. The more stringent an NTM, the higher the sourcing cost will be.

The *enforcement cost* relates to the diversion of managerial attention and staff time to proving compliance with the NTMs. This may involve dealing with paperwork, inspections by officials from enforcement agencies, or seeking/encouraging the certification of foreign suppliers under the national standard. Enforcement costs are conventionally measured by the 'standard cost model' of the Organisation for Economic Co-operation and Development, which consists of establishing, based on a survey, the time spent monthly by the staff of affected companies on proving compliance, multiplied by their salaries. The result is a monetisation of the time burden created by paperwork and dealing with NTMs in general. Typically, the more stringent an NTM, the more suspiciously it is enforced, complicating the burden of proving compliance; indeed, anecdotal evidence on the ground suggests that stringency and enforcement costs tend to correlate.

Both sourcing and enforcement costs can affect market structure through firm selection, but the importance of this effect is likely to depend on their nature. Enforcement costs are essentially fixed in the sense that they depend only weakly on the scale of production. In a model of trade with heterogeneous firms à la Melitz (2003), the level of fixed costs affects the entry decision; thus, higher enforcement costs discourage the entry of fringe firms. By contrast, sourcing costs are variable. For instance, if a technical regulation mandates that wire insulation material be fire-retardant, every unit will become more expensive. This will affect all firms in proportion to their sales, including large ones.

Which ones are likely to be most important for aggregate outcomes? The answer is shown in Figure 8.1. The horizontal axis ranks firms in terms of productivity from least to most productive. The distribution is shown by curve f, which roughly reproduces a Pareto distribution: lots of low-productivity (small) firms and fewer and fewer at higher levels. The scale of curve f, in terms of the number of firms, is measured on the left-hand-side vertical axis. Curve g_0 shows the cumulative output of those firms, measured in, say, US dollars on the right-hand-side vertical axis. The increments are initially small as the addition of more small, low-productivity firms does not raise cumulative output much. The increments then become increasingly steeper as one moves to progressively larger and more productive firms.

Suppose now that a certain country imposes an NTM with large enforcement costs. The costs induce the massive exit of small firms, shown by the thick arrow,

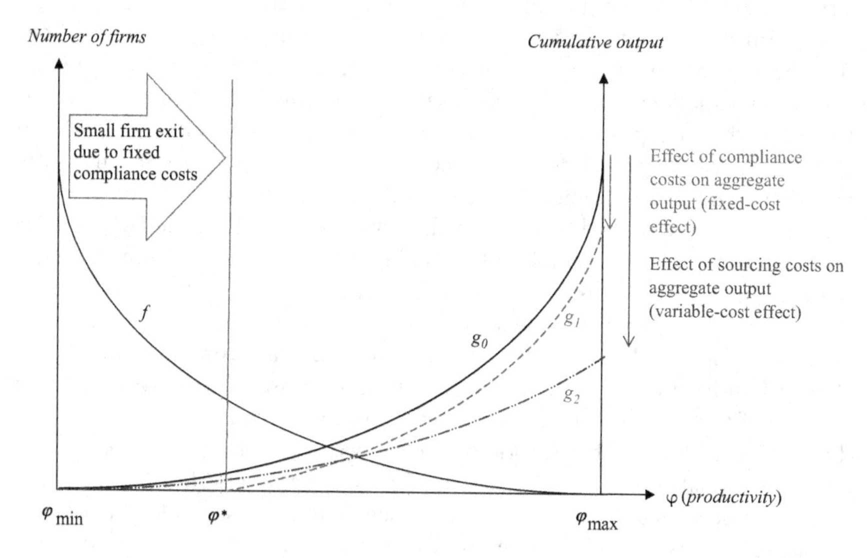

Figure 8.1 Why Variable Sourcing Costs Matter More than Fixed Enforcement Costs.
Source: Authors' description.

with only firms above a critical productivity level, φ^*, able to survive. Although the exit, as shown, is massive, the effect on aggregate production, shown by the downward shift of the g curve from g_0 to g_1, is small because the exit affects the low-productivity fringe firms only. In contrast, sourcing costs affect the pricing and output decisions of all firms, including the largest and most productive ones. The effect on aggregate output, shown by the drop of the g curve from g_0 to g_2, is now much larger. This is one of the insights of the recent heterogeneous-firms models: policy interventions affecting fixed costs typically have smaller effects than those affecting variable costs. In that sense, the salience of cumbersome procedures and costly certification in surveys should be put in perspective; as long as the enforcement costs are not variable, they should not be overemphasised in the policy debate.

Figure 8.1 shows that fixed-cost increases related to the enforcement of NTMs may end up having small aggregate effects on production and trade as they affect essentially the smallest and least-productive firms. However, this does not mean that these effects are irrelevant to the policy debate: small firms may provide employment outside of agglomeration centres or employ vulnerable populations, and so on. NTMs that make compliance difficult for small firms may thus have detrimental social effects. We will return to these considerations[3] in Section 8.4.

8.2.2 Fragmentation effects

The fragmentation effect of NTMs is the barrier between markets created by differing NTMs, irrespective of their stringency. It is particularly important economically, as it affects not just the level of firm costs, but also the market structure and the degree of competition. When countries impose different technical regulations, producers incur differentiation costs to adapt products to them. As a result, they tend to specialise by market, reducing the extent of competition. To see this, imagine that Country *A* imposes a technical regulation prohibiting the use of certain pigments in paint for domestic use, while Country *B* prohibits only the use of lead in paints. A producer manufacturing paint for sale in Country *B* may want to use pigments banned in *A* because they are cheaper, provided that they contain no lead. But then paints produced in the same facility using only pigments permitted in *A* will be polluted by residues left from the batch destined for *B* unless a costly clean-up is performed between batches. As a result, tacit arrangements may arise whereby some producers manufacture according to *A*'s standard and sell only there, while others manufacture according to *B*'s standard and sell only there. Under certain conditions, this may well suit their interests if the forsaken economies of scale are more than compensated by reduced competition and higher prices. In other words, the fragmentation effect is akin to a regulation-induced collusive device. Note that this effect is not directly related to the stringency of *A*'s standard: the maximum residual level (MRL) of banned pigments could be relaxed up to a certain level in *A* without changing the incentive for firms to specialise by market.

Stringency and fragmentation effects affect regional and multilateral trade through essentially the same channels because modern NTMs apply on a most-favoured-nation (MFN) basis. That is, by Article III of the General Agreement on Tariffs and Trade (GATT), technical or SPS regulations must apply equally to all 'like' products irrespective of origin – domestic, preferential, or other imports. Indeed, it would not make sense to loosen SPS regulations on shrimp for preferential partners. We will discuss later what institutional arrangements (harmonisation, mutual recognition, etc.) can reduce compliance costs selectively at the regional level. This section is concerned with ways to assess empirically how NTMs affect regional trade, irrespective of the fact that they are notionally MFN. We will describe two relatively crude, but nevertheless useful, ways of getting towards such an assessment and point towards methods that could improve on them.

8.3 Measuring the effects

This section uses the analysis from the last section to assess empirically the effect of NTMs and various modes of harmonisation on estimated compliance costs and trade flows. The assessment is constrained by key data limitations, including the absence of price data, replaced by trade unit values, and the current state of NTM data collection, the coverage of which is only partial. Therefore, the results should be interpreted cautiously. Be that as it may, they suggest that deep-integration clauses in regional trade agreements (RTAs), such as on harmonisation and mutual recognition, have identifiable, albeit limited effects in reducing compliance costs. However, their effects on trade patterns are complex when development levels differ in the bloc, with possible adverse effects in the presence of a 'premature harmonisation' syndrome.

8.3.1 Can NTMs inadvertently hurt regional trade?

Even when applied in a non-discriminatory way in accordance with GATT Article III, NTMs can still penalise trade more with certain partners than others just because coverage ratios differ depending on the product composition of bilateral trade. For instance, SPS measures fall more heavily on trade with partners having a comparative advantage in foodstuffs, and TBTs on those with a comparative advantage in manufactures. The same reasoning applies at the regional level. If intra-regional trade has a strong component in foodstuffs relative to trade with the rest of the world, it will be affected more than proportionately by SPS measures.

This suggests a simple approach to measuring the potential of NTMs to affect regional trade using coverage ratios. A coverage ratio, in general, measures the proportion of trade covered by one or more NTMs. Here we adapt the concept to measure the share of regional versus out-of-region trade that is covered by NTMs, depending on their respective product compositions. The formulae we use are derived in the Appendix.

Figure 8.2 shows the result of this calculation for four regions of the world for which data are available (without particular reference to formal trading blocs). For each importing country labelled by its ISO3 code, the red bar corresponds to formula (9) in the Appendix (coverage ratio for intraregional imports) and the grey one to formula (8) (overall coverage ratio). When the former is higher than

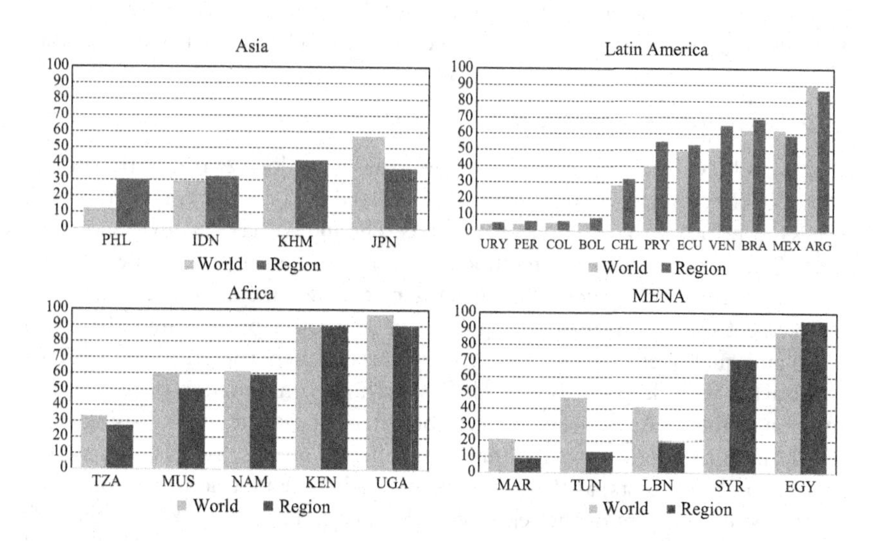

Figure 8.2 Coverage Ratio for Imports from Regional Partners.

Notes: PHL = Philippines; IDN = Indonesia; KHM = Cambodia; JPN = Japan; URY = Uruguay; PER = Peru; COL = Colombia; CHL = Chile; PRY = Paraguay; ECU = Ecuador; VEN = Venezuela; BRA = Brazil; MEX = Mexico; ARG = Argentina; TZA = Tanzania; MUS = Mauritius; NAM = Namibia; KEN = Kenya; UGA = Uganda; MAR = Morocco; TUN = Tunisia; LBN = Lebanon; SYR = Syria; EGY = Egypt.

Source: Authors' calculations based on COMTRADE database.

the latter, NTMs fall disproportionately on regional trade, and vice versa. This is the case for the Philippines, whose NTMs fall disproportionately on regional trade. For Indonesia and Cambodia, the coverage of NTMs is roughly balanced between regional and non-regional imports. For Japan, in contrast, their weight falls more on out-of-region imports.

Except in the case of the Philippines, patterns of NTM imposition in documented ASEAN countries do not suggest that they fall disproportionately on regional trade due to the composition of intra-regional trade. At a broad level, this is consistent with the heavy content of regional trade in capital equipment, high-tech intermediates, and electronics components, which are affected by relatively few NTMs compared with food products.

8.3.2 Does deep integration actually help?

In this section, we explore what could be expected from harmonisation or, more broadly, from regulatory convergence as part of RCEP through a quantitative ex post assessment of how deep-integration clauses (harmonisation or mutual recognition) in RTAs have reduced NTM compliance costs and enhanced trade. First, we assess the effects on compliance costs using a price equation. Then, we assess the trade effects using a gravity equation, highlighting a 'premature harmonisation' syndrome that has been discussed only recently in the literature. Results from both approaches suggest that expectations should not be set too high on the benefits to be derived from deep integration but that the mutual recognition of conformity-assessment procedures might provide a possible quick win with sizable benefits.

8.3.2.1 Reducing compliance costs

Here we follow the novel approach of Cadot and Gourdon (2015) for the estimation of NTM ad valorem equivalents (AVEs) based on a comparison of trade unit values (i.e. prices) with versus without NTMs. The approach is thus an econometric generalisation of the price-gap method widely used in trade law. Price increases are interpreted as a combination of compliance costs (essentially sourcing costs, since enforcement costs, principally being fixed, should affect prices only indirectly if at all) and quality-enhancement effects. In a second step, the presence of NTMs is interacted with deep-integration clauses, such as harmonisation or mutual recognition in the RTA, to assess whether the latter mitigates the price-raising effect of NTMs. If this is the case, the mitigating effect is interpreted as a reduction in NTM compliance costs, as there is no reason to believe that deep-harmonisation clauses would mitigate quality-enhancement effects. That is, let $p_{cc'k}$ be the unit value of product k exported from country c to country c' without an NTM; $p_{cc'k}^{\text{NTM}}$ its price in the presence of an NTM; and $p_{cc'k}^{\text{NTM},h}$ its price in the presence of the same NTM, but combined with a harmonisation clause between countries c and c'. Also, suppose that

$$p_{cc'k} < p_{cc'k}^{\text{NTM},h} < p_{cc'k}^{\text{NTM}}. \tag{8.1}$$

The log-price differential $\ln\left(p_{cc'k}^{\mathrm{NTM}}\right)-\ln\left(p_{cc'k}\right)$ is the NTM's AVE on product k, interpreted as a combination of compliance costs and quality-enhancement effects, while $\ln\left(p_{cc'k}^{\mathrm{NTM}}\right)-\ln\left(p_{cc'k}^{\mathrm{NTM},h}\right)$ is the AVE reduction, which we ascribe entirely to reduced compliance costs, brought about by harmonisation.

The analysis focusses on SPS (Type-A) and TBT (Type-B) measures as deep-integration clauses concern essentially those. Let h stand for standard harmonisation, m for mutual recognition, and a for mutual recognition of conformity-assessment procedures. We define a set of dummy variables marking the type of RTA based on the deep-integration clause $l=\{h,m,a\}$ as coded by Piermartini and Budetta (2009):

$$I_{cc'}^{l}=\begin{cases}1 & \text{if } c \text{ and } c' \text{ have an RTA with deep-integration clause } l\\ 0 & \text{otherwise.}\end{cases} \tag{8.2}$$

The estimation is carried out separately product by product, as in Kee et al. (2009). Let δ_c and $\delta_{c'}$ be country fixed effects; $t_{cc'k}$ the tariff imposed by c' on product k imported from c; $\mathbf{x}_{cc'}$ a vector of country-pair determinants, such as distance or common language; and $I_{c'k}^{n}$ a dummy variable marking the imposition of NTM n on product k by country c', as defined in (4). Recall that there is only one year of data, so no time indices are needed. The estimation equation is then

$$\ln p_{cc'k}=\delta_c+\delta_{c'}+\sum\nolimits_{n=A,B,\text{other}}\alpha_1^n I_{c'k}^n+\sum\nolimits_{n=A,B,\text{other}}\beta_1^n\left(I_{c'k}^n\times I_{cc'}^l\right)+ \\ \beta_2\ln\left(1+t_{cc'k}\right)+\mathbf{x}_{cc'}\gamma_1+u_{cc'k}. \tag{8.3}$$

Equation (3) is estimated on a database with the largest number of observations available, i.e. with all countries for which data on NTMs and deep-integration clauses exist.[4] The results are shown in a synthetic form in Table 8.1, suggesting that the mutual recognition of conformity-assessment procedures is susceptible to yielding the largest gains across the board in terms of the compliance-cost reduction for TBT measures. The mutual recognition of technical and SPS regulations (second line) yields the lowest reduction in compliance costs, while the remaining three approaches yield roughly equivalent reductions. One way of interpreting the low results for the mutual recognition of TBT and SPS measures is that it happens typically between countries that have bridged their regulatory distances through partial harmonisation, yielding few additional gains.

The results are decomposed by sector presented in Figure 8.3. Each bar measures the reduction in NTM AVEs, again as a percentage of the baseline AVE and not in 'raw' percentage points.[5] In 11 Sections (HS classification at the 2-digit level of aggregation), the mutual recognition of conformity-assessment procedures brings the largest reduction in NTM costs; on average, mutual recognition of conformity assessment procedures reduces by one-sixth the AVE of SPS measures and by one-quarter that of TBT measures. The footwear sector stands

Table 8.1 Mutual Recognition of Conformity-Assessment Procedures Yields Large Reductions in Compliance Costs

		SPS (A)	TBT (B)
Mutual recognition	Conformity-assessment procedures	−15.1	−27.6
	Technical/SPS regulations	−3.6	−9.9
Harmonisation	Conformity-assessment procedures	−11.8	−20.0
	Technical/SPS regulations	−13.6	−20.3
Transparency requirements		−15.4	−21.1

Note: The reduction shown is in percentage points of the baseline AVEs, not in 'raw' percentage points. Thus, the first entry (−15.1) means that the average AVE of SPS regulations (2.8 percent) is reduced by 15 percent or 0.4 percent points, to 2.4 percent, by the mutual recognition of conformity-assessment procedures.
Source: Cadot and Gourdon (2015).

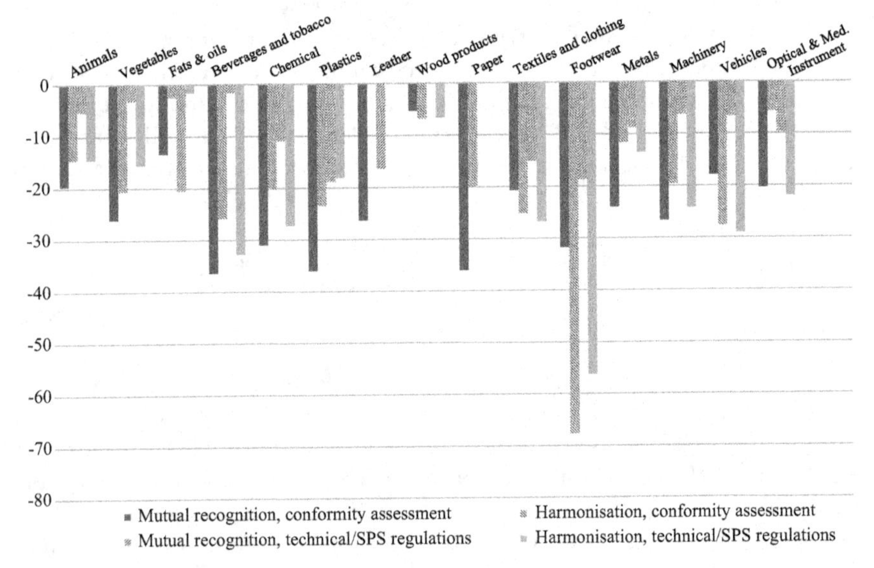

Figure 8.3 Mutual Recognition of Conformity-Assessment Procedures Yields Large Cost Reductions.

Note: SPS = Sanitary and Phytosanitary.
Source: Cadot and Gourdon (2015).

out as a sector where harmonisation seems to yield very large gains in terms of cost reduction.

All in all, the results presented here seem to suggest that harmonisation is not much more powerful than mutual recognition for mitigating the cost of complying with NTMs, even though it is perhaps the most ambitious and politically difficult route. Most strikingly, the mutual recognition of conformity-assessment procedures, which is relatively easy to achieve and has low visibility, seems to deliver substantial gains. As some countries in ASEAN are struggling to get their conformity-assessment infrastructures up to speed, this suggests a strategy whereby the ASEAN Secretariat could target conformity-assessment infrastructures (standards bureaus and testing laboratories and other related measures) for technical assistance with a view to achieving area-wide mutual recognition within a short time horizon.

8.3.2.2 Trade diversion from 'premature harmonisation'

Here we go one step further and assess whether deep-integration clauses in RTAs seem to enhance trade, with particular emphasis on the distinction between North–South and South–South trade, a distinction that is particularly relevant in ASEAN, where development levels vary substantially. The policy question is as follows. Suppose that Southern or relatively poor country c harmonises its SPS or TBT regulations with a Northern or richer country, c'. In most cases, regulations are most stringent in c' (see Maur and Shepherd, 2011), so the burden of adjustment falls on c, where producers must adopt the relatively expensive technology compliant with the stringent standard in c'. Is it possible that in so doing, c's producers price themselves out of *other* Southern markets where the level of standard imposed by c' is irrelevant? In this case, the North–South RTA's deep-integration clauses would create or reinforce a hub-and-spoke trade pattern where relatively poor countries trade with the richer one but not with potential Southern, out-of-bloc partners. This would be akin to an unusual form of trade diversion, whereas standard, Vinerian trade diversion predicts that the bloc's *imports* shrink; this form predicts that the bloc's *exports* shrink.

The analysis is based on the gravity equation and draws from Cadot et al. (2015). The sample of bilateral trade flows (covering 1990–2006) is split into two subsamples corresponding, respectively, to North–South and South–South trade relations,[6] dropping North–North relations. The definition of deep integration clauses in RTAs draws again from Piermartini and Budetta (2009), updating it with recent North–South RTAs.

The variable explained by the model is bilateral trade flows; for North–South trade relations, the treatment variable is a dummy equal to one when countries c and c' both belong to the same North–South RTA, interacted with the same deep-integration clauses used in the previous section, with a further refinement depending on whether harmonisation is on regional (*ad hoc*) or international standards (like the Codex Alimentarius). For South–South relations, the treatment is whether c or c' belongs to an RTA with a Northern country, again interacted with deep-interaction clauses.

The results are shown synthetically in Table 8.2, which reports only the coefficients on the variables of interest. All coefficients on standard gravity variables (importer and exporter GDP, fixed effects and distance) have the expected signs and magnitude and are omitted.

The first two lines of Table 8.2, pertaining to North–South trade, i.e. intra-bloc trade in North–South RTAs, suggest that trade agreements between rich

Table 8.2 Deep Integration between Rich and Poor Countries, a Non-Conventional Trade Diversion

	Coefficient[a]
North–South trade[b]	
RTA with SPS/TBT harmonisation:	-0.20
On regional standards	
On international standards	0.52
South–South trade[c]	
Importer belongs to an NS RTA	-0.11
Exporter belongs to an NS RTA:	
Any RTA	-0.20
RTA with SPS/TBT harmonisation	-0.22

Note: RTA = Regional trade agreement; SPS = Sanitary and phytosanitary; TBT = Technical barriers to trade; NS = North–South.
Source: Adapted from Cadot et al. (2015).
[a]Coefficients are from the PPML estimator and therefore their magnitude cannot be interpreted the same way as ordinary least squares (OLS) coefficients. All coefficients reported in the table are significant at the 1 percent level.
[b]1,731 observations (only country pairs documented in the Piermartini–Budetta database); fixed effects by exporter-year, importer-year, and exporter-importer dyad.
[c]24,803 observations; year and dyad fixed effects.

and poor countries with deep-integration clauses foster intra-bloc trade only to the extent that harmonisation takes place on international standards. When regional standards are promoted instead, the effect on trade is negative, possibly because regional standards are often *ad hoc* and influenced by special interests.

The third line is suggestive of standard, Vinerian trade diversion as Southern countries belonging to North–South RTAs tend to import less from other Southern countries. The most interesting results are in the last two lines. They show that North–South RTAs also tend to generate non-conventional trade-diversion effects, as Southern members also tend to *export* less to out-of-bloc Southern markets and even less – although the additional effect is small – in the presence of deep-integration clauses.

These results suggest two observations. First, the benefit of North–South RTAs for Southern countries – enhanced access to Northern markets – depends on the quality of regulatory convergence at play in the bloc. If it is based on international standards, i.e. best practices, the market-access effect is positive; if it is based on *ad hoc* regional standards, likely to be tainted by special-interest politics, there is no market-access gain anymore. Second, the benefits, when they exist, come at a cost –a reduced export by choice due, effectively, to quality upgrading, partly, presumably, because of a compliance-cost effect. Note that these results are consistent with those discussed in the previous section, where it appeared that the harmonisation of technical and SPS regulations carried the lowest benefits in terms of a compliance-cost reduction.

Thus, there is a 'dark side' to harmonisation. Moreover, in practice, harmonisation can be driven by special interests; for instance, harmonisation to stiff standards can be pushed by large players to drive out smaller ones for whom compliance is more difficult to achieve (recall the exit of small players illustrated in Figure 8.1). As large players are likely to have better access to policy processes, manipulations of this sort may be frequent in practice.

8.4 Towards regulatory convergence: how distant are partners?

Before reducing the regulatory differences potentially responsible for the fragmentation of regional markets, one needs a way to assess the size of the differences. We propose here a broad, two-way categorisation: at the 'extensive margin' and at the 'intensive margin', with a conceptual and visual tool to measure those differences. The tool could be useful as a way of assessing, prior to the launch of regional negotiations on harmonisation/mutual recognition, how wide is the gap between member states' practices. While this would not replace technical work by industry experts to assess what measures could or should be harmonised and what adaptation costs would be involved for producers, it would help assess the overall difficulty and chances of success of negotiations. It could also be useful to identify quick wins to gather momentum in the negotiations.

The regulatory distance at the extensive margin (RD–EM) captures the differences in the patterns of imposition of NTMs of different types (particular forms of SPS or TBT measures, as classified by the Multi-Agency Support Team (MAST) nomenclature) on different products. Regulatory distance at the intensive margin measures differences in the stringency of measures of the same type on a given product: for instance, differences in the MRLs of a given toxic substance for a given product.

8.4.1 Extensive margin

RD–EM answers the following question: do countries tend to apply the same type of measure (e.g. quotas or inspection requirements) to the same products? It can be measured for pairs of countries for which NTM inventories classified according to the MAST nomenclature are available from data available on WITS, the World Bank's trade data portal. The RD–EM variable is built up from the product-measure level. Suppose that Country *A* imposes one type of NTM, say B840 (inspection requirements), on a given product defined at the 6-digit level of the harmonised system, say HS 840731 ('spark ignition reciprocating piston engines of a kind used for the propulsion of vehicles of HS Chapter 87, of a cylinder capacity not greater than 50cc'). If Country *B* imposes the same type of measure (coded as B840) on that same product for the given measure-product pair, countries *A* and *B* are said to be 'similar'. We then code the regulatory distance variable as zero. By contrast, if *B* imposes a different regulatory requirement, but not B840, or if it imposes no NTMs at all on that product, then *A* and *B* are 'dissimilar' for measure-product pair (B840, 840731) and the regulatory-distance variable is coded as one.

Formally, let *c* index countries, *k* HS6 products, and *n* NTM types, and let

$$I_{cnk} = \begin{cases} 1 & \text{if country } c \text{ applies NTM type } n \text{ to product } k \\ 0 & \text{otherwise.} \end{cases} \tag{8.4}$$

Regulatory distance at the measure-product level is

$$d_{cc'nk}^{EM} = \left| I_{cnk} - I_{c'nk} \right|.$$

Letting $N = \max\{N_c; N_{c'}\}$ be the total number of NTMs used by any of the two countries and $K = \max\{K_c; K_{c'}\}$ the total number of products covered in any of the two countries, the aggregate regulatory distance between c and c' is

$$D_{cc'}^{EM} = \frac{1}{NK} \sum_{n} \sum_{K} D_{cc'nk}, \tag{8.5}$$

i.e. the sum of the absolute values of the differences in NTM application status. Because regulatory distance is normalised by the grand total of product–NTM combinations, it lies between zero and one and is typically a small number.

The complete matrix of bilateral regulatory distances between countries in the United Nations Conference on Trade and Development (UNCTAD)'s NTM database is shown in Table 8.A1. Large tables can be unwieldy to use, so Figure 8.4 shows a new and alternative way of representing regulatory distance. The idea is to project bilateral distances onto a plane akin to a map. Mathematical details of the method are given in the Appendix.[7] To interpret Figure 8.4, note that the axes are arbitrary: they are scaled so as to fit the range of bilateral distances and merely represent the cardinal points in which distances are mapped.

Figure 8.4 suggests several observations. First, a small number of countries stand out for unusual patterns of NTM imposition. Those include Nepal (NPL), Sri Lanka (LKA), China (CHN), Morocco (MAR) and Namibia (NAM).[8] Second, there is a 'core' of countries with similar patterns of NTM imposition at the product level. Interestingly, all ASEAN countries for which we have data are well inside that core, suggesting either that national governments have developed regulatory patterns that are inspired by international experience or that ASEAN's efforts to bring regulatory convergence have had some effect.

Is there any evidence that FTAs, in general, foster regulatory convergence? As a first pass, Table 8.3 shows the results of a regression of regulatory distance on RTA dummies using Piermartini and Budetta's database (Piermartini and Budetta, 2009). The dependent variable in the regressions is the bilateral regulatory distance measure shown in Table 8.A1, which we regress on dummy variables marking whether a given country pair belongs either to any FTA (Column 1) or to a particular one (Column 2).

The coefficient in the first column of Table 8.3 is negative and statistically significant (at the 1 percent level), suggesting that, on average, RTAs reduce the regulatory distance between their members. The effect is quantitatively very large; the average regulatory distance between country pairs in our sample is 0.079. Thus, the average RTA cuts regulatory distance by 0.033/0.079 = 42 percent. The second column breaks down this effect by individual agreement. The estimated effect for the Asociación Latinoamericana de Integración (ALADI) is also negative and highly significant. For other agreements, we do not have enough observations to estimate statistically significant effects,

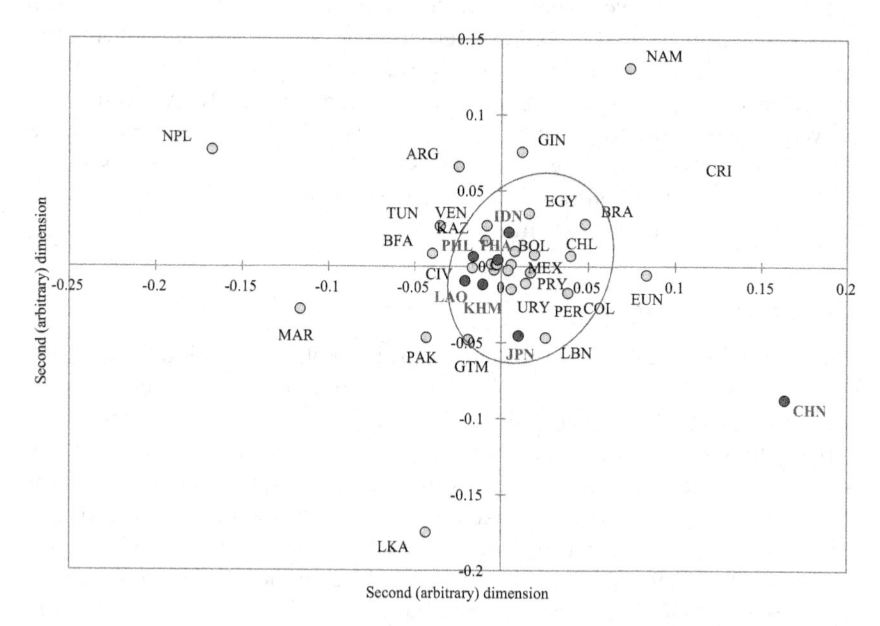

Figure 8.4 Map-Like Representation of Regulatory Distances.
Source: Authors' calculations.

Table 8.3 Regression Results, Regulatory Distances, and Regional Trade Agreements

	(1)	(2)
Both in the same RTA (any)	-0.033***	
	(8.07)	
Both in ALADI		-0.029***
		(2.83)
Both in Andean Community		-0.023
		(0.77)
Both in CACM		-0.049
		(0.72)
Both in COMESA		-0.033
		(0.85)
Both in SADC		-0.045
		(1.14)
Both in SAFTA		0.018
		(0.46)
Constant	0.086***	0.0831***
	(24.33)	(26.15)
Observations	992	992
R-squared	0.01	0.01

Note: Estimator: OLS; dependent variable: bilateral regulatory distance.
Robust t-statistics in parentheses.
*significant at 10 percent; **significant at 5 percent; ***significant at 1 percent.

but they are all negative except for the South Asian Free Trade Area (SAFTA). More research is needed to assess whether those results can be confirmed on a larger sample and with adequate controls, but the prima facie results are encouraging. From a policy perspective, they suggest that RTAs do induce a convergence of regulatory systems 'at the extensive margin'; i.e. member states tend to apply the same type of measures to the same products. This should facilitate further harmonisation at the intensive margin, i.e. convergence in the level of stringency of the measures.

8.4.2 Intensive margin

The concept of regulatory distance can also be applied at the intensive margin (RD–IM), where it answers the following question: For a given (homogeneous) type of measure and a given product, how distant is the measure's stringency between two countries? As an example, consider a fungicide called Imazalil used to reduce the perishability of oranges during transport and storage. The Imazalil molecule, known as enilconazoleis, is listed as 'known to the state to cause cancer' under California's Proposition 65 (Safe Drinking Water and Toxic Enforcement Act of 1986) and carries a warning label in the US.[9] It was developed by Janssen, a New Jersey chemical company, part of the Johnson & Johnson group, which, however, divested from it in 2006.[10] Table 8.4 shows, for selected countries (including all ASEAN members with published data), the MRLs of Imazalil in citrus fruit, expressed in parts per million (ppm) (last column), and the regulatory distance calculated as the difference between the MRLs of each country pair as a proportion of the maximum level (10 ppm for the whole database). For instance, the US accepts 10 ppm, the world's highest level, while Cambodia accepts only 5 ppm; their regulatory distance is then 5/10 = 0.5.

In terms of regional blocs, although there is no formal mechanism to harmonise SPS regulations in the North American Free Trade Agreement (NAFTA) (the US exerts a *de facto* leadership), all three members share a high 10 ppm MRL for Imazalil, while practically all other countries, except Australia, have a substantially lower MRL at 5 ppm.

With several regulated substances, the principle of regulatory distance at the intensive margin illustrated for one pesticide in Table 8.4 can easily be extended as follows. Let x_{ck} be the MRL on substance s imposed by country c for product k measured in, say, ppm. The multi-dimensional regulatory distance at the intensive margin between countries c and c' for product k is then

$$d_{cc'k}^{IM} = \frac{1}{N_{sk}} \sum_{s} \left| x_{csk} - x_{c'sk} \right| \tag{8.6}$$

where N_{sk} is the number of regulated substances for product k. When a country does not impose an MRL for a given substance, the MRL database codes it as a missing value; x_{csk} is then undefined and substance s drops out of the sample when taking the differences in (6), which only include cases where both c and c' impose MRLs on the same substance.

Table 8.4 MRL on Imazalil in Oranges, Selected Countries, and Codex Alimentarius

Regulatory Distances, Intensive Margin	*Australia*	*Cambodia*	*Canada*	*China*	*Codex*	*EU*	*India*	*Indonesia*	*Mexico*	*NZ*	*Philippines*	*Singapore*	*Taiwan*	*Thailand*	*US*	*Viet Nam*	*MRL Level*
Australia		0.5	0	0.5	0.5	0.5	0.5	0.5	0	0.5	0.5	0.5	0.5	0.5	0	0.5	10
Cambodia			0.5	0	0	0	0	0	0.5	0	0	0	0	0	0.5	0	5
Canada					0.5	0.5	0.5	0.5	0.5	0	0.5	0.5	0.5	0.5	0.5	0	0.5
China					0	0	0	0	0.5	0	0	0	0	0	0.5	0	5
Codex						0	0	0	0.5	0	0	0	0	0	0.5	0	5
European Union							0	0	0.5	0	0	0	0	0	0.5	0	5
India								0	0.5	0	0	0	0	0	0.5	0	5
Indonesia									0.5	0	0	0	0	0	0.5	0	5
Mexico										0.5	0.5	0.5	0.5	0.5	0	0.5	10
New Zealand											0	0	0	0	0.5	0	5
Philippines												0	0	0	0.5	0	5
Singapore													0	0	0.5	0	5
Chinese Taipei														0	0.5	0	5
Thailand															0.5	0	5
US																0.5	10
Viet Nam																	5

Note: EU = European Union; NZ = New Zealand; US = United States; MRL = maximum residual levels.
Source: https://www.globalmrl.com.

While only illustrative, these calculations are suggestive of the kind of analysis that could be conducted in preparation for future ASEAN negotiations on harmonisation and mutual recognition to assess the 'distance' that must be bridged, overall, in order to achieve convergence.

8.5 Regulatory convergence in ASEAN: the way forward

This section explores ways of moving forward a deep-integration agenda in ASEAN, based on existing international experience as well as recent initiatives in Southeast Asia. While top-down efforts have proved only moderately successful in other regions so far, a bottom-up approach based on 'dynamic disciplines' and technical cooperation between national regulatory agencies offers promise.

8.5.1 Lessons from international experience

As multilateral efforts to reduce NTBs have progressed only slowly, a number of regional secretariats have tried to give an impulse to NTB reduction, harmonisation, and mutual-recognition agendas to reduce regulatory differences and the abuse of regulatory measures for protectionist purposes. This section briefly reviews the experience of selected regional arrangements, including the EU, NAFTA, ASEAN, the East African Community (EAC), the Southern African Development Community (SADC), and the Common Market for Eastern and Southern Africa (COMESA)[11] as well as a number of North–South bilateral agreements. To preview the result of the discussion, whereas the EU and (to a much lesser extent) NAFTA have adopted a top-down approach to regulatory convergence, South–South agreements have attempted to set up bottom-up approaches based on the identification of NTBs by the private sector, but with very limited success.

The reduction of NTBs to trade features prominently in ASEAN's efforts to promote economic integration in the region, reflecting a widespread view that NTBs have superseded tariffs as relevant barriers to trade. In particular, the ASEAN Economic Community blueprint has mainstreamed the reduction of NTBs in regional integration efforts, together with improvements in trade facilitation through single windows.

The ASEAN Trade in Goods Agreement (ATIGA), adopted in 2008, set a schedule for the elimination of NTBs in three stages (see ASEAN (2012)). The approach consisted of classifying NTBs into three categories: green for NTMs that were not NTBs, i.e. justified measures; amber for NTMs whose trade restrictiveness could be discussed; and red for clear-cut NTBs. ASEAN member countries were supposed to submit lists of NTMs, which the ASEAN Secretariat then classified into green, amber, or red. The secretariat's classification was reviewed by member countries, after which measures were examined and prioritised for elimination by a number of negotiating bodies, including the

Coordinating Committee on the Implementation of the Common Effective Preferential Tariff (CEPT) for the AFTA.[12]

Several action plans involving the removal of the core NTBs have been set up, by 2010 for ASEAN-5 (Brunei Darussalam, Indonesia, Malaysia, Singapore and Thailand), by 2012 for the Philippines, and by 2018 for Cambodia, Lao PDR, Myanmar and Viet Nam. On top of that, a number of regulation harmonisation efforts in cosmetics, automobiles, electrical and electronic equipment, medical devices, pharmaceuticals, and information and communication technology (ICT) have been endorsed and conducted. ASEAN has recently also set up the ASEAN Consultative Committee on Standards and Quality, which works with the sectors mentioned and also prepares food and rubber products.[13] However, the ATIGA mechanism suffers from an incentive problem, as governments are expected to provide information that will then be put on a bargaining table, although they have an incentive to hoard it instead. It also expects governments to set up inter-ministerial coordinating mechanisms to centralise information on regulations issued by various agencies. The problem is that governments are expected to overcome a collective-action problem to provide a public good – market access for regional partners.

What lessons can be drawn from international experience on streamlining NTMs? The EU's experience is probably the most advanced, but its replicability is limited by the fact that the EU integration project was from the start a more ambitious deep-integration project than most other regional blocs. Still, it is useful to note that mutual recognition was the key step forward when the European Court of Justice (ECJ) adopted the 'Cassis de Dijon' decision in 1979. Since then, mutual recognition and harmonisation have played complementary roles and progressed in parallel, with the European Commission setting broad guidelines through regulations and directives or, alternatively, decisions on particular issues and mutual recognition applying to all other cases.[14]

Politically, the impetus for regulatory convergence in the EU has come from the implicit cooperation of the European Commission and the ECJ, with the ECJ breaking up national barriers to trade and competition and the commission replacing them with new EU-wide regulatory regimes (Dzabirova, 2010). Some member states had feared that mutual recognition would set off a race to the bottom, with some countries loosening regulations in order to attract manufacturing. But those fears do not seem to have materialised, possibly because the commission's legislative activity pushed the model towards increasing reliance on harmonisation. The model's reliance on two powerful and driven supranational institutions (the European Commission and the ECJ) limits its replicability in the ASEAN context, which lacks such supranational institutions.

However, two lessons emerge from the EU model – (i) mutual recognition appeared as a simpler initial step than attempting to negotiate common rules between governments; and (ii) it did not trigger a race to the bottom in spite of uneven starting points in terms of development and regulatory stringency between Mediterranean and Northern countries.

The NAFTA was always much less ambitious than the EU in terms of deep integration, although the agreement contains specific provisions on regulatory convergence. For instance, for SPS measures, Chapter 7B encourages member states to consider each other's measures when developing their own. For TBT measures, Chapter 9 encourages them to make their regulations compatible. The NAFTA does not have a universal mutual-recognition principle like the EU's Cassis de Dijon decision; what comes closest is Article 714, which states that 'an importing Party shall treat another NAFTA country's SPS measure as equivalent to its own if the exporting country demonstrates objectively that the measure achieves the importing Party's appropriate level of protection'.[15] The wording suggests that the burden of proof is on the exporting country, which must demonstrate that its regulations are equivalent to those of the importing country, rather than the other way around, which is quite different from a blanket mutual-recognition principle. A number of proposals have been periodically floated for further integration (Irish, 2009 or Manley et al., 2005), in particular when enhanced security measures at US borders hampered Canadian exports after 11 September 2001.[16]

Interestingly, in the post-9/11 era, a key motivation for further integration in North America was security rather than trade, with the recognition that enhanced security might imply the emergence of supranational regulatory bodies (unless US agencies were given hegemonic power over the entire bloc, which other nations would be unlikely to accept). However, few of the new ideas have been put into practice. Some degree of regulatory convergence took place, or at least enhanced tripartite cooperation, under the 2005 Security and Prosperity Partnership, although on a limited agenda. Proposals on how to move forward include one that is directly relevant for ASEAN and will be discussed in more detail in the next section – to check for regulatory convergence (possibly through mutual consultation) *prior* to the issuance of new regulations as part of routine regulatory impact analysis, so as to end the 'tyranny of small differences' (Hart, 2006). Where the NAFTA has made substantial progress is in the mutual recognition of conformity assessment procedures contained in Articles 906(6) and 908(6) (Coffield, 1998), which the econometric analysis of the previous section found to be particularly important.

Beyond the NAFTA and the EU themselves, preferential agreements involving the EU and the US often involve commitments to reduce NTBs (Horn et al., 2009) that fall into two broad types: 'WTO+' commitments that go beyond WTO agreements (Trade Facilitation Agreement, particularly on SPS or TBTs) but build on them and 'WTO–X' commitments covering areas not covered by the WTO (e.g. labour and environment).

Many US and EU agreements have WTO+ clauses, typically deeper for those involving the EU, although relatively few make them enforceable. Lesser (2007) notes that most of the North–South and South–South agreements signed by Chile, Mexico and Singapore rely on mutual recognition of conformity assessment results and transparency/notification requirements. Many also call for the establishment of joint bodies to monitor the implementation of TBT provisions and facilitate cooperation and include dispute-settlement mechanisms for regulatory disputes. Mutual recognition arrangements for conformity assessment have often been adopted in sectors like telecoms, electrical, electronic and medical equipment.

Three key factors seem to influence the depth of regional TBT commitments. The first is the level of development of the parties. Standards harmonisation and even more mutual recognition of conformity assessment results are much easier among countries with similar levels of development. The second factor is the agreement's degree of integration. Deeper agreements, such as customs unions and common markets, can go more easily beyond WTO commitments. The third factor is the presence of the EU or the US as one of the parties to the agreement. Agreements involving the US often include acceptance of partner technical regulations as equivalent, alignment on international standards, and mutual recognition of conformity assessment. Agreements involving the EU often rely on alignment with the EU's own regulations, standards, and conformity assessment procedures, especially with close partners, such as Mediterranean countries.

In a review of over 70 preferential trade agreements covering several regions, levels of development, and depth of integration, 58 of them with TBT provisions, Piermartini and Budetta (2009) also found that harmonisation is more frequent than mutual recognition for technical regulations (29 agreements against 15), but mutual recognition of conformity assessment is the most frequent approach (39 agreements), followed by harmonisation of conformity assessment procedures (25 agreements). Harmonisation of technical regulations is a characteristic of EU agreements, sometimes, as noted, implying adoption of the EU *acquis communautaire* by RTA partners.

In South–South agreements, progress on regulatory convergence has been both more recent and shallower. Article 6 of the SADC Trade Protocol calls for the elimination of all NTBs and for member states to refrain from imposing new ones, but implementation has been haphazard, essentially bearing on monitoring through yearly implementation audits and the creation of the SADC Trade Monitoring and Compliance Mechanism (TMCM) in 2008. The TMCM's idea was to offer an online portal for private-sector complaints and a dispute-settlement mechanism, but the workflow from private-sector complaints to settlement of the issues has been largely ineffective. Similarly, Article 49 of the COMESA Treaty obliges member states to remove all existing NTBs to imports of goods originating from the other member states and thereafter refrain from imposing any further restrictions or prohibitions (Imani Development, 2009).

Regarding the EAC, Kirk (2010) shows that most NTBs prioritised for removal (so-called 'Category A') are still in place. All in all, only half the complaints received by SADC and 20 percent received by COMESA have been resolved under the Tripartite (SADC–COMESA–EAC) Monitoring Mechanism. Reasons for the failure of efforts to reduce NTBs and foster regulatory convergence include weak administrative capabilities at the national level and in regional secretariats. Indeed, the complaint portals have largely been developed by donors like TradeMark East Africa, with limited appropriation or active participation by governments or regional secretariats. But there is no doubt that beyond capability issues, many political-economy issues lurk in the background.

All of the mechanisms discussed in this section rely essentially on moral persuasion rather than binding commitments with enforcement mechanisms. However, for such mechanisms to work, there must be a political drive for deep integration at the highest level, which typically must go beyond the mere issue of regulatory convergence. What can be hoped for from capacity-building efforts is to tackle at least those problems that can have technical solutions and to gather momentum for reform from observed successes.

8.5.2 An institutional setup to foster convergence

The discussion suggests that the dominant approach in South–South agreements, with the possible exception of ASEAN, was at least designed as bottom up, relying on the private sector to identify problems and on intergovernmental negotiation forums to pick up and address issues. However, implementation has been largely donor driven and plagued by a lack of political commitment and weak capacity. In view of its achievements so far, it seems fair to say that this approach apparently offers limited promise.

While the degree of high-level political commitment must be taken as a given, the objective of this section is to offer an alternative institutional setup, potentially offering more promise, based on the World Bank's recent experience with a number of ASEAN countries, and offering a blueprint which, if adopted at the regional level, could generate sustainable and, most importantly, self-fuelling progress.

The approach is based on the World Bank's 'toolkit' for NTM streamlining (World Bank, 2011) and centres around the creation of regulatory supervisory bodies at the national level. Such bodies are viewed as having a twin role:

- i Promote inter-ministerial dialogue and cooperation to internalise 'regulatory externalities' (the fact that a regulation addressing one issue, say plant health, may have effects on competitiveness and trade).
- ii Provide an evidence-based analysis of regulatory costs and benefits based on the WTO principles of necessity and proportionality, and using relevant international evidence, so as to ground the regulatory process on a sound assessment of the economic and societal benefits and costs.

If implemented in earnest, this approach has the potential to bypass some of the constraints that have plagued past efforts to reduce the economic cost of poorly designed regulations and to bring multiple benefits, in particular if coordinated at the regional level.

First, past approaches have been aimed at existing regulations – the hardest battles to win as rent-creating regulations have had time to generate special interests willing to fight for them – while no disciplines were imposed on the flow of new regulations. Thus, there was a danger that if battles against existing regulations were won, which was difficult to start with, they could simply lead to the displacement of the problem with new regulations replacing the old. The creation of a 'dynamic discipline' in the form of a quality-control process imposed on all new regulations can thus close a potentially important loophole in NTM streamlining efforts.

Second, best-practice regulations tend to follow similar patterns; for instance, best-practice SPS regulations often follow the *Codex Alimentarius*. Such international standards do not fragment markets because they are the same everywhere. On the contrary, regulations that fragment markets are often idiosyncratic ones that are at odds with international standards and best practices. A regulatory supervisory agency would systematically promote the use of international standards in all areas because this would be part of its mandate. If similar agencies were set up in parallel in all ASEAN countries, their collective influence would be to reduce fragmentation simply by fostering convergence towards best practices *even in the absence of formal coordination mechanisms.*

Third, the approach draws on the experience of countries using Regulatory Impact Assessment (RIA) and tries to strike a balance between full-fledged cost-benefit analysis, which is much too burdensome to be used systematically, and 'box-checking' RIA, which is often too shallow to be useful, by relying on sound economic analysis and evidence. Moreover, if more advanced countries in ASEAN were doing evidence-based RIA (which, when technically complex, could be pooled between countries and/or outsourced to research bodies), less advanced ones with limited capabilities could in many cases take those analyses 'off the shelf' and adapt them to their context, which would be much less demanding in terms of capabilities. This, again, would not require formal coordination mechanisms, but simply a willingness to share the results of technical analyses.

Fourth, regulatory supervisory bodies should be merged with competition authorities at the national level. Several arguments militate in favour of having the same agency in charge of both missions. On the one hand, bad regulations often create monopoly power by restricting entry (sometimes on purpose); thus, competition and regulation issues are deeply intertwined. Moreover, the skills required to investigate collusion or abuses of dominant positions are typically the same as those required to investigate the impact of regulations – law and economics, with an emphasis on microeconomics and industrial organisation. On the other hand, the key problem for regulatory supervisory bodies is one of clout: to have teeth in battles with special interests, they must be able to dominate the debate analytically and enjoy widespread respect. An agency with a mandate to impose welfare-enhancing disciplines on both the private and public sectors will have much more clout than two separate ones.

The creation of such agencies in all ASEAN countries does not require explicit coordination and could even be seen as an ambitious reading of the Trade Facilitation Agreement, signed in Bali in 2013. The Trade Facilitation Agreement mandates the creation of trade portals and trade facilitation committees. These obligations could be fulfilled *a minima* by the creation of a committee to discuss doing-business issues and a trade portal giving basic information on customs procedures. However, a more ambitious reading of the agreement would use it as the impulse towards the creation of trade-centred regulatory supervisory bodies with a mandate to cover both the issues discussed earlier and the maintenance of up-to-date inventories of all trade-relevant regulations, all made accessible via the trade portal. Singapore, Malaysia, Indonesia and Thailand have been developing trade portals, and lately followed by the Philippines, Brunei, Viet Nam, Cambodia, Lao PDR and Myanmar.

Although explicit coordination at the regional level is not a prerequisite for the blueprint discussed here, it could substantially enhance the speed of regulatory convergence. For instance, technical staff in supervisory agencies (whether called NTM committees, as in Cambodia, or otherwise) could be trained in common sessions open to all or subsets of ASEAN countries. Through common training, staff would acquire and build a common vision and establish networks of contacts that could facilitate future consultations when new regulations are designed. Such prior consultations have been discussed in the context of NAFTA's deepening (see supra) or the Transatlantic Trade and Investment Partnership (TTIP). While difficult to impose as a systematic requirement, they could be greatly facilitated by personal familiarity between the agency personnel of member states.

In this, the ASEAN Secretariat could play a key role through advocacy, raising the visibility of successful experimentation, providing technical assistance (e.g. in collaboration with development partners), and pushing for a general approach to regulatory convergence based on a 'better-regulations' philosophy rather than the usual 'give-and-take' approach adopted in failed NTB-elimination efforts.

8.6 Concluding remarks

This chapter shows that regulatory convergence is a complex matter where ultimate effects can be different from those expected and where the results of past efforts have been uneven. When levels of development differ, regulatory needs differ. In such a context, forcing harmonisation may be counterproductive and does not necessarily lead to enhanced efficiency. Moreover, with the very strong political drive of the EU being absent, political commitment for regulatory convergence has been slow to emerge.

These difficulties should not be construed as meaning that regulatory convergence does not matter or is too ambitious to be achievable. First, it matters. Poorly designed regulations are pure deadweight losses that hamper business and trade without bringing any revenue (unlike tariffs) and that often fail to achieve legitimate non-trade objectives. The approach proposed here is based on 'soft' harmonisation through convergence on best practices while leaving space for slow convergence for the least advanced member states. The idea is to put in place at the country level an institutional setup ensuring that regulations pass tests of economic rationality and properly internalise key societal trade-offs (e.g. between environmental protection and competitiveness).

Solving trade-offs explicitly is the right approach to maximising social welfare, but it is well known that governments are exposed to pressures from various lobbies intent on hijacking regulations to further special interests. Technical regulations are often difficult to understand and therefore offer ways of distorting markets while obfuscating the issues. In the presence of such distortionary intents, no well-wishing regulatory setup can ensure that flawed decisions will not be taken. Sometimes, battles will need to be fought, and there is no guarantee that they will be won.

However, even when politically important jobs or commercial interests are at stake, regulations often offer only third-best options. WTO-consistent trade remedies, while having many drawbacks of their own, can often achieve the same result at a lesser cost in terms of economic distortions. When poorly designed regulations are proposed based on a fudge of trade and non-trade objectives, a smart regulatory supervisory body would be able to tell motivations apart and propose specific solutions to each at a lesser cost, including trade remedies to protect jobs and regulations to protect health. Thus, even in the presence of political-economy considerations, the naïve welfare-maximising proposal in this chapter may not be naïve after all.

Disclaimer

The work was conducted when Lili Yan Ing was with ERIA. The view expressed by her here are personal and do not represent the view of the Ministry of Trade of Indonesia.

Notes

1 For instance, the US reacted to the 1986 Three Mile Island nuclear accident with a freeze on all nuclear energy projects, whereas Europe kept on steaming ahead with its own. Conversely, the European Union (EU) reacted to the bovine spongiform encephalopathy crisis of the 1990s with super-precautionary SPS regulations, whereas the US was going ahead with the marketing of genetically modified organisms. In both cases, the underlying force was the fear of catastrophic events, but the triggering crises were not the same. On these issues, see, for example, Vogel (2012).

2 NTMs are defined as policy measures – other than ordinary customs tariffs – that can potentially have an economic effect on international trade in goods, changing quantities traded, prices, or both. Some of measures can be perceived as barriers or so-called NTBs. NTBs are a subset of NTMs.

3 Another consideration outside of the Melitz framework is on market structure from an IO perspective: if dominant firms are constrained by a competitive fringe and that fringe is laid to waste by these higher fixed costs then that can have anti-competitive effects in terms of surviving firms' domestic behaviour.

4 Unfortunately, there are not enough data for ASEAN countries alone to separate the estimation between ASEAN and non-ASEAN countries, so the results are for the worldwide averages.

5 For instance, for animals, the combined estimated AVE of all NTMs is 26.2 percent. Mutual recognition of conformity-assessment procedures (the dark blue bar) would reduce that by 20 percent, i.e. 0.2×26 percent = 5.2 percent, bringing back the AVE of combined NTMs to 21 percent.

6 In addition, a Chow test suggests that the estimated coefficients on both subsamples differ significantly and confirms this divide.

7 The mapping cannot be perfect; with 33 countries to place on the map (we treat the EU as one, as the regulatory distance amongst the EU member states is zero) and arbitrary distances between them, only a 32-dimensional space could provide a perfect representation. As the number of dimensions shrinks, the distortion in the representation of distances grows. The distortion for a two-dimensional projection is shown in the Appendix Table 8.A1. If there were no distortion, all points would lie on the 45° line; it can be seen that the distortion remains moderate.

8 We recoded Chinese data to transform all NTMs erroneously coded as B for products other than agri-food products (Chapters HS01 to HS24) into A, keeping the last three digits the same.

9 It is rated by the US Environmental Protection Agency (EPA) as only moderately toxic. See http://pmep.cce.cornell.edu/profiles/extoxnet/haloxyfop-methylparathion/imazalil-ext.html.

10 www.janssenpmp.com.

11 Information on regulatory convergence in Mercosur is virtually non-existent and the issue is not discussed in the Inter-American Development Bank's reports.

12 See Ando and Obashi (2009) for more details.

13 For details, see Prassetya and Intal (2015), Pettman (2013), and ACCSQ (www.asean.org/news/item/accsq).

14 A regulation is similar to a national law with the difference that it is applicable in all EU countries. Directives set out general rules to be transferred into national law by each country as they deem appropriate. A decision only deals with a particular issue and specifically mentioned persons or organisations. See http://ec.europa.eu/legislation/index_en.htm.

15 See Irish (2009: 339) or Meilke (2001).

16 Amongst the proposals, Irish (2009: 335) lists 'investment in border infrastructure, law enforcement and military cooperation, support for economic development in Mexico, a North American energy strategy, a permanent North American tribunal for dispute resolution, a unified approach to anti-dumping and countervailing duty actions, a trinational competition commission, labour mobility between Canada and the US, mutual recognition of professional standards and degrees, a North American education programme, an annual North American summit meeting of the leaders of government, a North American Advisory Council and a North American Inter-Parliamentary Group'.

References

Ando, M. and A. Obashi (2009), *The Pervasiveness of Non-tariff Measures in ASEAN: Evidences from the Inventory Approach*. Tokyo, Japan: Keio University.

ASEAN Consultative Committee on Standards and Quality, the Association of Southeast Asian Nations, www.asean.org/news/item/accsq (accessed in August 2015).

Baldwin, R. and M. Kawai (2013), 'Multilateralizing Asian Regionalism', *Trade Working Papers* 23553, East Asian Bureau of Economic Research.

Cadot, O., A.-C. Disdier, and L. Fontagné (2015), 'Harmonizing Non-tariff Measures: Always a Blessing?' in P. Delimatsis (ed.), *The Law, Economics and Politics of International Standardisation*, pp. 242–272. London: Cambridge University Press.

Cadot, O. and J. Gourdon (2015), 'NTMs, Preferential Trade Agreements, and Prices: New evidence', *CEPII Working Paper* 2015-01 February.

Coffield, S. (1998), 'Commonality of Standards – Implications for Sovereignty – A US Perspective', *Canada–United States Law Journal*, *24*, p. 235.

Dzabirova, L. (2010), 'New Developments in the EU Internal Market – Harmonisation vs. Mutual Recognition', *mimeo*.

Evenett, S. and M. Wermelinger (2010), 'A Snapshot of Contemporary Protectionism: How Important are the Murkier Forms of Trade Discrimination?' in ESCAP (ed.), *Rising Non-Tariff Protectionism and Crisis Recovery*, pp. 8–26. New York, NY: United Nations Economic and Social Commission for Asia and the Pacific (ESCAP).

Hart, M. (2006), *Steer or Drift? Taking Charge of Canada–US Regulatory Convergence*, Commentary No. 229. Toronto, Canada: C.D. Howe Institute.

Horn, H., P. Mavroidis, and A. Sapir (2009), 'Beyond the WTO? An Anatomy of EU and US Preferential Trade Agreements', *Bruegel Blueprint Series* Vol. VII, Brussels, Belgium: Bruegel Foundation.

Imani Development (2009), *Corporate Social Responsibility in Sub-Saharan Africa – Built In or Bolted On? A Survey on Promoting and Hindering Factors.* Eschborn, Germany: Deutsche Gesellschaft für Technische Zusammenarbeit [GTZ] GmbH/BMZ/ British High Commission South Africa.

Irish, M. (2009), 'Regulatory Convergence, Security and Global Administrative Law in Canada–United States Trade', *Journal of International Economic Law 12*, pp. 333–355.

Kee, H.L., A. Nicita, and M. Olarreaga (2009), 'Estimating Trade Restrictiveness Indices', *The Economic Journal 119*(January), pp. 172–199.

Kirk, R. (2010), 'Addressing Trade Restrictive Non-Tariff Measures on Goods Trade in the East African Community', *World Bank Africa Trade Policy Note No. 7*, Washington, DC: The World Bank.

Lesser, C. (2007), 'Do Bilateral and Regional Approaches for Reducing Technical Barriers to Trade Converge Towards the Multilateral Trading System?' *OECD Trade Policy Working Paper* No. 58, Paris: OECD.

Maur, J.-C. and B. Shepherd (2011), Preferential Trade Agreements and Development: Issues and Implications. Washington, DC: The World Bank.

Manley, J., P. Aspe, and W. Weld (2005), *Building a North American Community.* Report of an Independent Task Force, sponsored by the Council on Foreign Relations with the Canadian Council of Chief Executives and the Consejo Mexicano de Asuntos Internacionales. New York, NY: Council on Foreign Relations.

Meilke, K. (2001), *An Appraisal of the SPS Provisions of the North American Free Trade Agreement.* Washington, DC: Chemonics International.

Melitz, M.J. (2003), 'The Impact of Trade on Intra-Industry Reallocations and Aggregate Industry Productivity', *Econometrica 71*, pp. 1695–1725.

Pettman, S. (2013), 'Standards Harmonisation in ASEAN: Progress, Challenges and Moving Beyond 2015', *ERIA Discussion Paper Series* No. 30, Jakarta, Indonesia: ERIA.

Piermartini, R. and M. Budetta (2009), 'A Mapping of Regional Rules on Technical Barriers to Trade', in Estevadeordal, A. R. and K. Suominen (eds.), *Regional Rules in the Global Trading System.* Cambridge, UK: Cambridge University Press.

Prassetya, R. and P.S. Intal, Jr. (2015), 'AEC Blueprint Implementation Performance and Challenges: Standards and Conformance', *ERIA Discussion Paper Series* No. 42, Jakarta, Indonesia: ERIA.

Vogel, D. (2012), *The Politics of Precaution: Regulating Health, Safety and Environmental Risks in Europe and the United States.* Princeton, NJ: Princeton University Press.

World Bank (2011), *Streamlining Non-Tariff Measures: A Toolkit for Policy Makers.* Washington, DC: The World Bank.

Appendix A

Regional and out-of-region coverage ratios

Let M_{jk} be Country j's imports of product k from all of its partners in the world, and let

$$I_{jk}^{\text{NTM}} = \begin{cases} 1 & \text{if country } j \text{ imposes one or more NTM on product } k \\ 0 & \text{otherwise.} \end{cases} \tag{8.7}$$

The NTM coverage ratio on Country j's imports is

$$c_j = \frac{\sum_k I_{jk}^{\text{NTM}} M_{jk}}{\sum_k M_{jk}} \tag{8.8}$$

Similarly, let M_{jrk} be Country j's imports of product k from regional bloc r; the NTM coverage ratio on Country i's regional imports is

$$c_{jr} = \frac{\sum_k I_{jk}^{\text{NTM}} M_{jrk}}{\sum_k M_{jrk}} \tag{8.9}$$

That is, a country's regional coverage ratio is the proportion of its imports from the regional bloc covered by one or more NTM. The out-of-bloc coverage ratio can be calculated similarly. Let $M_{i,-r,k}$ be Country i's imports of product k from all countries outside of bloc r. The equivalent of for out-of-bloc imports is

$$c_{i,-r} = \frac{\sum_k I_{ik}^{\text{NTM}} M_{i,-r,k}}{\sum_k M_{i,-r,k}}. \tag{8.10}$$

Regulatory distances

Let i be index countries, k HS6 products, and j NTM types; and let I_{ilk} be an indicator function defined by

$$I_{ilk} = \begin{cases} 1 & \text{if country } i \text{ applies NTM } l \text{ to product } k \\ 0 & \text{otherwise} \end{cases} \tag{8.11}$$

The Regulatory Distance measure at the measure-product level is the absolute value of the difference between this indicator function between the two countries:

$$r_{lk} = \left| I_{ilk} - I_{jlk} \right|.$$

In the second step, regulatory distances at the measure-product pair level are aggregated into an overall measure of dissimilarity or 'regulatory distance' at the country-pair level. That is, let N be the total number of observed product–NTM combinations. The country-level regulatory distance measure for countries i and j, D_{ij}, is

$$D_{ij} = \frac{1}{N} \sum_k \sum_l r_{ilk} \tag{8.12}$$

As D_{ij} is normalised by the grand total of product–NTM combinations, it lies between zero and one. In our sample, it ranges from 0.009 between Madagascar and Tanzania to 0.304 between China and Nepal.

We now turn to the two-dimensional projection of regulatory distances in Section 8.3. Let i and j index countries and D_{ij} stand for the distance between i and j. The dissimilarity matrix is

$$\Delta = \begin{bmatrix} D_{11} & \cdots & D_{1m} \\ \cdots & \cdots & \\ D_{m1} & \cdots & D_{mm} \end{bmatrix} \tag{8.13}$$

which is a square, symmetric matrix with zeros on the diagonal and bilateral distances off the diagonal. The Δ matrix of regulatory distance is shown in Table 8.A1. Multidimensional scaling (MDS) consists of finding m coordinate vectors $\mathbf{x}_i$ (one for each country) such that, using an appropriate distance metric (noted $\| \; \|$),

$$D_{ij} \simeq \left\| \mathbf{x}_i - \mathbf{x}_j \right\| \tag{8.14}$$

i.e. the projection of the individual country distance onto a space of less than m dimensions represents reasonably well their true dissimilarity. If the space had m dimensions, the representation would be perfect; as the number of dimensions shrinks (e.g. to two in a plane projection) the distortion potentially grows. The most usual way of formulating the problem of choosing these $\mathbf{x}$ vectors is to minimise a quadratic loss function:

$$\min_{\mathbf{x}_1,\ldots,\mathbf{x}_m} \sum_{i<j} \left(D_{ij} - \left\| \mathbf{x}_i - \mathbf{x}_j \right\| \right)^2. \tag{8.15}$$

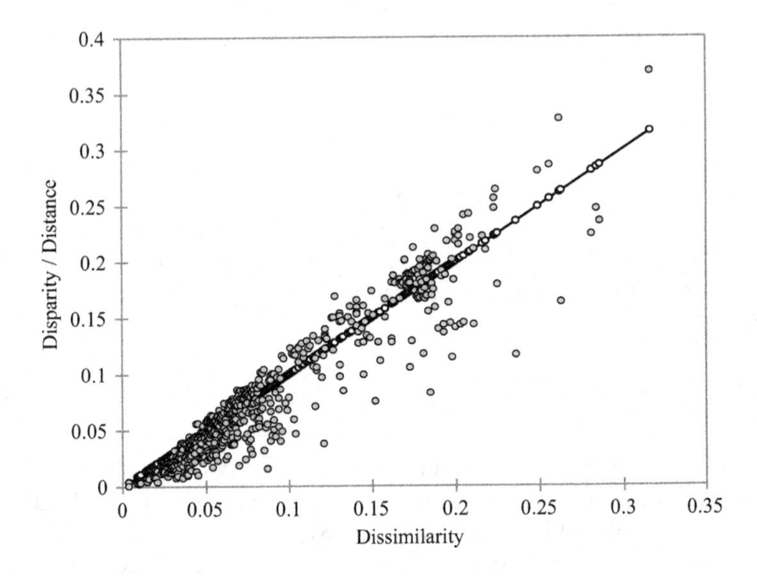

Figure 8.A1 Shephard's Diagram (Distortions due to the 2-Dimensional Projection).
Source: Authors' calculations.

Table 8.A1 Bilateral Regulatory Distances

	ARG	BFA	BOL	BRA	CHL	CHN	CIV	COL	CRI
ARG	–	0.091	0.064	0.070	0.075	0.208	0.081	0.085	0.072
BFA	0.091	–	0.047	0.083	0.072	0.200	0.048	0.072	0.052
BOL	0.064	0.047	–	0.053	0.043	0.173	0.029	0.047	0.027
BRA	0.070	0.083	0.053	–	0.057	0.196	0.068	0.075	0.059
CHL	0.075	0.072	0.043	0.057	–	0.184	0.056	0.062	0.051
CHN	0.208	0.200	0.173	0.196	0.184	–	0.184	0.193	0.179
CIV	0.081	0.048	0.029	0.068	0.056	0.184	–	0.059	0.034
COL	0.085	0.072	0.047	0.075	0.062	0.193	0.059	–	0.051
CRI	0.072	0.052	0.027	0.059	0.051	0.179	0.034	0.051	–
ECU	0.074	0.053	0.029	0.062	0.052	0.177	0.039	0.046	0.034
EGY	0.091	0.067	0.044	0.077	0.066	0.192	0.049	0.071	0.049
EUN	0.111	0.106	0.080	0.096	0.090	0.198	0.090	0.104	0.084
GIN	0.121	0.070	0.075	0.103	0.098	0.216	0.076	0.095	0.076
GTM	0.097	0.082	0.055	0.083	0.073	0.192	0.066	0.078	0.060
IDN	0.080	0.056	0.035	0.069	0.059	0.184	0.040	0.061	0.039
JPN	0.096	0.078	0.054	0.078	0.066	0.188	0.061	0.076	0.057
KAZ	0.078	0.054	0.032	0.066	0.053	0.179	0.039	0.056	0.036
KHM	0.080	0.050	0.030	0.068	0.056	0.181	0.033	0.060	0.035
LAO	0.069	0.041	0.020	0.057	0.045	0.173	0.024	0.049	0.025
LBN	0.106	0.078	0.055	0.094	0.082	0.211	0.059	0.085	0.059
LKA	0.205	0.199	0.173	0.202	0.189	0.281	0.182	0.186	0.176
MAR	0.162	0.133	0.113	0.150	0.137	0.256	0.117	0.141	0.118
MDG	0.071	0.042	0.020	0.058	0.046	0.175	0.023	0.050	0.025
MEX	0.069	0.056	0.031	0.058	0.048	0.179	0.040	0.055	0.038
MUS	0.065	0.041	0.020	0.056	0.047	0.172	0.025	0.049	0.025
NAM	0.181	0.158	0.138	0.173	0.154	0.286	0.141	0.151	0.142
NPL	0.203	0.197	0.174	0.209	0.200	0.316	0.178	0.200	0.178
PAK	0.116	0.087	0.064	0.102	0.089	0.218	0.068	0.095	0.070
PER	0.073	0.053	0.025	0.062	0.050	0.176	0.038	0.046	0.035
PHL	0.081	0.051	0.029	0.068	0.056	0.186	0.032	0.060	0.034
PRY	0.061	0.044	0.021	0.052	0.041	0.173	0.028	0.044	0.028
SEN	0.081	0.053	0.035	0.071	0.057	0.185	0.039	0.051	0.039
THA	0.068	0.038	0.016	0.055	0.043	0.172	0.019	0.046	0.021
TUN	0.095	0.070	0.050	0.081	0.066	0.188	0.055	0.074	0.056
TZA	0.067	0.037	0.015	0.054	0.042	0.171	0.018	0.045	0.020
URY	0.069	0.052	0.029	0.057	0.050	0.181	0.039	0.047	0.037
VEN	0.077	0.060	0.035	0.068	0.058	0.184	0.043	0.059	0.041

(*Continued*)

	ECU	EGY	EUN	GIN	GTM	IDN	JPN	KAZ	KHM
ARG	0.074	0.091	0.111	0.121	0.097	0.080	0.096	0.078	0.080
BFA	0.053	0.067	0.106	0.070	0.082	0.056	0.078	0.054	0.050
BOL	0.029	0.044	0.080	0.075	0.055	0.035	0.054	0.032	0.030
BRA	0.062	0.077	0.096	0.103	0.083	0.069	0.078	0.066	0.068
CHL	0.052	0.066	0.090	0.098	0.073	0.059	0.066	0.053	0.056
CHN	0.177	0.192	0.198	0.216	0.192	0.184	0.188	0.179	0.181
CIV	0.039	0.049	0.090	0.076	0.066	0.040	0.061	0.039	0.033
COL	0.046	0.071	0.104	0.095	0.078	0.061	0.076	0.056	0.060
CRI	0.034	0.049	0.084	0.076	0.060	0.039	0.057	0.036	0.035
ECU	–	0.052	0.089	0.079	0.062	0.043	0.060	0.036	0.040
EGY	0.052	–	0.100	0.089	0.078	0.054	0.074	0.052	0.048
EUN	0.089	0.100	–	0.131	0.106	0.092	0.092	0.089	0.088
GIN	0.079	0.089	0.131	–	0.108	0.082	0.104	0.079	0.080
GTM	0.062	0.078	0.106	0.108	–	0.068	0.078	0.066	0.065
IDN	0.043	0.054	0.092	0.082	0.068	–	0.063	0.041	0.035
JPN	0.060	0.074	0.092	0.104	0.078	0.063	–	0.063	0.060
KAZ	0.036	0.052	0.089	0.079	0.066	0.041	0.063	–	0.040
KHM	0.040	0.048	0.088	0.080	0.065	0.035	0.060	0.040	–
LAO	0.029	0.040	0.081	0.069	0.054	0.032	0.051	0.029	0.025
LBN	0.066	0.074	0.116	0.106	0.092	0.067	0.087	0.065	0.060
LKA	0.180	0.195	0.211	0.223	0.174	0.186	0.190	0.179	0.178
MAR	0.122	0.131	0.170	0.163	0.145	0.123	0.142	0.121	0.115
MDG	0.030	0.040	0.080	0.070	0.057	0.031	0.051	0.030	0.024
MEX	0.039	0.052	0.079	0.083	0.063	0.042	0.058	0.040	0.040
MUS	0.030	0.041	0.077	0.071	0.054	0.033	0.051	0.032	0.023
NAM	0.146	0.155	0.193	0.185	0.170	0.145	0.163	0.144	0.141
NPL	0.185	0.194	0.224	0.225	0.184	0.186	0.202	0.183	0.177
PAK	0.074	0.084	0.122	0.115	0.074	0.075	0.094	0.074	0.069
PER	0.031	0.052	0.088	0.080	0.061	0.041	0.056	0.039	0.039
PHL	0.040	0.049	0.091	0.079	0.067	0.040	0.061	0.039	0.033
PRY	0.028	0.043	0.077	0.073	0.052	0.033	0.052	0.032	0.029
SEN	0.040	0.053	0.094	0.082	0.067	0.043	0.063	0.041	0.039
THA	0.026	0.036	0.077	0.066	0.053	0.027	0.048	0.025	0.020
TUN	0.056	0.068	0.101	0.099	0.082	0.059	0.071	0.054	0.053
TZA	0.025	0.035	0.076	0.065	0.052	0.026	0.047	0.024	0.019
URY	0.036	0.053	0.084	0.079	0.062	0.042	0.059	0.041	0.039
VEN	0.040	0.056	0.093	0.086	0.067	0.044	0.064	0.045	0.044

LAO	LBN	LKA	MAR	MDG	MEX	MUS	NAM	NPL
0.069	0.106	0.205	0.162	0.071	0.069	0.065	0.181	0.203
0.041	0.078	0.199	0.133	0.042	0.056	0.041	0.158	0.197
0.020	0.055	0.173	0.113	0.020	0.031	0.020	0.138	0.174
0.057	0.094	0.202	0.150	0.058	0.058	0.056	0.173	0.209
0.045	0.082	0.189	0.137	0.046	0.048	0.047	0.154	0.200
0.173	0.211	0.281	0.256	0.175	0.179	0.172	0.286	0.316
0.024	0.059	0.182	0.117	0.023	0.040	0.025	0.141	0.178
0.049	0.085	0.186	0.141	0.050	0.055	0.049	0.151	0.200
0.025	0.059	0.176	0.118	0.025	0.038	0.025	0.142	0.178
0.029	0.066	0.180	0.122	0.030	0.039	0.030	0.146	0.185
0.040	0.074	0.195	0.131	0.040	0.052	0.041	0.155	0.194
0.081	0.116	0.211	0.170	0.080	0.079	0.077	0.193	0.224
0.069	0.106	0.223	0.163	0.070	0.083	0.071	0.185	0.225
0.054	0.092	0.174	0.145	0.057	0.063	0.054	0.170	0.184
0.032	0.067	0.186	0.123	0.031	0.042	0.033	0.145	0.186
0.051	0.087	0.190	0.142	0.051	0.058	0.051	0.163	0.202
0.029	0.065	0.179	0.121	0.030	0.040	0.032	0.144	0.183
0.025	0.060	0.178	0.115	0.024	0.040	0.023	0.141	0.177
–	0.051	0.171	0.109	0.015	0.030	0.016	0.131	0.169
0.051	–	0.205	0.141	0.050	0.066	0.051	0.167	0.202
0.171	0.205	–	0.263	0.172	0.178	0.171	0.262	0.249
0.109	0.141	0.263	–	0.109	0.122	0.109	0.223	0.236
0.015	0.050	0.172	0.109	–	0.030	0.015	0.131	0.168
0.030	0.066	0.178	0.122	0.030	–	0.030	0.147	0.183
0.016	0.051	0.171	0.109	0.015	0.030	–	0.132	0.167
0.131	0.167	0.262	0.223	0.131	0.147	0.132	–	0.284
0.169	0.202	0.249	0.236	0.168	0.183	0.167	0.284	–
0.059	0.094	0.162	0.152	0.059	0.075	0.061	0.175	0.187
0.029	0.065	0.179	0.122	0.028	0.037	0.029	0.145	0.183
0.024	0.058	0.183	0.117	0.023	0.040	0.025	0.141	0.178
0.019	0.055	0.171	0.112	0.019	0.026	0.019	0.136	0.173
0.030	0.067	0.182	0.120	0.031	0.045	0.032	0.128	0.186
0.011	0.045	0.169	0.104	0.010	0.027	0.011	0.127	0.164
0.045	0.082	0.198	0.131	0.047	0.056	0.046	0.158	0.200
0.009	0.044	0.168	0.103	0.009	0.025	0.010	0.126	0.162
0.031	0.067	0.180	0.123	0.031	0.035	0.029	0.148	0.183
0.034	0.070	0.187	0.127	0.034	0.042	0.033	0.149	0.167

(*Continued*)

	PAK	PER	PHL	PRY	SEN	THA	TUN	TZA	URY	VEN
ARG	0.116	0.073	0.081	0.061	0.081	0.068	0.095	0.067	0.069	0.077
BFA	0.087	0.053	0.051	0.044	0.053	0.038	0.070	0.037	0.052	0.060
BOL	0.064	0.025	0.029	0.021	0.035	0.016	0.050	0.015	0.029	0.035
BRA	0.102	0.062	0.068	0.052	0.071	0.055	0.081	0.054	0.057	0.068
CHL	0.089	0.050	0.056	0.041	0.057	0.043	0.066	0.042	0.050	0.058
CHN	0.218	0.176	0.186	0.173	0.185	0.172	0.188	0.171	0.181	0.184
CIV	0.068	0.038	0.032	0.028	0.039	0.019	0.055	0.018	0.039	0.043
COL	0.095	0.046	0.060	0.044	0.051	0.046	0.074	0.045	0.047	0.059
CRI	0.070	0.035	0.034	0.028	0.039	0.021	0.056	0.020	0.037	0.041
ECU	0.074	0.031	0.040	0.028	0.040	0.026	0.056	0.025	0.036	0.040
EGY	0.084	0.052	0.049	0.043	0.053	0.036	0.068	0.035	0.053	0.056
EUN	0.122	0.088	0.091	0.077	0.094	0.077	0.101	0.076	0.084	0.093
GIN	0.115	0.080	0.079	0.073	0.082	0.066	0.099	0.065	0.079	0.086
GTM	0.074	0.061	0.067	0.052	0.067	0.053	0.082	0.052	0.062	0.067
IDN	0.075	0.041	0.040	0.033	0.043	0.027	0.059	0.026	0.042	0.044
JPN	0.094	0.056	0.061	0.052	0.063	0.048	0.071	0.047	0.059	0.064
KAZ	0.074	0.039	0.039	0.032	0.041	0.025	0.054	0.024	0.041	0.045
KHM	0.069	0.039	0.033	0.029	0.039	0.020	0.053	0.019	0.039	0.044
LAO	0.059	0.029	0.024	0.019	0.030	0.011	0.045	0.009	0.031	0.034
LBN	0.094	0.065	0.058	0.055	0.067	0.045	0.082	0.044	0.067	0.070
LKA	0.162	0.179	0.183	0.171	0.182	0.169	0.198	0.168	0.180	0.187
MAR	0.152	0.122	0.117	0.112	0.120	0.104	0.131	0.103	0.123	0.127
MDG	0.059	0.028	0.023	0.019	0.031	0.010	0.047	0.009	0.031	0.034
MEX	0.075	0.037	0.040	0.026	0.045	0.027	0.056	0.025	0.035	0.042
MUS	0.061	0.029	0.025	0.019	0.032	0.011	0.046	0.010	0.029	0.033
NAM	0.175	0.145	0.141	0.136	0.128	0.127	0.158	0.126	0.148	0.149
NPL	0.187	0.183	0.178	0.173	0.186	0.164	0.200	0.162	0.183	0.167
PAK	–	0.073	0.068	0.064	0.074	0.054	0.089	0.053	0.074	0.079
PER	0.073	–	0.039	0.027	0.041	0.025	0.056	0.024	0.033	0.040
PHL	0.068	0.039	–	0.028	0.040	0.018	0.056	0.017	0.040	0.043
PRY	0.064	0.027	0.028	–	0.034	0.015	0.049	0.014	0.025	0.031
SEN	0.074	0.041	0.040	0.034	–	0.027	0.055	0.026	0.044	0.047
THA	0.054	0.025	0.018	0.015	0.027	–	0.042	0.004	0.027	0.030
TUN	0.089	0.056	0.056	0.049	0.055	0.042	–	0.041	0.057	0.063
TZA	0.053	0.024	0.017	0.014	0.026	0.004	0.041	–	0.026	0.029
URY	0.074	0.033	0.040	0.025	0.044	0.027	0.057	0.026	–	0.043
VEN	0.079	0.040	0.043	0.031	0.047	0.030	0.063	0.029	0.043	–

Source: Authors' calculations.

9 The impacts of services trade restrictiveness on the productivity of manufacturing sectors in East Asia

Cosimo Beverelli, Matteo Fiorini and Bernard Hoekman

9.1 Introduction

Services trade liberalisation is gaining momentum in the context of domestic reforms as well as in international agreements. Trade costs for services are much higher than trade costs for goods (Miroudot and Shepherd, 2016). Moreover, restrictions to trade in services span a broader set of policies than is the case for trade in goods. They include measures affecting the physical movement of foreign services providers and the establishment of a commercial presence (or being engaged in foreign direct investment, FDI). All firms use services as inputs into the production of goods and other services. If input costs are higher than they would be in an environment where services trade costs were lower, they will act as a tax on domestic industries and reduce their competitiveness.

This chapter reviews the literature on services trade liberalisation with a focus on those services that are used as intermediate inputs downstream in the supply chain. While there exists evidence of a strong positive effect of removing barriers to trade in services for downstream firms and sectoral performance (Arnold et al., 2016; Beverelli et al., 2017), trade agreements that aim at maximising the gains from liberalisation need to account for the heterogeneous effects of services trade policy depending on the institutional differences across countries. Recent empirical studies, discussed later, demonstrate that broad aspects of governance institutions, such as the control of corruption, regulatory quality, and the rule of law, are relevant factors that shape the actual effects of policy action to reduce barriers to services trade. This is consistent with the intangibility and non-storability that applies to many services sectors and that requires at least part of the economic activity of services exporters to be performed in close contact with the governance institutions prevailing in the importing country.

The present chapter conducts a quantification exercise on the effects of services trade liberalisation for ten Asian economies, including several members of the Regional Comprehensive Economic Partnership (RCEP) launched in 2012. The analysis highlights substantial heterogeneity among the covered RCEP economies. Differences exist not only in terms of the effort required to reach further

DOI: 10.4324/9780429433603-9

openness in services markets but also with respect to the quality of governance institutions, which is likely to shape the effects of services trade policy across the partnership's members. This implies that the same policy objective negotiated in the context of RCEP could require very different political efforts and trigger very different economic gains across the manufacturing firms and sectors of the RCEP Member States. A policy implication of the findings presented in the chapter is that the objective of removing barriers to services trade should not be pursued in isolation or unconditionally. Account should be taken of the existing quality of domestic economic governance and the operation of the relevant institutions across RCEP members.

The rest of the chapter is organised as follows. Section 9.2 discusses the economic mechanisms governing the impact of services trade liberalisation on downstream manufacturing performance, including how this effect is moderated by governance institutions. Section 9.3 presents the econometric framework, the data, and the results of a quantification exercise for selected Asian economies, including several RCEP members. Section 9.4 concludes.

9.2 Services trade policy and manufacturing productivity

9.2.1 Services trade policy and input-output linkages

A variety of services, such as finance, insurance, information and communications technology (ICT), transport, logistics, and professional services, are inputs into modern production processes. Because of their relevance as inputs for downstream producers, they are often referred to as 'producer services'. Services used as intermediate inputs in production are different from intermediate manufactured goods (parts and components). The key property of services inputs is that they help to coordinate and control complex operations involving other factors of production. For instance, ICT, transport, and logistics services can connect labour and/or capital units across space; financial and insurance services allow firms to manage the risk of routine as well as innovative production operations. For this reason, services are essential for successfully managing market integration and new trade opportunities, especially in a world of global value chains (GVCs), where production involves the coordination in space and time of intermediate inputs produced by different firms located in different geographical regions. As 'facilitators' of production processes, services inputs directly affect the degree of specialisation and the scale of downstream economic activity (Francois, 1990; Francois and Hoekman, 2010).

By looking at services trade patterns in Organisation for Economic Co-operation and Development (OECD) economies through the lens of input-output analysis, Miroudot et al. (2009) find that 73 percent of all services trade between 1995 and 2005 was accounted for by trade in services inputs. This is a much larger figure than in the case of trade in goods, where manufactured intermediate inputs accounted for 56 percent of total trade flows in the same period. These patterns, together with the standard implications from trade theory, suggest that international services markets are important channels for firms to gain access to the cheapest and most efficient services inputs.

The discussion so far of the properties of services inputs and of the role of international transactions for firms' access to intermediates implies that restrictive trade and investment policies that impact on the degree of competition in services markets, and thus on markups and sectoral efficiency, will negatively affect downstream manufacturing sectors.

This argument is also consistent with the recent literature on input tariff liberalisation, which focuses on the downstream effects of tariffs that apply to manufactured goods used as intermediate inputs in production. In a seminal paper featuring Indonesian firm-level data, Amiti and Konings (2007) show that reducing input tariffs by 10 percent increases the productivity of those Indonesian firms importing their inputs by 12 percent. This strong positive effect is consistent with three theoretical mechanisms: lower input tariffs can have a positive causal effect on downstream firms' productivity as they result in (i) firms' access to more varieties of intermediate inputs, (ii) firms' access to higher quality inputs, and (iii) firms' learning from the foreign technology embedded in the imported input (Amiti and Konings, 2007). Analogous evidence comes from the case of Indian firms studied by Goldberg et al. (2010) and De Loecker et al. (2016). The first study finds that lower input tariffs in India accounted for 31 percent of the new products introduced by Indian firms from 1987 to 1997. The second study shows how input tariff liberalisation reduces properly estimated marginal costs at the level of downstream Indian producers.

While these results are derived from the study of the effects of input tariffs applying to manufactured intermediate inputs, the same motivating mechanisms apply to the case of services inputs.

In fact, a number of empirical studies analysing the linkages between services trade policies and downstream productivity identify sizeable positive effects of liberalising services trade for the productivity and export performance of firms operating in downstream industries (notably manufacturing).[1] Among these country-specific case studies using firm- or plant-level data, three focus on two important Asian economies. Duggan et al. (2013) look at Indonesian manufacturing firms and their total factor productivity (TFP) over the period 1997–2009. The authors find that liberalisation in services trade through commercial presence (FDI, or Mode 3 services trade in General Agreement on Trade in Services jargon) accounted for 8 percent of the observed increase in TFP over that period. Moving to the case of India, Bas (2014) shows how reforms (including trade liberalisation) in upstream markets for energy, telecommunications, and transport services benefited, on average, the export performance of almost 6,000 Indian manufacturers over a decade from 1994 to 2004. Similarly, Arnold et al. (2016) show how reforms in banking, insurance, telecommunications, and transport had a significant positive effect on the TFP of 4,000 Indian firms between 1993 and 2005.[2]

The link between the markets of producer services (upstream) and the economic performance of downstream firms or sectors is not limited to services trade policy measures targeting market access and being discriminatory in nature. This link extends to services sectors' performance (productivity, inward FDI, markup) as well as to non-discriminatory policies and conduct regulations that affect the degree of competition in services markets. The downstream effects of indicators capturing services sectors' performance as well as of services' domestic regulatory framework have been investigated in many studies. Analysis using firm-level data is conducted by Arnold et al. (2008) on a number of selected African countries; by Fernandes and Paunov (2011) for Chile; by Forlani (2012) for France, and by Hoekman and Shepherd (2017) for a wide set of developing economies. Barone and Cingano (2011) and Bourlès et al. (2013) both look at OECD economies and conduct empirical exercises based on sector-level data. The general implication associated with the findings in these studies is that better performance and domestic regulation of services markets can have sizeable effects for downstream economic outcomes, such as productivity and/or export performance.

9.2.2 The role of governance institutions

In a recent contribution to this literature, Beverelli et al. (2017) (henceforth, BFH) revisit the empirical assessment of the downstream effects of services trade policy by studying sector-level data for a sample of 57 economies, including many low- and middle-income countries. Their econometric framework has the advantage of the possibility to investigate whether and how the positive effects of services trade and investment liberalisation found in the case studies discussed (Czech Republic, Indonesia, and India) apply across a sample of heterogeneous economies. The key finding by BFH is that policies resulting in reduced barriers to services trade increase productivity in downstream manufacturing sectors conditionally on the characteristics of the economy implementing the services trade reforms. These conditioning characteristics pertain to governance institutions, namely the institutional framework undermining all economic activities that take place in a country. The standard dimensions of governance institutions, those that have most commonly been operationalised and captured in quantitative measures, are the control of corruption, the general quality of domestic regulation, and the rule of law. BFH show that the positive effects of services trade liberalisation on downstream manufacturing are significantly reduced, if not nullified, in countries where there is low control of corruption, bad regulatory quality, or weak rule of law.

It is well established in the economic literature that in the long run, the quality of institutions will affect the level of comparative development (Acemoglu et al., 2001). It has also long been known that economic governance and related institutions represent an important source of comparative advantage in certain industries, notably the ones where economic governance is more important, such as those that are more contract intensive (see Nunn and Trefler (2014) for a review). Finally, there exist some consensus and evidence in the literature that the benefits from trade liberalisation depend on country-specific conditioning factors, such as the quality of local governance institutions (see Rodriguez and Rodrik (2001) and Freund and Bolaky (2008)).

In the short and medium run, governance institutions can directly shape the downstream effects of services trade policies in several ways. As argued by BFH, removing barriers to cross-border services trade can be largely ineffective in cases where pervasive corruption, weak rule of law, and the absence of effective regulation impose economic uncertainty and insecurity on traders. This is consistent with Anderson and Marcouiller (2002) and Ranjan and Lee (2007), whose findings show how insecurity driven by low-quality institutions can reduce a country's inward trade flows. Moreover, eliminating restrictions on foreign firms on establishing a commercial presence and selling products locally may fail to induce a positive downstream effect if weak governance institutions in the host country discourage foreign firms from entering the market (in the expectation of too many institutions-driven frictions to their economic activity), or, if they enter, force them to operate inefficiently (see Dollar et al. (2005); Dort et al. (2014)).[3]

A corollary finding in BFH is that the moderating role of institutional quality for the downstream effects of services trade liberalisation is found to be driven by the conditionality of the effects of those liberalisation policies targeting services trade through commercial presence (Mode 3). This is consistent with the pattern of international services provision, where trade through commercial presence plays a much bigger role than cross-border, arms-length type transactions. This pattern is specific to the international services markets as it reflects the 'proximity burden' imposed on international services transactions by the intangibility and non-storability of many services. Given this corollary result, the following quantification exercise will focus on the effects of Mode 3 services trade policies, such as foreign equity quotas, discriminatory licensing criteria, and nationality requirements for key personnel.

As discussed later in the chapter, the finding on the role of institutions has potential implications for the design of trade agreements that include services. The following section uses the cross-country econometric framework developed in BFH to quantify the impact of services trade and investment reforms for downstream manufacturing sectors in ten East Asian economies, including eight RCEP countries. The quantification explicitly accounts for the role of institutions in shaping this effect.

9.3 Quantification exercise for selected Asian economies

9.3.1 Background econometric framework and data

The quantification exercise proposed in this chapter is based on the econometric framework and data used in BFH.

Following the approach initially proposed by Rajan and Zingales (1998), the authors estimate the following model:

$$y_{ij} = \alpha + \beta \mathrm{CSTRI}_{ij} + \mu\left(\mathrm{CSTRI}_{ij} \times \mathrm{EG}_i\right) + \gamma x_{ij} + \delta_i + \delta_j + \varepsilon_{ij} \qquad (9.1)$$

where y_{ij} is the natural logarithm of productivity in downstream sector j in Country i; $CSTRI_{ij}$ is a measure of the effective restrictiveness of services trade policy confronted by downstream sector j in Country i; EG_i is a measure of the economic governance in Country i, x_{ij} is a control capturing the average level of tariff protection for non-services inputs used by downstream manufacturing sector j; and δ_i and δ_j are country- and sector-level fixed-effects. While Equation (9.1) represents the baseline specification used by BFH, several extensions to the empirical model are tested in their paper. In particular, the results discussed in the following are robust to the inclusion of controls at the country-sector level that account for the degree of openness (output tariffs) and comparative advantage.

The regressor of interest, $CSTRI_{ij}$, is constructed as $\sum_s STRI_{is} \times w_{ijs}$, where $STRI_{is}$ is the level of services trade restrictiveness for Country i and service sector s, and w_{ijs} is a weighting coefficient that reflects the use of service s by manufacturing sector j in Country i.[4]

The baseline measure of productivity (y_{ij}) is the output per worker in 2008, constructed using the United Nations Industrial Development Organization's Industrial Statistics database. The variable capturing Mode 3 services trade policy ($STRI_{is}$) is taken from the World Bank's Services Trade Restrictiveness Database (STRD), which provides information on discriminatory trade policy for five aggregate services sectors and 103 countries. The STRD provides quantitative measures of policy stances prevailing in the mid-2000s. In the database, policy measures go from zero as complete openness to 100 as full restrictiveness. The four services sectors included in the analysis are finance, communications, transport, and professional services. Borchert et al. (2012) offer a detailed discussion and descriptive assessment of the STRD. Finally, the baseline proxy for the quality of governance institutions (EG_i) is given by a measure of control of corruption sourced from the World Bank's Worldwide Governance Indicators database.

The estimated coefficients on $CSTRI_{ij}$ ($\hat{\beta}$) and on the interaction term ($\hat{\mu}$) allow for the qualitative assessment of the impact of higher input-services trade policy restrictions on downstream industries. As already discussed, BFH find that higher STRIs are associated with lower productivity performance in downstream sectors but that the effect is highly dependent on the quality of governance, as measured by indicators such as the strength of the rule of law, regulatory quality, and control of corruption.

This result can be seen in the formal notation of the econometric model by looking at the estimated marginal effect of reducing barriers to services trade on downstream productivity, which accounts for heterogeneity in economic governance. This effect is given by

$$-\widehat{\frac{\partial y}{\partial CSTRI}} = -\hat{\beta} - \hat{\mu} \times EG_i.$$

The minus sign in front of the marginal effect reflects the fact that reducing barriers to services trade means decreasing the value of STRI, which in turn results in lowering the value of CSTRI. This marginal effect increases with the quality of governance (as $\hat{\mu} < 0$) and is significantly positive (at the 0.05 percent level of statistical significance) for 65 percent of the sample observations in BFH. For the 33 countries (out of 57) corresponding to these observations, reducing barriers to input-services trade has a positive effect on downstream productivity.[5] The positive effect is more pronounced the higher the quality of governance institutions. This conditionality result holds across a number of robustness checks that address the measurement and endogeneity issues embedded in this econometric exercise.[6]

To quantitatively assess the economic magnitude of the downstream effects of services trade liberalisation as well as the degree of their dependence on institutional quality in a country, the estimated coefficients from model (1) can be used to calculate the productivity changes associated with a hypothesised trade policy reform. For the sake of simplicity and cross-country comparability, the BFH paper focuses on the effects of a policy platform that results in the complete removal of all restrictions to Mode 3 services trade.[7] Because in the STRI database a fully unrestricted trade policy regime corresponds to an STRI value of zero, the policy change required by a country to remove all existing barriers to trade in services sector s in Country i is given by $0 - \text{STRI}_{is}$. The (negative) variation in the explanatory variable CSTRI reflecting full liberalisation of trade across services sectors is then given by:

$$\Delta \text{CSTRI}_{ij} = \sum_{s} (0 - \text{STRI}_{is}) \times w_{ijs}.$$

The associated change in productivity (expressed in levels) implied by the estimated coefficients ($\hat{\beta}$ and $\hat{\mu}$) can be computed as follows:

$$\%\Delta Y_{ij} = 100 \times \left(\hat{\beta} + \hat{\mu} \times \text{EG}_i \right) \times \Delta \text{CSTRI}_{ij}. \tag{9.2}$$

This expression is country-sector specific. The productivity effect of services trade policy is a function of the services input intensities at the downstream sector level and of two variables at the country level. The first variable is the policy change required to reach complete openness; the second is the quality of economic governance. This methodology allows for counterfactual exercises to quantify the effects of policy changes for Country i assuming different levels of economic governance quality. The quantification exercise to follow uses this approach to assess the relative importance of – and interaction between – the level of services trade restrictions and the quality of economic governance in Country i.

9.3.2 Quantification for East Asian economies

The empirical exercise in this section consists of the quantitative assessment of the effects of services trade policy reforms on the productivity of downstream manufacturing industries. The exercise is based on the same hypothesised policy reform as in BFH: i.e. the complete removal of all barriers to Mode 3 services trade in four producer services sectors – finance, transport, communications, and professional services. The available data across the different sources allow for quantifying this effect for ten countries in the region of focus in the present analysis. These countries are Mongolia, Sri Lanka and eight members of RCEP: Indonesia, Malaysia and Viet Nam from ASEAN, and China, India, Japan, the Republic of Korea (henceforth, Korea) and New Zealand. For these countries, sector-specific effects can be computed for up to 18 manufacturing sectors, as defined by the ISIC Rev. 3 at the 2-digit level classification.

The quantification is conducted in the following steps. First, Equation (9.1) is fitted with the estimation sample of BFH, augmented with a few datapoints for the US to increase estimation precision (this increases the estimation sample size from 912 to 930). Second, the resulting estimates of $\hat{\beta}$= 0.055 (robust standard error 0.030) and $\hat{\mu}$ = −0.037 (robust standard error 0.011),[8] together with the country-specific values of institutional quality, EG_i, and the country-sector specific values of the policy change needed to remove all restrictions to Mode 3 services trade, $\Delta CSTRI_{ij}$, are used to compute values of $\%\Delta Y_{ij}$ according to Equation (9.2).

It is important to notice how the variability of $\%\Delta Y_{ij}$ across manufacturing sectors (j) is completely accounted for by the technological dependence of each sector on the set of producer services, which are the target of the hypothesised reform. Our assumption – in line with the existing literature since the seminal work by Rajan and Zingales (1998) – is that these technological relationships do not vary across countries and that they can be accurately derived from the US input-output tables.[9]

Figure 9.1 plots services input intensity as captured by the shares of intermediate consumption of four producer services for 18 manufacturing sectors in the US. Often, more than 10 percent of all direct input consumption in manufacturing is accounted for by producer services. Transport and professional services tend to cover the largest value shares across downstream sectors. Financial services are relatively more heavily used in a number of sectors, including office, accounting, and computing machinery; radio, television and communication equipment; and medical, precision, and optical instruments. Finally, telecommunication services represent usually the smallest value share among the four producer services considered.

Country-level variability in $\%\Delta Y_{ij}$ has instead two dimensions. The first dimension is given by the services trade policy stance – in the four services sectors selected for the analysis – prevailing across countries. Descriptive evidence based on the World Bank's STRD shows that the ASEAN members covered in the 2008 STRD survey had relatively high barriers to services trade compared to other regions in the world, except for the Gulf States. Moreover, a second wave of survey data collection in 2012 for ASEAN countries highlighted only a modest average change towards liberalisation, with significant heterogeneity across countries and sectors (ASEAN Secretariat and World Bank, 2015).[10]

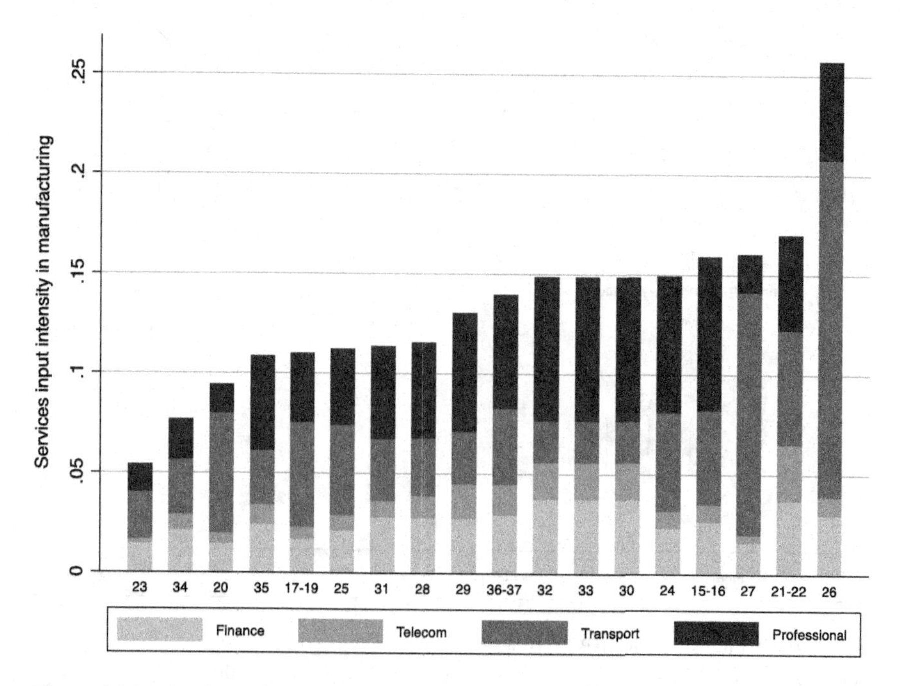

Figure 9.1 Technological Dependence from Producer Services.

Notes: The figure plots services input intensity across manufacturing sectors. Services input intensity is given by the value shares of intermediate consumption of each (upstream) services sector by each (downstream) manufacturing sector. Manufacturing sectors are sorted with respect to total producer services input intensity, and they are identified through ISIC 2-digit Rev. 3 numeric codes. 15–16 correspond to food products, beverages, and tobacco; 17–19 to textiles, textile products, leather, and footwear; 20 to wood and products of wood and cork; 21–22 to pulp, paper, paper products, printing, and publishing; 23 to coke, refined petroleum products, and nuclear fuel; 24 to chemicals and chemical products; 25 to rubber and plastics products; 26 to other non-metallic mineral products; 27 to basic metals; 28 to fabricated metal products except machinery and equipment; 29 to machinery and equipment n.e.c.; 30 to office, accounting, and computing machinery; 31 to electrical machinery and apparatus n.e.c.; 32 to radio, television, and communication equipment; 33 to medical, precision, and optical instruments; 34 to motor vehicles, trailers, and semi-trailers; 35 to other transport equipment; 36–37 to manufacturing n.e.c. and recycling.

Source: Authors' calculation based on OECD STAN IO Table, mid-2000s.

Figure 9.2 plots the values of $STRI_{is}$ from the 2008 World Bank's STRD for the covered members of the RCEP (grouped into ASEAN members and other RCEP members), distinguishing between restrictions to all modes of provision versus Mode 3 services trade. These policy variables are organised in radar charts, where each line corresponds to a sector among four selected producer services sectors: *finance*, including both banking and insurance services; *telecom*, which comprises fixed-line and mobile telecommunications; *transport*, aggregating policy stances across air, maritime, road and rail transports; and *professional*, consisting of accounting, audit and legal services.

We can detect several patterns. With the notable exceptions of Viet Nam, Australia and New Zealand, professional services emerge as the sector where

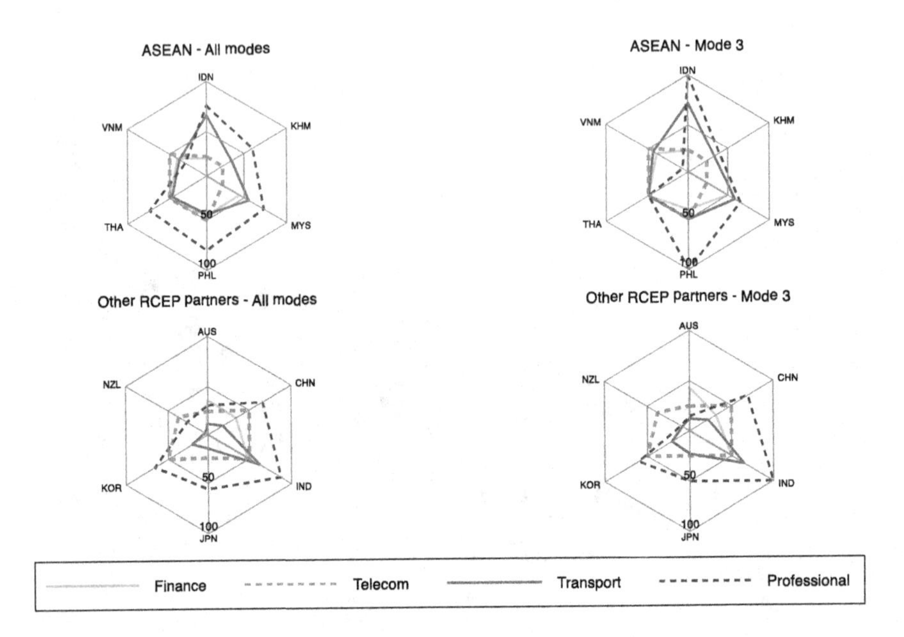

Figure 9.2 STRI across RCEP Members.
Source: Authors' calculations based on World Bank STR Database, mid-2000s.

restrictions are the highest. The sector appears as completely closed to FDI in the Philippines and India. Among the ASEAN members, barriers to international transactions in financial services and telecommunications are relatively moderate: going from the case of Cambodia where the values of STRI suggest no restrictions in place for trade in financial services and very little restrictions in telecommunications, to Thailand, where both finance and telecommunications score a value of 50 out of 100. Barriers to trade in telecommunication services are higher relatively than in other sectors in New Zealand but still below the value of 50. New Zealand and Japan present no restrictions to trade in financial services. India, instead, with the same score as Thailand, represents the most restricted country for finance and telecoms among the group of non-ASEAN RCEP members. International transactions in transport services appear more restricted than finance and telecoms for the case of ASEAN members, especially for Indonesia and Malaysia, where the STRI scores are above 50. Relatively fewer barriers are found in the case of non-ASEAN members, with the exception of India, for which the STRI scores are above 50 for both all modes policies and Mode 3 ones.

The general implication of these descriptive patterns in the context of the proposed quantification exercise is that a thought policy scenario, which consists of the complete, unilateral removal of all discriminatory barriers, represents a substantial policy reform for all members of RCEP at least in some sectors.

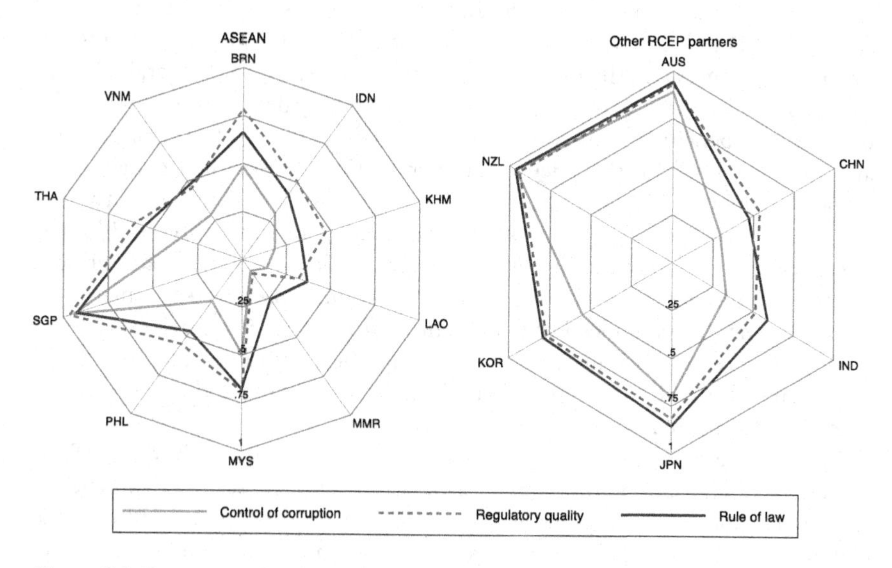

Figure 9.3 Governance Institutions across RCEP Members.

Notes: ISO codes in the left figure refer to the following countries: BRN, Bahrain; IDN, Indonesia; KHM, Cambodia; LAO, Laos; MMR, Myanmar; MYS, Malaysia; PHL, Philippines; SGP, Singapore; THA, Thailand; VNM, Viet Nam. ISO codes in the right figure refer to: AUS, Australia; CHN, China; IND, India; JPN, Japan; KOR, South Korea; NZL, New Zealand.

Source: Authors' calculation based on World Bank Worldwide Governance Indicators, 2006.

The second dimension of country-level variability is given by heterogeneous institutions across economies. Figure 9.3 plots the scores of three indicators from the Worldwide Governance Database managed by the World Bank: control of corruption, regulatory quality, and the rule of law. The support of all variables has been rescaled from 0 to 1, with higher numbers denoting better quality of governance institutions.

The key pattern here is that there exists a high degree of heterogeneity across countries in terms of governance institutions both within and – most of all – across the two country groups of ASEAN members and other RCEP partners. Descriptive evidence presented here highlights the nature of RCEP as a group of rather diverse economies in terms of the degree of services trade liberalisation and the quality of governance institutions. This heterogeneity can potentially be reflected in the effort needed to achieve further liberalisation in RCEP as well as in the economic implications of such policy action.

Before presenting and discussing the results, a few considerations are in order for a cautious interpretation of the findings. First, complete removal of all FDI restrictions is an example of liberalisation reform that may not be achievable in practice. This might be the case even when the producer services used in the analysis are in sectors where full liberalisation should in principle be possible. Practical difficulties to implement such an extreme policy might stem from political-economy forces, such as lobbying opposition or stakeholders' mobilisation against the reform. Second, the measures reported in the World Bank's STRD reflect discriminatory-policy stances, which are relevant towards all foreign partners and therefore do not capture bilateral or plurilateral relationships. These two features of the proposed methodology define the quantification exercise as a benchmark assessing the effects of services trade reforms, which are ambitious both for their degree of liberalisation and for their geographical scope. Therefore, in the context of RCEP negotiations, the output of the following quantification exercise must be considered as an upper threshold for the effects of services liberalisation. Finally, the methodology is partial equilibrium in nature, limiting the focus to sector-specific productivity effects (estimation of the overall net gross domestic product effects from removing services trade restrictions is precluded). This aspect implies that the magnitude of the results for any given sector will be the upper bounds, as factor demand and the investment diversion effects are not accounted for.[11]

Table 9.1 presents the quantification results. For each country, the effect of services trade liberalisation is presented for the manufacturing sectors that generate the highest and second-highest average value added in the period 2000–2007. Columns (1) and (4) report the names of the corresponding manufacturing sectors. Columns (2) and (5) list the values of $\%\Delta Y_{ij}$. When the quality of the governance institutions is low enough, and the country-specific marginal effect used to compute $\%\Delta Y_{ij}$ is not statistically different from 0, $\%\Delta Y_{ij}$ is set equal to 0. In these cases, the impact based on the estimated value of the marginal effect is reported in brackets. Columns (3) and (6) report – respectively, for the largest and the second-largest manufacturing sector – the effect of the same hypothesised policy reform but for the counterfactual situation in which each country's governance indicator is replaced with that of the best-performing country in the sample (New Zealand). This reveals how much of a difference in better institution can potentially make in augmenting the productivity effects of services liberalisation in economies with weak governance performance. The last two columns of Table 9.1 report each country's relative rank with respect to the level of prevailing openness to Mode 3 services trade in services (the average value of STRI across the four producer services sectors) and the quality of domestic economic governance. Finally, the results are organised in three vertically appended panels depending on the governance indicators used as the moderator factor in the empirical framework. These are, respectively, the control of corruption (Panel A), regulatory quality (Panel B) and the rule of law (Panel C).

The case of Indonesia can be discussed as an illustration. On the one hand, Indonesia ranks 9th out of 10 with respect to openness. High existing barriers to services trade imply a sizeable policy change to reach full liberalisation and therefore a high positive downstream effect from the hypothesised policy reform. On the other hand, Indonesia ranks quite low in terms of the quality of institutions across all three indicators (panels) in Table 9.1. Weak governance institutions reduce the potential downstream positive effect of liberalisation, making it statistically non-different from zero (zero is the value in Columns (2) and (5) across all panels). Moving to Columns (3) and (6), it is apparent how better institutions

Table 9.1 Potential Increase in Labour Productivity (%ΔY_{ij})

	Biggest Manufacturing Sector			*Second-Biggest Manufacturing Sector*			*Country Ranking*	
	Sector	*Impact Current Inst.*	*Impact High Inst.*	*Sector*	*Impact Current Inst.*	*Impact High Inst.*	*Openness*	*Institutions*
	(1)	*(2)*	*(3)*	*(4)*	*(5)*	*(6)*	*(7)*	*(8)*
Panel A: Control of Corruption								
China	Metals	0 (7.12)	58.05	Food/bev	0 (11.57)	94.28	6	8
India	Coke/oil	0 (24.71)	142.62	Metals	0 (22.99)	132.72	10	6
Indonesia	Food/bev	0 (18.5)	146.73	Textiles/app	0 (12.06)	95.66	9	7
Japan	Autos	14.79***	22.4	Machinery	32.37***	49.01	3	2
Korea	Machinery	27.78**	60.9	Radio/TV	31.68**	69.43	4	3
Malaysia	Radio/TV	38.62**	100.62	Coke/oil	14.36**	37.41	8	4
Mongolia	Textiles/app	0 (2.13)	20.44	Textiles/app	0 (2.04)	19.54	1	10
New Zealand	Food/bev.	18.18***	18.18	Paper prod	24.57***	24.57	2	1
Sri Lanka	Textiles/app	17.05*	62.92	Food/bev	24.42*	90.14	7	5
Viet Nam	Food/bev	0 (5.89)	53.29	Textiles/app	0 (4.94)	44.69	5	9
Panel B: Regulatory Quality								
China	Metals	0 (12.65)	50.15	Food/bev	0 (20.54)	81.45	6	5
India	Coke/oil	0 (25.32)	123.21	Metals	0 (23.56)	114.66	10	8
Indonesia	Food/bev	0 (23.13)	126.75	Textiles/app	0 (15.08)	82.64	9	9
Japan	Autos	14.82***	19.35	Machinery	32.43***	42.34	3	2
Korea	Machinery	35.85***	52.61	Radio/TV	40.87***	59.98	4	3
Malaysia	Radio/TV	45.81***	86.92	Coke/oil	17.03***	32.32	8	4
Mongolia	Textiles/app	0 (3.67)	17.66	Textiles/app	0 (3.5)	16.88	1	6
New Zealand	Food/bev	15.71***	15.71	Paper prod	21.23***	21.23	2	1
Sri Lanka	Textiles/app	0 (11.23)	54.36	Food/bev	0 (16.09)	77.87	7	7
Viet Nam	Food/bev	0 (4.55)	46.04	Textiles/app	0 (3.82)	38.61	5	10

(Continued)

	Biggest Manufacturing Sector			*Second-Biggest Manufacturing Sector*			*Country Ranking*	
	Sector	*Impact Current Inst.*	*Impact High Inst.*	*Sector*	*Impact Current Inst.*	*Impact High Inst.*	*Openness*	*Institutions*
	(1)	*(2)*	*(3)*	*(4)*	*(5)*	*(6)*	*(7)*	*(8)*
Panel C: Rule of Law								
China	Metals	0 (5.78)	52.79	Food/bev	0 (9.39)	85.73	6	9
India	Coke/oil	42.29*	129.69	Metals	39.35*	120.69	10	6
Indonesia	Food/bev	0 (2.64)	133.42	Textiles/app	0 (1.72)	86.99	9	10
Japan	Autos	16.39***	20.37	Machinery	35.85***	44.57	3	2
Korea	Machinery	37.86***	55.38	Radio/TV	43.17***	63.13	4	3
Malaysia	Radio/TV	44.03**	91.49	Coke/oil	16.37**	34.02	8	4
Mongolia	Textiles/app	0 (2.49)	18.59	Textiles/app	0 (2.38)	17.77	1	7
New Zealand	Food/bev	16.53***	16.53	Paper prod	22.35***	22.35	2	1
Sri Lanka	Textiles/app	19.54*	57.22	Food/bev	28*	81.96	7	5
Viet Nam	Food/bev	0 (6)	48.46	Textiles/app	0 (5.03)	40.64	5	8

Notes: 'Impact' refers to the percentage change in sectoral labour productivity of removing all barriers to Mode 3 services trade in financial, transport, communication, and professional services. Columns (2) and (5) report the estimated impact considering the prevailing quality of governance institutions in the corresponding country and measured according to the governance indicator specified depending on the panel (rule of law, regulatory quality, and control of corruption in Panels A, B, and C, respectively). When not statistically significant, the point estimate is reported in parentheses next to an impact value of 0. Columns (3) and (6) report impact values computed with governance variable at level of New Zealand (country with highest quality of governance institutions in the regional sample). Sectors based on ISIC 2-digit classification Rev. 3 (Food/bev: 15+16; Textiles/apparel: 17+18+19; Paper products: 21+22; Coke/oil: 23; Metals: 27; Machinery: 29; Radio/TV: 32; Autos: 34). Statistical significance: *$p < 0.1$; **$p < 0.05$; ***$p < 0.01$.

Sources: Governance variables from the World Bank Governance Indicators. Services trade policies from the World Bank's STRD. Labour productivity (output per worker) from UNIDO industrial statistics database.

would have allowed Indonesia to benefit much more from the hypothesized ambitious liberalisation reform. The effects under the counterfactual scenario where the quality of Indonesian governance institutions is raised to the higher level of New Zealand are always above 100 percent for the food and beverage product sector.

We can make several observations. First, the potential downstream productivity impacts vary widely, ranging from zero effect for China, Indonesia, Mongolia, and Viet Nam to more than 30 percent for Malaysia, Korea (Panels B and C) and India (Panel C). Second, many countries with high estimated potential productivity improvements following services liberalisation have high levels of Mode 3 restrictions and/or a high quality of institutions. Third, across the two reported sectors, the potential productivity impacts are also relatively heterogeneous, reflecting differences in the intensity of service input use across industries. Fourth, countries that stand to benefit the most in terms of the size of the potential productivity boost are countries that have the best economic governance. The lower the quality of governance, the lower the productivity effect of services trade liberalisation. Weak economic governance explains why the estimated productivity benefits for a country such as Indonesia are low, despite Indonesia having barriers to FDI in services that are among the highest in the sample, which should imply high gains from liberalisation.

9.3.3 The effect of trade policy targeting specific services sectors

The analysis conducted so far rests on the assumption that, conditional on input penetration, the effects of services trade policy do not vary across individual targeted services sectors. The present section relaxes this assumption by defining four services-sector-specific composite services trade policy variables: $\text{CSTRI}_{ijs} = \text{STRI}_{is} \times w_{ijs}$ for each s equal to finance, communications, transport, and professional services. The quantification exercise is then replicated for each of these four policy instruments. The (negative) variation in CSTRI_{ijs} reflecting the full liberalisation of trade in services sector s is then given by $\Delta\text{CSTRI}_{ijs} = -\text{STRI}_{is} \times w_{ijs}$. The associated change in productivity (expressed in levels) is instead $\%\Delta Y_{ijs} = 100 \times (\hat{\beta}_s + \hat{\mu}_s \times \text{EG}_i) \times \Delta\text{CSTRI}_{ijs}$.

The regression estimates required for the quantification ($\hat{\beta}_s$ and $\hat{\mu}_s$ for all s) are reported in Columns (2)–(5) of Table 9.A1, together with graphical representations of the marginal effects of each service-specific CSTRI, as functions of the quality of economic governance (see Figures 9.A1–9.A4).[12] We can make several observations. (i) The qualitative pattern governing the downstream effect of services trade openness and the way this impact is shaped by the quality of governance institutions is stable across all individual sectors. The only exception is professional services when governance is proxied with regulatory quality or rule of law (Panels B and C of Table 9.A1). However, in these cases, no significant pattern is identified. The general implication is that liberalising one sector in isolation tends to benefit downstream economic activity, and such a positive effect can fail to take place when governance institutions are weak. (ii) Statistical significance is always low for professional-services-specific regressions as well as – to a lesser extent – for financial services and telecommunications. (iii) The magnitudes of the estimated marginal effects of trade policy in these two sectors are larger than that of the marginal effects of transport liberalisation.

Table 9.2 reports the estimates for $\%\Delta Y_{ijs}$ for all ten Asian economies covered in the database for 18 manufacturing sectors and four services sectors (finance, communications, transport, and professional services). The estimated effects are computed based on the results in Panel A of Table 9.A1, where economic governance is measured by the degree of control of corruption in the economy. Each observation is identified by the country implementing the reform, the specific services sector for which trade barriers are removed, and the manufacturing sector whose productivity is potentially affected by the reform. The statistical significance of the estimates depends on the country and services sector, and is in the standard threshold of 10 percent for the few country-services sector pairs, reflecting lower statistical significance of the services-sector-specific regression estimates.[13] The sample reported in the table consists of 630 observations plus 90 datapoints labelled as 'NA'. These cells identify the services sectors already fully opened to trade in the respective country. The shades of grey reflect the segments of the distribution of $\%\Delta Y_{ijs}$ in the sample, excluding NA observations. Four tones of grey – from the lightest to the darkest – denote observations in the 25th percentile (equal to 2.06) of the distribution, between the 25th and the 50th (6.80), between the 50th and the 75th (12.72), and above the 75th, respectively.

For each manufacturing sector (column), Table 9.2 gives a first insight of the heterogeneous effects of services trade liberalisation across countries and specific services sectors (rows). However, the low statistical significance of the reported point estimates reveals that for many countries, the quality of governance institutions is too low. These effects would linearly increase and become statistically different from zero with higher institutional quality. The regression results show that the proportionality coefficient in this linear relationship is particularly high for the effects of trade liberalisation in financial and telecommunications services.

9.4 Conclusions and policy implications

The analysis presented in this chapter has shown that good governance institutions, as captured by broad indicators of the control of corruption, regulatory quality, and the rule of law, are important factors for the positive impact of services trade liberalisation on downstream economic performance. The quantification exercise suggests that effort should be made to improve broad economic governance across countries. The measures of governance institutions used in the analysis are horizontal in nature in the sense that they apply to all economic activities. Because of this, they are likely to capture to a greater or lesser extent the effects of more specific dimensions of regulatory institutions that determine the conditions of entry into a market. Examples include the scope of state-owned enterprises in the economy, government involvement in price setting (price controls), licensing and permit systems, and services-sector-specific regulations.

Determining the extent to which the latter types of economic governance impact on the benefits of services trade liberalisation is important from a policy perspective as it may be both easier to change sector- or activity-specific regulation than it is to improve the rule of law or to combat corruption and, as importantly, more feasible to do so in the short run.

In order to go beyond policy implications in terms of broad institutions, analysis needs to be conducted to assess and quantify economic governance performance at a fine-grained, sector-specific level and to identify services sectors where the removal of discriminatory barriers needs to be flanked with measures to improve domestic economic governance. A first attempt in that direction is given by Fiorini and Hoekman (2017b), where the authors investigate the relationship between the downstream effects of services trade policy and detailed, sector-specific governance institutions based on information contained in the OECD's Product Market Regulation databases. Their findings in the context of EU economies suggest that different moderating roles of institutions apply across services sectors and dimensions of governance. Replicating this type of analysis would be an important contribution in the context of RCEP.

Concretely this analysis could translate into enhanced transparency and policy dialogue type mechanisms that provide opportunities for a broad set of actors to engage in both market access and related economic governance matters. These could range from self-evaluation and peer review (mutual evaluation) on the one hand, to the negotiation of binding policy commitments that can be enforced by businesses and natural persons (citizens) on the other. The interactions between sectoral regulation/governance and market access barriers in services sectors will differ across countries and will also change over time. Thus, priorities and solutions cannot be determined ex ante, but call for analysis and deliberation involving government officials, regulators, and stakeholders focused on reviewing and assessing the performance of economic governance institutions. Such deliberation will also generate information on capacity constraints, including at the local level, that need to be addressed, such as the lack of knowledge or uncertainty on the part of implementing agencies as to what is required of them (Fiorini and Hoekman, 2017a).

The key implication in the context of RCEP is that the objective of removing barriers to services trade is best not pursued in isolation or unconditionally. The existing quality of domestic economic governance and the operation of the relevant institutions across RCEP members should be accounted for. RCEP should explicitly consider the relationships between services trade and investment restrictions and the quality of economic governance and regulation. It should also include provisions that target the performance of economic governance institutions. The quantitative estimates of the potential gains from services liberalisation suggest that these can be substantial but are conditional on the quality of domestic economic governance: if weaknesses in the latter are not addressed, gains from services liberalisation may not materialise. Addressing economic governance weaknesses in trade agreements will enhance the gains from services trade liberalisation while, at the same time, it will improve the prospect of attaining good institutions.

Table 9.2 Potential Increase in Labour Productivity ($\%\Delta Y_{ijs}$)

Countries Removing Trade Barriers in Specific Services Sectors		*Food products, beverages and tobacco (15-16)*	*Textiles, textile products, leather and footwear (17-19)*	*Wood and products of wood and cork (20)*	*Pulp, paper, paper products, printing and publishing (21-22)*	*Coke, refined petroleum products and nuclear fuel (23)*	*Chemicals and chemical products (24)*	*Rubber and plastics products (25)*	*Other non-metallic mineral products (26)*	*Bas met (27)*
CHN	Finance	10.85	7.05	6.04	15.24	6.02	9.55	8.83	12.28	6.5
	Telecom	6.68	4.61	4.16	21.87	1.71	6.65	5.94	7.15	3.
	Transport	−0.38	−0.42	−0.48	−0.46	−0.19	−0.39	−0.36	−1.35	−0.
	Professional	14.36	6.46	2.71	8.89	2.57	12.77	7.12	9.19	3.
IDN	Finance	8.77	5.70	4.89	12.32	4.87	7.72	7.14	9.93	5.
	Telecom	3.37	2.33	2.10	11.04	0.86	3.36	3.00	3.61	1.
	Transport	−1.08	−1.20	−1.37	−1.31	−0.54	−1.13	−1.03	−3.87	−2.
	Professional	20.55	9.25	3.88	12.72	3.68	18.28	10.19	13.16	5.
IND	Finance	21.79	14.17	12.14	30.62	12.09	19.18	17.74	24.66	13.
	Telecom	7.64	5.28	4.76	25.02	1.96	7.61	6.79	8.18	3.
	Transport	0.81	0.90	1.03	0.99	0.41	0.84	0.77	2.90	2.
	Professional	21.10	9.50	3.98	13.06	3.77	18.77	10.46	13.50	5.
JPN	Finance	NA	NA	NA	NA	NA	NA	NA	NA	NA
	Telecom	8.46	5.84	5.26	27.68	2.16	8.42	7.51	9.05	3.
	Transport	6.77	7.49	8.57	8.23	3.39	7.05	6.45	24.23	17.
	Professional	13.36	6.01	2.52	8.26	2.39	11.88	6.62	8.55	3.
KOR	Finance	NA	NA	NA	NA	NA	NA	NA	NA	NA
	Telecom	13.03	8.99	8.11	42.65	3.33	12.97	11.57	13.95	5.
	Transport	3.68	4.08	4.66	4.48	1.84	3.84	3.51	13.18	9.
	Professional	14.61	6.58	2.76	9.04	2.61	13.00	7.24	9.36	3.
LKA	Finance	15.30	9.95	8.53	21.50	8.49	13.47	12.45	17.31	9.
	Telecom	9.50	6.56	5.92	31.11	2.43	9.46	8.44	10.17	4.
	Transport	3.55	3.94	4.50	4.32	1.78	3.70	3.39	12.72	9.
	Professional	11.11	5.00	2.10	6.88	1.99	9.88	5.51	7.11	2.
MNG	Finance	NA	NA	NA	NA	NA	NA	NA	NA	NA
	Telecom	NA	NA	NA	NA	NA	NA	NA	NA	NA
	Transport	−0.75	−0.84	−0.96	−0.92	−0.38	−0.79	−0.72	−2.70	−1.
	Professional	1.02	0.46	0.19	0.63	0.18	0.90	0.50	0.65	0.
MYS	Finance	40.77	26.51	22.72	57.28	22.63	35.89	33.18	46.14	24.
	Telecom	5.82	4.02	3.63	19.07	1.49	5.80	5.17	6.24	2.
	Transport	7.86	8.70	9.95	9.56	3.93	8.19	7.49	28.13	20.
	Professional	15.29	6.88	2.88	9.46	2.73	13.60	7.58	9.79	3.
NZL	Finance	NA	NA	NA	NA	NA	NA	NA	NA	NA
	Telecom	17.53	12.10	10.91	57.38	4.49	17.46	15.57	18.77	7.
	Transport	4.10	4.54	5.20	4.99	2.05	4.28	3.91	14.69	10.
	Professional	3.06	1.38	0.58	1.90	0.55	2.72	1.52	1.96	0.
VNM	Finance	13.01	8.46	7.25	18.28	7.22	11.45	10.59	14.72	7.
	Telecom	6.45	4.45	4.01	21.11	1.65	6.42	5.73	6.90	2.
	Transport	−1.07	−1.18	−1.35	−1.30	−0.53	−1.11	−1.02	−3.83	−2.
	Professional	2.04	0.92	0.38	1.26	0.36	1.81	1.01	1.30	0.

ricated al products pt chinery equipment)	*Machinery and equipment n.e.c (29)*	*Office, accounting and computing machinery (30)*	*Electrical machinery and apparatus n.e.c (31)*	*Radio, television and communication equipment (32)*	*Medical, precision and optical instruments (33)*	*Motor vehicles, trailers and semi-trailers (34)*	*Other transport equipment (35)*	*Manufacturing n.e.c.; recycling (36-37)*
46	11.38	15.42	11.53	15.42	15.42	8.80	10.09	12.11
54	13.42	14.34	6.43	14.34	14.34	6.11	7.47	11.95
23	−0.21	−0.17	−0.25	−0.17	−0.17	−0.22	−0.22	−0.30
93	11.08	13.40	8.67	13.40	13.40	3.76	8.79	10.66
27	9.20	12.47	9.33	12.47	12.47	7.11	8.16	9.79
31	6.77	7.24	3.24	7.24	7.24	3.08	3.77	6.03
66	−0.60	−0.48	−0.71	−0.48	−0.48	−0.63	−0.62	−0.87
79	15.85	19.18	12.41	19.18	19.18	5.38	12.58	15.25
93	22.86	30.97	23.17	30.97	30.97	17.67	20.26	24.33
77	15.35	16.40	7.35	16.40	16.40	6.99	8.54	13.67
50	0.45	0.36	0.53	0.36	0.36	0.47	0.47	0.65
12	16.27	19.69	12.74	19.69	19.69	5.52	12.92	15.66
	NA	NA	NA	NA	NA	NA	NA	NA
31	16.98	18.14	8.13	18.14	18.14	7.73	9.45	15.12
14	3.76	2.98	4.44	2.98	2.98	3.92	3.91	5.43
31	10.30	12.47	8.07	12.47	12.47	3.49	8.18	9.91
	NA	NA	NA	NA	NA	NA	NA	NA
55	26.16	27.95	12.53	27.95	27.95	11.91	14.57	23.30
25	2.04	1.62	2.41	1.62	1.62	2.13	2.13	2.96
9	11.27	13.64	8.83	13.64	13.64	3.82	8.95	10.85
7	16.05	21.74	16.27	21.74	21.74	12.41	14.23	17.08
4	19.08	20.39	9.14	20.39	20.39	8.69	10.62	17.00
7	1.97	1.57	2.33	1.57	1.57	2.06	2.05	2.85
1	8.57	10.37	6.71	10.37	10.37	2.91	6.80	8.25
	NA	NA	NA	NA	NA	NA	NA	NA
	NA	NA	NA	NA	NA	NA	NA	NA
6	−0.42	−0.33	−0.49	−0.33	−0.33	−0.44	−0.44	−0.61
3	0.78	0.95	0.61	0.95	0.95	0.27	0.62	0.75
8	42.78	57.95	43.35	57.95	57.95	33.07	37.92	45.52
4	11.70	12.50	5.60	12.50	12.50	5.33	6.51	10.42
1	4.36	3.46	5.15	3.46	3.46	4.55	4.54	6.31
1	11.79	14.27	9.24	14.27	14.27	4.00	9.36	11.35
	NA	NA	NA	NA	NA	NA	NA	NA
0	35.20	37.61	16.86	37.61	37.61	16.03	19.60	31.36
1	2.28	1.81	2.69	1.81	1.81	2.38	2.37	3.29
1	2.36	2.86	1.85	2.86	2.86	0.80	1.88	2.27
4	13.65	18.49	13.83	18.49	18.49	10.55	12.10	14.52
4	12.95	13.84	6.20	13.84	13.84	5.90	7.21	11.53
5	−0.59	−0.47	−0.70	−0.47	−0.47	−0.62	−0.62	−0.86
7	1.57	1.90	1.23	1.90	1.90	0.53	1.25	1.51

s: The table reports the percentage change in labour productivity in the manufacturing sector specified in the first associated with the removal of all barriers to Mode 3 services trade in the services sector specified in the second mn (Finance, Telecom, Transport, Professional). The estimated effects are computed based on the results in Panel Table 9.A1, where economic governance is measured by the degree of control of corruption in the economy. Each rvation is identified by the country implementing the reform, the specific services sector for which trade barriers are ved and the manufacturing sector whose productivity is potentially affected by the reform. The statistical signifi- of the estimates depends on the country and services sector, and it is in the standard threshold of 10 percent for the wing country-services pairs: JPN-telecom; JPN-transport; KOR-finance; KOR-telecom; LKA-finance; LKA-telecom; -finance; MYS-telecom; NZL-finance; NZL-telecom; NZL-transport. The sample reported in the table consists of observations plus 90 datapoints labelled as 'NA', which reflect services sectors already fully opened to trade in the ctive country. Shades of grey reflect the distribution of the sample of 630 observations. Four tones of grey – from ghtest to the darkest – identify observations in the 25th percentile (2.058) of the distribution, between the 25th and 0th (6.796), between the 50th and the 75th (12.724), and above the 75th, respectively. Manufacturing is classified wing the ISIC 2-digit classification Rev. 3. ISIC codes are in parentheses following sectoral labels in the first row. stical significance: *p < 0.1; **p < 0.05; ***p < 0.01.

ces: Governance variables are from the World Bank Governance Indicators. Services trade policies from the World 's STRD. Labour productivity (output per worker) from the UNIDO industrial statistics database.

Disclaimer

The views expressed in this paper are those of the authors. They are not meant to represent the positions or opinions of the WTO or its members and are without prejudice to members' rights and obligations under the WTO.

Notes

1 Country studies include Duggan et al. (2013) on Indonesia and Bas (2014) on India. Cross-country analyses include Barone and Cingano (2011), Bourlès et al. (2013) and Hoekman and Shepherd (2015).
2 In a previous paper Arnold et al. (2011) found similar results for the case of manufacturing producers in the Czech Republic.
3 The econometric framework in BFH is not designed to identify in the data these individual mechanisms. In particular, it is not possible to identify the causal impact of services trade reforms on the productivity of services sectors. The existence of a direct, positive effect of services trade liberalisation on the performance and competitiveness of services sectors is consistent with the positive indirect effect (from upstream services to downstream manufacturing sectors) found in the literature. Further research on the empirical assessment of the direct effect of services trade policy would represent a relevant contribution, and it will crucially depend on the availability of good data for the performance of services sectors and services firms across countries.
4 In order to minimise potential endogeneity issues, the input-output matrix for the US is used to calculate these weights. The weights are given by shares of intermediate consumption.
5 The economic interpretation of the estimated marginal effect in BFH and in this chapter can be justified in two ways: first, by considering CSTRI as a direct proxy of input-services trade policy; or second, by assuming the actual services trade policy STRI to have no effect on manufacturing sectors other than the effect channelled by the input-output linkages.
6 The robustness checks in BFH include instrumentation and placebo simulation of the policy component ($STRI_{is}$) of the composite restrictiveness indicator, estimation with alternative input-output weights or alternative productivity measures, and variations in country and industry coverage.
7 Alternative exercises can be conducted, assessing the quantitative impact of a policy reform that brings the degree of services liberalisation to match the most open policy stance in the region. This would consist of a vector of heterogeneous policy objectives across services sectors: the most open policy regime for financial services in the region coincides with complete openness (for instance, in Korea), while this is not the case for transport services. By construction, services sector heterogeneity cannot be captured in $\Delta CSTRI_{ij}$. For this reason and for the fact that the most liberal policy stance in the region is often quite close to complete openness, the common policy objective for all services sectors of complete removal of all trade policy barriers remains the most straightforward counterfactual scenario for an insightful quantification exercise.
8 These results are obtained using control of corruption as a proxy of economic governance. The full set of regression results for three alternative measures of economic governance are reported in Column (1) of Table 9.A.1. The estimates obtained for the quantification exercise in this chapter are almost identical to those in BFH. From the corresponding specification in BFH (see Column 4 in Table 9.2 of BFH), the estimated coefficients are $\hat{\beta} = 0.054$ (robust se 0.031) and $\hat{\mu}=-0.037$ (robust se 0.012).
9 A thorough discussion of this assumption can be found in BFH and other papers (e.g. Rajan and Zingales, 1998; Bourlès et al., 2013).

10 A detailed discussion of STRI evolution across ASEAN members and sectors is given in ASEAN Secretariat and World Bank (2015).
11 Issues of trade/investment diversion are likely to be less salient in the case of agreements such as the Transatlantic Trade and Investment Partnership (TTIP), given that the EU and the US are both large and have competitive markets.
12 The measure of economic governance used in the Appendix figures is control of corruption.
13 The country-services sector pairs for which estimates satisfy the standard threshold of statistical significance of 10% are: JPN-telecom; JPN-transport; KOR-finance; KOR-telecom; LKA-finance; LKA-telecom; MYS-finance; MYS-telecom; NZL-finance; NZL-telecom; NZL-transport.

References

Acemoglu, Daron, Simon Johnson, and James Robinson. 2001. 'The Colonial Origins of Comparative Development: An Empirical Investigation'. *American Economic Review* 91 (5): 1369–401.

Amiti, Mary, and Jozef Konings. 2007. 'Trade Liberalization, Intermediate Inputs, and Productivity: Evidence from Indonesia'. *The American Economic Review* 97 (5): 1611–38.

Anderson, James E., and Douglas Marcouiller. 2002. 'Insecurity and the Pattern of Trade: An Empirical Investigation'. *Review of Economics and Statistics* 84 (2): 342–52.

Arnold, Jens Matthias, Beata Javorcik, and Aaditya Mattoo. 2011. 'Does Services Liberalization Benefit Manufacturing Firms? Evidence from the Czech Republic'. *Journal of International Economics* 85 (1): 136–46.

Arnold, Jens Matthias, Beata Javorcik, Aaditya Mattoo, and Molly Lipscomb. 2016. 'Services Reform and Manufacturing Performance. Evidence from India'. *Economic Journal* 126 (590): 1–39.

Arnold, Jens Matthias, Aaditya Mattoo, and Gaia Narciso. 2008. 'Services Inputs and Firm Productivity in Sub-Saharan Africa: Evidence from Firm-Level Data'. *Journal of African Economies* 17 (4): 578–99.

ASEAN Secretariat, and World Bank. 2015. *ASEAN Services Integration Report*. Washington, DC: World Bank.

Barone, Guglielmo, and Federico Cingano. 2011. 'Service Regulation and Growth: Evidence from OECD Countries'. *Economic Journal* 121 (555): 931–57.

Bas, Maria. 2014. 'Does Services Liberalization Affect Manufacturing Firms' Export Performance? Evidence from India'. *Journal of Comparative Economics* 42 (3): 569–89. doi:10.1016/j.jce.2013.06.005.

Beverelli, Cosimo, Matteo Fiorini, and Bernard Hoekman. 2017. 'Services Trade Policy and Manufacturing Productivity: The Role of Institutions'. *Journal of International Economics* 104: 166–82.

Borchert, Ingo, Batshur Gootiiz, and Aaditya Mattoo. 2012. 'Policy Barriers to International Trade in Services: Evidence from a New Database'. *World Bank Economic Review* 28 (1): 162–88.

Bourlès, Renaud, Gilbert Cette, Jimmy Lopez, Jacques Mairesse, and Giuseppe Nicoletti. 2013. 'Do Product Market Regulations in Upstream Sectors Curb Productivity Growth? Panel Data Evidence for OECD Countries'. *Review of Economics and Statistics* 95 (5): 1750–68.

De Loecker, Jan, Pinelopi K. Goldberg, Amit K. Khandelwal, and Nina Pavcnik. 2016. 'Prices, Markups, and Trade Reform'. *Econometrica* 84 (2): 445–510.

Dollar, David, Mary Hallward-Driemeier, and Taye Mengistae. 2005. 'Investment Climate and Firm Performance in Developing Economies'. *Economic Development and Cultural Change* 54 (1): 1–31.

Dort, Thibaut, Pierre-Guillaume Méon, and Khalid Sekkat. 2014. 'Does Investment Spur Growth Everywhere? Not Where Institutions Are Weak'. *Kyklos* 67 (4): 482–505.

Duggan, Victor, Sjamsu Rahardja, and Gonzalo Varela. 2013. *Service Sector Reform and Manufacturing Productivity. Evidence from Indonesia.*

Fernandes, Ana, and Caroline Paunov. 2011. 'Foreign Direct Investment in Services and Manufacturing Productivity: Evidence for Chile'. *Journal of Development Economics* 97 (2): 305–21.

Fiorini, Matteo, and Bernard Hoekman. 2017a. 'Economic Governance, Regulation and Services Trade Liberalization'. *EUI RSCAS Working Paper N.2017/.27.*

———. 2017b. 'Services Trade Policy, Domestic Regulation and Economic Governance'. *European Commission Discussion Paper.*

Forlani, Emanuele. 2012. 'Competition in the Service Sector and the Performances of Manufacturing Firms: Does Liberalization Matter?'

Francois, Joseph F. 1990. 'Producer Services, Scale, and the Division of Labor'. *Oxford Economic Papers* 42 (4): 715–29.

Francois, Joseph, and Bernard Hoekman. 2010. 'Services Trade and Policy'. *Journal of Economic Literature* 48 (3): 642–92.

Freund, Caroline, and Bineswaree Bolaky. 2008. 'Trade, Regulations, and Income'. *Journal of Development Economics* 87 (2): 309–21.

Goldberg, Pinelopi Koujianou, Amit Kumar Khandelwal, Nina Pavcnik, and Petia Topalova. 2010. 'Imported Intermediate Inputs and Domestic Product Growth: Evidence from India'. *Quarterly Journal of Economics* 125 (4): 1727–67.

Hoekman, Bernard, and Benjamin Shepherd. 2017. 'Services Productivity, Trade Policy, and Manufacturing Exports'. *The World Economy* 40 (3): 499–516.

Miroudot, Sébastien, Rainer Lanz, and Alexandros Ragoussis. 2009. 'Trade in Intermediate Goods and Services'. 93. *OECD Trade Policy Paper.* OECD Publishing. https://ideas.repec.org/p/oec/traaab/93-en.html.

Miroudot, Sébastien, and Ben Shepherd. 2016. 'Trade Costs and Global Value Chains in Services'. In *Research Handbook on Trade in Services*, edited by Pierre Sauvé and Martin Roy. Research Handbook on the WTO. Edward Elgar.

Nunn, Nathan, and Daniel Trefler. 2014. 'Domestic Institutions as a Source of Comparative Advantage'. In *Handbook of International Economics*, edited by Gita Gopinath, Kenneth Rogoff, and Elhanan Helpman, 263–315. Elsevier.

Ranjan, Priya, and Jae Young Lee. 2007. 'Contract Enforcement and International Trade'. *Economics & Politics* 19 (2): 191–218.

Rajan, Raghuram G., and Luigi Zingales. 1998. 'Financial Dependence and Growth'. *American Economic Review* 88 (3): 559–86.

Rodriguez, Francisco, and Dani Rodrik. 2001. 'Trade Policy and Economic Growth: A Skeptic's Guide to the Cross-National Evidence'. In *NBER Macroeconomics Annual*, edited by Ben S. Bernanke and Kenneth Rogoff. Cambridge, MA: MIT Press.

Appendix

Table 9.A1 Regression Estimates

CSTRI *Type*	*Aggregate*	*Finance*	*Telecom*	*Transport*	*Professional*
	(1)	(2)	(3)	(4)	(5)
Panel A: EG as control of corruption					
CSTRI	0.055*	0.259	0.097	0.074*	-0.018
	(0.030)	(0.303)	(0.227)	(0.042)	(0.047)
CSTRI × EG	-0.037***	-0.204*	-0.132*	-0.037**	-0.004
	(0.011)	(0.121)	(0.078)	(0.016)	(0.019)
Adjusted R-squared	0.591	0.589	0.589	0.589	0.586
Panel B: as regulatory quality					
CSTRI	0.073**	0.211	-0.026	0.116**	-0.051
	(0.032)	(0.264)	(0.230)	(0.044)	(0.060)
CSTRI × EG	-0.042***	-0.193*	-0.093	-0.053***	0.009
	(0.011)	(0.115)	(0.088)	(0.016)	(0.025)
Adjusted R-squared	0.591	0.589	0.589	0.590	0.586
Panel C: EG as rule of law					
CSTRI	0.077**	0.086	0.013	0.121***	-0.036
	(0.032)	(0.328)	(0.255)	(0.042)	(0.050)
CSTRI × EG	-0.044***	-0.132	-0.102	-0.054***	0.003
	(0.012)	(0.128)	(0.091)	(0.016)	(0.021)
Adjusted R-squared	0.592	0.588	0.589	0.591	0.586
Observations	930	930	930	930	930

Notes: All regressions include country and sector fixed-effects as well as the input tariff regressor x. Robust (country-clustered) standard errors in parenthesis. Statistical significance: *p < 0.1; **p < 0.05; ***p < 0.01.

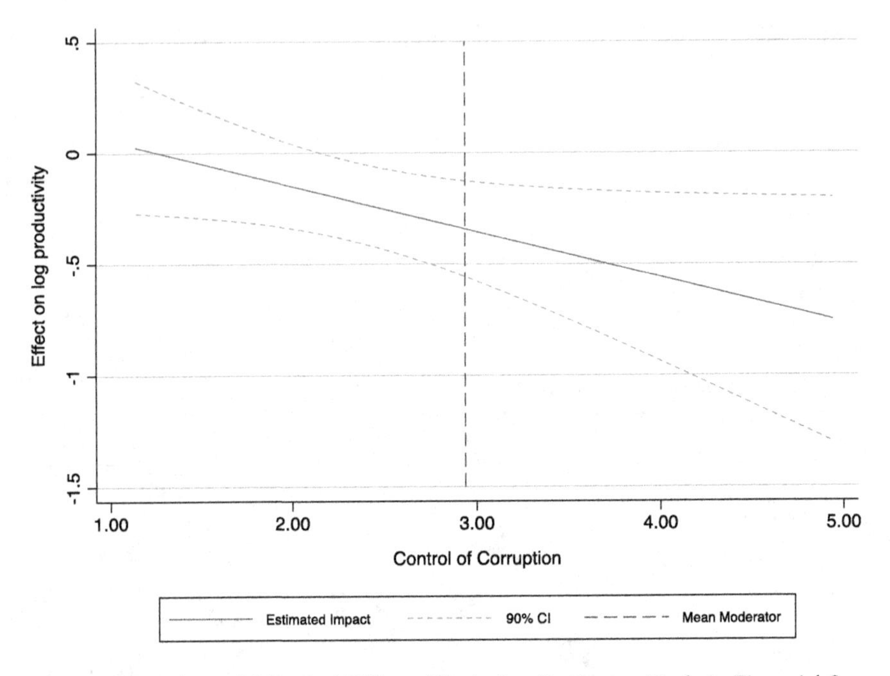

Figure 9.A1 Estimated Marginal Effect of Reducing Barriers to Trade in Financial Services as a Function of Economic Governance.

Source: Derived from estimated coefficients in Table 9.A1.

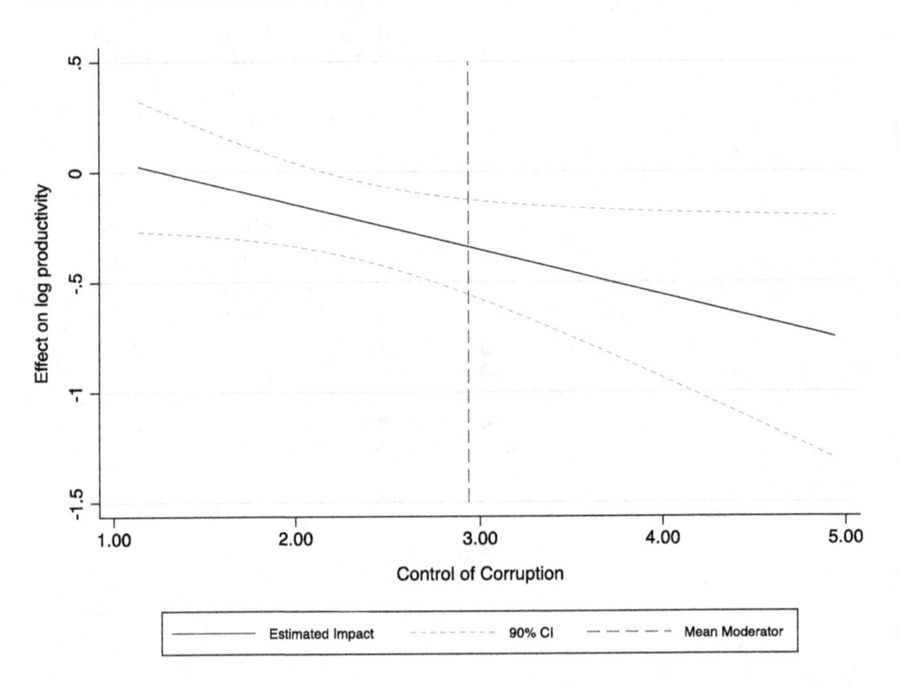

Figure 9.A2 Estimated Marginal Effect of Reducing Barriers to Trade in Telecommunications Services as a Function of Economic Governance.

Source: Derived from estimated coefficients in Table 9.A1.

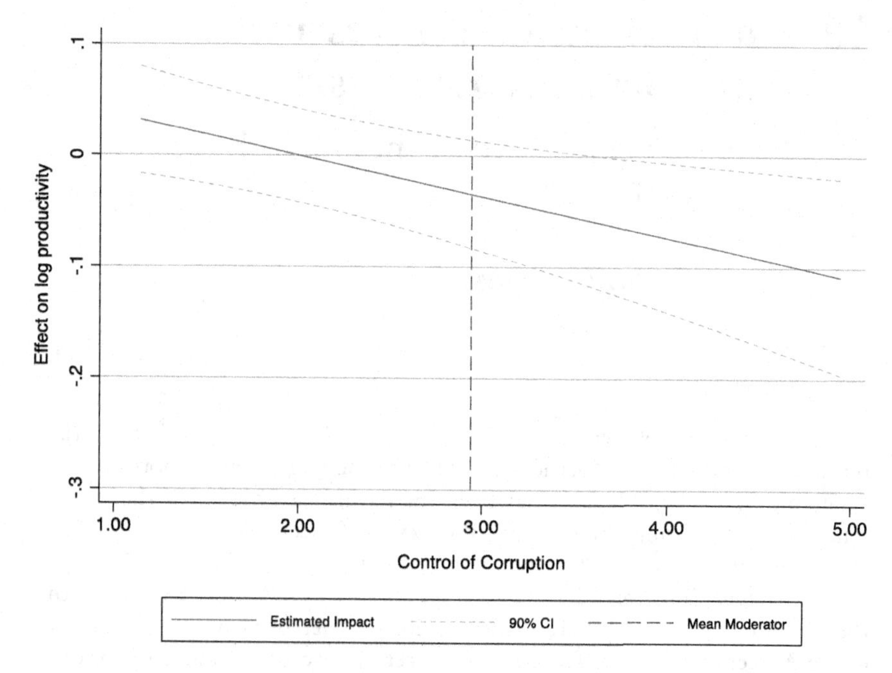

Figure 9.A3 Estimated Marginal Effect of Reducing Barriers to Trade in Transport Services as a Function of Economic Governance.

Source: Derived from estimated coefficients in Table 9.A1.

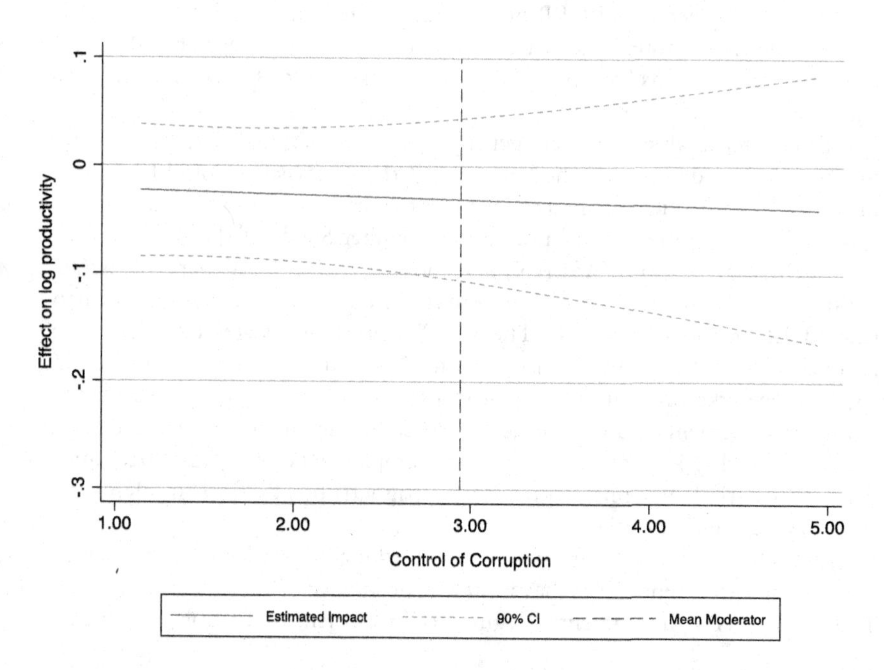

Figure 9.A4 Estimated Marginal Effect of Reducing Barriers to Trade in Professional Services as a Function of Economic Governance.

Source: Derived from estimated coefficients in Table 9.A1.

10 An international investment agreement for East Asia

Issues, recent developments and refinements

Junianto James Losari

10.1 Introduction

The Regional Comprehensive Economic Partnership (RCEP) will potentially replace the Trans-Pacific Partnership (TPP) as the largest trade cooperation by economic size. The TPP pact has been revived in the absence of the US and renamed as the Comprehensive and Progressive Agreement for TPP (CPTPP), and it retains most of the negotiated elements in the TPP.[1] The CPTPP is expected to enter into force in December 2018. CPTPP Article 1 provides that the provisions of the TPP are incorporated, by reference, into and made part of the Agreement *mutatis mutandis*, with certain exceptions and suspension of application of certain provisions specified in its Annex. Therefore, reference to the text of the TPP in this chapter refers to the CPTPP. At this stage, it may be premature to declare RCEP's new title because the negotiating states are yet to conclude the agreement. RCEP negotiations commenced in November 2011; by the time this chapter was written, more than five years have passed, and 20 rounds of negotiations have been held, but the timing for the conclusion of the agreement remains unclear.

This chapter analyses the new generation of international investment agreements (IIAs) to determine whether some of their provisions could be adopted into RCEP's investment chapter in an effort to create a modern and consolidated investment protection regime among the Member States of the Association of Southeast Asian Nations (ASEAN) and their six dialogue partners – Australia, China, India, Japan, the Republic of Korea (henceforth, Korea) and New Zealand (the RCEP negotiating states). The RCEP negotiating states have concluded more than 80 IIAs among themselves. This has led to parallelism – overlapping legal frameworks, including bilateral investment treaties (BITs),[2] regional investment agreements, and investment chapters in various free trade agreements (FTAs) – which potentially adds a layer of complexity (UNCTAD, 2013) and is what Bhagwati (1995) referred to as the 'spaghetti bowl' effect in reference to the growing number of FTAs.

Although there have been attempts to conclude a multilateral framework of investment agreements, they have not yet been successful (Koschwar, 2009). This has left us with fragmented regimes of investment protection, which allow

DOI: 10.4324/9780429433603-10

companies to structure their investments in such a way as to enjoy the benefits from the best regime(s). This has become easier with studies to map the various provisions in different IIAs (Alschner and Skougarevskiy, 2016; UNCTAD, 2017).

Section 10.2 stresses the importance of understanding the objects and purposes of an IIA. Section 10.3 analyses the main traditional pillar in IIAs. Section 10.4 explores the development of other pillars – liberalisation, promotion, and facilitation. Section 10.5 concludes.

10.2 Understanding the object and purpose of an IIA

The object and purpose of an IIA should be defined as a matter of priority for the purposes of negotiation as well as interpretation of the IIA's contents at a later stage when disputes arise. By understanding the objectives and purpose, negotiating states can better customise the agreement to advance their own objectives and purpose.

The lack of clarity in most investment protection provisions in existing BITs or the bilateral FTAs of the RCEP negotiating states provides a wide margin for discretion for investor-state arbitral tribunals in interpreting the provisions. In this process, arbitral tribunals often look at the object and purpose of the agreement (Sauvant and Ortino, 2013).[3] Unfortunately, the object and purpose of some IIAs are often not clearly stated. Some tribunals have simply relied on the preamble of a BIT to find that the object and purpose were 'to encourage and protect investment'[4] or 'to promote greater economic cooperation'.[5] Such a liberal interpretation put states at a disadvantage, especially if their measures have legitimate reasons despite the effects on some investors.

To overcome this issue, ASEAN in its ASEAN Comprehensive Investment Agreement (ACIA)[6] declares its purpose is to create a favourable investment environment that will enhance the freer flow of capital, goods and services, technology and human resources, and, eventually, overall economic and social development in the region. This purpose is an elaboration of the bigger goal of creating ASEAN as a competitive single market and production base (ASEAN Secretariat, 2008).[7] Ewing-Chow et al. (2014) claim that while production networks in several sectors have actually been established within ASEAN, IIAs among ASEAN countries remain useful for preventing the backsliding of countries on their commitments and ensuring that the freer flow of capital, goods, and investment can be achieved to create even stronger production networks.[8]

In the context of the RCEP, the region's aggregate gross domestic product of 17.2 trillion USD dollar and population of more than 3.4 billion reveal a huge potential that can be explored further through economic integration.[9] One of the general guiding principles for RCEP negotiations is to have broader and deeper engagements with significant improvements over the existing ASEAN+1 FTAs.[10] In order to achieve these, the RCEP should push for greater economic integration. In particular, the investment chapter should facilitate the creation of a more conducive investment environment for foreign investors in each of the negotiating states by providing access and protection for foreign investors. In general, foreign investors perceived that they need to be protected from expropriation, arbitrary decisions of government officials which negatively affect their investments, or denial of access to justice. Despite the importance of protecting foreign investors, RCEP's investment chapter should also mention explicitly the object and purpose of creating a more refined agreement that maintains the balance between investment protection and the preservation of the negotiating states' policy space to pursue their legitimate policy objectives, including the protection of public health and the environment. This is important because states should not sacrifice the public interest altogether in favour of investment protection. This particular theme should be reflected throughout the investment chapter (Table 10.1).

10.3 Traditional pillar in an IIA: investment protection

This section analyses the different investment protection provisions of the various IIAs of the Member States and the newer IIAs and recommend how the RCEP negotiators should approach these provisions. Investment protection provisions have become ever more important due to foreign investors' perception of the public sectors of some countries in the region, as reflected in the 2017 Corruption Perception Index (CPI), Table 10.2.

Investment protection provisions magnify the negotiating states' commitments to uphold the rule of law in the region. Yet governments have realised that the existing IIAs (particularly the earlier generation BITs) often contained vaguely drafted provisions without explicitly specifying the rights of states to regulate certain matters for public purposes, such as protection of public health or the environment. This is not ideal given that governments often need to take measures that may affect foreign investments in ways that potentially constitute violations of IIAs.

During the last decade, states have attempted to address the problem by entering into newer generation IIAs, which expressly provide states with the policy space to regulate. In the Asia-Pacific region, the ACIA and the ASEAN-Australia-New Zealand Free Trade Agreement (AANZFTA) are good examples. Further refinements can be found in various newer IIAs, e.g. in the investment chapters of the TPP, Canada Comprehensive Economic and Trade Agreement (CETA), and the European Union (EU)-Viet Nam Investment Protection Agreement (IPA). As illustrated further in this section, there is no definitive formula for striking such a balance. A balance is struck by ensuring that a state will not be held liable for a breach of its protection obligations under the relevant IIA when the breach is meant to address public interest that is greater than the interest of an investor. However, in doing so, host states must act in good faith and demonstrate that the measure is genuinely necessary and that no less damaging measures are available at the relevant time.

Table 10.1 FTAs with Investment Chapters or Regional Investment Agreements (Reviewed IIAs)

No.	*Name*	*Date of Entry into Force*
ASEAN + Dialogue Partners		
1	ASEAN Comprehensive Investment Agreement (ACIA)	29 March 2012
2	ASEAN-Australia-New Zealand Free Trade Agreement (AANZFTA) Investment Chapter	1 January 2010: Australia, Brunei, Malaysia, Myanmar, Philippines, New Zealand, Singapore and Viet Nam 12 March 2010: Thailand 4 January 2011: Cambodia and Lao PDR
3	Agreement on Investment of the Framework Agreement on Comprehensive Economic Cooperation between the ASEAN and the People's Republic of China (ASEAN-China Investment Agreement)	01 August 2010
4	2009 Agreement on Investment under the Framework Agreement on Comprehensive Economic Cooperation among the Governments of the Member Countries of the ASEAN and the Republic of Korea (ASEAN-Korea Investment Agreement)	01 September 2009
Singapore + Dialogue Partners FTAs		
5	Singapore-Australia FTA	28 July 2003
6	Singapore-India Comprehensive Economic Cooperation Agreement	01 August 2005
7	Agreement between Japan and Singapore for a New-Age Economic Partnership	30 November 2002
8	Korea-Singapore FTA	02 March 2006
9	Agreement between New Zealand and Singapore on a Closer Economic Partnership	18 August 2011
Malaysia + Dialogue Partners FTAs		
10	Malaysia-Australia FTA	01 January 2013
11	Malaysia-New Zealand FTA	01 August 2010
12	Malaysia-India Comprehensive Economic Cooperation Agreement	01 July 2011
13	Malaysia-Japan Economic Partnership Agreement	13 July 2006
Thailand + Dialogue Partners FTAs		
14	Thailand-Australia FTA	01 January 2005
15	Thailand-New Zealand Closer Economic Partnership	01 July 2005
16	Thailand-Japan Economic Partnership Agreement	01 November 2007
Philippines + Dialogue Partners FTA		
17	Philippines-Japan Economic Partnership Agreement	11 December 2008

(*Continued*)

No.	*Name*	*Date of Entry into Force*
Indonesia + Dialogue Partners FTA		
18	Japan-Indonesia Economic Partnership Agreement	01 July 2008
Other IIAs		
19	Agreement among the Government of Japan, the Government of the Republic of Korea, and the Government of the People's Republic of China for the Promotion, Facilitation, and Protection of Investment (Trilateral Investment Agreement)	17 May 2014
20	Comprehensive and Progressive Agreement for Trans-Pacific Partnership (CPTPP)	Signed on 8 March 2018, expected to enter into force in December 2018
21	EU-Canada Comprehensive Economic and Trade Agreements (CETA)	Signed on 30 October 2016, entered into force provisionally on 21 September 2017
22	EU-Viet Nam Investment Protection Agreement (EU-Viet Nam IPA)	Agreed final text as per July 2018

Source: Author's compilation from data provided in UNCTAD (2017).

Table 10.2 2017 Corruption Perception Index, Ranking of RCEP Countries

Ranking	*Country*	*Global Ranking (180 Countries and Territories)*
1	New Zealand	1
2	Singapore	6
3	Australia	13
4	Japan	20
5	Brunei Darussalam	32
6	Korea	51
7	Malaysia	62
8	China	77
9	India	81
10	Indonesia	96
11	Thailand	96
12	Viet Nam	107
13	Philippines	111
14	Myanmar	130
15	Lao PDR	135
16	Cambodia	161

Source: Transparency International.

	ASEAN-China	*AANZFTA*	*ACIA*	*CETA*	*TPP*
Covered investment, e.g. approval in writing	Yes, for Thailand (Art. 3 (3))	Yes, for Thailand and Viet Nam (Art. 2(a))	Art. 4(a) and Annex 1	–	–
NT (both pre- and post- establishment)	(Art. 4) – no pre-establishment	Art. 2(d) on def. of investor and Art. 4	Art. 4(d) and Art. 5	Article 8.6 – but pre-establishment NT is not subject to ISDS	Article 9.4
MFN treatment (both pre- and post-establishment)	Art. 1(1)(e) and Art. 5 – excludes ISDS	No MFN clause, Art. 16(2)(a)	Art. 6(1) – excludes ISDS	Article 8.7 – but pre-establishment MFN is not subject to ISDS	Article 9.5
FET (limited scope: not to deny justice or admin. proceedings)	Art. 7(2)	Art. 6(2)	Art.11	Article 8.10, with a broader scope than ACIA	Article 9.6
Expropriation	Art. 8 –exception for land and compulsory licences (CL)	Art. 9 – annex on expropriation, and exception for land and CL	Art. 14 – annex on expropriation, and exception for land and CL	Article 8.12 – annex on expropriation and exception for CL	Article 9.8 – annex on expropriation, and exception for land, CL, and non-issuance or non-renewal of a subsidy or grant
Prohibition on performance requirement	–	Art. 5	Art. 7	Article 8.5 – but pre-establishment is not subject to ISDS	Article 9.10
Freedom of transfer and its exception	Art. 10	Art. 8	Art. 13	Article 8.13	Article 9.9
Balance of payment/ prudential measures	Art. 11	Chapter 15	Art. 16	Articles 28.4–28.5	Article 29.3
General exceptions	Art. 16	Chapter 15	Art. 17	Article 28.3	–
Denial of benefits	Art. 15	Art. 11	Art. 19	Article 8.16	Article 9.15
ISDS	Art. 14	Art. 18	Section B – Article 29	Section F – Articles 8.18 – 8.45	Section B – Articles 9.19 – 9.30

Note: CIL – customary international law; NT – national treatment; MFN – most-favoured-nation; FET – fair and equitable treatment; ISDS – investor-state dispute settlement; SMBoD – senior management and board of directors.
Source: Author's compilation from data found in UNCTAD (2017).

10.3.1 Scope and coverage

Determining the scope and coverage of an IIA is important for regulating the investments and the investors entitled to benefit from the agreement. In order to illustrate this, I will discuss several provisions that have evolved from older IIAs, including (i) admission provisions and (ii) provisions on relationships with other chapters or agreements.

10.3.2 Admission provisions – approval in writing

Admission provisions govern the entry of investments into host states. In some IIAs, the provisions require investments to be admitted in accordance with the host state's national laws (investment-control model). In fact, this model is the one most commonly used. It allows a host state to control all inward foreign direct investment (FDI) (Pollan, 2006). For example, under the Foreign Acquisitions and Takeovers Act 1975 and the Foreign Acquisitions and Takeovers Regulation 2015, the Foreign Investment Review Board of Australia screens potential foreign investments in Australia above the threshold value of 252 million Australian dollar and 1,094 million Australian dollar (for certain countries) in non-sensitive businesses. In 2013, Archer Daniels Midland's proposed 2.8 billion Australian dollar purchase of Australian grain handler GrainCorp was rejected by the Office of the Treasurer based on this regulation.[11]

All of the reviewed IIAs contain admission provisions, but some of the ASEAN-plus dialogue partners' FTAs are unique. For example, Article 4(a) of the ACIA requires an investor to obtain specific approval in writing, without which the investor and its investment may not be protected.[12] Although such an approval requirement may be burdensome for investors, ACIA Annex 1 clarifies to an extent the specific procedure for obtaining approval.

Having an approval procedure may be useful, but the RCEP negotiating states can improve further the approval requirement by clarifying the procedures and contemplating the focal point in each host state to obtain the approval.

10.3.3 Relationship with other chapters and agreements

An investment chapter in an FTA normally overlaps with other chapters in the FTA, e.g. services, financial services, or even intellectual property. The relevant provision is titled 'Scope of Application', and appears to attempt to limit the scope of market access liberalisation. Unfortunately, the draft provision maintains the formulation in the ACIA, which is unclear as it does not define the term 'liberalisation'. 'Liberalisation' of investment can also mean better protection of foreign investors. It is thus essential for further East Asian integration to clarify this in order to avoid confusion and potential conflict regarding the meaning of the term.

Further, due to potential overlaps between the provisions in the investment chapter and other chapters, the future agreement in East Asia should specify the prevailing chapter in the case of inconsistencies. For example, TPP Article 9.3 provides explicitly the following: 'In the event of any inconsistency between this Chapter and another Chapter of this Agreement, the other Chapter shall prevail to the extent of the inconsistency'. The agreement should also regulate not only the relationship between chapters in the FTA but also the relationship between the agreement and other agreements to which the negotiating states are parties. For example, TPP Article 29.1(4) provides as follows:

> Nothing in this Agreement shall be construed to prevent a Party from taking action, including maintaining or increasing a customs duty, that is authorised by the Dispute Settlement Body of the WTO or is taken as a result of a decision by a dispute settlement panel under a free trade agreement to which the Party taking action and the Party against which the action is taken are party.

This type of provision is new, and it envisages the resolution of a potential situation whereby a (retaliating) state needs to take lawful retaliatory action (or a lawful countermeasure) against another (retaliated) state, as authorised by the World Trade Organization Dispute Settlement Body (WTO DSB) or a dispute settlement panel under an FTA (to which both states are parties). In such a circumstance, there is a possibility that the retaliatory action may cause losses or damages to foreign investors in the retaliating state. For example, a retaliatory action in the form of an increase of customs duties or withdrawal of intellectual property rights protection may affect a foreign investor in the retaliating state and so may lead to an investor-state arbitration claim. With TPP Article 29.1(4), a lawful retaliatory measure of a retaliating state will not amount to violation of the agreement (including the investment chapter). Thus, an investor's claim will not succeed. Indeed, this provision is essential in this ever more integrated world of international trade and investment, where multinational companies structure their companies in various countries in order to effectively and efficiently operate their global value chains (Losari and Ewing-Chow, 2016). Without this type of provision, there is great likelihood that states will be subject to many claims for lawful retaliatory actions under their other trade agreements.

In a broader context, the RCEP negotiating states must also consider the relationship between the RCEP and the existing IIAs among them – BITs, FTA with investment chapters, and regional investment agreements (Losari, 2016). This is particularly important to prevent foreign investors from cherry picking the most favourable provisions among different IIAs, particularly when the underlying IIA contains a most-favoured-nation (MFN) clause as elaborated further in Section 10.3.6. The RCEP negotiating states should consider including a provision to terminate the existing IIAs upon the entry into force of the RCEP, such as the following.

Article X

Transitional arrangements relating to other international investment agreements

1 Subject to Paragraphs 2, 3, and 4 of this paragraph, nothing in this Agreement shall derogate from the existing rights and obligations of a Member State under any other international agreements to which it is a party.
2 Upon the entry into force of this Agreement, the agreements amongst the Member States (as listed in Annex X) shall be terminated.
3 Notwithstanding the termination of the agreements listed in Annex X, the Reservation List and Non-Conforming Measures of those agreements shall apply to the liberalisation provisions of the RCEP's Investment Chapter, *mutatis mutandis*, until such time as the Reservation List of the RCEP's Investment Chapter comes into force.
4 With respect to investments falling within the ambit of this Agreement, as well as under one of the agreements listed in Annex X, investors of these investments may choose to apply the provisions, but only in its entirety, of either this Agreement or one of the agreements mentioned in Annex X, as the case may be, for a period of ten years after the date of termination of the IIAs mentioned in Annex X.

10.3.4 Performance requirements

A performance requirement provision places an obligation on host states not to impose certain requirements, such as local content requirements, trade-balancing requirements, or export controls, on foreign investors during the operation of their investments.[13] Most of the reviewed IIAs contain performance requirement provisions that refer to the Agreement on Trade-Related Investment Measures (TRIMs) of the WTO.[14]

10.3.5 National treatment

National treatment (NT) is a contingent standard of treatment whose application requires a comparative analysis of whether a host state grants no less favourable treatment to foreign investments or investors than to its domestic investments or investors (UNCTAD, 2007).

In analysing whether the NT obligation has been breached, tribunals normally assess whether there is *de jure* or *de facto* discrimination (Bjorklund, 2008).

Additionally, some tribunals also consider whether the investors are in '*like circumstances*', including whether the difference in treatment was justified by the rational policy objectives of the relevant government (Antoni and Ewing-Chow, 2013).[15] Nevertheless, there is no uniform interpretation of the 'like circumstances' test.

Footnote 14 of TPP Article 9.4 clarifies that 'like circumstances' will depend on the 'totality of the circumstances, including whether the relevant treatment distinguishes between investors or investments on the basis of legitimate public welfare objectives'. Covered investments or investors in 'like circumstances' should be made on a case-by-case basis by considering, among others the sector the investor is in, the location of the covered investment, or the goods or services consumed or produced by the covered investment. This type of clarification provides states with more policy space because it recognises the circumstances where certain legitimate regulatory objectives may require states to treat foreign investors differently from domestic investors.

In terms of the scope of application of NT clauses, some IIAs contain NT clauses that grant only the right of post-establishment, while others also grant the right of pre-establishment. The latter can be in the form of market access commitments, such as allowing foreign equity ownership in certain sectors that were previously opened only to domestic investors. These commitments are reflected in each member's schedule and relate to the liberalisation pillar of an IIA.

Although some IIAs include pre-establishment protection, they only allow disputes to be resolved through a state-to-state dispute resolution mechanism, e.g. Article 32(a) of the ACIA and CETA Article 8.7. This demonstrates that market access is a sensitive issue to the Member States, and they prefer to resolve disputes regarding this matter amongst themselves. At the same time, without investor-state dispute settlement (ISDS), the number of disputes relating to a breach of the pre-establishment protection can be reduced significantly.

RCEP's guiding principles mention that investment liberalisation will remain as one of the pillars in the investment chapter. As such, an NT guarantee with pre-establishment rights and the selected approach for listing their pre-establishment commitments – whether it is a negative-list approach, a positive-list approach, or a hybrid approach – should remain as part of the chapter. The negative-list approach requires more resources, as the negotiating states must conduct a thorough audit of existing domestic policies. In the absence of specific reservations, a negotiating state commits to opening those sectors/activities that at the time the IIA is signed may not yet exist in the country. In contrast, the positive-list approach offers selective liberalisation. States create a list of industries in which investors will enjoy the rights of pre-establishment (UNCTAD, 2012).

In order to avoid the risk of not regulating market access to sectors that may not have existed at the time of the conclusion of the agreement, this shall not apply to any measure that a Party adopts or maintains with respect to existing or new and emerging sectors, sub-sectors, and activities set out in its Schedule in Annex 4. This can address the weakness of regulating by the negative-list approach because the reservation applies to new and emerging sectors. At the same time, this can be restrictive because it basically does not provide pre-establishment NT protection to any foreign investors who wish to invest in these sectors. Nevertheless, the provision clearly needs further refinement to provide more clarity. The draft provision suggests that new and emerging sectors are listed in Annex 4, but this would not make sense.

10.3.6 Most-favoured nation treatment

An MFN treatment clause in an IIA is meant to create a level playing field between all foreign investors of different nationalities. It can apply to conditions of entry and the operation of foreign investors (UNCTAD, 2010).

In practice, besides claiming the violation of MFN treatment, investors or claimants in an ISDS case normally use the MFN clause in the primary treaty – under which a dispute is brought – to incorporate/import more favourable substantive provisions[16] or Rules of Dispute Settlement[17] from a secondary treaty (to which the host state is a party) into the primary treaty. In fact, most MFN claims in ISDS cases have been invoked for such purpose rather than to claim against actual different treatment between foreign investors.

Although it is possible to import substantive protection standards from third-party agreements by virtue of an MFN clause, there are limitations. For example, investors may not invoke an MFN clause to eliminate the provisions of the primary treaty (UNCTAD, 2010).

The importation of more favourable Rules of Dispute Settlement is controversial (Ewing-Chow and Ng, 2008). While some tribunals are willing to incorporate Rules of Dispute Settlement from secondary treaties by virtue of an MFN clause,[18] others have been reluctant.[19]

Since the case of *Maffezini*, some states have decided to exclude the clause altogether[20] or have refined the MFN clause in their newer IIAs. Most of the ASEAN+1 dialogue partner IIAs, except the ASEAN-Korea Investment Agreement, contain refined MFN clauses that explicitly exclude the application of the clauses to dispute settlement procedures.[21]

However, CETA and the EU-Viet Nam IPA have gone further in preventing the use of the MFN clause to incorporate substantive standards of treatment contained in other IIAs of a host state. CETA Article 8.7(4) provides:[22] [...] Substantive obligations in other international investment treaties and other trade agreements do not in themselves constitute 'treatment', and thus cannot give rise to a breach of this article, absent measures adopted by a Party pursuant to such obligations [emphasis added].

This limitation is particularly important because, without it, efforts to negotiate more refined and balanced standards of protection in the RCEP could be futile, as investors will simply use the MFN clause to incorporate vaguer provisions in older IIAs of host states into RCEP's investment chapter by arguing that those provisions are more favourable. For this reason, the RCEP negotiating states should consider incorporating such limitations.

10.3.7 Fair and equitable treatment

In IIAs, fair and equitable treatment (FET) provisions (often referred to as minimum standards of treatment) often lack a precise meaning and have raised much controversy, leading to multiple interpretations by arbitral tribunals (UNCTAD, 2007). Some of the reviewed IIAs contain FET provisions which are linked to customary international law (CIL),[23] while FET provisions in other IIAs are very simply drafted (often referred to as the autonomous FET).

The so-called autonomous FET provision has often been interpreted broadly to include various guarantees, including non-arbitrariness, predictability, transparency, and the respect of investors' reasonable and legitimate expectations.[24] Similarly, even FET provisions linked to CIL were interpreted differently by various arbitral tribunals (Losari, 2016). Therefore, it is important to draft a clearer FET provision.

Some of the reviewed IIAs have attempted to limit the standard only to the guarantee against denial of justice (limited FET provision).[25] Although there has been no case suggesting how tribunals will interpret this type of provision, it is expected to limit any broad interpretation of the standard to mainly the guarantee for procedural matters and grossly arbitrary and unjust decisions (Bjorklund, 2005).[26] In *Flughafen v. Venezuela*, the tribunal ruled that to establish a denial of justice, two elements must be fulfilled: treatment that is clearly and manifestly anti-juridical, and exhaustion of all local remedies to challenge the decision (unless proven that such remedies would be futile).[27] Relevant to this, the due process principle also requires a host state to provide prior notice to the relevant party upon whom the state applies coercive power, and to provide an opportunity for the party to contest the application before an international tribunal including the right of legal representation (Vandevelde, 2010).

The RCEP negotiating states will have to consider whether to use the limited FET provision style or the EU FTA-style in formulating the RCEP's FET provision. In doing so, the consideration should be that the FET provision must provide investment protection that can provide comfort for foreign investors while at the same time also take into account the Member States' right to regulate. In this regard, the EU FTA-style offers a more comprehensive form of protection – namely, both procedural and substantive protections – to foreign investors. The future East Asian FTA may consider to adopt the EU FTA-style while at the same time ensure that the protections are properly caveated with a state's right to regulate where necessary.

10.3.8 Expropriation

Generally, states may expropriate foreign investments under the notion of lawful expropriation provided it is done on a non-discriminatory basis, for public purposes, in accordance with the due process of law and against the payment of compensation (UNCTAD, 2007). While in the past there were many cases of direct expropriation – the seizure of investments or transfer of legal title over investments – nowadays there are more claims of indirect expropriation, though still fewer than there are FET claims.

Unfortunately, expropriation provisions in older IIAs tend to be vague and fail to explain governmental measures that constitute indirect expropriation. This leads to different approaches by arbitral tribunals in interpreting what constitutes indirect expropriation, including measures having a permanent character that substantially deprive the investors' rights or conflict with its investment-backed expectations (Dolzer and Schreuer, 2008; Dugan et al., 2008) or measures which are not proportional to the public interest protected by them and to the protection legally granted to the investments (Newcombe, 2005; Dugan et al., 2008). Another more controversial interpretation[28] (known as the *Methanex* approach) suggests that a measure will not be expropriatory and no compensation will be owed to investors when the measure is non-discriminatory, in accordance with due process, and for public purpose (Weiler, 2005; Schneidarman, 2008).[29] This approach conflates itself with lawful expropriation as the criteria are the same, except for the obligation to compensate.

While all of the reviewed IIAs cover both direct and indirect expropriation, the difference lies in the elaboration of what constitutes indirect expropriation and in the exceptions (carveout). For example, the ACIA carves out the expropriation of land and the issuance of compulsory licenses in accordance with the Agreement on Trade-Related Aspects of Intellectual Property Rights (TRIPS) from the rule of expropriation. A similar carveout on the issuance of compulsory licences can also be found in CETA Article 8.12(5).

Annex 2 of the ACIA appears to adopt the approach developed by the tribunal in *Methanex*. Paragraph 3 of Annex 8-A of CETA attempts to refine this type of provision by adding another test that the measure must not be manifestly excessive. Otherwise, the measure will still constitute indirect expropriation. This reminds us of the 'necessity test' in the General Agreement on Tariffs and Trade 1994 (GATT) Article XX and the General Agreement on Trade in Services (GATS) Article XIV, and may be a better approach than that developed in *Methanex* as it provides more clarity and is different to the test of lawful expropriation. For example, if a country proposes that investors must pursue remedies before domestic courts or tribunals prior to initiating a claim under the agreement. This particular proposal may not be very appealing for foreign investors in certain host states where domestic judiciary systems are problematic, e.g. long delay in hearings or corrupt judiciary.

Besides providing further clarification as in Annex 8-A of CETA, RCEP's investment chapter could be improved further by including a procedural mechanism that has to be followed by a government seeking to exercise its regulatory power. This could be in the form of a requirement to notify affected investors prior to the implementation of the measure and/or a domestic review mechanism for investors to challenge the proportionality of the measure. The mechanism would prevent the potential abuse of a government's policy space and ensure balance with investment protection.

10.3.9 Transfers and exceptions

All of the reviewed IIAs contain provisions on the guarantee of transfers relating to a covered investment. The provision guarantees that such transfers can be made freely without delay into and out of a host state. Normally, the provision also contains a list of exceptions under which the host state may prevent or delay a transfer so long as it is done in an equitable and non-discriminatory manner and in good faith. The difference among various IIAs' transfer provisions mainly lies in the list of exceptions. For example, Article 13(3) of the ACIA lists the exceptions to freedom to transfer, such as bankruptcy, criminal offences, and taxation. Such a list is important because in certain situations, host states should be allowed to prevent investors from evading their obligations under domestic law.

CETA Article 8.13(2) is slightly different, as it also prevents a home state from requiring its investors to transfer income, earnings, profits, or other amounts derived from investments in the territory of the other party. This is a rather interesting provision that could potentially address the growing protectionism policy taken by some states in order to bring investments back into their respective countries. The future East Asian integration agreement should also consider incorporating a similar provision as CETA Article 8.13(2), considering the growing protectionism that we are witnessing nowadays.

10.3.10 Treaty exceptions

Treaty exception provisions are used as a policy tool to strike a balance between investment protection and the safeguarding of other values or objectives considered to be fundamental to the countries concerned, such as public health, environment, or national security (Ewing-Chow and Fischer, 2011). The provisions provide a host state with significant room to manoeuvre when facing circumstances that may justify derogation from its IIA obligations. If the host state successfully invokes a treaty exception provision, it is exempted from any liability arising from its measure (Dugan et al., 2008).

There are several types of treaty exception provisions, including (i) a simple essential security exception provision, as found in many BITs;[30] (ii) exceptions to the transfer of funds; (iii) measures to safeguard balance of payments; and (iv) general exceptions similar to the GATT Article XX exception – word by word with minor modifications.[31] To the best of my knowledge, exception (iv) has never been invoked in investment arbitration cases, but since the exception seems to be inspired by GATT Article XX, we can expect some tribunals referring to WTO cases for interpretation (Kurtz, 2008).

CETA Article 28.3(2) is similar to exception (iv), but it adds more exceptions to its list, such as exceptions applicable to culture as well as taxation matters.

Besides a general exceptions provision that relieves states from liability, certain exceptions are created in order to prevent a certain dispute being brought to investor-state arbitration or any dispute settlement forum. For example, Annex 8-C of CETA provides that Canada's decision regarding whether or not to accept an investment that is subject to review under the Investment Canada Act is not subject to any dispute settlement mechanisms under CETA. A similar exception can also be found in TPP Article 29.5, which provides that a party may elect to deny benefits of Section B of Chapter 9 (Investment) with respect to claims challenging a tobacco control measure.

Presumably, the general exceptions are included in a different chapter. However, if the clause has not been included, the RCEP negotiating states should consider including the clause to preserve their policy space. The various types of exception provisions in other IIAs can be a basis to formulate the exceptions that will work most effectively in balancing investment protection and states' legitimate right to regulate.

10.3.11 Denial of benefits

The denial of benefits provision is inserted into IIAs to prevent treaty shopping and nationality planning by investors, both domestic and foreign (UNCTAD, 2014). For example, Article 19 of the ACIA allows host states to deny the benefits of the agreement to non-ASEAN investors or domestic investors who establish a shell company with no substantive business operations in the territory of another ASEAN Member State.[32]

The effectiveness of a denial of benefits clause is rather questionable. Corporations, especially multinationals, often structure their subsidiaries for various purposes, including operational, taxation, or even legal protection. Law firms have been openly advising in favour of this[33] and some tribunals have openly allowed this type of corporate structuring.[34] However, in certain cases where the restructuring was done much later for the purpose of bringing a dispute, tribunals rejected the claims and found them to be abuses of rights despite the absence of the denial of benefits provision.[35]

If the RCEP negotiating states are eager to prevent treaty shopping, at the very least they should clarify the factors for determining the existence of 'substantive business operations'. Although several tribunals have interpreted similar phrases as having 'substance and not merely form', such a definition is not always helpful.[36] In practice, some investment-related activities and the employment of a small but permanent staff had been considered substantial.[37] Even a holding company may carry out substantial business activities, except if the activities were simply to hold assets of its subsidiaries.[38]

10.3.12 Dispute settlement – investor-state dispute settlement

10.3.12.1 Criticisms of ISDS

All of the reviewed IIAs contain both state-to-state dispute settlement (SSDS) and ISDS mechanisms. In this chapter, ISDS specifically refers to investor-state arbitration, which has been scrutinised by many countries; indeed, some have even decided to exclude ISDS altogether.[39] Several economics studies specifically analyse the effects of having ISDS provisions in investment treaties to FDI inflows. For example, Aisbett et al. (2016) suggest that BITs with ISDS provisions which are signed prior to a dispute between the host state and an investor from the host country will have positive impact on bilateral FDI flows. However, FDI flows from the BIT-partner will decrease more strongly following a dispute compared to FDI flows from investors of countries with whom the host state has no BIT. Slightly different, Kohler and Stähler (2016) find that ISDS increases aggregate welfare in their study involving a two-period model analysing the potential of ISDS mechanism to mitigate the holdup problem present with FDI. Nevertheless, it is beyond the scope of this chapter to elaborate further on this study. Instead, I focus mainly on several criticisms of ISDS from legal perspective.

First, a number of developed countries argue that they do not need any ISDS, because they have fair and competent courts. While this may be true, in reality, investments do not only go to developed countries but increasingly to developing countries, including those with problematic rule of law. Many of the RCEP negotiating states are becoming both capital-importing and capital-exporting countries. For this reason, it is important for them to ensure that their citizens have direct access to a competent and impartial judiciary when investing in the region.

Still related to the first criticism, some critics suggest that ISDS should be replaced by SSDS, including one such as the WTO DSB. There are several issues regarding this proposition. First, SSDS may re-politicise an investor-state dispute. Indeed, ISDS is one of the main innovations introduced by IIAs to enable an individual (investor) to bring a dispute directly against a state, instead of having to exhaust local remedies for a lengthy period and, if not successful, completely rely on its home state to exercise diplomatic protection (Roberts, 2014, p. 2). Second, a state may not litigate a case of an aggrieved investor due to resources concerns, particularly if the home state is a developing country and has numerous investors requesting the state to litigate their respective disputes. In that situation, the aggrieved investor would be left with no other recourse than the domestic court system (which may be problematic) in the host state.

Roberts (2014) argues that exercise of diplomatic protection in SSDS mechanism can be useful, e.g. for individuals or small companies who cannot afford bringing a direct claim themselves, for class actions where the injuries are individually small but collectively large, or for investors who fear retaliation by a host state if they were to launch an investor-state arbitration. However, in order to create a WTO DSB-like dispute settlement mechanism, it may require tremendous commitments of nations to agree on its establishment as well as amendments of the existing IIAs' dispute settlement clauses. As the effort to create a multilateral investment agreement has not even progressed since its failure in the late 1990s (Schill, 2009), it will be a while until this could be materialised. In the meantime, the WTO DSB could perhaps be a model to develop a permanent investment court system as being proposed by CETA and the EU-Viet Nam IPA.

Second, some critics argue that ISDS exposes governments to expensive litigation. This may be true, but it can be resolved by ensuring that ISDS is used only as a last resort. The creation of a dispute prevention mechanism in each respective RCEP member can alleviate this issue. The mechanism is meant to prevent a conflict from escalating into a dispute and should be implemented as an investor aftercare service (Echandi and Sauvé, 2013). Further, RCEP members must ensure transparency by publishing the procedures of the mechanism as well as ensuring the impartiality of the relevant office. An example is Korea's Office of the Foreign Investment Ombudsman.[40]

Third, some argue that ISDS leads to various, often contradicting, interpretations of investment provisions in IIAs. There are two ways to address this concern. First, the RCEP negotiating states can include a joint interpretation mechanism, as found in Article 40 (2) and (3) of the ACIA. Under this mechanism, the tribunal or a disputing party may request a joint interpretation of any disputed ACIA provision, and the interpretation of the parties to the agreement shall be binding on the tribunal. Second, the RCEP negotiating states can consider the proposals to create an independent appellate body to review decisions made by *ad hoc* tribunals (Sauvant and Ortino, 2013) or a permanent court mechanism (Bishop, 2005; Crawford, 2005). There are concerns that the mechanisms could undermine the finality of an arbitral award, 'repoliticise' the process, and replicate the difficulties in the current system (Sauvant and Ortino, 2013). Nevertheless, the need to ensure better governance and a more harmonised interpretation are paramount. This idea has been refined further in the EU's new FTAs.

Lastly, the last criticism is directed towards the decision makers (arbitrators) in investor-state arbitrations. Kauffman-Kohler and Potesta (2016) observe that criticisms are mainly focussed on the arbitrators' alleged lack of sufficient guarantees of independence and impartiality. It is often argued that arbitrators are concerned about their future appointments, and since investor-state cases are initiated by investors, they are, consequently, inclined to cater to the investors' interests. In addition, some practitioners act as both counsel and arbitrator in different proceedings, leading to the so-called issue conflicts (Kauffman-Kohler and Potesta, 2016). These concerns can be addressed more effectively with the proposal to create a more permanent investment tribunal.

10.3.12.2 A more permanent investment tribunal – a solution to address them all?

One of the most recent innovations that have been discussed extensively to improve the current ISDS mechanism is the creation of a permanent investment tribunal to resolve investor-state disputes.[41] Indeed, this innovation has been incorporated into CETA and the EU-Viet Nam IPA, though one is yet to see the implementation. Although it is called a permanent investment tribunal system, the system introduced by CETA is not the same as some other permanent courts, such as the International Court of Justice or the WTO DSB. The agreement does not create its own secretariat but appoints the ICSID Secretariat to carry out the function (presumably even for cases submitted under other Rules of Arbitration, e.g. UNCITRAL Arbitration Rules).[42] The only more permanent feature of this system is the Tribunal, which comprises members who serve for a five-year term with possible renewal for one term.[43]

The appointment system of the members of the Tribunal can potentially ensure better guarantees of impartiality and independence than the appointment of arbitrators on an *ad hoc* basis. The security of tenure would insulate members of a tribunal from powerful private interests and prevent critics from arguing that the arbitrators decide certain issues for their own interests to get reappointments. Having said this, it is also recognised that critics may argue that the appointment of members of the Tribunal by states in the first place raises issues of impartiality because the states that pay for these individuals may appoint only pro-state individuals (Kauffman-Kohler and Potesta, 2016). This can be addressed by other safeguards, e.g. the code of conduct binding on the members of Tribunal as well as the appeal mechanism for ensuring the proper checks and balance. Another way of dealing with this issue is to allow the disputing parties to choose from a roster of previously elected members of the Tribunal. In any event, the negotiating states must agree on the election mechanism of the members of the Tribunal – a mechanism that must at least be transparent and able to be clearly monitored by the various constituencies (Kauffman-Kohler and Potesta, 2016).

In addition to the permanent investment tribunal, CETA Article 8.28 establishes an appellate tribunal to review awards rendered by an investment tribunal. The grounds to review awards are broad and may address the concerns raised by many commentators regarding diverging interpretations issued by various arbitral tribunals. By allowing the appellate tribunal to review errors in the appreciation of facts, CETA Article 8.28 also addresses an issue that often hampers the effectiveness of the Appellate Body of the WTO of the lack of capacity to make further factual inquiry.

A multilateral investment court would be ideal, as contemplated by CETA Article 8.29, with a multilateral mechanism to replace the mechanism therein once it has been established. However, in the absence of such a multilateral arrangement, the RCEP can at least adopt a similar system as that in CETA whereby the members of Tribunal may be appointed from the Member States based on their professional qualifications.

10.3.12.3 Other enhancements to the ISDS

Besides the proposal for the permanent investment tribunal, CETA Section F extensively regulates various matters on ISDS. It contains, among other things, provisions regarding the scope of investment disputes that can be submitted to the tribunal,[44] the availability of a mediation mechanism,[45] the obligation to disclose third-party funding,[46] ethics for members of the tribunal,[47] transparency rules referring to the UNCITRAL Rules on Transparency,[48] the enforcement of awards,[49] and consolidation.[50]

CETA Article 8.18 also limits the submission of a claim to the ISDS if an investment has been made through fraudulent misrepresentation, concealment, corruption, or conduct amounting to an abuse of process. This type of provision seems to capture recent cases where tribunals deemed investments that were made involving bribery[51] and fraud to be inadmissible.[52]

All the aforementioned provisions should be considered by the RCEP negotiating states to address the concerns that they have about the current ISDS mechanism. After all, this mechanism is one that has been perceived to be relatively reliable by foreign investors compared to domestic courts in some countries.[53]

10.4 Additional pillars in an IIA: investment promotion, facilitation, and liberalisation

10.4.1 Investment promotion

BITs are normally titled 'Agreement on the Promotion and Protection of Investments'. However, most BITs' investment promotion provisions simply use the generic phrase of requiring the contracting parties to 'encourage and create favourable conditions for nationals and companies of the other Contracting Party to make in its territory investments that are in line with its general economy policy'.[54] This has evolved in some plurilateral IIAs, which clarify further the obligation by including a list of actions to be undertaken by Member States. For example, Article 24 of the ACIA requires Member States to cooperate in 'increasing awareness of ASEAN as an integrated investment area in order to increase foreign investment into ASEAN and intra-ASEAN investments through, among others ... (b) enhancing industrial complementation and production networks among multi-national enterprises in ASEAN'.[55] This is unique compared to other IIAs because the provision is tied to the object and purpose of the ACIA: namely, enhancing production networks in the region. Nevertheless, the effect should not be exaggerated given that the provision only imposes a 'duty to cooperate' in promoting the Member States collectively.

Compared to BITs, some newer generation IIAs, including the EU-Canada CETA and the EU-Viet Nam IPA, leave out investment promotion provisions altogether. Presumably, this is because the parties to these FTAs believe that the task of promoting investment lies with each Member State's government agency or chamber of commerce.

RCEP's guiding principle implies that the negotiating states want to maintain an investment promotion provision in the investment chapter; for this purpose, they could use the ACIA's investment promotion provision as a baseline to develop more concrete binding obligations, for example, an obligation for the developed members to build the capacity of the less-developed members to fulfil the obligations in the investment chapter.

10.4.2 Investment facilitation

Similar to the investment promotion provisions in most ASEAN-plus dialogue partners' FTAs, investment facilitation provisions in the discussed agreements also impose a duty to cooperate without any strong and binding obligations.

Investment facilitation measures will have more impact if they make it easier for foreign investors to invest and conduct their day-to-day operations in host states. UNCTAD suggests states enhance transparency, efficiency, predictability, and consistency in their investment policy frameworks so foreign investors can feel the immediate impacts. This could be done more effectively at the national level by each host state (UNCTAD, 2016, pp. 117–118).

Another successful investment facilitation initiative is Korea's Office of the Foreign Investment Ombudsman, which provides assistance in resolving difficulties companies face both in business management and in daily life. The office has specialists in various fields, such as labour, taxation, finance, and construction, who assist foreign investors in resolving their grievances while investing in the country. If the RCEP could push all negotiating states to create such a kind of office, it would greatly facilitate investment.

A senior management and board of directors (SMBoD) provision can also strengthen the investment facilitation pillar in an IIA. This provision is critical because foreign investors may need to place their senior management team (foreigners) who understands their business operations, in host states. On the other hand, host states often want to increase the spillover effects from foreign investments by requiring investors to employ domestic workers and, at the same time, to retain control over their immigration policies (UNCTAD, 2012).

TPP Article 9.11 and CETA Article 8.8 adopt a very liberal approach by preventing a party from requiring 'an enterprise of that Party, that is also a covered investment, appoint to senior management or board of director positions, natural persons of any particular nationality'. To further smoothen the process of integration, the future FTA should also consider allowing natural persons in managerial or executive positions or someone with specialised knowledge to enter and stay temporarily in its territory, subject to the host states' measures relating to public health and safety and national security applicable to the entry and sojourn. This is an example of an attempt to facilitate foreign investors without sacrificing the state's right to regulate. This can be further enhanced by including certain binding obligations on host states, e.g. to install a transparent and streamlined mechanism for the work permit applications of SMBoD. The investment chapter could also potentially incorporate a time frame as well as an obligation to provide reasons for refusing a work permit application of SMBoD.

10.4.3 *Investment liberalisation*

In order to add more value to the existing IIA, the RCEP must cover deeper and broader areas of liberalisation. Berger et al. (2013) find strong evidence that liberal admission rules – IIAs with pre-establishment market access commitments (NT and/or MFN treatment) – could increase FDI inflows into a host state by up to about 29% in the long run (Berger et al., 2013). In fact, this is the trend that we are seeing in newer generation IIAs, including the TPP and CETA. However, given that the discussion about investment liberalisation is very broad and can be a chapter in its own, it is not discussed further than the discussion regarding performance requirements and NT in Sections 10.3.4 and 10.3.5, respectively.

10.5 Conclusion

The decision of the US to abandon the TPP may be a catalyst for the RCEP negotiating states to conclude their regional trade agreement, which could potentially be the biggest in the world in terms of the economies involved. However, the current political climate with regard to trade and investment has been rather grim because of the rise of protectionism. It remains to be seen whether the RCEP negotiating states will push for further liberalisation or simply follow the wave of protectionism and conclude an agreement that is not much different from the status quo.

Since the beginning of the RCEP negotiations, there have been many developments and innovations introduced in newer generation IIAs. On top of adding value from the liberalisation and treaty consolidation perspectives, RCEP can also become a benchmark of a modern investment agreement that strikes a proper balance between investment protection and states' right to regulate.

In order to become a benchmark of a modern investment agreement, RCEP should enhance further the investment protection provisions by refining and adding clarity. RCEP can also contribute further to the provisions on investment promotion and facilitation by providing a better list of the various actions to be undertaken by Member States to make investing easier and consequently boost the confidence of foreign investors in the region. This should be complemented with capacity building for the less developed members to fulfil those obligations.

RCEP negotiations have been ongoing for more than five years. In order to be relevant, the investment chapter must progress further. It must be ambitious enough to add more value to the existing regime and must address the criticism voiced against the existing regime, including ISDS.

Disclaimer

The author is a lawyer at the international arbitration department of Allen & Overy LLP, Singapore. The work was conducted when the author was with the Centre for International Law. The views expressed here do not reflect any opinion or view of Allen & Overy LLP.

Notes

1 Alana Petroff, 'The Pacific trade deal Trump quit is back on' (CNN: 23 January 2018), http://money.cnn.com/2018/01/23/news/economy/trade-deal-tpp-agreement/index.html.

2 Note that several ASEAN Member States have terminated the BITs among themselves, particularly Indonesia which has notified the termination of its BITs with Laos, Malaysia, Cambodia, Viet Nam, and Singapore. However, it has not terminated its BIT with Thailand presumably because the notification period has passed.

3 *Vienna Convention on the Law of Treaties,* 23 May 1969 (entered into force on 27 January 1980) (VCLT), Article 31(1).

4 *Azurix v. Argentina,* ICSID Case No. ARB/01/12, Award, 14 July 2006, 307.

5 *LG&E v. Argentina,* ICSID Case No. ARB/02/1, Decision on Liability, 3 October 2006, 124.

6 *ASEAN Comprehensive Investment Agreement* (entered into force 29 March 2012).
7 Declaration on the ASEAN Economic Community Blueprint (signed 20 November 2007).
8 There have been separate studies on whether investment rules affect foreign direct investment (FDI) flows. It is acknowledged that establishing a clear link between changes in FDI flows and the existence of investment provisions in itself is difficult.
9 Ministry of Trade and Industry of Singapore, 'Factsheet: What you need to know about RCEP', available at: www.mti.gov.sg/MTIInsights/SiteAssets/Pages.pdf (last access: 16 February 2018).
10 ASEAN (endorsed by the RCEP Ministers on 30 August 2012), 'Guiding Principles and Objectives for Negotiating the Regional Comprehensive Economic Partnership', available at: https://asean.org/storage/2012/05/RCEP-Guiding-Principles-public-copy.pdf (last access: 15 November 2018).
11 Lincoln Feast and Colin Packham, 'Australia surprises with rejection of 2.55 billion Australian dollar GrainCorp takeover by ADM' (*Reuters:* 28 November 2013), www.reuters.com/article/us-graincorp-adm-idUSBRE9AR0SG20131128.
12 *Yaung Chi Oo Trading Pte Ltd. v. Government of the Union of Myanmar*, ASEAN ID Case No. ARB/01/1, Award, 31 March 2003 (ICSID Additional Facility Rules).
13 For example, *Mobil Investments Canada Inc. and Murphy Oil Corporation v. Canada*, ICSID Case No. ARB(AF)/07/4, Decision on Liability and Principles of Quantum, 22 May 2012, 45–46, 237–238, and 242.
14 See, for example, Article 6 of the ASEAN-Korea Investment Agreement.
15 *Pope & Talbot Inc. v. Canada*, NAFTA, Award on the Merits of Phase 2, 10 April 2001, 103; *Archer Daniels Midland Company and Tate &Lyle Ingredients Americas, Inc. v. United Mexican States,* ICSID Case No. ARB(AF)/04/5, Award, 21 November 2007, 196–197; *Apotex Holdings Inc. and Apotex Inc. v. United States of America,* ICSID Case No. ARB(AF)/12/1, Award, 25 August 2014, 8.15.
16 *Bayindir Insaat Turizm Ticaret Ve Sanayi AS v. Islamic Republic of Pakistan*, ICSID Case No. ARB/03/29, Award, 27 August 2009, 227–235.
17 *Emilio Augustin Maffezini v. The Kingdom of Spain*, ICSID Case No. ARB/97/7, Decision of the tribunal on the objections of Jurisdiction, 25 January 2000, 62–63.
18 *Maffezini, supra* note 26, 62–63; *Impregilo S.p.A. v. Argentine Republic,* ICSID Case No. ARB/07/17, Award, 21 June 2011, 104–108.
19 *Plama Consortium Ltd. v. Republic of Bulgaria,* ICSID Case No. ARB/04/15, Decision on Jurisdiction, 8 February 2005, 202, 215; *Tza Yap Shum v. Republic of Peru,* ICSID Case No. ARB/07/6, Decision on Jurisdiction and Competence, 19 June 2009, 220.
20 For example Investment chapters of AANZFTA, the ASEAN-India Investment Agreement, and some bilateral FTAs between ASEAN Member States and the dialogue partners.
21 See also Malaysia–New Zealand FTA, Article 10.5(2); AANZFTA, Article 16(2)(a); ACIA, Article 6 footnote 4(a).
22 See also EU-Viet Nam IPA, Article 2.4.5.
23 *Agreement between Japan and the Republic of the Philippines for an Economic Partnership* (signed 9 September 2006), Article 91.
24 *Técnicas Medioambientales Tecmed, S.A. v. United Mexican States,* ICSID Case No. ARB (AF)/00/2, Award, 29 May 2003, 154; *Enron Corporation and Ponderosa Assets, L.P. v Argentine Republic*, ICSID Case No. ARB/01/3 (also known as *Enron Creditors Recovery Corp. and Ponderosa Assets, L.P. v The Argentine Republic)*, Award, 22 May 2007 [*Enron Award*], 262.
25 ACIA, Article 11(2); ASEAN-China Investment Agreement, Article 7(2)(a); AANZFTA, Article 6(2)(a).
26 *Rumeli Telekom AS and Telsim Mobil Telekomikasyon Hizmetleri AS v Republic of Kazakhstan,* ICSID Case No. ARB/05/16, Award, 29 July 2008, 653.
27 *Flughafen Zürich AG and Gestión e Ingeniería IDC SA v Bolivarian Republic of Venezuela,* ICSID Case No. ARB/10/19, Award, 18 November 2014, 635, 642.

28 For example, see *Fireman's Fund Insurance Company v. The United Mexican States,* ICSID Case No. ARB(AF)/02/01, Award, 17 July 2006, 176; *Glamis Gold, Ltd. v. United States of America,* UNCITRAL, Award, 14 May 2009, 356.
29 *Methanex Corporation v. United States of America,* Final Award on Jurisdiction and Merits, 3 August 2005 Part IV Chapter D, 7.
30 This clause had been interpreted differently in many cases involving Argentine during the financial crisis there, including: *CMS Gas Transmission Co. v. Republic of Argentina,* ICSID Case No. ARB/01/08, Award, 25 April 2005, 349–352; *CMS Gas Transmission Co. v. Argentine Republic,* ICSID Case No. ARB/01/8, Decision on Application for Annulment, 21 August 2007; *LG&E, supra* note 43; *Sempra Energy International v. Argentina,* ICSID ARB/02/16, Award, 28 September 2007, 366–368; *Sempra v. Argentine Republic,* Decision on Argentina's Application for Annulment of the award, 10 June 2010; *Enron Award, supra* note 30, 324–326; *Enron v. Argentine Republic,* Decision on the Application for Annulment, 30 July 2010; *Continental Casualty Co. v. Argentine Republic,* ICSID Case No. ARB/03/9, Award, 5 September 2008, 183.
31 Losari (n 3) pp. 248–249.
32 See also similar stipulation in TPP Article 9.15.
33 Herbert Smith Freehills, 'Indonesia Update: What are the Possible Consequences of Termination of Indonesia's Bilateral Investment Treaties?' Jakarta, May 2014 <http://www.herbertsmithfreehills.com/-/media/Files/ebulletins/2014/20140512 – Indonesia update what are the possible consequences of termination of Indonesias Bilateral Investment Treaties.htm>.
34 *Tokios Tokeles v Ukraine,* ICSID Case No. ARB/02/18, Decision on Jurisdiction, 29 April 2004, 29.
35 *Tidewater Inc., Tidewater Investment SRL, Tidewater Caribe, C.A., Twenty Grand Offshore, L.L.C., Point Marine, L.L.C., Twenty... v. The Bolivarian Republic of Venezuela,* ICSID Case No. ARB/10/5, Decision on Jurisdiction, 8 February 2013, 146; *Phoenix Action Ltd v Czech Republic,* ICSID Case No. ARB/06/5, Award, 15 April 2009, 140,142; see also *Philip Morris Asia Ltd v Australia,* UNCITRAL, Award on Jurisdiction and Admissibility, 17 December 2015, 585.
36 *Limited Liability Company Amto v. Ukraine,* Arbitration Institute of the Stockholm Chamber of Commerce, Case No. 080/2005, Final Award, 26 March 2008, 61–62, 69.
37 *Ibid.*, 69.
38 *Pac Rim Cayman v. El Salvador,* ICSID Case No. ARB/09/12, Decision on the Respondent's Jurisdictional Objections, 1 June 2012, 4.72, 4.74, and 4.78.
39 *Agreement between Japan and Australia for an Economic Partnership* (entered into force 15 January 2015).
40 The office was established in October 1999. For further information: www.i-ombudsman.or.kr/eng/index.jsp.
41 CETA Chapter 8, Section F; EU-Viet Nam IPA, Article 3.38.
42 See www.uncitral.org/uncitral/en/uncitral_texts/arbitration/2010Arbitration_rules.html, last accessed: 19 February 2018. From a technical point of view, if the parties decide to submit their dispute under the International Chamber of Commerce (ICC) Rules of Arbitration (as allowed under CETA Article 23(2)(d)), this may raise an issue because the ICC Rules provide that the ICC International Court of Arbitration is the only body authorised to administer arbitrations under the Rules.
43 CETA Article 8.27.
44 CETA Article 8.18.
45 CETA Article 8.20
46 CETA Article 8.26.
47 CETA Article 8.30.
48 CETA Article 8.36.
49 CETA Article 8.41.
50 CETA Article 8.43.

51 *World Duty Free Co. Ltd. v Kenya*, ICSID Case No. ARB/00/7, Award, 4 October 2006, 188.
52 *Churchill Mining PLC and Planet Mining Pty Ltd v Indonesia*, ICSID Case No. ARB/12/14 and 12/40, Award, 6 December 2016, 528.
53 Office of the United States Trade Representative, 'The Facts on Investor-State Dispute Settlement: Safeguarding the Public Interest and Protecting Investors' 27 March 2014: www.ustr.gov/about-us/press-office/blog/2014/March/Facts-Investor-State%20 Dispute-Settlement-Safeguarding-Public-Interest-Protecting-Investors (accessed 21 October 2014).
54 *Cambodia – Singapore Bilateral Investment Treaties* (entered into force on 24 February 2000), Article 3.1.
55 *ASEAN Comprehensive Investment Agreement*, Article 24.

References

Aisbett, E., M. Busse, and P. Nunnenkamp (2016), 'Bilateral Investment Treaties Do Work: Until They Don't', *Kiel Working Paper No. 2021.*

Alschner, W. and D. Skougarevskiy (2016), 'Mapping the Universe of International Agreements', *Journal of International Economic Law, 19*(3), 561–588.

Antoni, A. and M. Ewing-Chow (2013), 'Trade and Investment Convergence and Divergence: Revising the North American Sugar War', *Latin American Journal of International Trade Law, 1*(1), 315–351.

ASEAN Secretariat (2008), *ASEAN Economic Community Blueprint.* Jakarta, Indonesia: ASEAN Secretariat.

Berger, A., M. Busse, P. Nunnekamp, and M. Roy (2013), 'Do Trade and Investment Agreements Lead to More FDI? Accounting for Key Provisions Inside the Black Box', *International Economics and Economic Policy, 10*(2), 1–17.

Bhagwati, J. (1995), 'U.S. Trade Policy: The Infatuation with Free Trade Agreements', *Discussion Paper Series* No. 726, New York, NY: Columbia University.

Bishop, D. (2005), 'The Case for an Appellate Panel and Its Scope of Review', *Transnational Dispute Management, 2.*

Bjorklund, A. (2005), 'Reconciling State Sovereignty and Investor Protection in Denial of Justice Claims', *Virginia Journal of International Law, 45*, 809–894.

Bjorklund, A. (2008), 'National Treatment', in A. Reinisch (ed.), *Standards of Investment Protection.* New York, NY: Oxford University Press.

Crawford, J. (2005), 'Is There a Need for an Appellate System?', *Transnational Dispute Management, 2.*

Dolzer, R. and C. Schreuer (2008), *Principles of International Investment Law*, New York, NY: Oxford University Press.

Dugan, C.F., D. Wallace Jr., N. Rubins, and B. Sabahi (2008), *Investor–State Arbitration.* New York, NY: Oxford University Press.

Echandi, R. and P. Sauvé (eds.) (2013), *Prospects in International Investment Law and Policy.* New York, NY: Cambridge University Press.

Ewing-Chow, M. and G. Fischer (2011), 'ASEAN IIAs: Conserving Regulatory Sovereignty While Promoting the Rule of Law?', *Transnational Dispute Management, 8*(5), 1–12.

Ewing-Chow, M., J.J. Losari, and M.V. Slade (2014), 'The Facilitation of Trade by the Rule of Law: The Cases of Singapore and ASEAN', in J.M. Jallab (ed.), *Connecting to Global Markets*, WTO Publication, available at: www.wto.org/english/res_e/booksp_e/cmark_chap9_e.pdf.

Ewing-Chow, M. and W. Ng (2008), 'Caveat Emptor: Three Aspects of Investment Protection Treaties', *Asian Yearbook of International Law, 14*, 27.

Kauffman-Kohler, G. and M. Potesta (2016), 'Can the Mauritius Convention Serve as a Model for the Reform of Investor State Arbitration in Connection with the Introduction of a Permanent Investment Tribunal or an Appeal Mechanism?: Analysis and Roadmap', *CIDS Research Paper*, available at www.uncitral.org/pdf/english/commissionsessions/unc/unc-49/CIDS_Research_Paper_-_Can_the_Mauritius_Convention_serve_as_a_model.pdf.

Kohler, W. and F. Stähler (2016), 'The Economics of Investor Protection: ISDS versus National Treatment', *CESifo Working Paper No. 5766*.

Koschwar, B. (2009), 'Mapping Investment Provisions in Regional Trade Agreements: Towards an International Investment Regime?', in A. Estevadeordal, K. Suominen, and R. Teh (eds.), *Regional Rules in the Global Trading System*. New York, NY: Cambridge University Press.

Kurtz, J. (2008), 'Adjudging the Exceptional at International Law: Security, Public Order and Financial Crisis', *Jean Monnet Working Paper* 06/08, New York, NY: The Jean Monnet Center.

Losari, J. J. (2016), 'Searching for an Ideal International Investment Protection Regime for ASEAN+ Dialogue Partners (RCEP): Where Do We Begin?', in L.Y. Ing (ed.), *East Asian Integration*, 1st Ed. ERIA Research Project 2014–6, Jakarta, Indonesia: ERIA, 225–260.

Losari, J. J. and M. Ewing-Chow (2016), 'A Clash of Treaties: The Lawfulness of Countermeasures in International Trade Law and International Investment Law', *Journal of World Investment & Trade*, *16*, 274–313.

Newcombe, A. (2005), 'The Boundaries of Regulatory Expropriation in International Law', *ICSID Review – Foreign Investment Law Journal*, *20*(1), 1–57.

Pollan, T. (2006), *Legal Framework for the Admission of FDI*. Utrecht, The Netherlands: Eleven International Publishing.

Roberts, A. (2014), 'State-to-state Investment Treaty Arbitration: A Hybrid Theory of Interdependent Rights and Shared Interpretative Authority', *Harvard International Law Journal*, *55*(1), 1–70.

Sauvant, K.P. and F. Ortino (2013), *Improving the International Investment Law and Policy Regime: Options for the Future*. Helsinki, Finland: Ministry for Foreign Affairs of Finland.

Schill, S. (2009), *The Multilateralisation of International Investment Law*. Cambridge, UK: Cambridge University Press.

Schneidarman, D. (2008), *Constitutionalizing Economic Globalization: Investment Rules and Democracy's Promise*. New York, NY: Cambridge University Press.

Transparency International, *Corruption Perceptions Index 2016*, www.transparency.org/news/feature/corruption_perceptions_index_2017#table (last accessed: 13 July 2017).

UNCTAD (2007), *Bilateral Investment Treaties 1995–2006: Trends in Investment Rule-making*. Geneva, Switzerland: United Nations.

UNCTAD (2010), *Most-Favoured-Nation Treatment: UNCTAD Series on Issues in International Investment Agreements II*. Geneva, Switzerland: United Nations.

UNCTAD (2012), *World Investment Report 2012: Towards a New Generation of Investment Policies*. Geneva, Switzerland: United Nations.

UNCTAD (2013), *World Investment Report 2013: Global Value Chains: Investment and Trade for Development*. Geneva, Switzerland: United Nations.

UNCTAD (2014), 'Recent Developments in Investor–State Dispute Settlement (ISDS)', *IIA Issues Note No. 1*, Geneva, Switzerland: United Nations.

UNCTAD (2016), *World Investment Report 2016: Investor Nationality: Policy Changes*. Geneva, Switzerland: United Nations.

UNCTAD (2017), *Investment Policy Hub: IIA Mapping Project*, http://investmentpolicyhub.unctad.org/IIA/mappedContent#iiaInnerMenu (last accessed: 21 February 2018).

Vandevelde, K.J. (2010), 'A Unified Theory of Fair and Equitable Treatment', *New York University Journal of Int'l Law & Politics, 43*, 43–106.

Weiler, T. (2005), 'Methanex Corp. v. U.S.A.: Turning the Page on NAFTA Chapter Eleven?', *Journal of World Investment and Trade, 6*, 903–921.

Index

Note: **Bold** page numbers refer to tables and page numbers followed by "n" denote endnotes.

Printed in the United States
by Baker & Taylor Publisher Services